Slow Manifesto

Slow Manifesto

———

Lebbeus Woods Blog

———

Clare Jacobson, editor

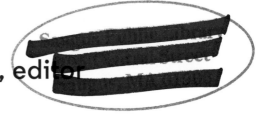

Princeton Architectural Press, New York

Contents

2007

2008

2009

2010

2011

2012

Foreword

Christopher Hawthorne

The book you're holding is a work of architecture criticism. As an architecture critic myself, perhaps that should have been clearer to me from the start, but it took me a while to figure it out. I read several of the blog entries that make up this collection when they first appeared online, beginning in 2007, and even as I turned to them again recently, in preparing this essay, they struck me primarily as extensions of the work Lebbeus Woods did throughout his career as an architect, which is to say prose versions of his drawings and sketches of complex, forbidding landscapes. Woods, it seemed to me, was working through on the keyboard the same issues he was hashing out with his pencil. And in a superficial way I was right about that: there are entries in this volume about Sarajevo, about resistance, about ethics, about approaches to drawing—the same subjects and preoccupations that animate Woods's work on paper or stand at the heart of his career-long, largely solitary, and often underappreciated effort to broaden the traditional, hidebound definition of what architecture is and what architects do.

Yet the more time I spent reading and thinking about these entries the more I realized that they exist markedly apart from the rest of Woods's work. The most obvious way in which this is true has to do with tone. Woods's drawings are feverish. They are not merely full of but propelled by a sense of dislocation, rupture, and even violence. They are impatient not in the sense that Woods didn't take his time creating them but from a political point of view: you can feel looking at them that he is deeply disturbed by the way things are (in cities and corporate architecture offices alike) and is in a hurry to suggest a different way of making buildings and arranging those buildings into a functioning society. A fissure or a tear in the fabric of a Lebbeus Woods drawing is never decorative; it is meant as a bit of crucial evidence, or quite sincerely as means to an end.

The blog entries, by contrast, are notable for their evenness. If despairing, they are also cool. They are curious about the work architects produce and how that work is received by clients, the public, the press, and fellow architects. And if you think of them as criticism *qua* criticism, you might even say that they are conservative, which is of course not a word that is often, if ever, applied to the Woods we know from the drawings. The writing accepts the constraints of the blog form. The pieces are not fragmented or sharpened to a shard-like point but rational, well argued, and cogently shaped.

This is not to say that they are not full of surprises—only that those surprises are matters of content (ideas and turns of phrase, for example) rather than form. The first surprise is the appealing directness of Woods's writing style, how nimbly he avoids cliché and professional jargon. The second is how wide ranging the subject matter turns out to be. Woods writes about homeownership, abstraction, Pierre Boulez, architectural education, and the late-career work of Eero Saarinen, in whose firm, not long after its namesake's death, Woods briefly worked; he also writes with great energy and care about sidewalks, the sort of topic the adventurous architects of his generation typically left to new urbanists.

Concluding that there was, in the latter stage of Woods's career, something of a gulf between the architecture and the writing leads to a trickier set of questions. To write radical prose (particularly when you are publishing that prose yourself, without relying on the gatekeeper of an agent or editor) is easier in some ways than to maintain, as Woods did for more than three decades, a radical architecture practice. What was the appeal, for Woods, of limiting his response to complex topics to short, standalone posts? What did he find compelling about this particular form?

Perhaps writing was a solace. If architecture is war, as Woods said, writing was—if far from peace—a kind of DMZ, a place to repair to, to find quiet, to think. A place from which to survey the wreckage of contemporary culture and political life. Throughout his career Woods proposed variations of what he called "freespaces": rooms or even buildings, as he describes them here, "without predetermined programs of use," places that might operate as "crucibles for the creation of new thinking and sociopolitical forms, small and large." His impulse in maintaining a blog seems to have been to carve out a freespace in his own intellectual work. Just as one cannot write in a sustained, intense way for more than a few hours per day, surely one cannot draw in the way Woods drew without needing some kind of respite, a way not to turn off the brain but to use it in a different way. And just as the freespace was for him a place for people to find an intellectual or political community, one appeal of the blog format for him was the way it enabled a conversation in the comments section.

One thing seems clear: writing was a way for Woods to fill what he saw as a significant vacuum in architecture criticism. He was unhappy that most of the newspaper and magazine critics during the period he was maintaining his blog were either not covering subjects he considered instrumental or not covering them with sufficient rigor. Critics who reflexively defended the most influential and famous architects in the world—so-called starchitects—came in for the harshest scorn (though Woods did go out of his way to defend Zaha Hadid, Thom Mayne, and a few others with the architectural equivalent of bold-faced names). In response he produced precisely what he judged to be missing: regular, skeptical, politically engaged, and highly informed posts on contemporary architecture and cities, the most impressive of which are reprinted here.

It is notable, finally, that these entries came so near the end of Woods's working life. Woods's own deep allergy to nostalgia keeps most of them free of sentiment. Yet from a philosophical standpoint, although they tackle a combination of contemporary and historical subjects, they suggest a backward gaze, a reckoning with what a career adds up to. Woods apologizes to his readers when he pulls some old drawings out for inspection, but he pulls them out all the same.

This was surely another advantage of the blog format for Woods, that its directness and speed allowed him to communicate, in a relative rush, his opinions, memories, and thoughts on a diverse, shifting range of topics related to architecture. (Here again, that sense of impatience.) Setting aside the question of whether he knew the end was near, there was quite a bit he was anxious to get to as a writer. Perhaps "determined" is a better word.

Preface

Clare Jacobson

Architect Lebbeus Woods established his reputation through meticulously hand-rendered drawings and beautifully crafted books. Yet from 2007 to 2012—what proved to be the final years of his life—he turned to a blog as his primary form of expression. The blog took good advantage of its electronic form, actively integrating texts, art, links, and readers' comments. Its posts show the variety of Woods's interests. Theoretical propositions. Political commentaries. Construction updates. Breaking news. Challenges to readers. Poems. As one of the last major works of an extensive career, the blog stands as a testament not only to Woods's significance to contemporary architecture but also to his appreciation of the possibilities of new media.

So why, dear reader, this attempt to represent the breadth and depth of the Woods blog within the antiquated and necessarily abbreviated form of a book? Because we, and Woods himself, recognize the benefits of the form. (In answer to a blog reader's query, "How many books in that library of yours?" he responded, "A few thousand."/1) We trust that the collection on paper is the definitive collection, the cream that has risen to the top and made it from the ubiquitous World Wide Web to the rarefied world of print. We run our finger down the table of contents and recognize the narrative that the collection creates. We appreciate the refined layout of the page and perhaps scribble some comments in its margins. We associate the weight of the book with the weight of its ideas. In making Woods's blog bookish, we provide it with a new life and a new audience.

Of course some things are lost in transforming a blog to a book. Most significantly, this book prioritizes Woods's submissions over those of other blog contributors. Omissions include texts by disparate writers and series by Manuel De Landa and Cheng Feng Lau. Only three of thirteen posts of Woods's students' work have been reproduced herein. Images from other architects and artists have been minimized. Readers' comments, which were moderated by Woods yet still include harsh criticism and feisty debate, are absent from this book. It may seem a questionable decision to exclude these other voices in the work of a man well known as a collaborator. Yet these omissions allow for the most complete representation of Woods's contributions to the blog. Woods's own intentions for his website have been reproduced as the introduction to this volume. The complete blog—http://lebbeuswoods. wordpress.com—remains as an online archive as this book goes to press.

The responsibility for what is in and what is out of this book is mine, and it is a responsibility that bears heavy on me. I come to this project as an outsider, a woman who was not a regular reader of—and never a contributor to—the Woods blog while it was active. And so I read it and edited it as a posthumous piece rather than an evolving work. At the same time, I come to this project as an insider, a woman who edited Woods's *OneFiveFour* in 1989 and had the pleasure of working on four additional books with him over the course of many years. While I had numerous doubts as to my judgment during the production of this volume, I took solace in Woods's longstanding respect for my work and a 2009 email request from him: "I would like to make a book with you. Perhaps it can be based on my blog writings and postings."/2

I necessarily took a heavy hand to the material available, cutting over half of the original posts and roughly two-thirds of the images. The texts themselves received a much lighter touch, with just minor corrections to grammar, spelling, and facts, while the images in this book faithfully reproduce those in the blog, with a few unavoidable exceptions. The reader should note that Woods produced all artwork and texts herein unless otherwise noted. All footnotes are his and all endnotes mine. Narrative captions are also Woods's work, while identifying captions have been added here for consistency and issues of copyright.

There is a lot of "I" in the previous paragraphs, but goodness knows there were a lot of "we" in this book's realization. Thanks to all who made it possible. To Aleksandra Wagner for trusting me with this collection and for providing a complementary voice in setting its scope and focus. To Ellen E. Donnelly for her work with the images. To Princeton Architectural Press: publisher Kevin Lippert and editorial director Jennifer Lippert for taking on this title, editorial assistant Marielle Suba for her helpful research, senior designer Jan Haux for his elegant treatment, and especially senior editor Megan Carey for her passionate attention to every aspect of this project. To the Graham Foundation for Advanced Studies in the Fine Arts for providing the financial support that made this publication possible. Most importantly, to Lebbeus, who provided this editor with such rich material and with memories of an openhearted friendship that guided me in my work.

Introduction

Lebbeus Woods

The purposes of this website are several. First: to provide access to my and my collaborators' projects and writings that are not published elsewhere, or published a little. At this stage in my life and work—I would optimistically call it a middle stage—I have a clear grasp of what it is that I want to achieve, though I am still searching for the best realization of ideas that have driven me all along. Also, I am sitting on a large number of works, constituting a body of research that, while not fully developed, may be of value to others pursuing similar or parallel ideas and aims. This site enables their widest possible dissemination. The works presented here are—necessarily—protected by international copyrights and may not be used for any commercial purposes, yet they are free to all who might use them for study or enjoyment. Second: to provide a means of publishing new works in a form increasingly available to all possibly interested in them. Third: to create a forum for discussing the ideas and issues raised by this work, which carries an open invitation to all who have something to say about them, and thereby to contribute to the knowledge and practice of architecture. Unlike the past decades, the present moment is lacking in architectural discourse, generally. In particular, there is an absence of criticism of works and ideas, except in terms of efficacy, and that—at a time of critical changes of every kind—is not good enough.

2007

Outsider Architecture

Rudolf Steiner, Goetheanum II, 1928

Over the past few years, I've had occasion to think about architects who have produced work of various kinds outside the mainstream certified by the historians and critics who make up architectural academia, or otherwise influence the climate of opinion. To some degree, my thinking was prompted by my own work and where it might be placed in today's critical categories. Yet, what interests me here is other architects whose work has had enough impact on the mainstream to be visible, but is kept by the critics at arm's (or barge pole's) length from the historical canon.

Part of my interest comes from a conversation I had in 1997 with Toshio Nakamura, the legendary editor of Japan's *A+U* (*Architecture and Urbanism*), who wanted to commission from me an "alternative history" of modern architecture to be published serially in his journal. I, of course, accepted immediately. What an exciting prospect it was! However well done most histories of modern architecture are, one gets tired of reading about the same buildings, the same architects; tired of shuffling time and again along the same worn path. Maybe the conventional histories get it right—maybe contemporary architecture is influenced most by a score of canonical buildings about which we have all read countless times. Or maybe the repetition creates an influence at least equal to that of the buildings themselves. Maybe we become so influenced by the historical certification that we gullibly follow along, drawing on what we've "learned" in school and beyond.

In any event, there have been a number of buildings, and their architects, whose influence has more or less seeped through the filters of architectural education—and mainstream architectural journalism—and yet has impacted architectural thought and design, despite the inattention of critics and historians. What a history that would make!

Well, Mr. Nakamura left *A+U* shortly after our conversation. Otherwise, I would have been obliged to write the history I had promised to him. Maybe I'm still obliged. If so, I'm taking my time, and I haven't lost my interest, and bits and pieces of progress are visible—at least in my files. Who are these "outsider" architects? Which of their buildings, or unbuilt designs, are significant? What is important to say about them? How do we bring them into our thinking today? Or should we? Maybe they should stay outside, in the cold, a little longer. Here are several at the top of my list:

Rudolf Steiner (Goetheanum I and Goetheanum II)
Hermann Finsterlin (speculative projects)
Frederick Kiesler (Endless House)
John Hejduk (Masques, Cathedral)

Surely there are others, and it would be very interesting to hear who they are, and to discuss and debate their ideas, buildings, and their place in the ongoing flow of modern architecture.

October 10, 2007

Criticism

Friedrich Nietzsche said, "I never attack persons, but only ideas, and only after they have become successful."

His critics were not so scrupulous about ad hominem attacks. He was labeled a madman (before he actually lost his mind), unscholarly (he never used footnotes), an anti-Semite (his writings condemn anti-Semitism), and a proto-Nazi (the Nazis liberally quoted him out of context), among other choice things. Granted, his concept of the "overman" was easy to parody, as George Bernard Shaw did in his play *Man and Superman* (certainly one source of the comic book hero's moniker), or twist into a likeness of Der Führer. His concept of "the eternal recurrence" has the earmarks of a half-digested Hindu precept, though forecasts by modern physicists of the fate of the universe are not entirely dissimilar. His most often quoted dictum, "God is dead," is something he never wrote or said. What he said was, "Truly, all the gods are dead. When one old greybeard of a god said, 'I am the only god,' they laughed themselves to death!" Misquoting someone on such an important point of his work is about as ad hominem as it gets. It is certainly not a reasonable form of criticism, by anyone's standards.

What successful ideas did Nietzsche criticize? Well, German nationalism, for one—it was the time of Otto von Bismarck and German unification. For another, Christianity. He saw the church as a betrayal of Christ's ethics. And Wagnerism. Richard Wagner's music dramas were the rage of Europe, but Wagner was both a German nationalist and a declared anti-Semite. Nietzsche had been close to Wagner early on, but detested the fawning cult that formed around him later, and the pseudo-Christian stance of his last work, *Parsifal*. Nietzsche's criticisms didn't win him many friends at the time, in academia or elsewhere, but they laid the foundation for modern thought—and art—to come.

But this isn't a post about Nietzsche. It's about criticism, and especially criticism in the field of architecture. Nietzsche's standards are very precise, but also very tough to live up to. He asks us to be fearless and, even harder, to be honest—in public, or at least in print, which amounts to the same. He asks us to risk offending people we might like or respect, colleagues who take any criticism of their work very personally. Nietzsche considered honesty the truest sign of respect. Most of us don't feel that way. We just want the good news.

Criticism as we think of it today didn't emerge until the nineteenth century, with the rise of the middle class and the newspapers and journals they needed to give them an edge in cultural matters, which had formerly been the province of the aristocracies needing no critics to tell them what to like or reject. The aristocrats, and royal families, had made "taste" by simply commissioning the art, music, and architecture they liked. It was up to the artists, composers, and architects to invent new ways to attract and enchant their patrons. No critics were needed.

But the merchants and factory owners of the late eighteenth and the nineteenth centuries were not so self-assured. Emerging from a lower social stratum solely by virtue of their new wealth, they, as the new aristocracy, needed help in knowing what to like. Enter the critics. The art, music, theater, literature, and architecture critics were the avant-garde of the culture of experts who came to dominate bourgeois society, right up to the present. The expert critics were, and remain, the middlepersons of culture, in all its aspects. They mediate between the artists and the public. They make art intelligible—and digestible—to a public who considers the arts somehow important, but doesn't have as much leisure time as royals to actually listen and see what's available and to make choices. Hence, the power of the critics, who are paid to have the time, and of their written (for newspapers, magazines, blogs) and spoken (for radio, television, podcasts) pronouncements. They decide what's important.

But who are the critics? Where do they come from? What is the basis of their expertise? Whatever it might be, it is certainly not from being architects. The critics are a separate class. Architects are never critics. And why not? Because architects do not feel comfortable criticizing their colleagues. "Judge not, lest ye be judged," goes the old Biblical admonition. So everyone judges the critics, and usually not approvingly. But the critics don't care—they do the dirty work and have the power to shape opinion and, in effect, write the first page of new history.

There is another reason architects are loathe to criticize other architects. They don't want to appear jealous if the work they criticize is more esteemed than their own ("Sour grapes!") or mean-spirited if it is not. So, what's to be gained by writing criticism?

Two things, for sure. Most importantly, the development of critical thinking that can be useful in one's own work. Analyzing (that's what writing is, one way or another) exactly what it is we like or dislike about a work of architecture inevitably feeds back into evaluating our own efforts. Self-criticism is a discipline vital to creative work. Secondly, if one chooses to publish criticism of ideas or works of architecture, it creates discussion among architects about what is important in architecture today. What are the important questions to be asked? Which answers work, which don't—and why? Which colleagues do we share crucial interests with, opening possibilities of correspondence and cooperation? So much lip service is given to architecture being a collaborative effort, yet architects are so busy competing with each other for commissions that they isolate themselves from one another.

One consequence of that isolation is, in the broad sense, political: the profession of architecture is weakened in the social scheme of things. Architects are thought of not as principled professionals, but as businesspeople, competing like everyone else in the marketplace. That's all right, if we think of architecture as the making of commodities, subject only to the vicissitudes of fashion and taste. But it's a disaster if we think of architecture as a field of knowledge put into practice. The creation of knowledge involves occasional flashes of inspiration, but a lot of slow and steady critical thought between. And it is always a collaborative effort.

I'll close this post with a comment on making criticism of one's own or others' works. There are ways of criticizing that are harsh, brutal, and destructive. These are, needless to say, counterproductive. But also there are ways to criticize that are honest and direct, but emphasize what is valuable in a given work, leaving what is not to simply fall away. Einstein's critique of the "aether" concept in his first relativity theory was simply to not mention it at all./₃ Thereafter, no one else did either. Generally, criticism should show the way forward.

October 20, 2007

Taking a Position

We do indeed live in a dry time for theories of architecture. It's as though we've reached the "end of history" proclaimed in 1989 by Francis Fukuyama./₄ "What we may be witnessing," he wrote, "is not just the end of the Cold War, or the passing of a particular period of post-war history, but the end of history as such: that is, the end point of mankind's ideological evolution and the universalization of Western liberal democracy as the final form of human government." An astonishing prospect!

Architects, often the handmaidens of politics, today seem more eager than ever to play the main game of liberal democracy, which is the pursuit of clients and their commissions. And who are the clients? Developers, exponents of liberal democracy's main activity: capitalist enterprise. In the age of Marshall McLuhan (and Guy Debord), they understand the value of the PR spectacular architecture delivers. Occasionally, governments—who need the same kind of upbeat PR—are clients. The "liberal democracies" of the UAE and Kazakhstan, for example. Or of Beijing, Shanghai, or Singapore. That's where the money is. That's where the developers and their architects (including many of the best we have) are, working feverishly at the end of history. Theory? Actually, it's excess baggage, even when the architects are flying first class.

Architects are not born theorists, that is true. Most of the world's best architects never wrote a line about their work, let alone proposed a theory—

they didn't have to. There were busy critics and professors who followed their works with great attention. Innovative architects were lucky to have Lewis Mumford, Sigfried Giedion, and Manfredo Tafuri, and, more rarely, Michel Foucault, Gilles Deleuze, and Jacques Derrida. The theories that the theoreticians spun around their works enabled a wide discourse to develop, elevating architecture to a form of knowledge, lifting it out of the venal chatter of the marketplace. Sadly, those critics and professors have died, leaving a conceptual—and critical—void.

Many of the critics and professors of the present day may be silent about the most recent works for a reason. The "Bilbao Effect" has dampened critical architectural writing. With its advent, interest shifted from the heady quarrels about deconstructivism and postmodernism to a concern with the much less intellectually taxing search for novel forms. Novel forms work well, from the viewpoint of promoting tourism and other spun-off enterprises. As for the Guggenheim Bilbao, there's not much that can be said about it beyond its great success. It encloses the same old museum program. If we look behind the curving titanium skin, we find swarms of metal studs holding it up—no innovative construction technology there. It hasn't inspired a new architecture, or a new discourse, other than that of media success. Herbert Muschamp was right—the building is the resurrection of Marilyn Monroe./5 Certainly the architect, like Marilyn, hasn't said anything of consequence. Sexiness just speaks for itself, no? Exeunt critics and professors.

I think architects themselves need to take up the task of writing theory and not wait for rescue from the quarters of academe. That may seem at first an absurd expectation, but I can think of two architects, very engaged in building, who have done just that: Rem Koolhaas and Steven Holl. They don't write theory, exactly, but they place their work in the context of ideas, not just opportunities. They take the risk of putting off potential clients. Think what you will of them, their buildings, and their books, but they have taken positions vis-à-vis other fields of knowledge and the contemporary world. That's not only admirable, but also imitable. All I can say is, let's have more from others—the architects who, by building or intending to build, are shaping the world.

November 6, 2007

Noblesse Oblige */

The interplay between the ethical aspects of exclusivity and those of ubiquity is operative in a clear way in the case of significant public buildings. Consider, for example, the Seagram Building in New York. The wealth and power of the client are immediately apparent, amply demonstrated by the haughty aloofness of the building's sober and restrained design and, at the same time, the sumptuous costliness of its materials and details. The

*/ This is the first in a series of posts on the relationships between aesthetics and ethics in architecture. [Other posts in this series include "The Corporate Model" (November 25, 2007), "The New and the Ugly" (January 8, 2008), and "Integrity" (March 20, 2008), which are reproduced in this volume, and "The Fountainhead" (September 22, 2008; http://lebbeuswoods .wordpress.com/2008/09/22/the -fountainhead/), which is not reproduced herein.]

large open space in front of the building seems almost extravagant, considering the staggering prices of land in Midtown Manhattan, and contrasts sharply with its more egregiously commercial neighbors, who have crammed the maximum square footage of leasable space onto their sites. To the average passerby, the building and its siting have the aesthetics of a civic monument, an architecture that goes far beyond advertising its client and becomes a kind of gift to the city, a form of noblesse oblige—the obligation the rich and powerful have to the society that made them so—that confirms the client's superior station. The Seagram Company assumes the aesthetic raiments of government, bestowing on the public space of the street an imposing demonstration of social hierarchy and the ethical relationships of New York's social classes. The rich give, the poorer receive. The rich are generous—they bestow on the teeming masses beauty and space for gathering and enjoyment. In return, they ask what the givers of all gifts ask: appreciation and a kind of fealty that amounts to a confirmation of the social arrangement the gift expresses. "I would rather be respected than loved," the old saying goes. That is the Seagram Building, in short. Respect is the essence of an ethics based on power and its separateness from more common, and ambiguous, everyday emotions. This is what the aesthetics of its architecture has achieved, in the name of a company that makes and sells everyday liquors and wines and stands for no lofty ideals of public life.

The Seagram Building, it is true, is an exception in the realm of commercial office buildings, but only in the extremity of its aesthetical qualities and, accordingly, its ethical implications. Today, all such buildings offer various forms of public plazas and usually street-level spaces for shopping, entertainment, eating.... Part of Seagram's uniqueness is the austerity of its offerings, its lack of conscious appeal to popular tastes, which characterize most examples of its building type today. No benches, no quaint lamps, no signs, no color, just hard-edged geometry in unapologetically, elegantly "timeless" materials. The public—the masses—have the rare opportunity to enter the living space of an intellectual and social elite and to feel the distance—the gulf, really—between. It is not, as it turns out, an alienating experience, but a rather popular one. The majority of people, or so it would seem, enjoy knowing—viscerally feeling—the presence of a higher, to them unattainable but not wholly inaccessible, stratum in the life of the city and its society.

November 13, 2007

What Is Architecture?

I would argue that any architect worthy of the name addresses in one way or another the prospect of building. That is to say, the architect's primary concern is the built environment, the physical domain of our experiences that is tangible, material, and constructed. However, I would also argue that this fact does not mean that an architect's work will necessarily be realized in the built environment. The reason is obvious: the architect is not the one who decides to build or not to build. That decision is made by others who control the financial and material resources necessary to build, those who own the land or represent the prevailing governmental and legal systems. Architects do not build—rather, they make designs that instruct others what and how to build, if those others should so decide.

If this is the case, then the question is: wherein resides the architecture? Is it only in the realized, built design? Many would argue this is so, and that the unbuilt design of the architect has only the potential of becoming architecture, and is not such in itself. It is hard to quarrel with this outlook, in that we have not yet invented an objective measuring device for detecting the presence of architecture. In this domain, architecture is detected by the attuned sensibilities of individual observers, which can and will vary widely.

Rather than challenge this outlook, however, I will interrogate it a bit more. If architecture is only in the building, what, we might say, puts it there? The labor and skills of the contractors and mechanics who build the building? If that were true then every building would be architecture, and not even the most skeptical of observers would claim that to be the case. Architecture is something different from building. So what makes it different?

The usual answer is: a concept. Architecture is the built realization of a particular concept, or idea. This idea can be about construction, or the way people will use a building, or how the building fits into a physical or a social landscape. But wait. Every building has such concepts, even warehouses, convenience stores, garages. They are embedded in its typology, so much so that we don't even need to discuss them. Everyone knows not only how to behave in such spaces, but also what they mean in simple, everyday terms. This is the basis of what we call "vernacular architecture," which is a vital part of architectural history. But a vernacular cannot account for, or lead to, the creative architecture that responds to the changes dramatically affecting the contemporary world. That architecture is something else. So, then, what is it?

I would say that architecture, as we understand it today, differs from building in that the concept, or ideas, it embodies are formulated in a unique, and not merely generic, way. In order for this to be so, it must originate in a single mind—the mind of an architect. One consequence of this understanding is that the architecture is in the architect's work—sketches, drawings, models—from the beginning. If this were not so, it would be impossible to somehow "inject" it later. Given this, it is merely a semantic debate as to whether the instrumental products of an architect's design process are architecture or only have the potential for architecture. In either case they cannot be dispensed with, if architecture is to exist.

And there is something else. The more that concepts and ideas formulated by the architect have an immediacy for contemporary conditions of living, thinking, and working, the higher we will value it as architecture. We want architecture to participate in the crucial changes affecting our lives, and not simply form a backdrop to them.

Why is this issue important? Because the idea of such an architecture today is disappearing. Developers, corporations, and politicians understand the marketing value of architecture, as long as it gets attention. But that cannot be all there is. Architects themselves—some of whom devote their unique minds and their talents for embodying ideas to serving the interests of developers, corporations, and politicians—are ignoring more urgently critical conditions. Continuing the struggle to understand what architecture is helps keep everyone—especially the architects—more honest.

November 25, 2007

The Corporate Model

One of the main roles of architecture, historically speaking, has been that of making a particular kind of impression on the public, and that is the impression of the power of a few over many. The few are those who control the wealth and resources of a society and have the financial capability to commission and realize large buildings in the public domain. The many are those who depend on the few for their livelihoods. The ascendancy of democratic—even populist—forms of government has done little to change architecture's role. Democracy has resulted in some redistribution of wealth; the merchant and the professional classes have a greater share of it than ever before, on the average and at their extremes, where many business owners, lawyers, doctors, and architects have become rich. Indeed, the professional and merchant classes have largely merged, a phenomenon that has occurred in the past thirty years or so.

For those who are willing to look back to an earlier era, the professional was distinguished from the businessperson by an ethical position. The aim of the businessperson was to make a profit. The aim of the professional was to provide a service. This position found an example in the United States by the fact that doctors, lawyers, and architects had fee schedules, agreed upon through their professional organizations, which set the amount they were to be paid for a particular service. While there were always the exceptions, on the high and low ends, professionals charged according to the fee schedule so that they would be judged (and hired) on the quality of the service they provided and on their reputation, and not on whether they charged a higher or lower fee. At a point in the early 1970s the distinction between product and service was challenged by the federal government, which said that the professional was a merchant whose product was a service. Fee schedules, it contended, were a form of price-fixing, which is illegal under "fair trade" laws, and could no longer be used. Professionals had to compete in the "marketplace," just like everyone else. While the ethical implications of this ruling by the government were enormous, it was little debated at the time in ethical terms. Most professionals accepted the change and joined the merchant class, setting up various forms of professional corporations that took the place, in more than just economic ways, of private practices.

In a real-world sense, the "practitioner" was by then an anachronism, one belonging to a social system that had functioned more on personal responsibility than the present system does. For example, in the pre–credit card era up to the early 1960s (when computerization made credit cards practicable), there were two ways to pay a merchant for a purchase. One was cash. As a result people carried more cash with them than they do today. The other was a personal bank check. The check is a promissory note that depends on the truthfulness—the personal promise—of the check giver and on the trust of the check receiver, the merchant, for its efficacy as a medium of exchange. This exchange was more personal than institutional. On a similar level, the professional practitioner had been judged by the efficacy of his or her service, no doubt, but also on a personal level. By the 1970s, this was being swept away society-wide by computerization and a homogenization of economic standards that effaced personal distinctions in favor of computable data. The loss of the personal—the intuitive—as well as of the lone professional practitioner who assumes personal responsibility for his work and its consequences has been the price to be paid for the expansion of economic opportunities gained through technology and globalization.

It is difficult to argue that the loss of the lone practitioner in architecture and the rise of the corporate architect have had a great effect on the way cities look or how cities impact people living in them. To do so, one would have to demonstrate that cities "after" are appreciably different from those "before." Still, the rise of corporatism has had one obvious effect. Architects, rarely leaders in society, have followed corporate trends toward the expansion and consolidation of markets by extending their practices first to the scope of the national, then to the international and global. One result has been the radiation of a new type of generic architecture, one that is reproduced in one city after another, around the world. This is not a universal architecture such as modernist theory proposed would be produced in the same way everywhere by different architects following a fixed (implicitly socialist) set of principles. Rather it is a generic of the idiosyncratic styles of highly individual architects, each practicing independently, not necessarily following any principles at all. It is the generic of the name brand, of the consumer commodity, of the franchise. Corporate architects market their styles globally, filling far-flung urban centers with their high-end products. This follows precisely the global corporate model.

December 19, 2007

Starchitects Defended

Nicolai Ouroussoff, the *New York Times* architecture critic, wrote an article published on Sunday, December 16, 2007, entitled "Let the 'Starchitects' Work All the Angles."*/ In particular, he singles out Frank Gehry, Jean Nouvel, Rem Koolhaas, and Santiago Calatrava as the subjects of what can only be called his apologia for their

*/ Nicolai Ouroussoff, "Let the 'Starchitects' Work All the Angles," *New York Times*, December 16, 2007, www.nytimes.com/2007/12/16 /weekinreview/16ouroussoff.html.

deals with various mega-developers to design large, high-profile commercial buildings around the world. Regardless of what we might think of the projects, the architects, and their deals, the Ouroussoff piece does them no service. It is a weakly conceived, sloppily written, wincingly defensive piece of PR.

Ouroussoff's underlying theme—the article's tagline—is that a big name on the blueprint doesn't mean sellout at play. It may mean visionary at work. But, only "may." It might also mean "sellout," after all? Apparently some people have thought so, and I guess the critic is worried that the architects in question might be stung by such doubts. After all, they are enjoying great success, so why should they be denied anything—including the admiration of "those inside the profession who see . . . the pact between high architects and developers [as] a Faustian bargain." After conceding "there's some truth to this, of course," the critic sets out to convince the skeptics.

He launches several arguments. The first of these is that the architects in question finally have a chance to test in the public domain their visionary ideas, which—he says—were once a critique of what was wrong with the profession. Sadly, he offers no examples of either the visionary ideas of, say, Calatrava or Gehry or the public projects where they have been/are being tested. It would have been helpful, maybe even essential to his argument.

Another argument is more nitty-gritty. "To my mind, if these architects are also getting a cut of the pie, why begrudge them?" It's not clear, exactly, which pie he's referring to, but it's clearly one that's rich in fat and carbohydrates. He continues, seeking to assuage any guilt involved, by saying, "In this new world, no hands are clean; there are good guys and bad guys on all sides." So much for ethical distinctions.

He goes on: "From the architect's perspective, working with mainstream developers is also a chance to step out of the narrow confines of high culture and have a more direct impact on centers of everyday life that were once outside their reach, from shopping malls to entire business districts." Sounds good. No doubt public culture will benefit from a Nouvel shopping mall or a Koolhaas business center. It would have been helpful, for the skeptics at least, if the critic had explained exactly how. The democratization of high culture? Or its banalization? How does the public benefit from visionary ideas reduced to mundane ones?

And on. "Architects have no control over a development's scale or density; nor do they control the underlying social and economic realities that shape it." True enough, once starchitects are in the game. But they don't have to join the game. Instead they could turn their visionary abilities to different sorts of problems, ones that we don't already know how to solve. Do we really need visionaries to solve the urgent problems of shopping malls and office towers? But, no. "Why should such an immense responsibility be turned over to hacks?" Someone's got to do blockbuster developments, why not "our most imaginative talents?" Sounds good. But if the architects are as powerless over the realities as the critic says, then it's a bring down, not a step up.

Ouroussoff stumbles badly here. The question remains, why did he feel the need to rise to the defense of several of the most powerful architects in the profession?

2008

The New and the Ugly

The art critic Clement Greenberg once wrote that the new is always ugly. This is because it confronts us with experiences and ideas that we haven't encountered before and don't understand or, at least, are not accustomed to. It follows that, because we live in a society and an urban landscape driven by the new, we are in for substantial, even perpetual, ugliness. His concern was the aesthetic, but also the ethical. He wrote in a post–World War II period not only of rapid expansion of American cities and the social landscape they created, but also of existentialism, which made ugliness—if it was "authentic," that is, if it emerged from the inner nature of a thing—a virtue. Prettiness was conventional, easily acceptable, and, in a time of rapid change, an ethical crime against truth. Prettiness was used as a cosmetic by advertisers and other commercial—and political—interests to disguise the difficult, even tragic, struggles that social, economic, and technological changes were forcing upon people and their ways of thinking and living. Prettiness was used by the powers-that-be not to make the new more digestible, but to disguise its deeper implications and ethical imperatives. It was a way of saying, "Don't worry, everything is normal—just go on as you always have." In other words, "Just let us keep running the world as we always have."

Occasionally artists manage to create the truly ugly. Jackson Pollock's drip paintings were prime examples of Greenbergian newness, hence ugliness. He was driven by ideas of the "automatic," which was a term for the uncontrollable forces of both the psyche and of society. Mega-scaled urban and suburban growth had made central control impossible, much the same as mass production and mass media had a generation before Pollock's time. The technological machinery was no longer guided by a single person or elite group; rather, the elite, to gain commercial advantage, had broken big machines down into ever smaller, more salable ones, relinquishing control of the changes they wrought to ever more dispersed and more ubiquitous "consumers." Pollock's tangled paint drippings and swirls were at once an assertion of one person's independence from the norms and a poignant expression of his surrender to the unpredictable, the vicissitudes of modern existence. Their violation of the aesthetic norms of beauty was at once exciting and challenging. They existed at an edge between order and chaos, balancing traditional notions of composition with inchoate scrawls and scribbles. Their ugliness indicated a way forward. We could live with uncertainty without abandoning all noble traditions.

If we follow through on Greenberg's thought, we realize that eventually things we didn't understand become familiar: yesterday's "ugly" becomes today's "pretty." It's telling that Pollock's paintings, even though they've become icons of modern art, are still considered ugly by many people—a sign of their enduring newness.

Question: have architects managed to create the truly new and enduringly ugly? If we look at Le Corbusier's chapel at Ronchamp, I think we can agree he succeeded in doing so there. Frank Gehry's Guggenheim Bilbao, which we might see as a play on Ronchamp's formal themes, seems glittering and pretty in comparison and won universal acceptance immediately, always the acid test. Ronchamp is a modernist icon, but is too strange in form and idea to have been, by now, more than superficially assimilated. It is still new, still ugly.

January 13, 2008

Haunted

Shandor Hassan, *Pawn Shop Austin Texas*, 1995, from the series *American Journey*, 1994–97

Shandor Hassan's photographs are of places that seem haunted. The feeling comes not only because we see the places at night and devoid of people, but also because of a different kind of emptiness, one that is haunted by a nonhuman presence or, rather, by the ghost of something more vague, more abstract. This ghost is not at rest, as the stillness of the images suggests. We sense its uneasy presence, even if we do not think or speak of it.

These are not places where we like to be. Yet they are here, ostensibly for us. The elements that comprise them are, if not exactly friendly, then at least familiar. They were made for us to use and appreciate. They are intended to welcome us, yet they do not. We enter these places reluctantly, only from necessity. Then we leave as quickly as possible.

But what, exactly, haunts them? I believe it is the ghost of American modernism. It is the ghost of a once-upon-a-time promise of a better life for everyone, a promise that never delivered. The convenience stores sell junk food that makes us fat. The service station dispenses endless fuel for gas-guzzlers that poison our atmosphere. The franchise restaurant is everywhere but belongs nowhere. The pawnshop may be easy, but it reminds us of our, and others', desperation. The promise haunts us and its ghost lingers at the edges of night, dreamlike and restless.

Then we come to a little illuminated house. How cheerful it is! But the ghost is there, too, mocking our optimism and good cheer.

January 21, 2008

Lost and Found

I want to be careful not to strain the indulgence of visitors to the Lebbeus Woods blog. With this post I might be pushing my luck. Still, I thought it might be of interest to people who know my work to see a few of my drawings that I came across in an old plan file. These are certainly the first drawings I made in which I tried to give visual, even tectonic, form to philosophical concepts. They were made in 1973.

The paired, dialogical drawings seem most alive to me. In them, the main ideational threads—conflict and transformation—that run through my work up to the present are visible. As is my excited embrace of contradictory modes and forms. This is seen in the interplay of the organic and the geometric, the fantastical and the mathematical, but also, less conventionally, in their subordination to both the premeditation and spontaneity of drawing. Architects make designs. Their designs have to embody—or at least allude to—the paradoxical nature of the human condition and of our personal experiences. These were early attempts that, it seems to me, still resonate with a degree of clarity.

In these same drawings, some nascent formal experimentation appears, the beginnings of a personal language and grammar of formation that I have developed over the years since then in numerous projects and studies. What is interesting—and a little frightening—is that the basic forms and ideas were there from the beginning.

The more identifiably architectural drawings are less interesting today. The ideas, while well enough drawn, are more conventional, more related to architectural developments of their time. So be it. We have to learn. And also, we must never forget, it takes a long time to understand architecture, let alone create it.

PS: The series of which these drawings are a part was intended to be a "treatise on architecture," but was never published. Naturally, it also included many pages of dialogical text.

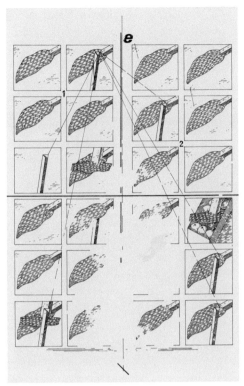

Lost and Found 1, 1973

Lost and Found 2, 1973

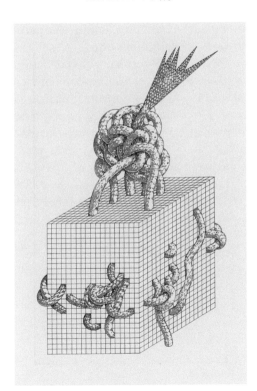

Lost and Found 5, 1973

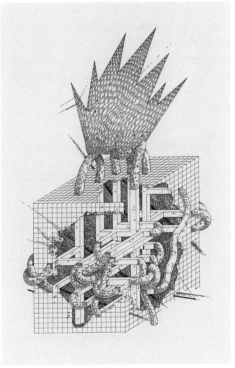

Lost and Found 6, 1973

The Reality of Theory

Sarajevo, from *War and Architecture*, 1993. Proposal for the reconstruction of the Electrical Management Building

The question of how theory relates to practice has come up several times in previous posts. The Electrical Management (Elektroprivreda) Building in Sarajevo, Bosnia, gives us a good chance to consider the issue.

First, a brief (as possible) history. Sarajevo is the capital city of Bosnia and Herzegovina, which in 1991 was one of the six republics incorporated into Yugoslavia, an independent Socialist Federation founded in 1945. With the end of the Cold War in 1990, Yugoslavia began to break up and its republics became independent countries. In the case of Bosnia, this was accompanied by massive violence. A war raged on its soil from 1992 to 1995, which the so-called Dayton Accords ended. Tens of thousands were killed and Bosnian Serbs carried out the worst genocide in Europe since the Holocaust against Bosnian Muslims. The city of Sarajevo was under blockade and military siege from 1992 to 1995, during which time it had no normal supplies of food or water, no electricity, gas, or heat, and no telephone links. It was almost completely cut off from the outside world.

The United Nations flew in canned food and basic medical supplies. Journalists were allowed to fly in and out on UN relief flights. A few cultural figures—prominently Susan Sontag—became "journalists" and came to Sarajevo during its darkest hours to give moral support, stage theater performances, and offer other gestures to encourage people, particularly Sarajevo's world-class artists and intellectuals. The city was dark and cold and under constant artillery and sniper fire.

The Bosnian Serb army surrounding Sarajevo had in mind to humiliate the people in the city, to punish the city for its cosmopolitan character and traditions. As much as anything, the siege was a terrorist act, a war on diversity and urbanity, and an attack on the very idea of "city." Thankfully—because of the strong spirit of its people—the terrorists ultimately failed.

In November 1993, I went to Sarajevo—as a "journalist"—at the invitation of Haris Pašović, head of the Sarajevo International Film and Theater Festival, who was aware of my work from a lecture I had given in Sarajevo two years earlier. I was accompanied by another architect, Ekkehard Rehfeld, who fully participated in all conversations and events. I brought with me forty freshly printed copies of *War and Architecture* (Pamphlet Architecture 15) and a roll of photocopy enlargements to make an exhibition. My goal, put simply, was to help architects in Sarajevo to begin thinking about the role architecture would play both during and after the siege. I was able to see firsthand what the people were enduring and the city's many damaged buildings.

The Electrical Management Building—along with the post office, parliament, national library, mosques, and churches—was symbolic of the civic life of Sarajevo and therefore was especially targeted by the besieging Bosnian Serb army. I met the architect of the building, Ivan Štraus, one of the most respected architects in Yugoslavia, who was very supportive of my presence and ideas. It was he, during a later visit, who asked me to design a reconstruction of the Electrical Management Building.

In this and other reconstruction projects I proposed for Sarajevo, my theory was clear: the siege, and the four-year-long war, changed everything. Socialism was out, and an uncertain privatization was in. The city was losing its ethnic diversity, as Serbs, Croats, Slovenes, and anyone who could left it and, for a while before the city was completely surrounded, Muslim refugees poured in. The infrastructure of utilities and services was severely damaged, with no idea of where the money would come from to repair them, or when that would even be possible. Buildings vital to the social and economic functioning of the city were damaged and unusable without extensive reconstruction, but, again, how reconstruction would be financed was unclear. More than all this, the people of the city had suffered years of deprivation, terror, and uncertainty, and many would be transformed by it. How, I asked, could architecture play any positive role in all of this?

My answer was that architecture, as a social and primarily constructive act, could heal the wounds by creating entirely new types of space in the city. These would be what I had called "freespaces," spaces without predetermined programs of use, but whose strong forms demanded the invention of new programs corresponding to the new, postwar conditions. I hypothesized that "90 percent of the damaged buildings would be restored to their normal prewar forms and uses, as most people want to return to their old ways of living. . . . But 10 percent should be freespaces, for those who did not want to go back, but forward." The freespaces would be the crucibles for the creation of new thinking and sociopolitical forms, small and large. I believed then— and still do—that the cities and their inhabitants who have suffered the most difficult transitions in the contemporary world (in Sarajevo and elsewhere) have something important to teach us, who live comfortably in the illusion

Actual reconstruction, Ivan Štraus, architect, 2005

that we are immune to the demands that radical changes of many kinds will impose on us, too.

The design for the reconstruction of the Electrical Management Building is a case study in the application of this theory. Most of the building would be restored to accommodate corporate offices of the known kind. However, in the space that had been literally blasted off by artillery fire, a freespace would be constructed. It would be inhabited by those who, in the reinvention of ways to inhabit space, would open the way to the future.

Architects are idea people. We have concepts and make designs that embody or implement them. We present them as clearly and openly as possible, and can only hope that others will find them useful to their ends, and build them. In the case of the Electrical Management Building in Sarajevo, my theory and design were not used. This does not mean that they are wrong or a failure. Nor does it mean that those who elected to ignore them were wrong to do so. More challenges await us, and the ideas here may yet become useful in ways that I could never conceive.

February 9, 2008

Slums: One Idea /6

Architects, as I said in the previous post, are idea people. We have concepts and make designs that embody or implement them. We present them as clearly and openly as possible, and can only hope that others will find them useful to their ends and build them. When it comes to the reformation of slums, we are a long way from having designs and are very much at the beginning of having ideas. It is in that spirit that I make this post. I count on the tough criticism of colleagues.

If we brainstorm a little, we can imagine, as one solution, a capsule—a material package—that can be inserted into a slum. With its use by a person living there, it immediately begins to transform that person's living conditions. What it does first of all is establish a demarcated space that is secure from without, clean and radiant with natural and artificial light within. The sheltered space provides distinct areas for sleeping, gathering, hygiene, and sanitation. It provides space for cooking, with adequate ventilation, and for work—whatever type of work the person and his family or friends do for their own benefit, economic or otherwise. The capsule is capable of configuring itself, or being configured, according to different patterns of work and living. It does not produce a module or standardized unit. If we think of it more like a nutrient, rather than a product, we understand that the results it creates are adapted in unique ways to particular persons or families, because it nurtures whatever is strong in a given situation, rather than imposing a uniform result based on a preconceived judgment of what is best. In this sense (letting our imaginations play freely), we can conceive of the capsule as something that organically enhances the living and working conditions of people who use it, beginning as something standardized—like a pill we take when sick—that morphs into a restorative source of energy, metabolizing into material form, enabling health, and enhancing the capabilities, whatever they may be, of those who use it.

If such a capsule could be designed by leading thinkers, engineers, architects; if it could be produced by the best technicians using advanced technological facilities; if it could be financed by institutions in the private and public sectors with a vision of the vast benefits it would create for everyone; then it would seem that such a project could actually be accomplished. If a large number of these capsules were to be inserted into a slum, the result over time would be growth of a healthier living environment, from within. Because the transformation would be incremental, both in time and scale, it is conceivable that an organic form of community could literally grow from the exchange and cooperation of people now inhabiting slums as they reform their living environments.

It is easy to imagine objections to such a "magic bullet," as the cure for syphilis was called in the nineteenth century. From the side of the slum dwellers, it might seem an unwelcome intrusion from outside, just another quick fix imposed by the economically advantaged on the desperately poor, serving the interests of the rich by transforming the slum according to their well-intentioned but—to the slum dweller—necessarily opposed values. It is especially important, then, that the transformative capsule enables the slum dwellers to achieve their goals, serving their values, and does not reduce them to subjects of its designers' and makers' wills. Inevitably, the values, prejudices, perspectives, and aspirations of the designers and makers will be imbedded in the capsule and what it does. Therefore the slum dwellers should, in the first place, have the right of refusal. Also, they must have the right to modify the capsule and its effects as they see fit. It cannot be a locked system, capable of producing only a predetermined outcome. The implication of these freedoms is that the capsule, whatever its capabilities, could be used to work against the intentions of its designers and makers. Because the effects of the capsule would be powerfully transformative, its possession would involve risk for all the groups and individuals involved. Because the sponsoring institutions in the economically enabled sector have the most to lose, it is more likely that resistance to the creation of such a capsule would come not from slum dwellers but from these sectors. For those who believe in such a project, it is imperative that leaders in the economically powerful sectors be convinced that creation of the capsule is a risk worth taking.

Even without institutional support and sanction, the conceptualization and design of the capsule can and should begin immediately. There is nothing to lose by moving in this direction. And moving independently is probably the only effective way to proceed, because issues of politics and economics, from institutional viewpoints, will slow down or frustrate the process of having ideas and developing them, as they often do in much less complex projects. What is needed now is free thinking by the most creative minds in order to innovate on the level required by the "unsolvable" problem of transforming slums on a local, let alone global, scale. Because the problem is urgently in need of a solution, the effort should be thought of in the same way as that to find a cure—or at least a treatment—for a virulent disease that is already affecting millions and spreading rapidly.

There is really no time to waste.

February 24, 2008

Common Ground

The sidewalks of New York are extraordinary, if overlooked, human documents. Found on them—as though on the tablets of a lost civilization—are accumulated inscriptions comprising a chronicle of the city's existential complexity. There are the marks and scratches of the ceaseless movement of people and vehicles; the stains of spills large and small; the ruptures and cracks of destruction and repairs; the often-jarring juxtaposition of diverse materials; both fresh and long-faded symbols indicating this and that; and everywhere mysterious black spots, which I thought were "the souls of the departed" that somehow sank into the gritty surfaces, but which my wife assures me are only the marks of chewing gum carelessly thrown away. /₇ The task of deciphering the stories imbedded in even a square meter of any sidewalk in the city would be overwhelming, particularly if we consider that a story they might reveal could read like this:

The light gray is the bottom layer, infused here and there with sandy tan and gravelly blue speckles, and even some dull red flecks that were part of the original matrix. Then comes an almost transparent layer of black soot, deposited unevenly across the entire surface, probably ten years ago when the building across the street almost burned down. Then comes a layer . . .

Or, like this: The Con Edison surveyor spray-painted a mark indicating where the water main is, six feet below the surface. A woman in soft-soled black shoes stopped abruptly just here, dropping a bottle of ketchup she'd gone out to buy while dinner was on the stove (she was in such a hurry that the ketchup was unbagged), unaware that the water main was slowly leaking. A drunken man stumbled and . . .

Not exactly compelling stuff. No beginnings, middles, or endings. No climaxes or conclusions (unless you consider the faded but still visible bloodstains of a fatal shooting, which only an experienced forensic investigator would recognize as such), just the on-and-on of everyday life. Yet we could fill books, even libraries, with such stories. Imagine what future anthropologists could make of them, if only the sidewalks would survive a few thousand years—but they won't. Like the daily lives they portray, they slip unnoticed past our consciousness and beyond the reach of memory. During the next street-digging project, the sidewalks will be broken up and carted in unrecognizable chunks to a landfill, even as new sidewalks are being laid down.

Without the stories, the sidewalks fall prey to gratuitous aestheticizing. They are visually very seductive, if we are not bound by classical standards of beauty. The layering, the diversity, the clashes, and the unexpected harmonies of textures, colors, tones, lines, dribbles and dots, cracks and joints. They combine to form a vast mini-terrain that is almost entirely of human invention, but not intention. Fusing accident and design, they form a visual field that is unique in part and whole, and inimitable. They can never be repeated or reproduced. Yet sidewalks can awaken the imagination of the visual artist who is easily intoxicated by a depth of possibility that seems, in its contradictions, inexhaustible. Just like the city, at once timeless and ephemeral, monumental and immemorial, they are close—very close—to the heart of things.

February 29, 2008

The Proto-Urban Condition

With cities on the rise—many existing ones expanding rapidly, and others, once mere towns, growing into full-fledged urban centers—the need to understand the urban condition becomes ever more urgent. While we would hope that local culture would be a major factor in the design and planning of particular cities in quite different parts of the world, we have to acknowledge that there are more universal factors, having to do with international economics and development, operating globally today. Architects

Cooper Union students and faculty review the master model, 2007.

are being asked to design buildings far from their home cities and cultures, and they inevitably transplant what they already know. What concerns me here is, what do they already know? The case for studying proto-urban conditions—conditions shared by cities anywhere—is made in the hope that what architects already know can be deepened to the level of principle. If such a deepening could occur, local variations on prototypical conditions would become more possible, and the present era of typological impositions of one culture upon others would gradually be brought to a close.

The rectilinear street grid—creating straight, continuous spaces lined with building walls—is a proto-urban condition explored by fourth-year students at Cooper Union School of Architecture, under the direction of a team of four faculty, in the spring semester of 2007. Rather than assign a site in the grids of, say, Manhattan, Barcelona, or Beijing, any of which would be heavily loaded with historical and cultural factors requiring extensive analysis, the given site was an abstracted version of a street space resulting from a rectilinear grid. This allowed us to immediately begin to develop new strategies for inserting programs of use that could inform not only this analogous site, but also Manhattan, Barcelona, Beijing, and other cities as well.

The commentary by Professor Kevin Bone sums up the procedure of the studio: "The studio set out to investigate the ideal of multiple architectural works woven together across an urban landscape and to look at the community of projects from various perspectives. Works were expected to operate in fields of non-specific boundaries. Where the limits of one individual architectural proposal began and another ended was not absolutely defined, allowing for new combinations of urban architectural interactions. To accomplish this, students worked in various groups on various stages of the investigations. Initially students were asked to pair up and develop architectural propositions that communicated with each other. This architectural conversation could be from one side of the wall to the other, through the wall, or at discrete positions along the wall, as long as the projects somehow addressed other proposals. As the studio evolved these works (in some cases) fused together into a single hybrid proposition. The pair ups then assembled in larger groups containing several pairs of students. These larger groups looked at all of the proposals of the class and attempted to place them in areas of operation within the site. These groups each produced a kind of spatial/zoning diagram, an architectural master plan for the work of the studio. The best ideas from each of these four 'planning' groups were incorporated into a general organizing structure. All students worked on a single idealized urban site and all projects existed simultaneously with each other. The assembly of works became an autonomous architectural work, with accidents and unintentional spaces provoking further architectural response. The proto-urban problem began to build its own context and its own history. The class and studio began to build its own community and negotiate its own rules for various architectural actions."

As can be seen in the master model, which was developed at eighth-inch scale, the rigor of the methodology combined with the freedom of the students to design for programs of their choosing resulted in a varied, complexly interwoven, highly articulated architectural landscape. Densely layered spatially and programmatically, it demonstrates a principle often considered paradoxical: given carefully considered circumstances, the interests of a community and its creative individuals can reinforce one another. The making of architecture is the key.*/

*/ The Proto-Urban Condition, ARCH 141 Architectural Design, spring 2007. The Irwin S. Chanin School of Architecture of The Cooper Union. Anthony Vidler, Dean. Faculty: Lebbeus Woods, Kevin Bone, Mersiha Veledar, and Christoph a. Kumpusch. Students: Evelyn Alejo, Oskar Arnorsson, Peter Ballman, Jessica Bayuk, Lis Cena, Paul Dallas, David Elzer, Jack Fowler, Christopher Fox, Anupama Garla, Daniel Garwood, John Greenberg, Iman Johnson, Ian Knight, Yevgeny Koramblyum, Christian Kotzamanis, Katerina Kourkoula, Joseph Lawrance, Aaron Lim, Stephen Martin, Bruno Navarro, Ido Nissani, Samuel Omans, Jesung Park, Yoonok Park, Graham Smith, Laura Steele, Erin Stephenson, Wahid Seraj, Rayyane Tabet, and Uri Wegman.

Slow Manifesto

Integrity

Hard as it is to believe, it was once thought that architecture had integrity. Not just the architects who practiced their profession with a principled, uncompromising sense of purpose or mission, but buildings themselves. Certainly, the attribution of human qualities to inanimate things like buildings is and always was what the literary critics call a "pathetic fallacy." A "sad moon" may work as a metaphor of our own emotions when we, on occasion, look at the moon, but no one would really believe that the moon itself experiences sadness, or anything else. And yet the belief that buildings had an uncompromising, principled reality about them was once widely held. As a student of architecture, nearly fifty years ago, I was taught that all good buildings had, in fact, three integrities, without which they could not be considered architecture.

The first was integrity of function. This meant that a building's form and spaces had to be designed to serve their intended purpose. Fifty years ago, everyone knew this meant its form had to accommodate a known building typology: school, hospital, house, museum . . . all of which had been established by exemplary precedents.

The second was integrity of materials. This meant that a material was always used according to its inherent properties. Wood, for example, was a "beautiful" natural material, so it should never be painted. The same with concrete—even though it was not beautiful or natural, its roughness and ugliness were integral with its "character," so it should always be left exposed.

The third was integrity of structure. This meant that whatever held a building up had to be clearly visible as part of its form. Structure was not to be disguised or hidden, as in Beaux-Arts buildings, burying, say, the steel frame structure of a building in masonry walls to achieve the effect of an ancient Roman or Gothic building. To do that was to betray the reality of the building, to turn it into something false, a lie, a mere stage set—the antithesis of architecture.

This idea holds that a building is—like a human body or a machine—an assemblage of parts having diverse purposes that must be integrated to form a coherent, working whole. In order to be integrated, each of the parts—function, materials, structure—has to be integral within itself, within its own, intrinsic nature, to join coherently with the others. It is rather like the old saying, "Be true to yourself, and you cannot be false to another." Each part has to have integrity before the whole can have it, too. In this way, architecture is the embodiment of an ethical, as well as aesthetic, ideal.

Such thoughts were once taken very seriously. We still see their residue in the buildings of some prominent architects in the over-sixty generation, who grew up with the idea that architecture had integrity. For the generations following them, however, a building's integrity—or lack of it—is no longer an issue. The idea is, in fact, never mentioned.

Newer ideas hold that a building—like any product of manufacture—is a unit serving a prescribed purpose within which its constituent parts are entirely subordinate to the whole. This means that the makeup of any part can vary, so long as the integrity of the unit is not violated. Perhaps the better word is "efficacy"—the effectiveness of the unit. The ease and speed with which the computer can integrate different systems has taken the emphasis off the different parts and placed it on the whole. In a practical as well as philosophical sense, the goal of design today is an overall synthesis of the elements of building— a form—that is achieved not as a result of assembling parts, but established at the beginning of the design process. Architects who work with any 3-D modeling program know that structure and materials are now subordinate to form. When concrete can be easily substituted for steel framing, or plastic for glass, or stressed-skin carbon fiber for riveted aluminum without sacrificing the coherence of the form, then the lines between the former distinctions are sufficiently blurred to be insignificant.

There is another factor. The global marketing of brand-name consumer goods has coincided with a social trend towards an effacement of differences based on racial, gender, economic, and other stereotypes. It has created a new type of diversity based, ironically enough, on sameness. In the products we buy, the places we go, and the ideas we have, we all share the same differences. In other words, we can have different designer clothing, or buildings by different well-known architects, but the differences between these brand-name products are not antithetical or opposed, like the old stereotypes (black/white, male/female, gay/straight, socialist/capitalist, modern/classical…), but are only variations on themes and trends dominating the marketplace at the moment. Ethical distinctions (right/wrong, good/bad…), which are seldom marketable themes, have—like integrity— become all but irrelevant.*/

*/ The critic gets it (almost) right: See Nicolai Ouroussoff, "Nice Tower! Who's Your Architect?" *New York Times*, March 23, 2008, www.nytimes.com/2008/03/23/arts/design/23ouro.html.

March 26, 2008

Raimund Abraham: Musikerhaus

Musicians' House. Four musicians will live here every year, one in each quadrant. Occasionally, they will meet in the center space and make music together, under the triangular opening to the sky. Music and mathematics and architecture. Rarely has geometry been considered so seriously in architecture or taken to such poetic lengths. Clarity is not a conclusion, but the threshold to a mystery that is archaic and prophetic, belonging at once to the first questions ever asked and the

Raimund Abraham, Musikerhaus, Düsseldorf, Germany, 2008. Construction view

last ones that ever can be asked. An epic cycle of time is evoked here, and it both exhilarates and threatens.

How accustomed we are to architecture entertaining us with its novelty, or its richness, or its melodrama! This building challenges us with its sober, still, enigmatic presence. We are discomfited, unprepared. And then we hear within it the sounds of music being played, crisp, equally clear and abstract, yet elusive, ephemeral . . . and we understand. This is what philosophers meant by "the dialectic." This is what the architect, Raimund Abraham, means by "architecture is a collision between ideas and matter."

Raimund Abraham's Musikerhaus in Düsseldorf is under construction and due to be completed this year. */

*/ See also Gregory Zucker, "A Conversation with Raimund Abraham," New York Architecture, http://www.nyc-architecture.com /ARCH/ARCH-RaimundAbraham.htm.

April 8, 2008

Dumb Boxes

Anyone familiar with my work knows that I reserve a special place in my feelings and thoughts for what I call "dumb boxes." These are buildings that are often little more than rectilinear solids of brick or stone facing with holes punched in them for windows and doors. Sometimes they are all glass, with no holes at all. Most architects today consider them the antithesis of creative design, but I believe they are essential to it. The worst thing I can imagine is an urban world of idiosyncratic buildings that jostle each other for attention with no reference to any deeper form of order. The next worst thing I can imagine, though, is a world of dumb boxes embellished by architects determined to disguise their dumbness with all manner of distracting shapes, colors, materials, or tectonic doodads. I say, a box is inherently dumb, so let it be dumb, by which I mean let it be what it is.

What is dumb about the box? Well, it's actually we, when confronting it, who are able to be dumb. We know what it is. We don't have to think about it. In the same way, we don't have to think about an urban street grid. Thirteen blocks up and two blocks to the right and we're there. What we find when we get to our destination is another matter, and it may shake, though probably not, our com- fortably routine world of assumptions. The same with the dumb box. Within it, we will probably find "normal" life, totally predictable. But we might find the abnormal, even the world shaking. Serial killers live in dumb boxes, as did Karl Marx and Wassily Kandinsky. Right now, a genius is sitting in a dumb box somewhere, thinking through a knotty problem that, if solved, will transform our ways of thinking, even of living. Alfred Hitchcock's *Rear Window* is a con- cise movie that plays on dumb boxes and their everyday, sometimes profound, human mysteries. Those of us who live in cities don't need a movie to tell us that we never really know, for sure, what lies around the next corner.

Architects, however, are today routinely indoctrinated against the dumb box. Even advertising urges us to "think outside the box." Why? Because it is thought we all hate the box for being too dumb, too boring, and we want to escape it. If we do escape by buying the advertised product, we usually find ourselves inside another dumb box populated by boring people just like us. It is clearly possible to live an extraordinary life inside a dumb box. Is it possible to lead an extraordinary life in anything other than a dumb box?

The extraordinary can only be measured against the ordinary. If the dumb box and all the predictability it embodies and symbolizes is the ordinary, then we need it in order to transcend it, if that is what we choose to do. In the world composed only of the extraordinary, the only extraordinary thing to do would be to design a dumb box.

Or, there is another way to look at it. In the world of the extraordinary—which becomes, in effect, the ordinary—the only way to transcend it is to design the more extraordinary—to up the ante. This is what seems to be happening in architecture today, in the post-Bilbao era. It brings to mind the comment by Eduard Hanslick, the nineteenth-century music critic, about the operas of Richard Wagner, which their author proclaimed as "The Music of the Future": Wagner's "style recognizes only superlatives; but a superlative has no future."/8

Perhaps, though, there is another way out of the trap of the extraordinary for its own sake, as a kind of "can you top this?" syndrome. Let us make the extraordinary only when extraordinary conditions demand it: radical social and political changes; recovery from war and natural disasters; the reformation of slums; cultural "paradigm shifts," such as computerization or the greening of technology. Let us refrain from dressing up old building types in extraordinary new forms that do nothing to transform the way we actually inhabit or use or think about them. Instead, let us deploy the extraordinary in architecture as a way of bringing about changes we believe are important to the improvement of the human condition.

In the meantime, let us inhabit our dumb boxes, striving for the extraordinary when it is necessary, at the same time sustaining as high a standard of the ordinary as we can. After all, it is the common ground—quite deep at that—we all share.

May 5, 2008

Line

Even though I am best known for my drawings and have spent many years as a teacher of architects, I have never taught drawing. The reason is that each person who wants to draw should devise his or her own way. It makes no sense to teach a method or style of drawing, because drawing is a way of thinking, and it would be wrong to didactically teach a method or style of thinking. People must learn from the drawers—and the thinkers—who appeal most to them, and then devise their own ways. Originality—in drawing and thinking—is important for the same reasons that individuality in all matters of existence is important: it confirms the wonder, and the terror, of the human condition.

Essentially, each of us is alone. Biologically and psychically we are separate not only from other living things, but also from others of our kind. We cannot feel or think what another person feels or thinks, nor can they know exactly our feelings or thoughts. Because we are social creatures and dependent upon each other, we spend much of our time and energy trying to communicate our thoughts and feelings, and also to understand, as deeply as possible, those of others. It is a uniquely human task and one that requires all our intellectual effort, emotional commitment, and expressive skills. Spoken and written languages are the foremost of these, but drawing—in all its variants—runs a close second. Indeed, as we know, there are ideas and feelings that can only be expressed in drawn form. If we look at the caves of Lascaux, we might imagine that drawing came before writing and was, in its narrative making of marks, its source.

When very young, let's say in my late teens and twenties, I had a fierce desire to communicate my thoughts and feelings through drawing. In high school I had some mechanical drawing courses, where I learned to use T square and triangles, but little else. For inspiration, I had to look in magazines and art books. I was tremendously moved by the etchings of Francisco Goya, the drawings of Pieter Bruegel, the ink and watercolor drawings of Paul Klee, and, of course, the drawings of Michelangelo Buonarroti and Leonardo da Vinci. Each artist conveyed something different in his work, something that resonated with my own sensibility but did not sum it up. Different as these artists were, they all had one thing in common: a mastery of line.

What I mean by "line" is exactly that: a single mark, short or long, drawn with a pen, pencil, stylus, or any sharply pointed instrument that is held in the hand and commanded by it, in coordination with the brain, to inscribe on paper, tablet, plate, or any chosen surface exactly that mark and not another.

This last qualification is important. When rubbing a piece of charcoal, pastel, or blunt pencil on a surface, one accepts (even hopes for) a certain degree of approximation, even of accident. The resulting tone is, from an analytical point of view, vague when compared with line. Line is precise and unequivocal. It is here, not there. Making a line is not about accidents. Rather, it is about contour, edge, and shape. It is about where one space begins and another ends. It can be spontaneous or studiously deliberate, but it always carves space in a decisive way. It has a clear ethical, as well as aesthetic, impact. The drawn line is one of the great human inventions, and it is available to all of us—a tool both common and esoteric, personal and universal.

May 7, 2008

O, Ordos

At first glance, the Ordos 100 project looks like a great chance for younger architects to build something exciting and significant. Located on a barren desert site near the Inner Mongolian city of Ordos, the development of a grouping of one hundred houses for the wealthy is in the planning and design stage. The developer, who has made his fortune in coal, asked the Chinese artist Ai Weiwei to plan and organize the project, and he, in turn, has asked the Swiss architects Herzog and de Meuron to select—from their personal "network"—a hundred architects to design the houses. The idea, apparently, is to create a showcase for up-and-coming design talent and a highly marketable, and profitable, real estate venture.

A hint of trouble appears when we notice that Ai Weiwei's design company is called Fake Design. Sure enough, when we look at his overall plan for the development, we find that it copies American suburban tract developments from the 1950s, say, in California's San Fernando Valley. Compare the movie *The Two Jakes*. Sand-blown, treeless, lifeless for all human purposes, but soon to contain "your dream house"—just sign here! The picture published in the *New York Times* of the invited architects surveying their desolate sites is absurdly comic and at the same time sad. What must be going through their minds? Is this the Weissenhof Siedlung for the new age? Can I make great architecture here? Will I be mentioned in the next *Times* article? Or, did I come halfway around the world for this? Am I here as an architect, or as a pawn in Ai's latest art game?

The idea of building large private houses on three-quarter acre plots jammed together without regard for the spaces between or the relationship of one house to the next must be unsettling to many of the invitees, especially considering the history of American suburbs. Some have questioned the lack of even basic design or ecological guidelines in the planning. They may be wondering, too, if Ordos, of all the rapidly developing places on the planet, really needs a retro typology—however updated and upgraded—as the most visible symbol of its future. It would be a more hopeful harbinger of the future for not only this city, but also the field of architecture in general, if a number of the Ordos 100 architects banded together and came up with a coordinated overall plan and insisted that it be adopted. And, if it were not, they would simply decline the opportunity.*/

*/ See Fred A. Bernstein, "In Inner Mongolia, Pushing Architecture's Outer Limits," *New York Times*, May 1, 2008, www.nytimes.com/2008/05/01 /garden/01mongolia.html.

May 19, 2008

Tower Space

High-rise towers rarely develop the verticality of spaces they create, remaining instead only iconic objects in the urban landscape. Their interiors consist of stacked-up floor plates, maximizing leasable or usable floor area. In urban centers where groupings of towers crowd together on the most expensive land, the spaces between the towers are ignored. No doubt, these conditions result from the single-minded interests of commercial developers and the isolation enforced by private property ownership. The potential remains, regardless of the limitations of current attitudes, to invest the latent and actual verticality of

Installation of the *Tower Space* project at Pratt Institute, New York, 2008

towers with new programs of habitation that expand the meaning and experience of urban tower space. This was the aim of the sixth-semester design studio in the Graduate School of Architecture at Pratt Institute this past semester. It was realized in a one-to-one installation constructed by the members of the studio in the main space of Steven Holl's recent addition to the architecture building.

"The studio set out to explore a 'proto-urban' condition observed in cities through-out the world," write the members of the studio. "Tower projects are rising to previ-ously unimaginable heights, employing the very latest in technology, materials, design, and construction methodology. While many such endeavors enjoy great acclaim, the proj-ects, typically 'single point' towers, rarely address the existing or emerging urban land-scape. In this way, the tower, despite the use of expressive shapes and complex skins, is rapidly becoming the world's generic building unit. Regulatory and eco-nomic realities often force this unit's construction in a kind of non-contextual vacuum. Our studio explores what might occur if a *complex* of interrelated towers were to be commissioned. What types of relationships, physical or otherwise, might be formed? How might these new relationships change (for better or for worse) the 'proto-urban' environment?

"Our proposal emerges from the spirit of research and is born of a commitment to an entirely collaborative design/build process. Our collective vision is the creation of four integrated towers. The structures are shaped and informed by a matrix of vertical urban planes based on an aggregate of the world's many urban grids. Three of the emerging towers stand vertically while a fourth is set on a diagonal. The complex composition permits rich rela-tionships between the structures and the ground plane while also giving rise to an entirely new form of public zone. The architecture will incorporate interactive expe-riences that fuse light, sound, and moving images in order to explore our studio's interest in programs for vertical-ity that relate primarily to the psychological desires and realities of 'proto-urban' dwellers."

The results are visually powerful and evocative of new possibilities. What remains to be accomplished is a critical discourse about them and a way to evaluate— or even answer—the questions invoked by "for better or for worse."*/

*/ Sixth-Semester Design Studio. Pratt Institute Graduate School of Architecture and Urban Design. Thomas Hanrahan, Dean; William MacDonald, Chair. Faculty: Lebbeus Woods. Students: Liam Ahern, Kurt Altschul, Dhruv Chandwania, Brian Choquette, Adam Grassi, Johanna Helgadottir, Rob Jarocki, Benjamin Keiser, Tia Maiolatesi, Andrew Miller, and Tapasi Mittal. Guest critics: Steven Holl, Christoph a. Kumpusch, Christopher Otterbine, and Narelle Sissons. This project was made possible in part by a generous grant from the Research Institute for Experimental Architecture (RIEA.ch), Bern, Switzerland.

Junk

Junk piles. They have always fascinated me, ever since, as a student, a drawing teacher took me to some railroad yards in central Illinois. There were many things to draw in the landscape of tracks, roundhouses, sidetracked train cars (including long-empty living cars for railway workers), old and empty brick utility sheds, and the monumental cylindrical grain elevators lined up along the tracks, all of which had fallen into some state of disuse or abandonment, for reasons that were never clear. The flat, treeless plain on which these wonders lay was heavy with a feeling of something lost, but not dead, something living if only as a mystery. Still, on the sunny day we first went to the yards, everything was sharp and clear and unburdened. We had come to make freehand drawings on our large drawing pads in the fresh spring air, and to spend an hour or two exploring the world of forms that we might find. Later, these drawings in pencil, charcoal, or ink would be slipped into our portfolios, judged and graded as a course requirement. On that first day, however, they were pure fun.

I was immediately drawn to the large metal scrap piles that lay near the tracks. Looking back on that attraction, I can understand it as a reflection of sensibilities deeply felt. Complexity. Richness of form. Accident. Undesigned design (they are entirely of human origin). The extraordinary in the ordinary. But also, the mystery of objects, in our apprehension of them and in their origins, their originality (every scrap pile is different, even if, at first glance, they all look the same). How does their sameness/difference call the reality of memory into question? And, it occurred to me then and still occurs to me, what is inside the junk pile that I cannot see? Are there different things piled inside, or only more of what is outside? In either case, what does light and darkness matter to them?

Then, of course, there is the question of space. Space is created between and around objects. What is the nature of these spaces? Do they have any meaning? For sure, they are nonsystematic—or are they the products of a new system? Or are they just meaningless accidents, the products of a randomness that human beings cannot devise, except (as Paul Virilio claims) indirectly, by creating the technological products that end up as scrap thrown into piles along railroad tracks? Is this, in fact, their meaning for us? Clearly, the scrap pile is loaded with meaning as the detritus of human striving, but is its meaning something more? Is it a model for a human future, in both negative and positive senses? Are they piles simply waiting to be recovered and converted into new objects, or, can we somehow inhabit them, and why would we?

None of my drawings from that first visit, and subsequent ones, survive, at least not in their original form. Looking back, I have to think that they—and the questions they provoked—have echoed down and through a lifetime of work.

Dead Words

There are words and terms that once had currency in architecture but have become, in effect, dead. This short, annotated list contains a few, but I'm sure there are more, and I invite readers to submit their own in the comments section./₉ The point here is not merely academic, but rather to note the shifts in thinking that impact the nature of our field's development. The words we use—and don't use—are important.

RADICAL: This term used to refer to paradigm shifts and other important changes in thinking and practice that contributed to human progress (see below). But today, it is associated with "extreme." In the era of terrorism and the so-called "war on terrorism," radicals are seen as the enemies of the currently hunkered-down system of social order—in short, as terrorists. They are to be shunned, especially in the application of the penultimate instrument of social order, architecture. It is certainly acceptable to propose extreme forms, now and then, but only in the service of already known and familiar programs of use, and therefore as a reaffirmation of the status quo. Proposing radical forms that implement radical programs is unacceptable. Indeed, radical programs of use are more unacceptable than they ever have been.

NEW: Advertising and media hype have used this word to death. But that, in itself, is not the reason for its demise. The application of the word—and concept—to many things that are not really new has effectively destroyed its credibility. The rapidity of change has made everything seem new, even if it is not. The "new" model of car and the "new" skyscraper concept are of the same ilk: new forms of what we already know and have. We embrace the contradiction, so we can have the illusion of newness, while clinging to the old.

ORIGINAL: In the present time of appropriation in art, as well as the mass-merchandising of brand-name products including those of famous architects, the idea of originality is not only of minimal interest, but also, being a form of the radical (see above), rather dangerous. Of far greater interest is the recycling of ideas, products, and modes. Appropriation acquired legitimacy in the postmodernism of the 1970s and 80s, when the recycling of historical styles—including modernism—was in vogue. Today, it continues in the guise of architectural populism and social realism, where low art, such as squatter architecture, is elevated to high and presented as avant-garde.

PRINCIPLES: Today, everything is about technique. "How" a building is conceived and made is of great interest, but not "why." Principles are concerned with "why." Principles are philosophical—they define basic, inflexible reasons to do a particular thing and not just anything. Today, principles only get in the way of architects who want to do as they are told by their clients, or who want to be free to adopt new styles and modes.

PROGRESS: Considered a hopelessly old-fashioned idea, progress means that things get better, that they somehow advance, reach a higher level. Developments in technology, political thinking, and architecture were once thought to be instruments of progress—that is, change for the better in the human condition. Today it's difficult to say in any general way what "better" is—in the cacophony of the marketplace, there are so many different voices, options, demands. Hence we surmise that things pretty much stay the same, changing in form, not in content. Architecture valorizes wealth and power and the egos of architects, as it always has. Architecture is for an elite who can afford to commission expensive buildings and for the architects willing to design them.

EXPERIMENTAL: While this word is bandied about in architecture, its meaning is all but dead. There is little architecture, or design, that truly experiments—that is, plays with the unknown. The single defining characteristic of an experiment is that no one knows at the outset how it will turn out. The experimenter is looking for something, has a hypothesis to prove, but has no idea if the experiment will verify the hypothesis, prove it wrong, or result in something entirely unexpected. Experiments are risky. Architecture is today, and generally has been, averse to this kind of risk.

CRITICAL: This word has two meanings for architecture, both of which have to do with time. There are critical moments in architecture, when profound ideas are at stake and the outcome of debates and discourse about them will impact the future (see below) of architectural ideals and practices. At present, there are no great debates on which the course of architectural thinking seems to hinge. And no ideals. The second meaning of the term is found in the idea of criticism. Criticism was once thought to be essential to high-stakes debates about architectural principles (see above), but, lacking those, has today become, at best, a matter of personal opinion and, at worst, the stuff of careerist maneuverings.

HOUSING: This word refers to large-scale developments, usually sponsored by governments, that provide living units massed into large building groups. These mass-dwelling projects were the products of "socialistic" thinking—that is, governance committed to the fair redistribution of a community's wealth and resources. Today, socialism in all its forms is dead, having been soundly defeated by globalized capitalism. Further, the idea of class has been flattened out to a quotidian middle by credit cards, retail franchises, and tourism—in short, consumerism. The middle class does not live in housing, but in houses and condos.

GENIUS: Like the word "new," genius appears to have lost its meaning. If everyone will be famous for fifteen minutes, then everyone will be a genius for about the same period of time. However, the main reason the word no longer applies is that it is too blatantly elitist. Today, the rich wear blue jeans, not top hats. In the age of consumerism triumphant, everyone is supposed to be, or at least to look, the same—somewhere in a "middle" class. The words "celebrity" and "starchitect" are as derogatory as they are flattering or honoring. Maybe the age of geniuses, of people who discover or invent great new principles (see above) about nature, science, or art—and architecture—has, for the present, passed.

FUTURE: Once upon a time, the future was where wondrous and terrible things were going to happen, where the present would be transformed, for better or worse, and in a sense reach fruition. The idea of the future has all but vanished from architectural conversation and discussion, perhaps because the present is one of self-satisfaction—there is nothing to ripen and mature, and no great chances being taken that can succeed, or fail. Perhaps the future has become just another place we already know, or hope we know.

October 1, 2008

American Dreams

Could there ever be an American Dream of non-ownership of one's house or apartment? Leaving aside the issue of who really owns them (for most, it is actually the "mortgage holder"—whoever that might be in today's arcane and shaky financial webbing), it is interesting to consider the concept of home-ownership itself, from the perspective of any idea of the cherished "dream of a good life and a better future."

The idea of owning your home has the sound of securing it, of making it a safe haven for you and your family. It is yours and, as long as you make the payments and pay your taxes and stay out of too much debt, will remain yours and your children's (if you have any) in perpetuity. Also, no one can violate your home or the land it sits on (if it has any) by entering without your permission—a sanctity the law says you can enforce with a gun, if necessary. Another part of this American vision is that homeowners are the most responsible citizens of their communities, for the practical reason that they have the most invested in them, not just in terms of money, but also of moral capital. They play by the rules of their communities, which is the basis for their being granted and sustaining ownership of a part of them. Or that's the way it used to be.

Increasingly, Americans buy their homes and condominiums as a financial investment. Far from seeing their homes as places to be handed down to their children or, for that matter, to live out their lives in, they are viewed as instruments for getting a return on their money, primarily through selling them at a higher price than they paid. Whether they are living in Denver suburbs or Lower Manhattan, homeowners have an eye on the real estate market. If they can sell at a high price, they can afford to move upward to a better and more expensive home. Leaving aside the issue of those who cannot keep up in this game (and there are many) and lose their homes (becoming effectively "home-less"), or who have to move because their jobs are lost or they get transferred and have to sell at any price, it is clear that the character of the American Dream of homeownership has changed radically.

Is it time for a new dream? Clearly it is, and Martin Luther King Jr.'s "I have a dream" is hopeful as a model of what it might be. Architects, locked for so long in the ideal of homeownership—from Frank Lloyd Wright's Broadacre City, where everyone would have their sovereign acre of prairie (and a Wright house planted squarely on it), to Frank Gehry's twisty luxury condo tower in Lower Manhattan—have difficulty generating any comparable vision of the

American home. It is telling that the most gifted designers today—American and not—can only come up with snappy new wrappers for prevailing, but finally fading, ideas. The current bursting of the "housing bubble" and the coming financial shakeout, which will be global in extent and giga in scale, could leave them with more time to consider the reality of how most people live and the nature of home in the contemporary world.

The concept of non-ownership would be a good place to start. Or, at least, with the idea that money is not at the heart of it.

October 2, 2008

Stonehouse

More than twenty years ago, Günther Domenig began to build a house for himself on a narrow sliver of lakeside property in the mountains of Carinthia, Austria. He conceived it as a work of architecture limited only by his imagination and skill, at once a manifesto and an experiment, the outcome of which he could not be sure of at the beginning. The structure grew year by year, piece by piece, following an ever-evolving set of sketches and technical drawings, and was financed from his own architectural practice in Graz. When he had a little extra money, he

Günther Domenig, Stonehouse, Carinthia, Austria, 2008

put it into the construction. While the building is called a house, it was never intended as a residence. In fact, when Domenig lived at the site over the years, he stayed in a small, boxlike metal trailer away from the house, not wanting, perhaps, to confuse its purposes. Its sole purpose was to be architecture.

On Sunday, October 5, 2008, the Stonehouse was officially dedicated and, in effect, declared complete. Various luminaries participated in the ceremony (orchestrated by MAK director Peter Noever), including architects Thom Mayne, Wolf D. Prix, Carl Pruscha, Hans Hollein, and Raimund Abraham. While it is easy to share the excitement of such a moment, one can secretly hope the idea of completion is provisional. Essential to the house is the vitality, power, risk, existential optimism, and idealistic doubt that have characterized its long gestation.

Domenig's own statement made during the years of work is candid and unflinching: "I have reached my limits in every respect. Here we shall see what I really can carry out in architecture. I have reached the limits of myself. I am standing in front of the limits of my technical and financial possibilities. There is no way out, no way back. I feel the hopelessness of my own consequence. The better I am, the better each step is, the harder the next one becomes. Maybe I will fail."

Written by Lebbeus Woods on the Occasion of the Official Opening of the Stonehouse:

One of my earliest statements about the meaning and purpose of architecture was: "We should make our buildings first, then learn how to live in them." Born into a world we did not create, this is always the task facing us: to adapt ourselves to the world as we find it, or the world to us.

Why should we find only architecture limited to some assigned purpose? Why should architecture limit its potential to create space to satisfying the demands for the already known, for some normal "program of use"? Architecture should be freed to follow its own rules and ways to its own spatial, and spiritual, conclusions. Architecture should awaken in us new understandings and knowledge, and inspire us to embrace previously unimagined experiences. It should demand from us a level of invention of our own lives at least equal to the level of invention that brought it into being.

This view of architecture is not widely held by architects themselves. But it is the view held by the architect of the Stonehouse, Günther Domenig. In its architecture he has invested his most poetic powers of analysis and his most inventive powers of the conception and design of spatial forms. He has gathered together over many years the diverse strands of a wide and celebrated building practice into a single building and presented us, his fellow architects, with a model of dedication and commitment to ideas and their realization. The Stonehouse presents us with difficulties, of course, the very difficulties that mark our present world: the clash of different forms and modes, the unresolved collision of different systems of thought and action; the ambiguity of meanings that do not declare their purposes in advance. The Stonehouse belongs to a different world than the one we normally inhabit, and it dares us to find ways to inhabit it, or even to talk about it. Yet here it is, both realized and real. How real are we, as we stand in confrontation with this difficult work of architecture? Let us be grateful to Günther Domenig for giving us a chance to find out.

October 7, 2008

Cities Without Names

The cities without names are those we see from a distance, often as a glow on the night horizon, but which we cannot approach and enter. Perhaps their distance is maintained because we are only passing by, on our way somewhere else more familiar; or perhaps, by our desire to keep them in our minds as inviolate and unknown, places for the future and not for now. All the elements of cities we know are there, the more-or-less familiar profiles of buildings where people like us, we imagine, live out their lives. But some differences are apparent. As we strain to see more, these differences reveal the utter strangeness of these cities, their remoteness in more than distance and time from us and what we have known. Any one of these cities seems—for want of a better word—uncertain. The structure of the city is tentative, as though it were a

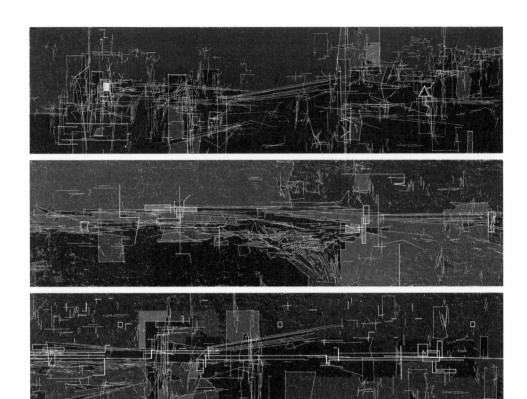

Formation, from *Cities Without Names*, 2008

series of inconclusive gestures in space, almost like the pentimenti of an artist's drawing, as he or she searches for a form not known in advance. Gone is the familiar sense of work accomplished and, in its place, the uneasy feeling that the work undertaken was not meant to be accomplished.

Our companion on one such journey, a distinguished architect, said, "Oh, don't be so surprised. Haven't you heard that those cities were designed by crazy fools? They started to build, but don't know how to finish. Still, they think they've created Utopia!"

October 19, 2008

Pagespace

Some poets and writers—even the occasional architect—think of a page as a space to be explored and defined by words. Whether typeset or handwritten, words are marks of a precise nature—they have shape, density, extension— that establish spatial boundaries and limits. In other words, they are the stuff of architecture. While the marks made by architects on a sheet of paper are most often abstractly pictorial, writers work with alphabets and languages, their form and syntax. The writer's work is complicated by the fact that the marks called words have a preassigned meaning that is shared by a community of people who use them as instruments of understanding. The writer's creative task is to make people see the words afresh, as though they were at the same time both new and known. Words used in too-familiar ways are clichés, trite and tired and worn, and refer in the reader's mind more to the writer's dullness than to what the words might potentially mean. The bad writer is one who does not arouse the reader to a fresh understanding of the familiar.

Even the best writers—those who enable us to read the same old words with new meaning—most often stay with the conventional arrangements of words on the page. A few of the best, and some of the less-than-best, employ the arrangement of the marks called words on the page to help us discover their familiar meanings in new ways. It is the most experimental, riskiest, and least often successful of techniques. All the more reason it remains a way of writing to be further explored.

October 23, 2008

The Politics of Abstraction

Representation occurs when one thing (say, colors smeared on a canvas) makes us think of something else (say, a mountain valley at sunset). Abstraction occurs when one thing (say, colors smeared on a canvas) makes us think of, well, colors smeared on a canvas.

Abstraction is shapes, lines, colors that represent only themselves—we might call it a special case of representation. Or, we might (as is most common) say it is a case of non-representation. Abstraction does not re-present anything. This does not mean, however, that it has no meaning, but only that its meaning lies in its own substance and structure. An abstract painting may evoke an idea (say, of movement, or of energy), as is often the case with abstract expressionist works. But this is only because most of us demand that a work of art "means" something. A mathematical equation, such as $E=mc^2$, is symbolic of a basic relationship between energy and matter, as opposed to a representational description of that relationship. As a symbolic expression, it is more scientifically useful than a picture of an atomic explosion, which re-presents that same relationship but only in terms of its effects. Most of us would agree, however, that a movie of a fireball and mushroom cloud rising over the desert or the city of Hiroshima gets the point across more vividly than the equation. The effects are what are important, or at least more understandable, to most people.

Architecture and music are the most abstract of the arts. They are both rooted in precise mathematical relationships played out across space and time. Still, their abstractness can become representational when it starts to symbolize something. What does a Gothic cathedral symbolize? Technological progress? The victory of ideas over matter? Or the power of religion? The importance of piety? For most people, it will be the latter more than the former, and in a quite literal way: the Gothic cathedral and all the buildings modeled on it are didactic symbols of devotion to Christianity. So, too, a Bach cantata cannot be heard entirely apart from its intended setting. Even the most agnostic listeners will feel the force of its religious passion.

What is the symbolism of a modernist icon such as the Tugendhat House? Technological progress? The victory of ideas over matter? Or…what? However wide its influence on the design of houses and other buildings that followed (and it was considerable), this seminal work of architecture somehow resists being symbolic. To the contrary, it remains emphatically abstract, even to those who know about it. Beethoven's late piano sonatas fall into the same category. They move us for what they are and not for what they represent.

It is fairly clear that political systems relying on propaganda to control the way people think and feel can make the most effective use of representational music and architecture. When the national anthem is played, everyone knows what it means and responds on cue. The same with the Capitol in Washington, DC, or the Arc de Triomphe in Paris. Abstract works cannot be used to the same ends. For example, the revolutionary Communist regime in the USSR, which for a brief period promoted an ideal of egalitarianism, encouraged the uncompromising abstractions of Constructivism and Suprematism. However, when this regime became a rightist autocracy, it tolerated only social realism—even Kazimir Malevich started painting colorful images of peasants—and a Stalinist version of classical architecture.

The same in Germany. During the liberal Weimar years, abstract art and architecture flourished, but, when the ultra-right Nazis took power, abstraction became "degenerate." Representational design was the only acceptable possibility: the classicism of Albert Speer, which symbolized, via Greece and Rome, Germany's historically superior moral authority over its decadent enemies; or the mock-rural styles of houses and other buildings that made the same point by extolling Germany's honest peasantry. In Rome itself, during the same period, the Rationalist movement in architecture was encouraged by socialists, one of whom was Benito Mussolini. The abstractions of futurism and Giuseppe Terragni's *astrattisti comaschi* were, however, pushed aside by Novecento art and a vaguely classical Fascist architecture, when Mussolini took a sharp right turn to absolute dictatorship.

Rightist, totalitarian rule needs to constantly enflame people's emotions with conflicting fears and hopes that can only be resolved in the person of a charismatic Führer, Duce, Maximum Leader, or Big Brother. Democracy and egalitarian systems employ propaganda, but it usually has a different message: think, understand, choose. Unlike autocracies, democracies rely on the intelligence of their people and believe that through education (as opposed to training) and the freedom to make difficult choices, people will act wisely in their collective self-interest. Here, abstract art and architecture—which demand personal interpretation and inventive adaptation to change—are appropriate challenges.

In the USA, which is arguably more egalitarian in its aspirations than many other societies, abstraction has had a hard time taking root, not to say becoming widely popular. Nevertheless the USA has been a sympathetic environment for artists, composers, and architects of radical abstraction, from Jackson Pollock to Mark Rothko, from Charles Ives to John Cage, from Richard Neutra to Gordon Bunshaft. Of course, abstraction is in retreat at the moment, as American politics has moved relentlessly to the right. It is no surprise that picturesque postmodernism emerged during the reactionary Nixon years and flourished under the charismatic leadership of Reagan, and has never retreated, even though its forms have mutated, on occasion mimicking even those of egalitarian modernism.

Today, there is nostalgia for the abstractions of modernism that amounts to reducing it to a mere style among many others. That appears to be finely democratic with regard to offering choices, but it is a false choice if the abstractions resemble the old ones, which have by now become comfortable representations of a lost innocence. Abstraction, like democracy, is demanding of each of us—often discomfiting, and always difficult to attain.

November 9, 2008

Zeroes and Ones

There is much talk today about computation in architecture, not only its implications for the design and production of tectonic objects—from chairs to buildings to cities—but also its inescapable philosophical consequences. Understandably, most of this talk, by a few theorists and many practitioners, centers on the digital computer and its capacity for rendering complexity and simulating reality. I say "understandably" not because this is a proper focus for issues raised by computation, but because very powerful digital computers have become handy and accessible tools for everyone. So . . . why not use them? Actually it is not the proper focus, especially if our interest is in philosophical domains such as aesthetics and ethics and how architecture both embodies and enables them. An even more powerful and accessible computing tool—the human brain—should be our primary subject, and object, of understanding the nature and consequences of computation for architecture and the world.

There are precise, historical reasons for this. It was advances in neuroscience during the 1930s and 40s—in understanding how the brain works as an electrical machine, a "biological computer"—that led to the rapid development of artificial, electronic computers. This advance—a leap, really—was prompted by dramatic discoveries in the 1910s and 20s in physics and mathematics, especially the invention of quantum mechanics and quantum theory. Niels Bohr's Copenhagen interpretation had radical and profound consequences not only for epistemology, but also for every branch of inquiry and practice. It states that when we describe with scientific precision any phenomenon, we must include in the description the manner in which we observed the phenomenon. The human brain and wider nature were thenceforth intertwined and inseparable; the old barriers between the "subjective" and the "objective" were shattered and a new era, the present one, began.

Architectural theorists and experimental practitioners would do well to give more attention to cognition theory—its origins and contemporary forms—when considering concepts of computation. One of the key concepts to come out of cognition theory is "self-referentiality," which has to do with the paradoxes created by the brain studying itself. Concepts such as "recursion," "feedback," "self-organization," and "autopoiesis" are secondary consequences. Technological application—such as software design, communications networks, and their relevance for architecture—comes further down the line.

Indeed, anyone who wishes to understand the role of computation in human thought and activity must study the developments in this recent history, particularly in the field of cybernetics, which in the 1950s and 60s laid the theoretical foundations for contemporary cognition theory, general systems, and information theories. These, in turn, underlay the rapid advances of computer technology.*/

*/ I close this post with a succinct essay by Heinz von Foerster, one of the founders of the transdisciplinary field of cybernetics. Hopefully, it whets your appetites for more. See Heinz von Foerster, "On Constructing a Reality," in *Understanding Understanding: Essays on Cybernetics and Cognition* (New York: Springer, 2003), 211–27. [An image of this essay has been omitted from this volume.]

November 23, 2008

Bad Faith

We seem poised to enter a new era of the control and regulation of private life by the public institutions of government. The reason, it is becoming clearer every day, is that too many individuals in key positions of authority and responsibility have abused their privilege of freely choosing their courses of action by serving their own interests at the expense of the interests of the wider public. This is equally true in politics (where ideological fantasies trumped reality), finance (where greed for short-term profits did the same), industry (felled by sloth and stupidity), and commerce (debt-financed consumerism and damn the consequences—won't the party go on forever?). So, new leaders are being brought in and must use their authority to try to repair the damage done and set the society on a new and healthier course. It is an extraordinarily difficult task that will require—given the complex interconnectedness of everything today— unprecedented degrees of centralized control. Regardless of anyone's political philosophy, there is no other choice. The sos has been sent. What we're talking about now is not the best of all possible worlds, but survival.

Architects, particularly many of the more recognized and celebrated ones today, share part of the blame for this unhappy state of affairs, along with leaders in other fields entrusted with the public's interests. For too long they've set the model for professional behavior by serving the narrow interests of clients who are primarily commercial developers and who are famously interested in making quick returns on their money. Spectacular new building wrappers for tried-and-true (presumably not risky) types of buildings have produced some amazing new shapes and surfaces, but little else. Developers will not risk their money on really new building types. Meanwhile, questions of new types of affordable living space in cities and of public spaces in an age of exploding population and diminishing direct contact go begging for some imaginative invention. And now, against all previously safe assumptions, we can begin to ask, who is going to buy all those luxury condos and lease all that corporate office space? We should care less if developers get burned in the current catastrophe, but we should care that some of the best and brightest of an innovative generation are going to suffer in the crises presently underway, and deepening.

On the other hand, it is difficult to feel badly about all the projects for skyscrapers, condos, resorts, luxury hotels, and shopping malls that are currently going on "hold," and will certainly die altogether. But it is not hard to feel sorry that so many gifted architects have devoted so much of their talents and energies to them. The ancient Greek conception of tragedy looms here, as even the greatest heroes are undone by fate. At the same time, existentialist voices keep whispering in our ears that we each choose our own fate.

For too long, architects have justified their servile attitudes (often accompanied by ostentatious displays of pride and independence, cleverly indulged by clients) with their belief that clients have more social agency than they do. In other words, by having lots of money or access to it and therefore the capability to commission large and expensive buildings (which use massive amounts of human and natural resources), developers prove that they speak for the public—the ultimate source of all wealth—and are acting in its best interests. As recent events show, this is far from true. Then again, no one expects developers to be moral or social philosophers, while we do hope that architects—the stewards of constructed human space—exhibit a wider perspective of and concern for the human condition. When they do not, especially at the top of the profession, it sets a bad example for the whole field.

All of us, regardless of our social or professional status, have not only agency within our own lives, empowering us to achieve our personal goals, but also social agency in that what we do affects others. Immanuel Kant's "categorical imperative" states that to be both rational and moral, each person must "act only according to that maxim whereby you can at the same time will that it should become a universal law."/10 Jean-Paul Sartre brought this idea into modern life by stating that each of us is responsible for all mankind. Our actions become the model for the actions of others. So, for example, if we decide to throw our used chewing gum wrapper on the street, we should not imagine that we are the exception, but the rule. If everyone threw their trash on the street, we would not be able to wade through it.

Sartre went further with his idea of "bad faith." We act in bad faith when we base our decisions on a socially assigned role, rather than our own inner sense of right and wrong. He had in mind the Nazi extermination camp commanders who defended themselves by saying that they were only following the orders of a legally constituted Nazi government, even though they did not personally believe in the murder of innocent people. A less dramatic example would be the judge who orders the execution of a prisoner "because it is the law," even though he or she does not personally believe in capital punishment.

A much more common example is the architect who accepts the commission for a project that he or she feels may be superfluous from a social standpoint, or perhaps redundant or even damaging, because "architecture is a service profession," displacing—in bad faith—the responsibility to the client.

By way of contrast, the great architect Cedric Price always asked potential clients, "Do we really need this building?" He inevitably tried to talk them out of building, saying, "The problem is not that we don't have enough buildings—rather, we have too many of them. The problem is, we don't know how to use the ones we have." He devoted his practice to addressing, in the most ingeniously innovative and inventive ways, how to use, and reuse, what we have.

We should lament that Price's sense of his social agency was not widely influential. Of course, he had few clients and commissions—hardly a model for today's globetrotting, international superstars, or those who dream of following their examples. Still, we might imagine that the current economic downturn and financial shakeout will give all of us in the field of architecture pause and some time to reflect on what we are—and should be—about.

November 29, 2008

Bad Faith 2

I deeply appreciate the seriousness and directness of those who have commented on the Bad Faith post so far./11 Each deserves an individual response. Still, one underlying question is clear: if architects are not to be the mere servants of developers, what are they to do? Because I have raised that question, I feel obliged to attempt an answer.

I mentioned Cedric Price in my post. His is certainly a fine model of practice to follow. He was not independently wealthy, nor did he live like a poor man. He enjoyed excellent cognac and fine cigars and never wanted for them. He had a fine marriage. His circle of friends and colleagues included the best and the brightest. And he turned down work he didn't believe in. He chose carefully, not making more than enough money to go forward with his work and his life. He also had a sense of humor and some perspective on himself, which enabled him to see things more fully. However, he is far from the only architect to uphold high standards in an often venal profession.

If you look at the lives of the best architects of the preceding generation, you'll discover that the esteem in which they are held had little to do with blockbuster developer projects, though they were often approached to design them, and just as often refused, because they believed that the critical issues of architecture lay elsewhere. Frank Lloyd Wright was always broke (by his own admission) because he devoted a large proportion of his time to questions of houses and housing and cities and researching the relationships between architecture, technology, and building crafts. Le Corbusier, the same. While the Plan Voisin was commissioned by a developer, it was Corbusier's program, and not the developer's, that prevailed. The number of urban studies he did for minimal or no fees is astounding. His research into typologies brought him little money, but just enough to carry on. Mies van der Rohe fared rather better financially, but not so much. His fees for the Seagram Building and 860–880 Lake Shore Drive no doubt financed his research into public housing projects and his conceptions of ideal civic space.

I could go on. Louis Kahn focused on public buildings of symbolic importance, where the integrity of the architecture resonated with ethical ideals of civic life. He wore rumpled suits and dreamed of a better city enabled by architecture. One can agree or not with the viewpoints or the architecture of each of these architects, but their devotion to the principle of architecture as a primary instrument of human agency is indisputable. These were architects who took personal responsibility for the place of architecture in the complex human world. And they were the role models for my generation.

Something happened in the 1970s. These and a few other exemplars of architectural thought and practice had died. The brief flowering of political populism of the 1960s was being translated increasingly into commercial projects. Robert Venturi, Denise Scott Brown, and Steven Izenour wanted architects to "learn from Las Vegas." Colin Rowe and Fred Koetter advocated "collage" cities, made up of implicitly commercial fragments of different, even conflicting, parts. It was an intellectually exciting time, as "paradigm shifts" always are. The marketplace of competing capitalism was equated with freedom of choice, hence social equality. Architectural thought—indeed its ideals—began to shift from singular visions of urban space to more commercially viable projects. The real estate developer emerged as the best social agent for a burgeoning consumer society. For younger architects the architectural role models were not the "old masters" like Mies or Wright or Corbusier, but corporate firms with mainly commercial projects like Skidmore, Owings & Merrill (SOM), offices that were servicing the rapid expansion of consumerism. Not only architects got on board, but municipal governments as well, by establishing various public "development" agencies and commissions and by giving tax breaks and other financial inducements to private developers. The real estate boom of the 1980s was on and, with some stumbles, has continued up to the recent crash.

The point here is not that the good old days were better and we should somehow go back to them. The world has changed too much, and going back never works, even if it were possible. But there are things to be learned from the past about the practice of architecture—ways of thinking and acting that might inspire us, bring a new sense of purpose, and give us renewed energy to go forward. As much as I dislike lists of dos and don'ts (they have a musty, superego-ish sniff to them), in this case it may help me get to the point. So, for architects, a short list:

Don't accept a commission (or a job) unless you believe that it makes a positive contribution to your community—however you define "community," and however you define "positive."

Don't convince yourself that taking on a project you have no such belief in is just a stepping stone to projects you can believe in. It won't work, and never has.

Do devote as large a portion of your time as you can to independent research and experimentation about problems that you think are important to architecture and your community. Don't wait for a client to ask for it—you are the only agent for such work. Be prepared to finance it from your own pocket. Then publish the results so they can be available to as many people as possible.

Do keep your office as small as possible. Creating a large overhead is a sure road to taking on projects and clients you don't want but "must" accept to pay your employees.

Do remember that your responsibility as an architect is first to the wider community you inhabit, and only then to your clients. Don't accept clients who do not share this understanding.

Do remember that what you do as an architect—at whatever level you practice—is vitally important to the field as a whole and to your community. Don't imagine that what you do doesn't matter, or is too small to make a difference.

There is one thing I failed to mention about the best architects of the former generation: they were all teachers. Wright had the Taliesin Fellowship; Mies the Bauhaus and the Illinois Institute of Technology; Kahn the University of Pennsylvania. Price had no fixed academic affiliation, but taught constantly at various schools in the UK and Europe. These architects believed in the coming generation and devoted much energy to it, earning a modicum of money with which they could carry on. They taught by the example of their work, but also by their direct engagement with young people aspiring to be architects. I cannot think of a happier form of practice.

December 1, 2008

Solohouse @ 20

The Solohouse is twenty years old. At my age, twenty years does not seem so long, except when I think that it is the length of time between 1940 and 1960, the period when I was growing up, and I can remember with amazement all the changes to myself and the world that took place during that span of years. And then I also remember how much has changed since 1988, the year of this project's birth. Considering that, I think the Solohouse has aged reasonably well. Of course, it no longer exists, except in photos and a few drawings, having been destroyed some years ago.

The Solohouse, I should explain, is as close as I have come (so far) to building a structure that could be called, in the usual sense, a building./12 It was built of steel and wood, about one-sixteenth full size. At five feet tall, it was not big enough to enter or physically inhabit, but nevertheless addressed the basic construction problems of an actual building—such as the selection and joining of materials, and constructional stability—in a highly tectonic sense. The architect and master builder Christopher Otterbine was my contractor and, as in all creative building projects, my design collaborator.

Solohouse, 1988–89

The concept of the Solohouse was, ostensibly, that it was a house for one person. But, even more so, I conceived it as an "atom" of architecture, one that embodied the essential properties of architecture that were fundamental to building up "molecules" and "compound substances," such as building groups and even towns and cities. The single dwelling is the fundamental space of human habitation, and there must be a clear idea in an architect's thought about it before he or she can talk about larger human settlements. The Solohouse was the embodiment of my ideas. Later, in projects for Berlin, Paris, Sarajevo, Havana, and San Francisco, the Solohouse mutated and combined many times— responding to different cultural, political, and geographical situations—but its underlying principles remained.

In a previous post—"Integrity"—I spell out basic ideas about materials, structure, and function in more or less orthodox Modernist terms that guided the design of the Solohouse./13 And yet Solohouse does not look like a Modernist building, and indeed it is not. Its thin steel-shell structure gains its strength though shape, not mass or an internal skeleton. Its materials are allowed to age and have no imperative to remain eternally new. Its function is ambiguity itself, the burdensome idea of "freespace"—one must invent the way to inhabit the house, because it is not predetermined. That's the way principles work, assuming many variations, shapes, and forms over time and changing the way we understand materials, structure, and function. Still, the human condition remains the same, joining us to the past, and also giving us not only inspiration, but also a guide for creating the future.

City of Fire

As I descended into one of the steep crevasses in the rocky terrain, I felt an updraft of warm air. Knowing this way down led to some of the mines, I remembered stories of how workers in the deepest mines were subjected to heat that rose upward from the earth's inner core of still-molten iron and nickel. At even three thousand feet below the earth's surface, miners suffer almost unbearable temperatures of a hundred and thirty degrees and more. I recalled as fact that geothermal wells, drilled downward from the surface to tap the heat within the body of the planet, provide virtually limitless sources of energy for various mechanical systems operating above. So my experience of the warm winds from below, in a darkness far from the sun, came not entirely as a surprise.

What did surprise, though, was what I found as I descended. Here, in strata upon strata of volcanic rock, were spaces inhabited by a community of people engaged in some sort of industry. There were dwelling spaces hollowed out from the dark earth masses. There were machines that captured an eerie form of light different from that far above. There were vast caverns in which I saw entangled, monumental forms that were like fragments of the lucid geometric volumes I had seen in the city above, but here broken into disparate parts and linked together by tendril-like passageways and conduits, creating a vast, indeterminate network rather than a geometrically coherent form. All of this was revealed by an inner-earth glow amid a constant, throbbing heat. It soon became clear that the harnessing of heat energy—as a source of motive power, I imagined—was the industry of this underground community.

To some extent, the existential philosophy of the community far above, which exalted as an end in itself its interaction with the physical body of the earth, was evident in the constructions I found, though in markedly different form. The architecture here was fragmented and tenuously connected. Lower down, though, in a region where humans' maximum tolerance of heat was reached, the rocks and buildings (if they can be called such) seemed to flow together. The resulting forms were, as on the airy ridges above, a fusion of the human and the natural, but here so much so that one could not be distinguished from the other. Indeed they were one, captured flows of energy—celebrated, I now believe, for their own sake. I called this place the City of Fire.

How I managed to ascend from this fearsome, strangely exciting domain I cannot say. Perhaps it was like waking from a dream. Or, more likely, I was taken upward by some of the inhabitants who saw my extreme discomfort and confusion and took it upon themselves to rescue me. In either case, or both, I left without understanding the ultimate purpose of engaging the heat and light, the quietly violent energy of the underworld. To drive the machines of the upper world? To, more simply, power their own machines and light their own dwellings? Or another possibility exists. I have since thought of the story

City of Fire, 1981

about the bull dancers of ancient Crete. In their sacred rituals, the point was neither to conquer the dangerous bull nor to spiritually merge with it. Rather, they danced with the bull as a form of artful play. It was all, and only, a very serious game.

December 31, 2008

City of Water

I stayed for some time in the forests bordering an inland sea, resting and considering the unusual places I had visited and recorded in my drawings. Determined to understand better the underlying ideas that had informed the different constructions, I began to puzzle together a theory of sorts. First of all, I decided that the two "cities," as I called them, were not built by two different communities of people but rather by the same community, living with the same philosophy under two differing sets of conditions. It struck me that "earth" and "fire" are different manifestations of the same vast pool of matter and energy comprising the planet, and two stages of a cycle of their necessary exchanges and transmutations.

The community, I reasoned, had as its motivation an active and continual engagement with some larger natural cycle. Its people were "nature worshipers" of a peculiar kind, considering the types of activities and structures they built. In my own community, now far away, we too had become sensitive to nature, which we referred to as the "environment," or the "ecosphere," but the activities we chose as participating with it were benign by comparison. We considered the idea of mining, of cutting into the earth, a violation of nature— something violent, exploitative, and wrong. Similarly, the idea of capturing the earth's latent heat and retaining it in strangely fragmented or fluid forms seemed an aggressive and almost pointless act of hubris. We preferred "passive" modes of energy exchange and gently left issues of architectural form to techniques of achieving what we called "sustainability," the maintenance of a perpetual equilibrium between human and natural forces. I decided that this community, in which I was a stranger, was a relatively primitive one compared with my own. What I encountered next confirmed, but then confounded, this estimation.

Near the shorelines I restlessly walked, I had come across large-scaled, almost architectural fragments among groves of trees, their geometrical forms overgrown and seemingly abandoned. Stranger than that, they seemed never to have belonged where I found them, but rather to have been brought there and left. This puzzled me, until I noticed one day, offshore, in the sea, some large structures. Thick plumes of white steam rose from some into the sky. Hurriedly taking a small boat and making sure I had paper and pencils, I set out across the water to explore.

The artificial islands on which the massive constructions stood were actually the upper parts of underwater structures I entered only after some

City of Water, 1981

time and difficulty. Once inside, in immense chambers surpassing in grandeur anything I had seen before, the detritus of a civilization had been accumulated. The pieces scattered near the shore were mere bits and parts compared to whole buildings and other monumental shards that I saw casually thrown together. The great assemblages comprised a chaotic tectonic landscape inhabited by workers and others busily arranging—almost composing—the more manageable elements, and dismantling them into precise, if convoluted, arrays of debris. All this activity was carried on with a sense of urgency. It was not long before the water came.

Falling in cataracts that inundated the complex landscape, the waters from the inland sea had been let in to transform the exotic terrain—not so much by force, I thought, as by erosion of the kind that water patiently produces on inert matter. Following the cataracts, I discovered older tectonic landscapes in progressive stages of erosion and decay. Some had been fused over time by the water into unexpected formations: great reefs of iron, glass, wood, and other materials formerly shaped by human craft and ingenuity for highly specific purposes, now melded into one with no apparent purpose whatsoever. It was then I remembered that water is the universal solvent, and that everything dissolves in water, eventually—everything returns to the sea. This, I decided, was a community devoted to the return to the earth of minerals taken from it—the completion of an epic cycle of human and natural struggle, interaction, and evolution. I called this place, accordingly, the City of Water.

Thinking of my own community and its disdain for polluting rivers, lakes, and seas, I felt that my sense of superiority over this culture and its practices was confirmed. But then I wondered: where were the plastics and toxic chemicals we used to make them; where was the industrial waste from the manufacture of countless consumer products; where, indeed, were the discarded consumer products, their discarded wrappers and containers; where was the garbage? Was I witnessing only a ritual of waste disposal? Where was waste of the kind that polluted our waters? Was it dealt with here in a different way? Did it exist at all? I was left with many questions and little sense of certainty.

2009

Slow Manifesto

The new cities demand an architecture that rises from and sinks back into fluidity, into the turbulence of a continually changing matrix of conditions, into an eternal, ceaseless flux—architecture drawing its sinews from web-bings of shifting forces, from patterns of unpredictable movements, from abrupt changes of mind, alterations of position, spontaneous disintegrations and syntheses—architecture resisting change, even as it flows from it, strug-gling to crystallize and become eternal, even as it is broken and scattered—architecture seeking nobility of presence, yet possessed of the knowledge that only the incomplete can claim nobility in a world of the gratuitous, the packaged, the promoted, the already sold—architecture seeking persistence in a world of the eternally perishing, itself giving way to the necessity of its moment—architecture writhing, twisted, rising, and pinioned to the uncer-tain moment, but not martyred, or sentimental, or pathetic, the coldness of its surfaces resisting all comfort—architecture that moves, slowly or quickly, delicately or violently, resisting the false assurance of stability—architec-ture that comforts, but only those who ask for no comfort—architecture of gypsies, who are driven from place to place, because they have no home—architecture of circuses, transient and unknown, but for the day and night of their departure—architecture of migrants, fleeing the advent of night's bitter hunger—architecture of a philosophy of interference, the forms of which are infinitely varied, a vocabulary of words spoken only once, then forgotten—architecture bending and bending more, in continual struggle against gravity, against time, against, against, against—barbaric architecture, rough and insolent in its vitality and pride—sinuous architecture, winding endlessly and through a scaffolding of reasons—architecture caught in sudden light, then broken in a continuum of darkness—architecture embracing the sudden shifts of its too-delicate forms, therefore indifferent to its own destruction—architecture that destroys, but only with the coldness of pro-found respect—neglected architecture, insisting that its own beauty is deeper yet—abandoned architecture, not waiting to be filled, but serene in its tran-scendence—architecture that transmits the feel of movements and shifts, resonating with every force applied to it, because it both resists and gives way—architecture that moves, the better to gain its poise—architecture that insults politicians, because they cannot claim it as their own—architecture whose forms and spaces are the causes of rebellions, against them, against the world that brought them into being—architecture drawn as though it were already built—architecture built as though it had never been drawn—

Type Casting

In various posts over the past year or so, I have stated outright or alluded to the need for architects to envision new types of constructed, inhabited space. What I refer to are not just recastings of already known building types, such as many innovative contemporary designs do—prominent examples being the Guggenheim Museum Bilbao and the CCTV Headquarters in Beijing. Spectacular though they are, they must be recognized as monuments to existing knowledge, a gloss on existing ways of living and thinking. One can admire the remarkable abilities of their architects while at the same time recognizing that they contribute nothing new to the typologies of museums or of office buildings, let alone to the concepts of preserving and publicly presenting artifacts or creating space for collective work. But, we might ask, why should they?

Why should architects concern themselves with conceiving new types of spaces? Is that not the prerogative of their clients, who represent the needs of society at a particular time?

The answer to the last question is not always. Clients do, indeed, represent the needs of certain financially empowered social elites who, understandably, want to serve their own interests. The wealthy and empowered believe that, by doing so, they serve the whole society, and they are right, at least in the case of museums. However, this does not mean that a museum must always be a big building with galleries, where things are lined up for display. Could there be other spatial solutions that re-contextualize works of art? That is a question of architecture and the invention of a new typology.

Throughout my working life, I have been most concerned with the changes happening in the world and how they impact architecture. Or, to put it differently, how architecture might impact these changes, and for the better. Early on, I developed the attitude that architecture is not a passive field, but an active one. Architecture should not merely follow, but lead in the conception of space for human use. Architecture should not merely express change, but should participate in creating it. Architects have a special responsibility because of the enormous impact architecture has on the lives of others. Ultimately, in a democratic society, it is up to others to decide whether architects' designs and, most especially, their innovations are useful and valuable. Architects need not worry that by making proposals, however unconventional, they are imposing them on others. Architects, thankfully, simply don't have that power. We are idea people—but we are, therefore, obliged to actually have ideas, and on occasion new ones, and to give them material form.

The changing needs of the majority of people who actually comprise society and who, in supposedly democratic political systems, count as much as elites rely on the advocacy of perceptive and inventive architects, when the elites' attention is focused elsewhere. The modernist movement in architecture was commissioned, as it were, by architects who saw the need for new types of housing, offices, factories, even cities, when those in government and business failed to do so.

New types of inhabited space with any value are not invented arbitrarily for the sake of novelty or mere interest. Rather, they are made necessary by changing needs for living, brought about by technological, cultural, political, and other changes that impact the lives of people of every social description. Architects should do their best to understand these changes and propose new types of spaces, when and where they believe conditions demand.

By way of giving some examples, I offer a partial list of new types of structures and spaces introduced in my projects over the past twenty years of tumultuous change in the world./14 A thorough survey will reveal many others, proposed by architects throughout the history of architecture.

LIVING-LABORATORIES: Spaces and structures performing as instruments for experimental living and working. Examples: the inverted (hanging) towers in *Underground Berlin*; *Solohouse*.

AERO-LIVING-LABORATORIES: Spaces and structures for living and working experimentally in the fluid terrain of the sky. Examples: the levitating aerial "houses" and communities of *Aerial Paris*.

FREESPACES: Spaces and structures for living and working that are 1) free of preassigned purpose or meaning and 2) difficult to inhabit; intended for those willing to invent ways to inhabit them. Examples: the hidden freespaces of *Berlin Free Zone*; the bridging, leaning, and suspended freespace structures in the streets of the *Zagreb Free Zone*; urban wall freespaces of *Old City, Havana*.

INJECTIONS, SCABS, SCARS: Spaces and structures creating three stages of the reconstruction of war-damaged buildings. Examples: numerous projects for Sarajevo, Bosnia.

HIGH HOUSES: Spaces and structures built on vertical beams stabilized by tension cables, occupying the air space above a site while still being physically connected to it. Example: *High Houses, Sarajevo*.

WALL CITIES: Urban-scaled, improvised megastructures built up incrementally using tectonic and spatial fragments. Examples: defensive wall for *Bosnia Free State*; *Quake City* from *San Francisco: Inhabiting the Quake*.

META-INSTITUTES: Structures presenting spatial conundrums, the solving of which contributes to a re-institution of an institution (e.g., a government). Examples: Parliament Building reconstruction, Sarajevo; *Meta-institute, Havana*.

HORIZON HOUSES: Structures that change their relationship to the horizon and, hence, to gravity, altering the nature and potential of the spaces they contain. Examples: *Wheel House*, *Block House*, and *Star House*.

BUOYANT BUILDINGS: Spaces and structures for living on and under the water, forming communities that reconfigure (self-organize) themselves according to fluid dynamics of the sea and shifting social arrangements. Examples: *Icebergs* from the San Diego project.

TERRAIN: Artificial landscapes reforming natural ones, according to the influence and impact of both human and natural forces of change. Examples: the terraforms of DMZ; the *Terrain* and the *Utopx* projects; the tilting beach of *Malecón, Havana*.

EARTHQUAKE HOUSES: Structures and spaces in seismically active regions that incorporate the forces released by earthquakes to transform them and the ways of living, working, and thinking they support. Examples: *Shard House*, *Slip House*, *Wave House*, and *Fault House* from *San Francisco: Inhabiting the Quake*.

VECTORSPACES: Structures and spaces formed by tectonic lines and their groupings embodying physical, emotional, and intellectual energy. Examples: installations of *The Fall* in Paris; *System Wien* in Vienna.

January 22, 2009

Sotirios Kotoulas: Seeing Space

Sotirios Kotoulas, *Map 5* (detail), 2003

Sotirios Kotoulas, photograph of electromagnetic circumpolar construction above the Arctic Circle, 2003

It is rare to encounter basic research in the field of architecture, but the publication of this project by Sotirios Kotoulas gives us a chance to do so. By its nature, basic research opens up new and unfamiliar domains that address the foundations of our knowledge. Architects, absorbed as they are in contemporary problems of design, devote little time to questioning the assumptions underlying their work. What is space? How do we know it? What constitutes its reality, its physical fabric? What material forces, lying beyond the realm of the visual, shape the physicality of space and human comprehension of it?

Our present world is greatly impacted by the invisible and, most extensively in Kotoulas's research, electromagnetic forces. Computers and the Internet, satellites and cell phones—indeed, all of the electronic instrumentation that our globally interconnected civilization increasingly relies upon for cohesion—engage the range of the electromagnetic spectrum of which visible light is but a sliver. In a palpable sense, we already inhabit electromagnetic spaces and are part of their constituency, as the term "cyberspace" attempts to acknowledge. The reason we do not know where cyberspace is, or when we are in it, or how it looks and feels when we are is because our conceptual and perceptual faculties are stuck in older ideas of space. We are hemmed in by our present assumptions and by our inability to visualize, and thus physically experience, space we cannot measure by means we already know.

Kotoulas aims to change this by bringing the invisible into the realm of the visible. Without losing his sense of awe or reducing the immeasurable, he accomplishes his mission by traveling to polar regions of the far north—to the geographical edges, if not the metaphysical limits, of our present civilization—where the visual dimension of our experience is distorted by extreme conditions. He recognizes this as a chance to not only extend our knowledge of ourselves and what we can create, but also to add something new to the apparatus of our understanding. His is a polar expedition of the mind, and the territories—philosophical and material—his rigorous and imaginative explorations reveal are claimed by him, quite appropriately, in the name of architecture. */

*/ Sotirios Kotoulas is an architect born in Winnipeg, Canada, who is currently working on several new projects, including his PhD in architectural theory at McGill University in Montreal. My text and Kotoulas's images are excerpted from the book Sotirios Kotoulas, *Space Out* (New York: Springer Verlag, 2005).

January 28, 2009

Architecture School 101

A school is—before all else—a faculty. It is obvious that without a faculty, a school could not exist, for there would be no one to teach the students who come to a school. Also, the better students—those who are most eager to learn, most ambitious for themselves, and most demanding, those, in short, with the most potential for becoming good architects—select a school partly because of its faculty. They understand well the dynamics of learning.

It follows that without a good faculty, a good school cannot exist. A mediocre faculty can only create a mediocre school, never a good one, regardless of how much potential its students have. Only a great faculty can produce a great school, and it does so by helping students realize their full potentials.

There are two aspects of a great faculty (let us put aside mediocre and say that good is fine, but why not calibrate higher?): they are very effective teachers, and they have active peer relationships. The latter refers to the exchanges they have with other teachers and critics within their school and to their creative activities outside the school, in the big, wide world of ideas and work. Peers demand of each other, first of all, a high level of dedication to architecture, meaning a high level of seriousness. A peer is an equal. No one who is serious (even playfully so) wants to waste time with anyone who is not. There is always a certain amount of competitiveness among peers, and not just for position. The true competition is for achievement—as teachers and as architects. Creative rivalry and intellectual disputation are good, even noble, forms of competition, and are to be encouraged and appreciated.

However, creative achievement does not necessarily make an architect an effective teacher. Teaching requires several qualities operating in parallel.

The first is *having something to teach*. An architect, or anyone else, who wants to instruct young people should feel strongly about what they know and have an equally strong desire to communicate it with others, particularly aspiring architects.

The second is *a commitment of time and energy* to teaching. Dipping in and out of a studio or seminar in distracted bits of time stolen from a busy career is no commitment. Teaching cannot simply be a line item on one's cv. A teacher must spend quality time with students, that is, must be personally, fully engaged in the time—of whatever duration—he or she is with students.

Third, a teacher must understand *the difference between training and education*. The term "training architects" is an oxymoron. The transdisciplinary nature of architecture—the depth and diversity of knowledge it requires as well as the complexity of integrating this knowledge into a broad understanding that can be called upon at any moment to design a building or project—goes far beyond what anyone can be trained to do. Still, some teachers try to train students, using all the finesse of training dogs. Even those who disclaim rote learning and "copy me" methods can carry vestiges of attitude that amount to the same. A good test is whether the students' work in a design studio is diverse and individual or is similar or even looks like the personal work—the "design style"—of the teacher. The best teachers preside over the flourishing of individuals and their ideas, and the resulting diversity. Diversity is the essence of *education.*

Schools of architecture must require that students pursue in some depth a broad range of subjects. This is because architecture is the most comprehensive field of knowledge one can enter. It engages the whole of society and must be informed by a society's knowledge, practices, and values. Philosophy comes first, as it provides a framework for ordering all the diverse bits and pieces. Then come the social sciences, literature, poetry, and art. These studies happen together with architecture and engineering courses and, ideally, coalesce in the design studio. It is the task of the studio teacher to set up projects and programs that enable this coalescence—far from easy. To accomplish it, a teacher must have the requisite knowledge himself or herself, and an almost uncanny ability to state in plain language a problem and lay out a methodical series of scheduled steps leading to an articulated and attainable goal. It is up to the teacher to make sure the intended work is actually accomplished within the given time. There is nothing more discouraging and dispiriting than work left unfinished.

Not least in importance is the study of history. Knowledge of the histories of the many communities we share today in global society, as well as the history of architecture, towns, and cities, is crucial. Johann Wolfgang von

Goethe said that the best part of history is that it inspires us. He was right. When we see what people have been able to achieve in the past, we realize that we can do the same, in our own inevitably different terms. Without a strong sense of this *spirit* of history, an architect can only drift with the currents of the moment. It is the responsibility of studio teachers to make this clear.

Students are the other half of any school's story. Without good students, a good school cannot exist. However, it is much easier to find good students than good faculty. It is far easier to find great students than great faculty. As Raimund Abraham once said, "There are no bad students." What he meant was that young people who aspire to become architects and have gone through an admissions and selection process have demonstrated in advance a potential that should be respected. If students try and yet do not produce really good work, it is, with few exceptions, due to the failure of their teachers. In contrast, many architects who become and remain teachers do so for reasons other than their potential as teachers. There are many—competent professionals—who should never be allowed any contact with young, eager students bristling with talent and ambition. Bad teachers, especially those who imagine themselves as good, do irreparable damage. They kill the spirit.

This does not mean that outstanding architects cannot emerge from mediocre schools—they can, and some have. But their being outstanding is more the result of their own drive to learn and develop, *in spite of* the mediocrity around them in school. They are, in effect, self-taught. However, even the most self-determined students need some help along the way: the encounter with a rare teacher who stirs their imaginations, ignites their passions about an idea, or sets an example by the teacher's own knowledge, integrity, and dedication. These are the qualities that describe the entire faculties of great schools.

This brings us to the other half of any school's story. Yes, there are three halves. The third is a school's administration, its dean and department chairs. . . . /15

February 7, 2009

Metastructure

In the last decade of the twentieth century, the newly recognized country of Bosnia and Herzegovina was under attack by two neighbors intent on destroying it and dividing the spoils between them. Croatia attacked from the north and west, making Mostar, the provincial capital of Herzegovina, the center of their assault. From the east, Serbian forces attacked, focusing on the national capital, Sarajevo. Both enemies of the fledgling nation claimed that the attacks were made by local militia, but it was clear that the materials of war and its strategies came from the two largest countries of the former Yugoslavia. The sieges of Mostar and Sarajevo, which lasted for years, and other towns such as Srebrenica were resisted by the undersupplied armies of the small nation at a great cost in lives, many of them civilians.

Metastructure, from *Bosnia Free Zone*, 1993. The wall of the Bosnia Free State

It was during this dark time that I imagined a defensive wall that could be constructed to protect Bosnia from the invaders. Aerial warfare had been effectively banned by the European powers and the United States through the creation of a no-fly zone over the entire country, enforced by NATO fighter aircraft. The war was fought, then, on the ground, in an almost medieval manner, though with tanks and artillery. My idea of the wall was not to build an armed fortification in order to repel invaders, but rather to make it function as a sponge and absorb them.

The wall would be built very high with a vast labyrinth of interlocking interior spaces, creating a structurally indeterminate system that would be extremely difficult to bring down by demolition charges or artillery fire. Tanks and mobile artillery could not be brought through the wall. Foot soldiers could not climb over the wall in large numbers, but would have to go through it. Once inside, they would become lost. Many would not be able to escape. They would either die, or, as it were, move in, inhabiting the spaces, even forming communities. Local farmers from the Bosnian side could arrange to supply food and water on a sale or barter basis. In time, they would move in, too, to be close to their market. Families would be living together. The wall would become a city.

Of course, it was a fantasy. There was not enough time to build such a wall, even if there had been the will, and not enough metal and industrial scrap-yards to supply the materials. I never proposed that it should in any way be realized, as I did with other reconstruction projects during and after the war. However, as a metaphor and even an architectural strategy, it has some value. Walls can be an armature for transformation, an instrument not for dividing and separating but for bringing opposing ideas and people together. It all depends on the design, the architecture of a wall. Later, in my proposals for *Old City, Havana* and the *Wall Game*, I pursued this idea at a less fantastic and more realistic, realizable scale.

February 12, 2009

Real Time

Recently, a journalist writing an article on how the present economic situation might affect the practice of architecture interviewed me. His particular question was: "Now that building commissions are getting more scarce, will architects turn to making 'paper architecture?'" By that term he meant speculative and theoretical projects that explore the possibilities of architecture outside the strictures imposed by clients, budgets, codes, and municipal building departments. The underlying question was, "With more time to reflect, will architects return to a more basic questioning of what architecture is and can be, even what it should be?"

My answer was: "No."

Architects who have not already been thinking about the deeper nature of architecture and speculating about it in drawings, writings, and models, either within their building practices or in independent research, are simply not able to pick it up because they find themselves with spare time. As the old saying goes, "It ain't that easy." To imagine that it is simply denigrates the field of architecture. Would someone ask the same of a physician: "Now that your patient load is diminished because of the escalating costs of health care and so many people losing their jobs and benefits, will you take up cancer research?"

Hardly. Research is a serious, lifelong vocation, not a sideline taken up when there is nothing better to do, then abandoned when there is. Perhaps the question speaks of a certain frivolousness architects have unwittingly promoted about what they do: creating new styles, new shapes, repackaging the old, the already known, but little else. If that is the case, architects cannot blame journalists who are "the messengers," but only themselves.

February 16, 2009

Architecture School 201

Once we have understood the basic structure of a school of architecture—its hierarchical, if paradoxical, composition of faculty, students, and administration—we can move on to the consideration of its content: what it teaches and why.

Most schools of architecture today are "professional" schools. This means that their goals, methods, and content are aligned with the demands and expectations of the profession of architecture, as generally accepted.

It is interesting that a great university, Harvard, was once reluctant to accept a school of architecture into its program because of its professional, not academic, orientation. The goal of Harvard's academic programs is to immerse students in different bodies of knowledge in order to prepare them to assume active, creative leadership roles in society. The university was and, perhaps, remains suspicious of professional training, which tends to be narrow by comparison, focusing on technical or other parochial skills. Even today, Harvard's Graduate School of Design (GSD) must support itself independently of the wider university's budget.

Schools that grant professional degrees must be accredited by professional groups, notably (in the United States) the National Architectural Accrediting Board (NAAB), which is comprised of professional architects and educators approved by professional organizations—such as the American Institute of Architects (AIA) and the National Council of Architectural Registration Boards (NCARB)—who continually visit schools, examine them, and decide whether they meet the standards they have set to be accredited to confer professional degrees. A professional degree is, today, a necessary step toward becoming a state-licensed professional practitioner. Because most graduating architects want to design buildings that will be built in the public domain and because that requires a state license, the accrediting process has an enormous influence on the content of almost any school's curriculum. The power of a dean to lead the school in any but an orthodox direction would seem to be very limited. But this is not always the case.

A historical example of the exception to the rule is the Irwin S. Chanin School of Architecture of the Cooper Union, in New York. When John Hejduk was dean of the school in the 1970s and 80s, he pursued a radical architectural design program and managed, at the same time, to maintain the school's accreditation to confer professional degrees. It was not easy.

During that time, his faculty included Raimund Abraham, Peter Eisenman, Bernard Tschumi, Elizabeth Diller, Ricardo Scofidio, and a host of lesser-known avant-gardists who brought their radical ideas into the design studios they taught. Hejduk himself taught the fifth-year undergraduate thesis course with an emphasis on innovative concepts of space and design. Seminars by the likes of Jay Fellows and David Shapiro added depth to the unconventional approach to architectural education. Often, accreditation committees would arrive at the school on their regular visits in a hostile mood. "What has all this to do with architecture?" they asked when they saw projects that did not resemble any buildings they had ever seen. While the school's catalog listed an orthodox program of architectural studies, the ways in which the studios and classes were conducted were utterly unorthodox, and this worried the examiners. Yet, time and again, Hejduk—with the support of his faculty and students—was able to convince them that this was a valid, indeed a valuable, approach to architectural education and practice.

How did this happen? Hejduk's charisma? The sheer quality of the student work, however unorthodox? The need for change, however grudgingly recognized? The allowance for exceptions in a vast field of sameness? Certainly all these were factors in the survival of the professional degree program by a radical school. By the 1980s, the worst fears of the more conservative critics and examiners were already being realized. With the publication of Hejduk's *Education of an Architect*, a book laying out the school's philosophy and methods, a revolution in architectural education had already been effected, as many schools adopted aspects of Cooper Union's innovative approach.*/

The Cooper Union story is a prime example of working within and at the same time extending the limits of a prevailing system of orthodoxy. Whether the same story could be written today is an open question. One can certainly argue that it is easier to transform an already working system of education

*/ John Hejduk et al., eds., *Education of an Architect: The Irwin S. Chanin School of Architecture of the Cooper Union* (New York: Rizzoli, 1988).

than invent an entirely new one. But the latter prospect may be necessary if and when the prevailing system has failed. To consider that we should look at the institution of the Bauhaus, as well as more contemporary examples of experiments in architectural education./16

February 20, 2009

Worlds Apart

The fragmentation of existing systems of order under the intense pressures of change has yielded new, more complex systems we have yet to formulate, hence understand, in clear terms. A period of exploration has been forced upon us, and we have no choice but to move deeply into a new landscape of unknowns. The previous systems of order, which are based on well-understood principles of unity, repetition, variation, and hierarchy, are useful only as points of origin and no longer as destinations. Entering the unknown terrain, we understand that unity, even totality, can no longer be rationally achieved. We must say good-bye to them as we would to old friends whom we will never see again.

We are confused by the apparent randomness—the seeming chaos—of the new conditions. We cannot easily accept the random as reasonable. Our self-consciousness insists on control, and the random resists control in the same way as a storm or an earthquake. The random pushes us toward mere reaction, and we lose initiative. We throw the dice or the straws. They land this way or that, and we struggle to interpret. Our creative powers become useless. But maybe not.

In our explorations and experiments, we discover that there is a human equivalent to randomness, and that is spontaneity. When we are spontaneous, that is, when we act without thinking, we are not really acting without any thought about what we are doing, but releasing our personal knowledge in other than the step-by-step way we—in the West—usually consider rational. We cannot be random in the same ways as the world fragmenting around us, but we can engage the randomness, not merely react to it, with our powers of spontaneity.

Architects are the most controlling of creators, who want to see the final result of their work in advance and then do all they can to see it realized. They are, accordingly, the least spontaneous of people. They work well, and always have, with autocrats in business and politics, who also have predetermined goals and are ruthless in their pursuit of them. Autocrats uphold the old systems of order, which they understand very well how to control, and so do architects.

A newer generation of architects will certainly take up the challenges of complex and confusing new systems of order by engaging the fragmentation and randomness with new principles of design that do not insist on controlling outcomes. They will integrate their own spontaneity with that of the many who build—and inhabit—our emerging worlds.

Up and Away

I live in a hole. Oh, the apartment is fine enough and has a large skylight that the occasional rain keeps reasonably well washed. However, it is the skylight that reveals daily the hole I speak of: a deep recess in Lower Manhattan made not by excavation but by building up. Tall buildings of varying heights loom all around, affording a bottom-up view of a higher world. It is a normal perspective when one is on the street, but there one rarely looks up, focusing instead on the eye-level landscape. Inside my apartment, the

View through the skylight of Woods's apartment toward Frank Gehry's 8 Spruce Street, 2009

skylight works like a lens that allows only upward views. In particular ways they are perfect for an architect—dramatically perspectival, only buildings and sky, pure geometry and space. But social and political aspects intrude on the pure aesthetic enjoyment. Who owns the buildings? For what purposes are they used? In this Financial District—the real site of contemporary disasters, from the destruction of the Twin Towers to the collapse of the American economy—what does all the ingenuity and investment of human and natural resources embodied in these buildings signify or, more simply, mean?

As is often true of vivid architectural experiences, the views through the skylight are both thrilling and troubling.

Notebook 98-3

For a period of ten years, a part of my practice was carried on in a space of ten by fifteen by two centimeters—one might call it an extreme space. Beginning in 1991, I was traveling a lot—lecturing, teaching, and working on the occasional project—and not often near my drawing board. As a way of coping with being on airplanes and trains, and living in hotel rooms, cafes, and bars, I began to keep notebooks in which I could draw and write while on the move. This was very important to me, as my thoughts were alive with new ideas that could not be put on hold. So the pages of the notebooks became a studio I could keep in my pocket, unfolding their nearly limitless space whenever I needed.

By the beginning of the new millennium, I was winding down my travels, though hardly the flow of new ideas. Still, I became a bit more settled and could work in a more settled spot. By that time making the notebooks had become a habit. For a while, I continued to work in them until I realized, reluctantly, that they were really finished, and I moved on to other ways of working. In all,

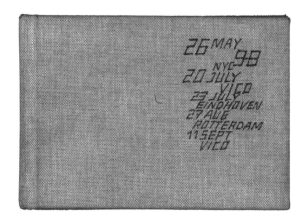

Cover, *Sketchbook*, 1998

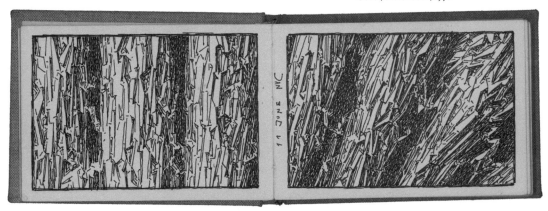

Pages from *Sketchbook*, 1998. Tectonic study

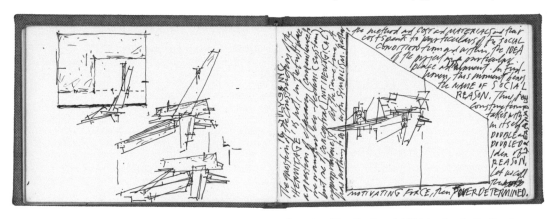

Pages from *Sketchbook*, 1998. Initial drawings for the Hermitage, Eindhoven, The Netherlands

I made some thirty notebooks of the same small size and a dozen of various larger sizes.

The notebooks turned out to be a wise decision, as many ideas that became projects for Sarajevo, Havana, Eindhoven, and elsewhere saw first light in transit. Not coincidentally, many of the ideas had to do with the transitory nature of living in social or political or natural conditions undergoing rapid, even extreme, forms of change. Shifting angles of view, abrupt arrivals and departures, and confrontations with the unexpected and the strange have become more than metaphors, but rather a way of living for many today.

Notebooks are portable. They can be kept secret or published. Technically, they are simple to make. Pen and paper. The hand, eye, and thought. Freed from any sort of burdensome apparatus, thought becomes more agile in confronting itself.

This is the first in a series of glances into the notebooks./17

March 15, 2009

Notebook 97-3

What makes home "home" are the constants. When we go out into the world, especially when traveling, we want a measure of discovery, adventure, the unpredictable, and the inconstant. But when we come home we want to find the familiar and the predictable, perhaps only to provide a frame of reference for considering all we did not know or understand from our experiences elsewhere. Home is a sanctuary where we feel safe. We can express how we feel, confide our fears and dreams. In these same ways, a notebook is something like a home, and it can be taken anywhere. In other words, we can have it both ways: to stay comfortably at home and to adventurously travel out and into the world.

The most important constant is the size of the notebook. It must always be the same. Also the paper, and the pen used to draw and write. It must be a pen and not a pencil, because a pencil smudges with the many openings and closings of the notebook, and the notebook would soon become a mass of blurs. Perhaps that is the nature of memories, but the notebook is not about memories. It is work, sometimes joyful, often difficult, and we want it to last as long as it can. Also, the pen—a cheap but reliable instrument that can be bought anywhere, but has real ink, not dyes that fade—makes precise lines that cannot be altered once drawn. The images and words placed on the pages are not tentative, but definite. They are built up a line at a time, without preliminaries, and thus they are an accurate record of ideas and the process of thought that brought them into being. Each line, each word, brings an idea closer to realization, to completion. In this sense, the contents of the notebook are not "sketches," preliminary attempts that will be finished later, but finished works in themselves.

The writer D. H. Lawrence once wrote in his *Apocalypse* about the difference between the idea of completeness in the ancient world and today.

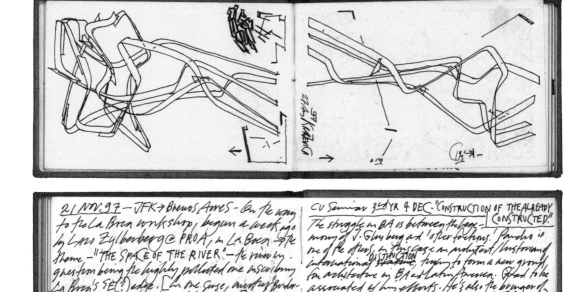

Pages from *Sketchbook*, 1997

Comparing today's "rational" process of thought to the dragging of an endless, linear "logical chain," he said that ancient thinkers would take a more circular or spiral approach. They would concentrate on a thought, following it deeper and deeper, until it reached a point of "fullness."/18 Both modes of thought have their virtues, and the possibility of fusing them in some way informs the notebooks shown here.

March 18, 2009

Architecture School 301

If there were to be a new and independent school of architecture formed today, what would be its philosophy, program, and course contents? The answers are as diverse as the faculties who would want to join them. But also, the direction of the school—and any school needs a clear direction—would be as precise as its dean and chairs could make it. In other words, there could be many new and independent schools, each offering a distinct approach to architecture.

It must be said that this prospect is radically different from today's situation, in which schools are homogenized by imposed professional standards enforced by accreditation boards and the like. Of course, the accreditation boards and their touring committees like to believe that they are encouraging diversity, not homogeneity. And, of course, each school likes to believe that it is unique—this is a very poignant human need: to believe in one's uniqueness. This holds the same for architects and students in schools of architecture. But the question remains: how best to achieve individuality in a field that is both interdisciplinary and collaborative and at the present time largely dominated by conformity?

The current design studio system in schools encourages students to work independently and to come up with their own ideas. These are then put up in reviews next to one another and judged in isolation. It is the perfect model of "free-market" competitiveness. The best students stand out and are praised. The less-than-best (by current standards) are less praised or criticized for not being good enough, which tacitly translates as losing in the competitive marketplace.

This approach, which emphasizes (at least for the present) uniqueness and originality, at the expense of camaraderie and the sharing of knowledge, does not work well after students graduate and enter the world of professional practice. Many graduates, entering practice and finding that their individuality is subordinated, become disillusioned and discouraged. Considering their experiences in school, this is understandably so. Of course, the occasional genius emerges and struggles to break out of the given hierarchy and establish himself or herself. But the genius will emerge from any sort of system, even the most rigidly conformist, and find a way. Our concern in education should not be to nurture geniuses but to encourage and help aspiring young people who want to contribute their idealism and talents—of whatever magnitude—to a common good and to do it through the design of architecture. This way of thinking should be encouraged in their schools, but as yet it is not.

It is clear that the corporate model as we know it in business and architectural practice today does not nurture individuality in this sense. It subsumes it in the process of attaining a corporate product. Thus, in effect, it discourages it, if in a different way than contemporary schools do.

I am convinced that a more embracive and ultimately more effective way to nurture individuality is to establish design studios that operate, paradoxically, on the basis of collaboration. I am not thinking of the sort of corporate collaboration where everyone's effort is blended anonymously into one result, but, rather, a type of collaboration where each individual work is still clearly legible within the collaborative whole, even while contributing to a collective effort, a common end result. This is an important distinction, though today not well understood because it is so seldom practiced.

We might think of a city as a model of individuality and collaboration. A city is an accumulation of many buildings built over time. Most buildings follow prescribed rules and are rather similar and, I suppose we would say, ordinary. A few bend the rules and stand out as singular achievements of thought and skill. On rare occasion, a building will break the rules and become literally "the exception that makes the rule," establishing new rules that amount to possible changes for the future. The point is, though, that each building, from the most ordinary to the most innovative, makes its contribution to the landscape of the city and the ways of living in it. In a city, at least a relatively democratic one, differences are accepted, and their terms of engagement, the conflicts between them, are negotiated. The ideal aim is not a homogenized whole, but a complexly evolving, dynamic balance of differences.

A new type of design studio and perhaps an entire school could be organized and conducted beginning with this type of urban condition as a model. However, being a school—in effect a laboratory for learning—there could be considerable experimentation with the ways individual projects might be combined in collaborative landscapes. Some preliminary explorations with this type of design education have already been made, with promising results.

March 23, 2009

Zaha Hadid's Drawings 1 [/19]

When I first visited her small studio in 1984, I saw a watercolor Zaha Hadid was working on taped to a drawing board. It was a delicate and intricate drawing related to her breakthrough project, *Peak*. Being one who drew, I asked her what brushes she used. Red sable? Without a comment, she showed me a cheap paint-trim "brush" that can be bought at any corner hardware store—a wedge of gray foam on a stick. I still remember my being shocked into silence. Years later, I came to understand her choice of tools as characteristic of her approach to architecture: a wringing of the extraordinary out of the mundane.

From the beginning of her creative work, Hadid has used drawing, to an unusual degree, as a means of visualizing her architectural ideas. Her way of drawing has changed over the years, as her practice has changed from that of a radical visionary—a reference most commonly applied to those who don't build—to an architect designing large-scale projects that are being built in various parts of the world. The evolution of her drawings and how they have affected the concepts of her architecture is my primary interest here.

Most architects make drawings. Yet Hadid's drawings of the 1980s are different, and in several ways. Most notably, she had to originate new systems of projection in order to formulate in spatial terms her complex thoughts about architectural forms and the relationships between them. These new projection methods were widely copied in their time and influenced, I believe, the then-nascent computer modeling culture. More to the point, they enabled her to synthesize entire landscapes within which a project she was designing may have been only a small part. This has been crucial to her thought because she sees architecture as an integral part of the wider world. She was a global architect long before the term acquired its present meaning.

There is another way these drawings are not only unique, but uniquely important to Hadid's idea of architecture: they must carry the entire weight of her intellectual investment. Her written statements about the work are, frankly, blandly descriptive, betraying little of her philosophy and even less

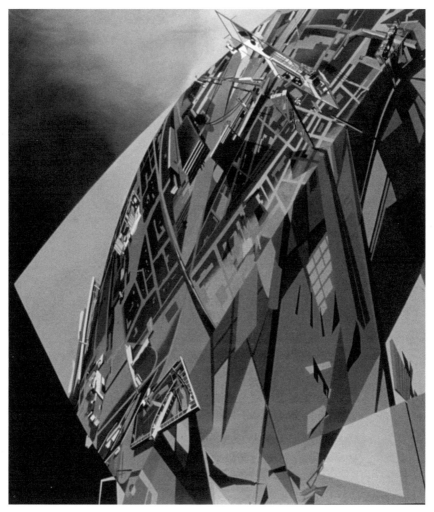

Zaha Hadid, *The World (89 Degrees)*, 1983

of her aspiration to employ her architecture as a unifying force in the world. Her lectures, while getting a boost from her charisma, are no more revealing. But her drawings speak volumes about her outlook, her intellectual depth, and her ambition to place architecture at the dynamic center of an ever more dynamic world.

Her detractors have often said her drawings are only about style, ignoring their systematic and obsessively analytical construction. On close examination, we find that the drawings reveal complex and subtle rearrangements and reinterpretations of what most of us would call "reality," portraying new forms of spatial order governing the relationships between sky and earth, horizon and ground, the artificial and the natural. Her drawing *The World (89 Degrees)* envisions a *tabula rasa* for a brave, new, Hadidian world. The seminal *Peak* drawings fragment both architecture and the mountainside overlooking Hong Kong, allowing them to intermingle in a startling, seemingly natural, synthesis. Who else had dared such all-embracing visions? Bruno Taut, in his

Alpine Architecture? Le Corbusier, in his *Radiant City*? Perhaps, but never in the context of projects so intended to be realized. This work was serious theory in visual form, and more. The drawings were manifestos of a new architecture that Hadid was clearly determined to realize in building, and against any odds.

Hadid's work of the 1980s was paradoxical. From one perspective, it seemed to be a postmodern effort to strike out in a new direction by appropriating the tectonic languages of an earlier epoch—notably Russian avant-garde at the time of the revolution—but in a purely visual, imagistic way: the political and social baggage had been discarded. This gave her work an uncanny effect. The drawings and architecture they depicted were powerfully asserting something, but just what the something was, in traditional terms, was unclear. However, from another perspective this work seemed strongly rooted in modernist ideals: its obvious mission was to reform the world through architecture. Such an all-encompassing vision had not been seen since the 1920s. Hadid alluded to this when she spoke about "the unfinished project" of modernism that she clearly saw her work carrying forward. With this attitude she fell into the anti-postmodern (hardly popular) camp championed by Jürgen Habermas. Understandably, people were confused about what to think, but one thing was certain: what they saw looked amazing, fresh, and original and was an instant sensation.

Studying the drawings from this period, we find that fragmentation is the key. Animated bits and pieces of buildings and landscapes fly through the air. The world is changing. It breaks up, scatters, and reassembles in unexpectedly new yet uncannily familiar forms. These are the forms of buildings, of cities, places we are meant to inhabit, clearly in some new ways, though we are never told how. We must be clever enough or inventive enough to figure it out for ourselves—the architect gives no explicit instructions, except in the drawings. Maybe we, too, must psychically fragment, scatter, and reassemble in unexpected new configurations of thinking and living. Or, maybe the world, in its turbulence and unpredictability, has already pushed us in this direction. */

*/ The above text was first published in Lebbeus Woods, "Drawn into Space: Zaha Hadid," in "Protoarchitecture: Analogue and Digital Hybrids," ed. Bob Sheil, special issue, *Architectural Design* 78 (August 2008), 28–35.

April 1, 2009

Within the Walls

In one sense, the town within a town that grew over many centuries within the Palace of Diocletian in Split, Croatia is an archetypal gated community. Bounded by the walls of the original Roman palace built around 305 CE, the town grew slowly and steadily through centuries of political, cultural, and religious change, each of which left its architecture in the town's landscape. The perimeter walls remained constant, as did a few key buildings. It was basically an infill process, with new buildings—constructed during the early Christian era, the Middle Ages, the Renaissance, and so-called modern times—being added to the ever more dense fabric. There was also the continual remodeling of earlier buildings to meet changing demands for contemporary living. It was an organic form of transformation, like many old cities, but one that ended in the twentieth century, when the town was fixed as a historical artifact and an object of international tourism. There is no contemporary architecture. From the standpoint of the spirit of urbanism that it embodies, this is a great pity, because it has become sacrosanct as a unique work of art and a document of history and can no longer serve as an active laboratory of urban building and living. Considering, however, the propensity of modernist architecture for erasing the past and of postmodernism for fashionable kitsch wherever it can be imposed, we should probably be grateful for the small town's ossification.

Today, walls that separate one community from another are considered to be problematic, or worse. Gated communities, planned as safe havens for the wealthy on the turbulent landscapes of urban diversity and conflicts between socioeconomic classes, are anathema to well-intentioned egalitarians. Still, this bounded town shows us that walls can also serve to concentrate energies, social and architectural. The dense layering and juxtaposition of differences and the continual rethinking of common space, its premises and purposes, can lead to admirable, even imitable—in principle—urban form.

April 2, 2009

Ends and Beginnings

When an architect such as Anthony Titus makes an installation in an art gallery, it is not an attempt to break into the art world, but a way of conducting experiments that can feed back into architectural thought. A gallery or a museum offers a controlled, laboratory environment where untested ideas can be tried out within a tight set of limitations and, at the same time, engage the public. Some ideas cannot be plugged directly into a building project but must be developed more modestly and economically. The temporary nature of installations works advantageously for this sort of research, not so much because it can be erased in preparation for starting over, but because of the intensity and focus imposed by time on both the architect and the public. Later, when ideas or even principles developed in the heat of the moment become clearer and more distilled, they can find their way into building design. But at their inception, experiments such as Titus's installation are risky, uncertain as to their outcome or potential for more practical uses—and necessarily so.

The pieces in this installation explore the material and conceptual aspects of designed space. Abstract geometrical elements are set up as spatial markers and boundaries, as is usual in architecture, but here in ways that introduce both surprise and anxiety. The elements are treated not as shapes designed to be together, but rather as found elements—in a sense, as idealized elements—that can only be brought together spontaneously, creating compositions and spaces from collisions and chance groupings. If one were

Anthony Titus, *The Light in the Window Is a Crack in the Sky*,
installation at Museum 52, New York, NY, 2008

to project a built landscape from them, it would be closer to that of a favela than, say, Brasilia. The evocative use of different materials, colors, and textures only underscores the impression that we are seeing the far outposts of another world, the meanings of which we must begin to grasp.

Entitled *The Light in the Window Is a Crack in the Sky*, this installation existed for a month about a year ago. The sky, as we know, is dark. The prevailing mood of the work is somber. The installation is not meant to entertain or distract us. There are dire problems pressing. We are unsure and sometimes afraid. Design—architecture—of this order intends to give us tools we may need on our journey to the light.

May 9, 2009

Architecture and Resistance

Apropos of nothing in particular—unless it is the general spirit of acquiescence pervading the field of architecture today—I have been thinking about the idea of architecture and resistance. Although many people might judge that my work in architecture has been nothing if not a form of resistance, I have never considered it as such. To say that you are resisting something means that you have to spend a lot of time and energy saying what that something is, in order for your resistance to make sense. Too much energy flows in the wrong direction, and you usually end up strengthening the thing you want to resist.

It seems to me that if architects really want to resist, then neither the idea nor the rhetoric of resistance has a place in it. These architects must take the initiative, beginning from a point of origin that precedes anything to be resisted, one deep within an idea of architecture itself. They can never think of themselves as resisters, or join resistance movements, or preach resistance. Rather (and this is the hard part of resistance), they must create an independent idea of both architecture and the world. It is not something that can be improvised at the barricades. It takes time and a lot of trial and error. This is only just, because the things to be resisted have not come from nowhere. They have a history built over periods of time, a kind of seriousness and weight that makes them a threat. They can only be resisted by ideas and actions of equivalent substance and momentum.

The word "resist" is interestingly equivocal. It is not synonymous with words of ultimate negation like "dismiss" or "reject." Instead, it implies a measured struggle that is more tactical than strategic. Living changes us in ways we cannot predict, for the better and the worse. One looks for principles, but we are better off if we control them, not the other way around. Principles can become tyrants, foreclosing on our ability to learn. When they do, they, too, must be resisted.

Resistance Checklist:
Resist whatever seems inevitable.
Resist people who seem invincible.
Resist the embrace of those who have lost.
Resist the flattery of those who have won.
Resist any idea that contains the word "algorithm."
Resist the idea that architecture is a building.
Resist the idea that architecture can save the world.
Resist the hope that you'll get that big job.
Resist getting big jobs.
Resist the suggestion that you can only read Jacques Derrida in French.
Resist taking the path of least resistance.
Resist the influence of the appealing.
Resist the desire to make a design based on a piece of music.
Resist the growing conviction that They are right.
Resist the nagging feeling that They will win.
Resist the idea that you need a client to make architecture.
Resist the temptation to talk fast.
Resist anyone who asks you to design only the visible part.
Resist the idea that drawing by hand is passé.
Resist any assertion that the work of Frederick Kiesler is passé.
Resist buying an automobile of any kind.
Resist the impulse to open an office.
Resist believing that there is an answer to every question.
Resist believing that the result is the most important thing.
Resist the demand that you prove your ideas by building them.

Resist people who are satisfied.
Resist the idea that architects are master builders.
Resist accepting honors from those you do not respect.
Resist the panicky feeling that you are alone.
Resist hoping that next year will be better.
Resist the assertion that architecture is a service profession.
Resist the foregone conclusion that They have already won.
Resist the impulse to go back to square one.
Resist believing that there can be architecture without architects.
Resist accepting your fate.
Resist people who tell you to resist.
Resist the suggestion that you can do what you really want later.
Resist any idea that contains the word "interface."
Resist the idea that architecture is an investment.
Resist the feeling that you should explain.
Resist the claim that history is concerned with the past.
Resist the innuendo that you must be cautious.
Resist the illusion that it is complete.
Resist the opinion that it was an accident.
Resist the judgment that it is only valid if you can do it again.
Resist believing that architecture is about designing things.
Resist the implications of security.
Resist writing what They wish you would write.
Resist assuming that the locus of power is elsewhere.
Resist believing that anyone knows what will actually happen.
Resist the accusation that you have missed the point.
Resist all claims on your autonomy.
Resist the indifference of adversaries.
Resist the ready acceptance of friends.
Resist the thought that life is simple, after all.
Resist the belated feeling that you should seek forgiveness.
Resist the desire to move to a different city.
Resist the notion that you should never compromise.
Resist any thought that contains the word "should."
Resist the lessons of architecture that have already succeeded.
Resist the idea that architecture expresses something.
Resist the temptation to do it just one more time.
Resist the belief that architecture influences behavior.
Resist any idea that equates architecture and ownership.
Resist the tendency to repeat yourself.
Resist that feeling of utter exhaustion.

Locus of Memory

Perspective view of *The Ascent*, from *World Center*, 2002

The building is called the World Center. It covers the site of the former World Trade Center and rises, for the present, to twice the height of the WTC Towers. It remains perpetually under construction, and its ultimate height is not yet known. It is the tallest building in the world and will, as it grows, always be the tallest building in the world. It is a symbol of regeneration and continual change. It is a project with a precise beginning—September 11, 2001—but no ending. Like New York City, it has a finite history, but a future that can be defined only in terms of potential.

The World Center contains vast amounts of leasable office space, though at any one time much of it is empty. There are equal amounts of public and private housing, as well as shopping malls, commercial facilities, sports and recreational facilities, and automobile parking, as well as several interlocking systems of vertical mass transit, which connect with the new Grand Central Station Downtown, which connects the site horizontally with the city and the region. The main feature of the new structure is a vertical memorial park called The Ascent, which reconstitutes in various ways experiences issuing from 9/11.

There are four ways to make The Ascent. The Pilgrimage (one month) is for the devout and consists of traversing a difficult vertical path through a series of stations, ordered by a narrative of the events and aftermath of 9/11. The Quest (one week) is for the ambitious and consists of a series of climbs up near-vertical faces, ledges, resting places, and camps, ordered by a narrative of the events and aftermath of 9/11. The Trip (two or three days) is for the vacationer, with or without family, and consists of a series of platforms, lifts, escalators, interactive displays, hotels, restaurants, vistas, and educational entertainment ordered by the story of 9/11, the histories of New York City, the skyscraper, and metropolitan life. The Tour (half a day) is for day tourists and consists of a rapid elevator ride to the summit of the park, with intermittent pauses at displays commemorating the events of 9/11 in the context of New York City history. All the ways occupy the same spaces of The Ascent. They interact yet remain separate, even opposed.

At the top of The Ascent is The Summit, a community dedicated to re-flection, study, and contemplative action, all related, directly or indirectly, to the events of 9/11. The Summit is a community made up of transients—pilgrims, climbers, vacationers, tourists, as well as workers in the World Center—who have made The Ascent and of permanent residents—scholars, students, philosophers, artists, and others—who have devoted themselves to the study of, reflection upon, and production of works concerned with the causes, events, and effects of 9/11, which are understood to be far reach-ing and wide ranging. It is a community that crowns the World Center with a continuously evolving network of interior and exterior spaces and serves as a window into old, present, and future worlds. At the same time, it is a commu-nity that brings together diverse social classes—a new egalitarian realm rising above the competitive tumult of the city below, a place where contentions can be informed by new perspectives and possibilities.

May 15, 2009

Architecture School 401

The use of analogy is the most radical and controversial aspect of the collabor-ative design studios mentioned here. The current "rehearsal" model for design studios in schools of architecture uses presumed actualities—actual sites and situations—and requires students to come up with pretend-to-be-actual transformations of them by means of architectural design. This approach has the advantage of walking would-be architects through a process resembling what they will encounter in practice as it is usually conducted. It is rather like a guided tour, with a teacher or design critic acting as a tour guide, but also as a client: giving the commission, assessing the architect's work, and "paying" the architect's fee with a grade. The fact that students in such design studios will have more freedom than in actual situations of practice does not diminish the psychological power of such a "real world" fantasy. It might, however, account for the disillusionment many students feel when they enter practice.

An analogical design studio operates very differently than this model. Its emphasis is placed on the design studio itself as a community analogous to communities anywhere. What binds together the studio community is a shared situation at the center of which is, first of all, an interest in architecture and all the ideas in orbit around it and the very act of designing. Then, of course, there is a problem or question that they agree to work on together and to answer through design.

The most important thing about the question placed before the collaborative analogical design studio is that it is one that can be answered by the members of the studio working together. This is not as simple as it seems. We are accustomed to thinking that students who address the design of a single building or an urban space, such as a streetscape or a park, do so in a way that is plausibly complete, in actual-world terms. The fact is, however, that the given buildings and public spaces are far more complex than can be dealt with in a single semester. The students, then, must be satisfied with creating the sketch of an answer or solution and cannot discover or be engaged with the completion of their designs. A central idea behind the analogical approach is that it is best to work with tangibles the students can grasp in the studio and its given time frame. Therefore, students are able to see their designs through.

There are two other ideas central to the analogical design studio. The first is that the design process be an active encounter between the individual and the collaborative, with the inevitable conflicts resolved—if at all—by negotiation. The second is that individual ideas and designs be legible within the ultimate result. The idea, again, is to create a collaborative design result that differs radically from what we know as a corporate product in which individual work is subsumed in a unified result. To the contrary, the form and content of the studio's work arises from diverse and expressive individuals. The result, therefore, is unified on a different plane of order.

A number of collaborative analogical studios have been conducted in different schools of architecture, at my instigation and under my leadership. In following posts, these will be presented in some detail, under headings beginning with "AS401."/20 Hopefully, they will clarify the general ideas presented here and provide a tangible basis for criticism and a refinement of their method and outcomes.

May 15, 2009

AS401: Buffalo Analog

The idea of an analog is to be like something else in some ways but not in others. If the something else is part of a city, therefore too complex for any definitive form of analysis, the analog can make manifest and analyzable some essential characteristics while leaving others, less important, aside. The analog is not an abstraction, though it uses abstraction as a tool. It is not a reduction or a simplification, for it remains complex in its own terms. Rather it is a shift in the angle of viewing and understanding a situation or complex set of conditions, one that gives the opportunity to see the familiar in new ways. This is extremely important when the familiar is, like a part of a city, overburdened with historical interpretations that inhibit the creation of new ones. By creating a parallel reality, the analog circumvents this historical overdetermination and liberates the imagination in ways that can impact the primary reality under consideration. In today's world of rapid changes, where history is less and less reliable as a guide to the future, intellectual freedom and inventiveness of the type enabled by the analog are increasingly important.

It is true that architecture as a practice and a form of production is bounded by precise practical considerations—technical, economic, legal, cultural—that restrict imagination and invention. But as cultural, technological, legal, and socioeconomic factors themselves undergo change, the boundaries of architecture require adjustment or even redefinition that cannot be devised by the simple extrapolation of old ones. This is where analogical thinking and the analog—as a model of constructed reality—become useful. This is especially the case in schools of architecture, where the next generation of practitioners, theorists, and teachers is being educated. The aim of their education must be less about understanding existing typologies and techniques and more about forging new ways of approaching old and new problems alike—that is, new ways of thinking about what architecture is, how it works, and what it may yet become.

The Upper Level Design Studio focused on spaces marked by conflict, beginning with particular sites in the city of Buffalo.*/ Spatial manifestations of conflict were given the highest priority among the spectrum of urban conditions and became the subject of our analogical analysis and projects. The idea was that conflict signals some sort of change that is trying to occur in the spatial structure of a particular site. This change requires an alteration of the existing spatial order and how it is used, and therefore calls for new spatial designs and constructions. Architecture, according to this thesis, arises as a creative engagement with conflict. Without conflict, there is no need for change, no need for architecture. The exception to this is when architecture must be introduced to create conflict where none exists, fomenting change in a social or spatial situation.

*/ Analogical Architecture, McHale Fellowship Studio, spring 2004. School of Architecture and Planning, University at Buffalo, the State University of New York. Directed by Lebbeus Woods, 2003–4 John and Magda McHale Fellow, with Dennis Maher, clinical assistant professor of architecture. Students: Timothy Beebe, Jose Chang, Keith Johnson, Brandon Lauricella, Zhiwei Liao, Tuan Luong, Peter G. Mendola, Derek Morgan, Caterina Onorati, Alexandria Rabuffo, and Christopher Romano.

The Buffalo Analog at the end of April, 2004,
with Lebbeus Woods at the right

Detail of the individual projects, Buffalo Analog,
Buffalo, New York, 2004

After the initial phase of identifying and analyzing spaces of conflict in existing urban situations, the work of the studio took a decisive turn. Rather than hypothesize about actual conditions in Buffalo, it was decided that we would treat the studio itself as a community, an analog of the wider community of Buffalo. Where it is the architect's usual practice to grasp the needs and motivations of groups and individuals from fragmentary and indirect sources, we would be able to work directly with people for whom the designs were intended—ourselves. We were, after all, a community in every sense of the word, having common interests, values, goals, and problems, and at the same time diverse, even conflicting, ideas, perceptions, and ways of working toward our common ends. Cannot we say that in one sense this was an ideal community, in that we would be able to work directly and together, without the need for inter-mediaries like developers, clients, and institutional representatives? Would not the ideal be that every community could design its own spaces, according to its uniqueness and demands? Politically, we might say this is the anarchist view, an extreme form of democracy in which liberty and choice are ordered not by imposed laws and ideology-based rules but rather by dialogue and critique within a community of individuals who understand from the beginning that their fate as individuals is tied up with the fate of the community. Enlightened self-interest is thus the operating frame of political and social reference.

Once the analyses of different urban conflicts were complete and codi-fied in visual terms (drawings and models), it was decided that we would build a construction, a spatial and conceptual analog of a community—ours—in con-tinuous self-definition and formation. It was decided that this construction would be within an eight-foot cube.

The apparent arbitrariness of this decision is important to consider. As an analog, the spatial frame of reference of our work could have been any number of other configurations: a pyramid, a sphere, an irregular vol-ume. Or, it could have been a volume more related to the origins of our work, the city of Buffalo. The latter option was rejected because it would be more representational than analogical, and it would be hard to escape from all the literal implications of that representation. Having to cope with the cube had implications that were more philosophical, typological, and conventional. The cube is the building block of the spatial reference system that is dominant in our society and culture. It is also the visible evidence that the complexity of human experience can be made coherent and practicable. The cube gives us coordinates in space, but also in time. Any form, any eccentricity, any accident or unpredictable occurrence can be contained within its system of coordinates and made intelligible, logical. So, somewhat less than purely arbitrary, it was chosen as a boundary, a limit, a structural frame, but also as a convention and critique. Our ideal community, we determined, would not abandon the known and accepted, but embrace and expand it.

The dimensions of the cube were determined by the available space in the studio. As such, it had no inherent scale. By tilting the cube up on one corner, shifting it off the ordinary Cartesian reference system of the room, the building, the campus, and the city, its three-dimensionality was fully liberated. But this created a problem of how to support the cube, to transfer its weight back to the Cartesian structure that would carry it to the ground. This required a compromise of the cube's autonomy that was the subject of heated debate. In what was probably the only consensus-driven decision of the project, the cube, a welded steel frame, was supported on a steel bracket at the corner and a short wall, constructed of plywood, at two raised points. The project began its move toward a tectonic hybridity that continued through its construction.

It was then decided that the space of the cube would be divided according to prevailing social practice as a series of volumetric properties. Each property, staked out by a member of the studio, was to embody a spatial construction related to the conflict originally identified in the analyses of urban spaces in Buffalo. Because these properties—irregular volumes estimated to best serve individual purposes—interpenetrated each other in the animated three-dimensional space of the cube, a set of new conflicts arose—the actual conflicts of our community, which had to be resolved through a long and difficult process of negotiation and design. Tempers flared. Factions formed and reformed. Mock-ups were tried, rejected, modified, and retried. There were moments when it seemed that the project could not go forward. The studio itself became the space of conflict, with the spaces of the cube at its conceptual center.

The designs for each of the properties within the cube were entirely determined by the individual architect occupying the spatial volume of a property. Adjacencies with other volumes and designs were matters of negotiation where abrasions demanded some resolution. Intersections of the volumes required active collaboration as differing, even opposing, tectonic systems met or collided. Each design had its unique narrative, each abrasion and confrontation its story. The final stage was only a moment in a living process incidentally truncated by schedule. It could have continued. It should continue, in some form or other, until it reaches the horizon. What we see is not a utopia, but a heterotopia—the spatial form of a community of differences, of conflicts, of personally determined spaces that work together in a complexly cohesive and communal way. It could be an analog of the most desirable city of tomorrow, one whose form and purpose arise not from the imposition of predetermined means and ends, but from a creative interplay of personal and communal means and ends.

Thoughts on the methodology: As the teacher in this design studio, I adopted the role of the senior member of the community. Having asked the initial questions, I became the arbiter, the counselor within an effort that I perceived to be the independent and collective work of the individuals in the studio. I preferred not to call them students, and myself teacher, because these terms put the wrong hierarchical emphasis on the generation of a project that could not be taught, in any traditional sense, but only created by the members of the class. This resulted in consternation and frustration among some members of the studio/community who wanted my direction as to what to do. It also led to their complaints and appeals to the hierarchy of the school, which I understood and had to seriously address.

Certainly there are aspects of architecture that need to be "taught," particularly at the beginning levels of architectural education. At the upper levels, when students have acquired skills of architectural drawing, model making, and design and face the prospect of leaving school and working in the architectural profession, it is time to "teach" individuals initiative, thinking, and action. Authority figures, such as teachers, must at this stage become mentors. Students not prepared for the degree of independence required by this work will not be prepared to practice architecture with an independent conscience and sense of responsibility.

It is hoped that the design studio also imparts the idea that architecture is, and can be more, a collaborative art. Buildings often are but should not be conceived in a social and political vacuum. At the same time, the best architecture cannot be designed by committee or consensus. New ways of approaching individuality and collectivity need to be developed in design if complex human living environments are not to be reduced to standards or to accumulations of randomly eccentric architectural gestures. The Buffalo Analog was and remains an exploration of the aesthetical and ethical possibilities of a methodology of collaboration that synthesizes community from conflict, and an analogical urban architecture from strongly articulated, highly individual differences.

May 26, 2009

When the World Was Old

When the world was old, all things became possible. Opposites remained opposed, yet found a unity in being so. Sameness was no longer the same, but different at each turn. Time remained infinite, but closed in finite cycles with distinct variations. There was reconciliation without compromise or surrender. Each thing remained true to itself, but joined with many others. Conflict became a form of harmony. Accordingly, the human and the natural embraced one another, almost by accident. It happened one day on the way to autonomy, when people finally saw and understood their reflections in "the mirror." That which can be controlled by them became reconciled with that which cannot.

Alas, the world was still young, too. When the world was young, nothing seemed possible, because possibility did not yet exist. There was only the immediate exchange between need and needed, between what was felt and hungered for and what could be grasped close at hand. Possibility came into being only when need could be delayed, when one could be hungry and wait to get the food one wanted to eat. Possibility is the acceptance of delay, acceptance of gratification's postponement, for a reason. When the world was young, there was no reason, as it was not needed, as long as gratification was easy. Reasoning became a need only when gratification became difficult, and only after the resulting wave of panic. Reason is the result of panic, in that it is the only way to keep panic from spinning out of control and consuming entirely our vital energy. Reason enables us to delay desire, to wait, to dream, and to plan.

June 5, 2009

Architecture of Energy

Any city is comprised of many systems—economic, technological, social, cultural—that overlay and interact with one another in complex ways. Each system is different, but from one point of view all share a common purpose—the organization of energy—and a common goal—giving the cumulative energy of the city a coherent form.

According to the second law of thermodynamics, the entropy in a system will increase (it will lose energy) unless new energy is put in. According to Newton's law of inertia, a system will stay at rest unless it is disturbed by an external force. Energy exists in two states: kinetic and potential. A brick sits on top of a wall—potential (it could fall). A brick is pushed from the top of the wall—kinetic (its potential is released).

Energy takes many forms, each created by a system that contains it for a particular purpose. Architecture is one such system that contains energy by establishing stable boundaries, limits, and edges. New energy—in the form of maintenance—must continually be added to the system of materials, or they will decay. Metaphysically speaking, new energy—in the form of human thought, emotion, activity—must continually be added to the system of boundaries, or they will lose their purpose and meaning.

The group of drawings, prints, models, and installations comprising the *System Wien* project develop an idea that the making of architecture can be understood as *the organization of energy*. The project explores how energy relations in public and private city spaces might be represented tectonically in the form of drawings and models; how existing energy relations in the city can be changed by the input of new energy in the form of highly temporary spatial interventions; and how the future of the city need not depend for creative energy

Lebbeus Woods in collaboration with Christoph a. Kumpusch, *System Wien*, 2005. The vector rod placement team in July, going into Vienna's First District

Lebbeus Woods in collaboration with Christoph a. Kumpusch, *System Wien*, 2005. A drawing used as a guide to the team for placing the vector rods

input on the development of building projects requiring large capital investments and institutional approval, but rather on the redistribution of energy at the human scale of the street and the room.

A portion of a city's potential energy is contained in its architectural constructions. A vast quantity of mechanical energy is stored in the materials used to make buildings—the energy it took to lift them into place above the surface of the earth and its center of gravity. The distance between the materials and the earth's surface determines the quantity of their potential energy, which can only be released when, responding to the gravitational attraction of the earth's mass, they fall.

The larger part of the city's potential energy is contained in its people. Each person has energy that can be activated, in thoughts and in actions, anytime in the future. In theory, just how and when this energy will be released and where it will be directed is unpredictable. Governments, businesses, and other institutions organizing the collective energy of a people work hard to ensure that the energy of individuals will conform to accepted standards and maintain a predictable continuity. In the fast-changing contemporary world, with its radical technological developments, political and economic crises, and abrupt cultural shifts, institutions often become more protective of the status quo, more resistant to changes in the established systems of organization. Like the build-up of energy in the Earth's tectonic plates, institutional resistance to change inevitably brings sudden and violent releases of energy, such as revolution and war. At the same time, institutional exploitation of the fear of violent change will polarize people of different opinions and beliefs. Energy that might otherwise be directed to collectively constructive projects is spent in attacking adversaries—a project that, while usually bent on destruction, is nevertheless part of the processes of creative change.

It is difficult to determine in advance the magnitude of any human being's energy—potential or kinetic. We can know the quantity of energy it takes to walk a given distance, but what is the energy of a person who assassinates a world leader? Do we measure it by cause or effect? Or the person who invents a new technology? Or the person who designs a housing project? Or the people who devote themselves to helping the poor? The energy of such persons' thoughts and actions cannot be measured quantitatively or qualitatively by applying any known formula. Their input is nominal—they think, move, speak in more or less normal ways—but their effects are vast. If we measure their input in nominal terms, it is not radically different from that of ordinary people going about their daily lives. The where, when, and how of the energy of such persons' acts have much to do with their effects.

But that cannot be all. If it were, then any person's thoughts and words and actions would sooner or later—under the right circumstances—produce vast effects. But they do not. The energy of persons who "change the world"— even the local world—must be extraordinary in ways that can be identified and measured. How, then, can that be done? How can it be represented in any analysis of the present and future organization of a city's energy? And, more importantly for our purposes here, how does the extraordinary inform the ordinary? How might we think of and portray the everyday differently as a result of knowing that at any human point it might become extraordinary?

If we could answer this question, we could immediately begin to establish a social and political order that recognizes the fact that any human life can and in some cases will change the course of human events at a scale larger than a personal scale. Steps have been made in that direction, in the form of legal and political instruments that guarantee fundamental human rights, including the right to be educated and the right to be employed within the institutional structure. In so doing they guarantee that any person's potential energies—physical, intellectual, moral, philosophical—can be applied to human conditions at the right place and time. It has taken many thousands of years for these first steps to be made, so we might imagine it will take considerably more time for steps that take us beyond the institutional to the direct application of human energies, without institutional mediation, foreseen by various utopians. Meanwhile, life goes on, struggling under imperfect conditions and circumstances. The city, the *polis*, is struggling to grow and to change, perhaps even toward that day when the idea of the human is recognized in the energy, the life impulse, and the actions of each human being.

The ethical implications of such a "toward" are enormous. If human society were to value each human life equally, then what about the murderers, thieves, pedophiles? How about the small-time cheaters, the dullards, the bigots, and the bores? Are they to be given the same value as the bright, the tolerant, the compassionate, the innovative, and the persons of "genius" who bestow gifts of wide value to the human world? The answer given by utopians is "no," because the human world will consist only of the latter and not at all of the former. All the disgusting and disagreeable human behaviors will have been eliminated by universal education and opportunity. But, as critic Aldous Huxley asks in his *Brave New World*, what if the perfect society is—against all odds and predictions—disturbed by savagery, that is, by atavistic urges and actions? It could be in the form of incest, or the belief in magic, or in rituals of racial superiority leading to genocide, or, in "my right to do whatever I want, regardless of what anyone else thinks." The very presence of these possibilities, indeed these potentialities that only wait to be released, brings us back to square one. Human perfectibility, we are forced to acknowledge, in either social or individual terms cannot be defined by any sort of fixed or universal standard of rectitude.

If that is the case—and history bristles with examples, including governments of the left and the right that tried to impose universal standards of thought and behavior—then some new and better system for the organization of human energy waits to be devised. The premise of the *System Wien* project is that the social, political, cultural, and ethical can be formulated in spatial terms, as indeed they already are. It opens a speculation on the possibility that this formulation can facilitate change more creatively—at once more wisely and spontaneously—than existing spatial systems allow.

"What exactly do the vectors represent?"

"They don't represent anything. They are just themselves—embodied energy."

"They contain energy?"

"Yes. Can't you see it?"

"I see white lines on a black surface."

"Tell me, what do you see when you look at that building? Bricks, windows, metal, glass?"

"Yes."

"That's all?"

"Yes."

"Ah, then that's the problem. You can't see energy, just its effects. . . . The vectors contain the energy that it took to make them. It is a measurable amount of energy, but it has not yet been measured. It consists of physical, intellectual, and emotional energy. Certainly we will be able to measure it by its effects, if and when there are any."

"So, then, the vectors are a form of energy?"

"Yes, that is what they are."

"Well, there's nothing new there. Any drawing, any word or act has the potential to have an effect. All you're doing is seeing it differently."

"Exactly!"

Architecture, we hope, is first of all a field of knowledge, and only then of action. Our hope is rooted in the judgment that actions are most constructive when informed by an idea that fits into a larger understanding of ourselves and the world. When we design and build, we demand that architecture embodies such an idea of human experience and how it is enabled by the conception, design, and construction of space. Our existing knowledge is important, because it is the structure of what is already here. Architecture, like other fields, reveals the structure of the familiar. It remains only for us to see this structure as though it has not been seen before, freshly, as though for the first time. This is, I believe, the task of architects.

It is true that most architects will continue to be kept busy designing buildings and spaces serving existing interests and points of view. It is entirely proper that there will be only a few who have the inclination or feel the necessity to invent new points of view, or who are willing to accept the risk, if not the probability, that their ideas will come to nothing. The truth is that in the day-to-day practices of architects building and rebuilding the familiar, a substantial part of the invention of new viewpoints will emerge, one building at a time. We might call the cumulative effect of these small steps a sociohistorical process, one that moves ahead inexorably but surely because it is intimately connected to everyday conditions and their own subtle and incremental transformations. Still, some leaps are needed if architecture is not only to keep up with today's accelerated changes, but also to get enough ahead to help lead them.

It is crucial that we invent strategies for seeing the familiar differently. If we rely solely on seeing it in familiar ways, we will only be able to reenact what we have already done and confirm what we already know. As changes occur to the familiar systems, either as a result of entropy or disturbances from outside forces, we will be poorly prepared with entrenched attitudes to control their transformations, the ways the energies they contain are released and to what ends they are employed. In order to adapt creatively to changing conditions, we must adapt our existing knowledge and skills. Accustomed though we might be to finding a new pill or product to solve critical problems, we cannot count on new knowledge alone to save us from becoming relics of our own history.

The first task of experimental works of architecture and art is to stake out new points of view on what already exists. The second task is to test them.

System Wien—a project made in collaboration with Christoph a. Kumpusch—begins with the existing system of spatial organization as embodied in Vienna's buildings, streets, and open spaces, and how they are presently inhabited.*/ It sees them not as organized matter, but rather as organized energy. The visual language through which this understanding is expressed is comprised of lines—constructed in two, three, and four dimensions—which we will call "vectors."

Vectors are mathematical symbols for expressing the direction and magnitude of forces active within or upon a system. In this project, the vector is expanded in meaning and application. It still retains its expressive function, only now including not only magnitude and direction of mechanical forces, but also the intensity and extensity of cognitive and affective forces both active and latent in the city. There is another aspect of the role vectors play in this project and in its projection of the present and future energy patterns of the city: the vectors not only express energy, *they embody energy*. Like other constructive elements used to build the city, they are elements of a system organizing

*/ See Peter Noever, ed., *Lebbeus Woods: System Wien* (Ostfildern, Germany: Hatje Cantz Verlag, 2005).

the mechanical, cognitive, and affective energy it took to make them, palpable energy that remains potential in their residual forms. If we can see vectors as forms of potential and kinetic energy, then we can see buildings and the city itself that way, too. If we can see these things not simply as objects, but as embodied energy, then we can see ourselves and others not as material objects, but as living systems interacting continuously with other systems, both animate and inanimate.

This is a new way of seeing the familiar, at least for architects. Ecologists and theorists from fields as diverse as cybernetics and the life sciences adopted similar points of view long ago. Architects retain a mechanical, materialist worldview, no doubt in part because of the nature of the people they work for, their clients, who see architecture as a product that relates only incidentally to other products, designed and paid for by others. The boundaries of a product are rigid, fitting into clients' ideas of property and consumers' ideas of buying and owning. Systems, on the other hand, have flexible, often porous or fluid, boundaries depending on their interactions with other systems.

The energy system's view of the city and its life has strong political implications, in particular regarding prevailing ideas of identity and, its corollary, property. Individuals, in such a view, are identified not so much by what they "own" or who they "are," according to the social roles they play, but by what they "do," how they interact with others, including the inanimate systems in their environment. In the same way, buildings, public spaces, and other forms of property can no longer be identified according to building types set by predetermined economic and functional categories but by how they perform in a landscape shaped by complex interactions. What architects do with their own initiatives or those of others seriously impacts networks of interacting human and other energy flows, as well as the energies latent in the city. Their ways of thinking and working need to integrate this reality more than they do at present. In doing so, the role of the architect will be transformed into a more expansive and more complex one in the evolution of the urban landscape. The identity of architects—like that for whom they design—will be based on the depth of their mastery of particular skills and knowledge, but, at the same time, on their agility in engaging an urban field of continually changing conditions. *System Wien* explores what the production of such architects might be.

June 8, 2009

Doom Time

Flashed around the world in September 2001, the pictures of the World Trade Center towers lying in ruins were both horrifying and—though few would openly admit it—strangely stimulating. The former because we instantly realized, with despair, that many people had died in the towers' collapse and that many others would suffer as a result of it for the rest of their lives. The latter because such a grand scale of destruction evoked an essential truth about human existence, a truth so disturbing that it is usually cloaked in denial: *we are all going to die.*

Not only will we die, but also all our works will die. The great buildings, the great works of art, the great books, and the great ideas on which so many have spent the genius of human invention will all fall to ruins and disappear in time. And not only will all traces of the human as we know it vanish, but the human itself will, too, as it continues an evolutionary trajectory accelerated by bioengineering and future technological advances. What all of this means is that we cannot take comfort in any form of earthly immortality that might mitigate the suffering caused by the certainty of our personal extinction.

It is true that, through works of art, artists can live on in the thoughts and actions of others. This, however, is more of a comfort to the living than to the dead, and while it may help a living artist maintain a denial of death effective enough to keep believing that working and striving is somehow lasting, it is an illusion, and a pretty thin one at that. In contrast, the solidarity that develops between people who accept the inevitability of oblivion is more substantial and sustainable. When we witness an accident or disaster, we are drawn to it not because of "prurient interest," or an attraction to the pornography of violence, but rather because it is an event that strips away the illusions of denial and reveals the common denominator of the human condition. For the moment of our witnessing we feel, however uncomfortably, part of a much larger scheme of things, closer to what is true about our existence than we allow ourselves to feel in the normal course of living.

Religions have promised immortality and certainty in afterlives of various kinds, but for many today this is an inadequate antidote to despair. There are people who want to focus on the present and to feel a sense of exultation in being alive here and now, not in a postponed "later." This desire cuts across all class, racial, gender, political, and economic lines. In some religious lore, the ruins of human forms will be restored to their original states, protected and enhanced by the omniscient, enduring power of a divine entity. But for those who feel this is too late, the postponement of a full existence is less than ideal. For them, the present—always both decaying and coming into being, certain only in its uncertainty, perfect only in its imperfection—must be a kind of existential ideal. The ruins of something once useful or beautiful or symbolic of human achievement speaks of the cycles of growth and decay that animate our lives and give them particular meaning relative to time and place. This is the way existence goes, and therefore we must find our exultation in confronting its ambiguity, even its confusion of losses and gains.

The role of art in all this has varied historically and is very much open to question from the viewpoint of the present. The painting and poetry of the Romantic era made extensive use of ruins to symbolize what was called the "sublime," a kind of exalted state of knowing and experience very similar to religious transcendence, lacking only the trappings of the church and overt references to God. Hovering close to religion, Romantic ruins were old, even ancient, venerable. They were cleansed of the sudden violence or slow decay that created them. There was something Edenic about them—Giovanni Battista Piranesi's Rome, Percy Bysshe Shelley's "Ozymandias," William Wordsworth's "Tintern Abbey,"

Lebbeus Woods and Kiki Smith, *Untitled (Firmament 1)*, 2004. Titled *The Kiss* in the Woods blog

Lebbeus Woods and Kiki Smith, *Untitled (Firmament 2)*, 2004. Titled *Serenade* in the Woods blog

Caspar David Friedrich's *The Wreck of the Hope*. The best of such works are unsentimental but highly idealized, located intellectually and emotionally between the programmed horror of medieval charnel houses and the affected nostalgia for a lost innocence of much architecture and painting of the late nineteenth century.

Taken together, these earlier conceptions are a long way from the fresh ruins of the fallen Twin Towers, the wreckage of Sarajevo, and the blasted towns of Iraq, which are still bleeding, open wounds in our personal and collective psyches. Having witnessed these wounds—and in a palpable sense having received them—gives us no comfortable distance in which to rest and reflect on their meaning in a detached way. Hence, works of art that in some way allude to or employ these contemporary ruins cannot rely on mere depictions or representations—today that is the sober role of journalism, which must report what has happened without interpretation, aesthetic or otherwise. Rather it is for art to interpret, from highly personal points of view, what has happened and is still happening. In the narrow time frame of the present, with its extremes of urgency and uncertainty, art can only do this by forms of direct engagement with the events and sites of conflict. In doing so, it gives up all claims to objectivity and neutrality. It gets involved. By getting involved, it becomes entangled in the events and contributes—for good and ill—to their shaping.

Thinking of Francisco Goya, Otto Dix, Käthe Kollwitz, and so many others who bore witness and gave immediacy to conflict and the ruins of its aftermath, we realize that today the situation is very different. Because of instantaneous, worldwide reportage through electronic media, there no longer exists a space of time between the ruining of places, towns, cities, peoples, and cultures and our affective awareness of them. Artists who address these situations are obliged to work almost simultaneously with them. Those ambitious to make masterpieces for posterity would do well to stay away, as no one of sensibility has the stomach for merely aestheticizing today's tragic ruins. Imagine calling in Piranesi to make a series of etchings of the ruins of the Twin Towers. They would probably be powerful and original, but only for a future generation caring more for the artist's intellectual and aesthetic mastery of his medium than for the immediacy of his work's insights and interpretations. Contemporary artists cannot assume a safe aesthetic distance from the ruins of the present, or, if they do, they risk becoming exploitative.

How might the ruins of today, still fresh with human suffering, be misused by artists? The main way is using them for making money. This is a tough one, because artists live by the sale of their works. Even if a work of art addressing ruins is self-commissioned and donated, some money still comes as a result of publicity, book sales, lectures, teaching offers, and the like. Authors of such works are morally tainted from the start. All they can do is admit that fact and hope that the damage they do is outweighed by some good. It is a very tricky position to occupy, and I would imagine that no artists today could or should make a career out of ruins and the human tragedies to which they testify.

Theodor Adorno stated that there could be no poetry after Auschwitz. His argument rested on the fact that the Holocaust could not be dealt with by the formal means of poetry, owing to poetry's limits in dealing with extremes of reality. Judging by the dearth of poetry about the Holocaust, I am inclined to believe he was right. Looking at a similar dearth of painting, sculpture, and architecture that engage more contemporary holocausts, I am inclined to extend his judgment into the present. Still, if we concede the impotence of plastic art in interpreting horrific events so close to the core of modern existence, we in effect say goodbye to them as vital instruments of human understanding. If we concede that, because of their immediacy, film and theater have been more effective, then we consign them to the limits of their own traditions. And so, we must ask, how have the arts dealt with the ruins of Sarajevo and Srebrenica, of Rwanda and Beirut and Iraq, of the Twin Towers site? How will they deal with the new ruins to come? Time itself has collapsed. The need is urgent. Can art help us here in the white heat of human struggle for the human, or must we surrender our hope for comprehension to the political and commercial interests that have never trusted art?

Today's ruins challenge artists to redefine both their roles and their arts. People need works of art to mediate between themselves and the often-incomprehensible conditions they live with, especially those resulting from catastrophic human violence. While not all works of art are universal, they share a universal quality—namely, the need to be perceived as the authentic expression of the artist's experience. Without the perception of authenticity and the trust it inspires, art becomes rhetorical, commercial, and, by omission, destructive. Today, what are the authentic forms of interpreting ruins—the death of the human, indeed ultimately of everything?

June 13, 2009

Total Design

The post-World War II world was one of hope and of fear. Hope for a future in which all people would benefit from the fruits of human progress. Fear that the rival global superpowers would destroy each other or, worse, that one would destroy the other, prevail, and force its way of life on all.

It was in this "age of anxiety" after 1945 that American design professions—building design, urban planning, furniture and interior design—reconstituted themselves for a postwar world. This involved experimentation with new, synthetic materials; a new degree of coordination between industrial manufacture and the design of everything from building panels to furniture; and, not least, a new degree of coordination of all the elements in a room, a building, or public spaces that became known as "Total Design." This was an important trend through the 1950s.

Total Design—as exemplified by Mies van der Rohe's Farnsworth House of 1950 and as conceived and practiced by Florence Knoll, Eero Saarinen, Charles and Ray Eames, and others in the 1940s and 50s—was arguably the fulfillment of a modernist vision of totality possible in a highly industrialized mass society, codified by the Bauhaus school and workshops in Weimar and Dessau, Germany, in the post–World War I era. This same vision had also flourished briefly in another defeated nation, Russia, just following the October Revolution in 1917. The promise of this vision was a society, democratic or egalitarian, that would live and work in buildings and cities that were both efficient, by modern industrial standards, and beautiful. It was an almost utopian vision that was in effect thwarted by the rise of totalitarianisms of an autocratic, reactionary nature during the 1930s.

The military defeat of these regimes in World War II encouraged some designers to think that this idealistic modernism could be picked up where it had been left and carried forward with industrial technologies vastly expanded and improved by the war effort. Many believed that America, with its newfound dominance, had a moral obligation to show the way forward, and the advocates of Total Design went about their innovative work with messianic fervor, driven by a sense of moral rectitude. Tacitly or not, they aimed at creating a benevolent totality that would improve the conditions of living for the many. And America, still under the influence of a soft form of New Deal socialism but with rapidly growing power and wealth, seemed to them the natural, perhaps inevitable, place for this to happen.

It should be noted that, in the simplest equation, design equals control. When buildings or chairs are designed, they are not yet made. The designs are instructions to the makers to make them in particular ways. No room is left for the makers' improvisations; rather the end product is controlled by the designer in coordination with builders and manufacturers, as well as with those who will market, distribute, and sell the products. While there is risk involved, the effort is made to eliminate chance as, for example, in using handcraft methods that will vary unpredictably. For a designer who designs, in a coordinated way, all the products in a working or living environment, the goal is to eliminate chance altogether. Total Design equals total control.

The design of private houses, office buildings, and their working spaces were prime subjects for Total Design in the 1950s. Not only were the buildings thoroughly designed and specified by the architect, but also the interiors, their furnishings, and decoration, usually in league with more specialized designers. In some extreme cases, custom-designed desks were arranged according to plan then screwed to the floor to insure they would not be moved. Carpets, draperies, paintings, and other decorations were selected by the designers, as were all colors used throughout. In company cafeterias, the kitchens and serving equipment were designed and also the uniforms of the servers, the menus, the flatware, and the china. Legally binding contracts were written between some more famous designers and their clients that none of these things could be altered without the designers' permission.

While the designers did not control the dress of the people using these places, dress codes were rigorously enforced according to corporate standards. The 1950s was the era of *The Man in the Gray Flannel Suit*, and women office workers never wore slacks. The behavior of the office workers, too, was controlled by corporate policies, all of which aimed ultimately at producing a predictable product that would be predictably consumed by a suitably "educated public." It was a time of moral priggishness: antigay, repressive of minorities, intolerant of any nonconformity. Not surprisingly, the era came to an abrupt and—in the sociopolitical sphere—a sometimes-violent end in the 1960s.

Total Design was expensive. As it had been with the Bauhaus, the ideal of the best furniture, fabrics, and household goods being mass-produced and available to all never came close to being realized and remained the exclusive domain of the well-off. Modernist buildings remained the option only for those who could afford unique "designer" houses or corporate buildings. What began as a movement that could inspire industry to provide efficiency and beauty to the many ended as a luxury goods business for a relative few. Total Design failed.

The reasons it failed are several. Certainly one reason was the inability of designers and architects to convince business and industry that its egalitarian mission would be profitable enough. Some attempts were made, such as the prefabricated metal Lustron Houses and the Eameses' Case Study Houses, which employed standardized materials and methods, but none of these found a positive reception with the broader public. The American people, it seems, were not ready for totality of design and control. Hopelessly insensitive to the virtues of innovative modern design, especially at the price of relinquishing their taste for the traditional, they appeared ready to accept less-than-total versions of modern design in the workplace, then retreat to a suburb of off-the-shelf, hand-built wooden houses decorated inside and out with references to the past.

Another reason Total Design failed is that, ultimately, designers themselves abandoned it. By the mid-1960s a chorus of leading architects and designers—led by Robert Venturi and Denise Scott Brown, as well as Reyner Banham and the Archigram group in England—rejected, for various reasons, modernist ideals of totality and argued for more eclectic or otherwise less-controlled methods of design. This corresponded with widespread political attitudes of the time, as well as radical changes in fields of philosophy and the humanities that became the position generally known as postmodernism.

June 28, 2009

Fluid Space

The surface space of this planet is filled with fluids—air and water—that we humans have adapted to by both natural and technological means. We not only live within veritable oceans of these fluids—with their ebbs and flows, their flux and interactions—but also have become entirely dependent upon them. Their lighter density relative to that of our own bodies allows us to move about with relative ease. We can walk, ride, fly, float, swim, sail, and dive, for the most part safely and increasingly with speed, even while the fluids themselves continuously swirl around us according to their own necessity.

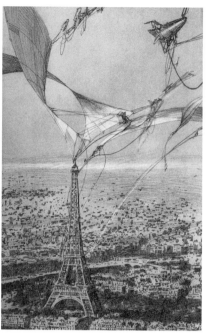

Icebergs, 1991. Icebergs: a community of inhabited structures floating outside the San Diego harbor. Much of their form—and interior space—is beneath the surface of the sea.

Aerial Paris, 1989. Aeroliving Labs: a community of heavier-than-air structures in the air over Paris. They drag immense sheets of lightweight material through the earth's magnetosphere.

Not only our physical existence but also our mental existence is intertwined with what we might call the life of the fluids we inhabit. It is telling that people will often begin a conversation by talking about the weather—how hot it is, how cold, or the rain or the snow or the coming storm. While this may be a way of keeping an emotional distance, it can also be understood as a common concern for the fluid space we share with all others, whoever they might be. This concern is also about our ability to move effectively, to travel, to get work and other important tasks accomplished. It is not mere coincidence that the arts and literature spend a fair amount of time concerned with human movement and its consequences, whether in the historical past or an imagined future, and the states of the fluids that enable it all.

In this regard, architecture, among the plastic arts, stands apart. Architecture, traditionally, is the anti-fluid. Or rather it is a primary form of resistance to the flux and flow of air and water, creating fixed points in their turbulence. In a similar way, architecture has always aimed at providing a refuge—"shelter from the storm"—from a sea of changes continuously occurring in the intertwined human and natural worlds.

Exceptions include the tent structures of nomadic people, recreational vehicles, automobiles, and mobile homes, but these are rarely considered architecture, precisely because they do not fit the standard model of resistance to the essential fluidity of space but instead celebrate it. Science fiction has proposed the occasional flying city, as did the Russian Constructivists when they speculated about the brave new worlds of the Socialist adventure. Archigram's Ron Herron proposed "walking cities," and Michael Webb designed "Suitaloons"—clothing that becomes a personal-scale living environment. But these have all been ignored by architects and even theorists as too far from architecture's essential mission: creating resistance to the natural flows of space.

There are, however, some benefits to be gained by speculating about architecture that moves. Such architecture does not simply have moving parts—from doors to moving sunscreens and the like—but wholly moves from place to place. The main idea at stake is that of social stability. If everything is moving all the time, and not even as predictably as the weather, how can a coherent, cohesive community of people be formed and maintained? It is fine if we have some wandering vacationers, itinerant poets, and migrant workers, and it is (for most) not so fine if we have roving bands of political insurgents and rebels. But in any event these nomads and their various modes of portable environment cannot serve as models for a viable human community. Or can they?

If we think about the quickly changing nature of contemporary society—its increasing mobility and dependence on ephemeral electronic systems of communication—as the connection between diverse people and places, it is useful to understand the spatial morphologies of "lateral," anti-hierarchical systems of order. The Internet is such a system, a network of constantly shifting centers occupied by individuals who come and go unpredictably. It does not work according to an overall, hierarchical "chain of command," but rather by the autonomous, uncoordinated actions of individuals following an agreed upon (or at least universally accepted) set of relatively simple largely technical rules or protocols. Beyond these, the overall form of the network is indeterminate, changing from moment to moment. Still, it works as a coherent whole, indeed as a community of people who do not otherwise know each other, much like a city. One architectural counterpart is, then, a community of autonomous structures moving freely in fluid space.

July 23, 2009

Political Machines

Cell phones are political machines par excellence. This has been shown several times in recent years but nowhere better than in the demonstrations against the government in Tehran over the past weeks. Twitter and instant messaging as well as texting were used to organize the resistance and to communicate its existence to the news media around the world. Still, people had to physically put themselves on the streets of the capital, claiming its public spaces as their own. The virtual world was still subordinate to the physical one, and actual space remained the prime contested territory, as the repressive, violent responses of riot police and the Basij militia demonstrated. If that is so, then we must concede that architecture—the design of physical space—still has a role to play in human affairs, even—or especially—those having to do with politics.

We are well acquainted with the monumental architecture of official power, the large and expensive buildings that demonstrate the wealth of private corporations, arts institutions, and stable governments. But what about the architecture of resistance to established authority? What about the architecture of rapid political change? Such architecture cannot be expensive because those who need it are not sponsored by banks and mortgage companies. Anyway, there isn't the time for the usual building process. Political architecture of this kind must be improvised, spontaneous.

Politics is, at its best, a mechanism for people to change their lives for the better. This means empowering those who have been disempowered by prevailing institutions. The architects of such architecture can only provide concepts of designs for spaces enabling political change, as well as models for structures that serve as its mechanisms. However, they cannot expect that these models will be followed to the letter. Rather, they serve as inspirations and guides for those who will actually invent an architecture of change, from the materials and situation at hand, be they educated as architects or not. Better, I believe, that they are the best of educated architects, so they can bring the scope of their knowledge to bear on the task and their instinct for the poetic in human experience.

August 1, 2009

Meta-institutes

We might imagine that the French Revolution failed because it installed itself in the buildings of the royalty it overthrew. While proclaiming a new social order, replete with new system of measure (the rational metric system), a new metric calendar (ten months to a year), a radical declaration of universal human rights new to Europe, and other innovative ideas, the revolution chose as its architectural setting the royal palaces of the *ancien régime*. While promising a new world order, it delivered an old world order of space and symbol. It was, perhaps, an understandable mistake—adopting the trappings of familiar power to borrow its authority—but it was fatal. Symbolically, the revolution offered itself as merely a substitute for the old order, just another form of elite, begging to be rebelled against and overthrown. What, we might ask, would have happened if the revolution had immediately proposed a new order of civic space, one reflecting its rational ideals—new town plans, a new plan for Paris (think of Le Corbusier's Ville Radieuse), and new types of public buildings, including those for the governing elite of the *nouvelle régime* itself? We will never know.

We might also imagine that the Russian Revolution learned a lesson from history and inaugurated itself with the most radical designs imaginable for buildings and towns, at least in its earliest phase. Constructivist design, which included a revolution in print graphics, clothing, theater, film, and music, as well as in architecture and urban planning, was based on the premise that changing the social order meant changing the aesthetic order, indeed that the ethical and the aesthetic were not only synonymous but synchronous—you cannot invoke one without invoking the other. Perhaps, we might speculate, the new socialist order failed because this understanding was abandoned after a decade or so, when the new order assumed the borrowed authority of the old royal, tsarist trappings in the form of a Stalinist dictatorship that housed itself in the imperial Kremlin and commissioned neoclassical "skyscrapers." What would have happened, we cannot help but ask, if the social revolution had been realized in the visionary Constructivist designs? In other words, what would have happened if the political revolution had proved to be more than words? Might we now be living in a brave, new socialist world? Perhaps not, but we will never know, for sure.

It is difficult to imagine carrying on government-as-usual in Vladimir Tatlin's spiraling Monument to the Third International, with its suspended, rotating chambers, which was intended to house a radically new socialist form of government. At the same time, it is easy enough to picture a labyrinthine bureaucratic regime carrying on quite as bureaucracies always have in the Kremlin, or in Albert Speer's pseudo-Greek buildings designed for the Nazi Reich. Phony revolutions are a perfect fit for phony architecture, or for architecture that inauthentically borrows its authority from a prerevolutionary past. It is fortunate that the United States is not undergoing a political or social revolution, given its pseudo-Roman Capitol and neoclassical White House; Barack Obama campaigned on a promise of "change" that culminated on a stage festooned with phony classical columns.

Tatlin's tower was actually a new building type, one with little history and even less foreseeable future, which I have called a "meta-institute." Simply put, it is a building designed to house an institution for the study of the very idea of institution. When a new form of government must be created, a study of government must, in itself, be the first order of business. A building that breaks out of the familiar models or types can become an experimental tool in the process, at the very least an example of new thinking and a stimulus to innovation. The very spaces where discussions and debates about the new form of government are offered and carried on should be as much a challenge to old ways of thinking as new laws and principles, thereby linking the intellectual to physical reality. In effect, a meta-institute should present a spatial problem to be solved that reflects the ideological one: solving one aids in solving the other.

August 12, 2009

Ars Brevis, Vita Longa

The truth is, knowledge does not endure but must be recreated anew by each person, by each generation.

Knowledge is created by and dies with the knower. Only data, or evidence that knowledge has existed, survives death in all the books and buildings and artifacts that people have created as demonstrations of what they knew or came to know through the hard-won process of living and working. These things are not knowledge itself, though some make the mistake of thinking so. Rather, they are the applications of knowledge, its effects.

This thought is easily tested when we try to directly reapply existing works to different or even, ostensibly, the same situations they address. So, for example, if we believe that William Shakespeare's knowledge of the human condition and behavior are actually embodied in his plays, it should be possible to use, say, *Hamlet*, to write a new play that is even better, considering that we are adding our knowledge to his. Alas, when we try to use *Hamlet* as a model for a new play, we find that we are only able to recast what Shakespeare has done (as countless knock-offs in film and theater show) and thus create a lesser form of the same. To write a new *Hamlet*, we will have to draw on our own experiences and imaginations, think through the relationships of the characters and their situations, just as Shakespeare did—creating knowledge—then apply what we come to know to the construction of a play, which most likely will not resemble *Hamlet* at all. We will have used *Hamlet* as an inspiration for our effort—"if he could do it so can I"—and also, perhaps, as a heuristic aid in understanding the idea, if not the particular techniques, of construction. In the creation of knowledge, *Hamlet* is important, but not absolutely necessary.

The point is, we must reinvent Shakespeare's knowledge—it is not available to us, even from his extant works. The evidence that these works give—that this knowledge once existed in a lone human mind—provides us with a light in the immense, dark terrain of existence.

The same is true of science and of technology. The breakthrough papers of Albert Einstein, which with their verbal and mathematical arguments opened up the modern era in physics, and those of Werner Heisenberg and then Richard Feynman, who advanced the crucial theories, can serve only as guides for the continual reinvention of knowledge. Language and mathematics have changed. Their works are no longer the most relevant, because the knowledge they had, which would no doubt be useful to solving the leading questions of today, is not contained in their extant works, but vanished with them.

So, too, in the age of computerization and satellites, the technology once used to launch spaceships to the moon and to land on it and return to Earth has been superseded and is, for us, useless. If we want to go to the moon again, we will have to invent all over again the technical means—and the moral reasons—to do so. The old ways and ambitions, just like the old technologies, remain inspirations, but they do not embody the knowledge we need. We of the present must invent that for ourselves. Yet, we must accept in advance that our knowledge will always be greater than can be contained by any construction we make with it. And that it will die with us. Contrary to received wisdom, it is Art that is short, and Life that is long.

Ars Brevis: Addendum

The reality that knowledge has to be reinvented by individuals in each new generation has an upside and a downside.

The downside is that civilization, which depends on knowledge of ourselves and the world and how they work together, is fragile. It can be lost in a single generation if the struggle for knowledge is abandoned in favor of simplistic thinking. This, indeed, happened in the last century—think of Nazism to start with—and could just as easily happen today if people act out of indifference or fear and not compassion, curiosity, and reason. Civilization could slip back into barbarism.

The upside is that all individuals, and each generation, can invent their own versions of the realities of being human, and on a changing planet. Nature is alive, and we are part of its aliveness. The wonder of discovering all over again what it is to be human and a part of a living, changing nature comes with being born into a world we did not create but, paradoxically, must each reinvent from our own experiences.

Today is, as they say, a challenging time, as most times have been, and perhaps more so now because of the lightning speed at which global events that affect all of us unfold. There is so much to be lost, and gained. All depends, it seems, on our commitment to knowing.

Notebook 01–3 (The Last)

2001 was a fateful year for many, and in different ways. Stanley Kubrick chose it as the year of rebirth and regeneration in his 1968 film *2001: A Space Odyssey* because it was the first year of the new millennium, according to those who consider Jesus to have been born in the Year One. In May 2001 I had a cardiac arrest and quadruple bypass heart surgery; I not only survived, but also began a new phase of my life. On September 11 came the attack on the Pentagon and

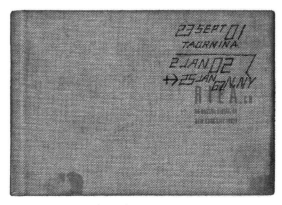

Cover, *Sketchbook*, 2001

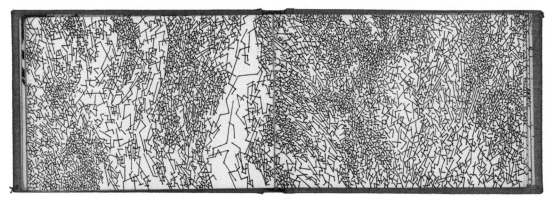

Pages from *Sketchbook*, 2001

the World Trade Center, the destruction of its blandly mighty towers and the beginning of a new era in American life and world affairs—the beginning, I suppose, of a slower-motion world war, number III. I traveled later that month to the fairy-tale mountain town of Taormina, Sicily, to lead a RIEA workshop on urbanism. When I returned to New York, I taught at Cooper Union and made an installation, *The Storm*. A notebook went with me as I traveled and I recorded ideas and events, but the world had changed, as had I, and this notebook was to be the last.

Slow Manifesto

Utopia?

The idea of utopia has all but vanished. The avant-garde architects of earlier generations rarely used the term—its meaning can cut both ways—but still proposed "ideal" urban designs that were, in effect, utopian. Now the avant-garde, such as it is, is focused on pragmatic matters, from innovative computer techniques of form making to issues such as sustainability. Utopian ideas are conspicuously absent. Why is this so?

The reasons, I think, are complexly interwoven. Foremost, there is a widely accepted feeling that we have reached "the end of history" (Francis Fukuyama) and the global triumph of capitalism and "liberal democracy." While the former is manifestly not the case, it is true that the demise of socialism as a human ideal has left no credible alternative to capitalism's global dominance. All utopian projects reach for not only formal or technical improvements, but also social ones as well. So, in the current climate, the only possible utopias are those perfecting capitalism and its present, consumerist forms of order. We can think of Rem Koolhaas as the visionary of consumerist utopias, celebrating their virtues and vices in equal measure. But we can also see shopping mall designers in nearly the same way, regardless or even because of their lack of design originality—very liberally democratic. In one sense, utopia has already been realized. Anyone can get a credit card; everyone can buy and be happy, at least until they max out their cards. So where is the inspiration to envision "another" utopia? Certainly, the present leaders in the field of architecture have not found it.

Then there is the "green" movement. Who can argue with its premises? Our priority is no longer to improve human society but to save the planet from human society. Changes to be made to the social system are more remedial than systemic: reducing air pollution and carbon footprints, recycling, refitting, redesign, and the like. Capitalist enterprise, far from being curtailed, is encouraged through tax incentives and government subsidies of new, green industries to expand its dominant role. Adaptivity is its keyword: anything can be turned to a profit. But who can argue with the goal and, since the very word "socialism" has become an insult, who would dare to? The green movement is important and necessary, but whether capitalism is really to be trusted with its fate remains to be seen. The lack of green utopias in a time increasingly obsessed with green issues may be due to capitalism's success and unchallenged dominance.

This idea is certainly reinforced by the ubiquity of information. The instant accessibility from anywhere of information about anything seems in itself a utopian achievement. Information has been radically democratized, and with this comes a belief that knowledge has, too. However, information is not knowledge (see the post "Ars Brevis, Vita Longa") and indeed it takes knowledge not present in the information to put it to any use./21 There is a continual stream of new information, with the result of keeping its recipients continually off balance. We never have enough and must continually return to the sellers—Internet sites that in one way or another are in the business of making money—to get more. Information is the ideal capitalist product. There is a cheap, inexhaustible supply of it and an insatiable market of consumers who believe it empowers them and keep buying. How much closer to utopia can we get? We might say that capitalism is a utopia of self-satisfaction and restlessness. Who, then, needs a better society? Alternative utopias would be out-of-date as soon as they would be written or drawn. Ideals and idealism can only slow us down. Utopias can only get in the way.

Then we come to architects themselves. Let us not consider the usual, even intelligent and talented practitioners. He and she have never, historically speaking, been interested in the hypothetical "what if?" as much as the down-to-earth "what now?" Instead, if we think about avant-garde architects who have some visible profile, we don't find work that envisions a social world widely improved by architecture—no utopias of the sort that dot the map of architectural history up through the postmodern era of the 1970s and 80s. Today their aspirations seem to have retreated before the advance of capitalism and liberal democracy.

Have we reached the end of utopia as well as the end of history? Let us listen to, and watch, the more ambitious and idealistic of the coming generation. Only they have the answer.

October 19, 2009

Constant Vision

Some time ago, I was speaking with Peter Cook, a founder of Archigram, about the Situationists and, in particular, Constant Nieuwenhuys—the artist and visionary architect. Cook told me a story: "In 1959 or 60, Mike Webb (co-founder of Archigram) and I attended a lecture given by Constant on his New Babylon project. We were just graduating from architecture school, but Mike leaned over to me during the lecture and whispered, 'We can do it better!'" And so, a couple of years later, they did it at least differently, setting off a revolution in architecture that reverberates to the present day. Both Constant and Archigram imagined architecture as a leading instrument of social change through the making of ideal or utopian architectural projects. The difference between them is that the projects and the ideals they expressed stand on opposite sides of a cultural divide. This takes a bit of explaining.

First of all, the historical divide. The late 1950s and early 60s was a period of global ferment and change. Eastern Europe and China were ruled by communist ideology. Western Europe and the Americas were ruled by capitalist ideology. Each was fearful of the other, and the result was a Cold War fought by propaganda and angst-raising demagoguery, as well as "contained" hot wars in smaller countries around the world. Growing numbers of people on both sides of this ideological divide were growing restless with the methods of domination and its values. Some looked to the opposite ideology for salvation and some to personal rebellion, while most quietly endured. In the early 60s, the spreading discontent began spilling into the open. In the East, "counter-revolutionary" movements were brutally repressed. In the West, political and intellectual challenges to the status quo were harder for governments to contain, until massive public protests and uprisings in the later 60s were violently suppressed. So at exactly the time that Cook and Webb attended the Constant lecture, the world was poised on a threshold of sweeping change.

Then there was the technological divide. Up to the 1960s, people living in cities—including those who worked in government and other corporate institutions—functioned in analog modes: typewriters, "snail mail," telegrams, telephones. Even many early data processors produced analog punch cards. After 1960, digital computation began to take over, owing to technological advances such as the transistor and microchip. These enabled—among other things, such as credit cards—the launching of geostationary satellites and instantaneous global communications. The contemporary world was born. Archigram, founded in 1964, quickly became a global phenomenon in a way that Constant never did. Using Archigram "comics," a traveling "opera," and other media-savvy tactics, its members spread the word of a new "instant city," alive with electronically propagated pop culture, spontaneous events and "happenings," and the light, temporary architecture of eternally migrating, even globe-trotting, urban dwellers. Constant, in his utopian New Babylon project, belonged to a seemingly settled and abruptly outdated past of heavy, fixed structures and, in a sense, of traditionally modernist architecture. These remarks are in the main correct, but do in fact exaggerate Archigram's break with the past (including Constant's work) and certainly do not do Constant's project justice, particularly with regard to its social aspirations. But more on this in a moment.

The last divide was architectural. The early 1960s saw the end of the dominance of modernist ideas about the beauty of the machine and the ethics of industrial technology, and the advent of postmodernist ideas focused on the virtues of the handily ambiguous term "culture," emphasizing imagery over structure. Robert Venturi's antimodernist manifesto, *Complexity and Contradiction in Architecture*, appeared in 1966 and quickly became the new ideal. While it eschewed the work of Archigram, I do not believe that it was ignorant of it and was at least tangentially inspired by its pop-culture imagery. In any event, the days of "heavy metal" architecture were over, and those of architectural pastiche based on history and popular culture were in. Constant's New Babylon, along with the works of many architects who were the inheritors of modernist ideals but had already extended them—Paul Rudolph and John Johansen, among others—was abruptly ignored. Such is the nature of any ideology, especially a newly risen one bent on securing its unrivalled dominance.

New Babylon was inspired by and contributed to the work of the Situationists, a group of intellectuals, theorists, writers, and artists who were anything but modernists in the classic capitalist mold. They were inspired by the irrational forms and practices of Dada and surrealism and were what we could call neo-Marxists, meaning inspired by Karl Marx's vision of revolutionary socialism but seeking to use the capitalist system to achieve their ends. Guy Debord and others invented tactics such as *derive*, *psychogeographie*, and *detournment*, which seized upon, then subverted, capitalist notions in order to develop radical ways of living that were meant to culminate in revolution. (Archigram first heard of these through Constant's lecture, no doubt.) Constant joined the Situationists early on and became their architect, much the same as Antonio Sant'Elia had done with the Futurists half a century before. The spaces of New Babylon were intended to be spaces of disorientation and of reorientation, from rational, functionalist society to one that would be liberated and self-inventing. The project was meant to replace capitalist exploitation of human labor and emotion with anarchist celebration of them. Its architecture was to provide a complex armature on which could be woven endlessly new, unpredictably personal urban experiences, determined by ever-changing individual desires. In the end, however, the architecture of the New Babylon seemed to overwhelm such playful, radical spontaneity by its sheer weight and monumental scale.

Is Constant's epic project of other than historical interest today? I believe it is. Aside from the visual strength and sometimes-poetic nuances of his models, paintings, and drawings, New Babylon raises many questions related to issues of contemporary interest. What role can architecture play in social and political change? What role should an architect take in determining the direction and character of change? How important is the design of space in the mix of human activity? Can design "change the world?" If so, who should control it? Constant and New Babylon can still inspire us—as they once did the young Peter Cook and Michael Webb—in spirit, if not in form. */

*/ Relevant link: Constant, http://members.chello.nl/j.seegers1/situationist/constant.html.

November 8, 2009

The Light, the Dark

Once I lived in an apartment on the thirteenth floor (called, of course, the fourteenth) of a building overlooking midtown Manhattan. The windows of the small room where I worked faced south and east, so I could watch, every day and night, the passage of light over and within the dense landscape of buildings. Over a period of eight years that I lived in this room—drawing, writing, looking from the windows—I knew each day that I was privileged to have the time to think and work, when so many must labor at jobs simply for survival, and also to have the views of an epic landscape that inspired much of what I was doing.

This inspiration was not to reproduce what I saw, or even its effects, though I must say it was a schooling in the drama of an intricate play between light, geometry, and materials. No, I would say that what I beheld inspired in me a feeling of calm and reflection that was liberating. I had nothing to prove. It was all there already. This city in which most of the buildings would not pass as architecture was complete and whole in its embrace of light and its implications. I had only to celebrate the order and beauty in my own terms, the task of any architect inhabiting a particular time, and I would do this unburdened by received notions of what architecture was or should be. Light freed me yet at the same time demanded a level of invention beyond any I had known before. Freedom is like that—it raises the stakes.

I had long thought that architecture measures light. Light flows everywhere in space but can only be perceived when it is reflected from an object—a mountain, a cloud, a building. A building is a special case because of its regular geometry. A rectangular wall shapes light and gives it a rational form, taking it out of a seeming chaos and making it comprehensible, thus useful. I think of architecture as an instrument—such as a ruler or a telescope—something we use to understand the world and create knowledge. I also believe that architecture is an instrument—such as a hammer or a violin—that enables our actions. Architecture is instrumental, active, and only incidentally symbolic or representational—that is, passively present.

Walls such as those I observed through my high, but not too high, windows measured the intensity and color of the light they reflected from the universal flow of waves, and by so doing selected a part of the universal, reserving it for human use. Light becomes local, particular, accessible, and unique—the same as with individuals. No two reflections of light are ever exactly the same, owing to the complexity of atmosphere, geography, and the slow but tangible transformations of the reflecting materials of the walls. The light we see one day will be different from what we see the next, either dramatically (it is cloudy, then sunny) or subtly (it is always sunny), but the sun itself has shifted a degree from one day to the next, at any rate enough to make today's sunlit wall different from yesterday's. Though we may not be perceptive enough to gauge such a small difference, intellectually we know it exists, and that is enough to transform our experience. In this way, light itself is a reflection of our evolving consciousness.

With light, we know, comes darkness. Darkness is not the absence of light. Rather, it is a product of light—an active, opposing presence created by it. Without light we would not think of darkness as we do. It would be all we know, and we would live in a visually monologic world. But we do not. We live in a world of contrasts between light and darkness, indeed a dialogical world of infinite gradations of the two. Urban darkness is still suffused with light. The darkest shadows on the brightest day are alive with soft echoes of light, moving from surface to surface. The struggles between light and darkness set the ground-tone of our human condition.

A city such as the one I observed from a high place many years ago is the ultimate landscape of this condition, and its architecture is the instrument of continual reformation. But one need not have a grand view of the city to understand what I am saying here. Any street, any set of walls, any window opening onto them will do.

Moss Is More

Complexity is a major theme that runs through
Eric Owen Moss's work. Nothing is as simple as we have been led to believe. Nothing
can be taken as given or assumed. Entering
a building. Walking up a stair. Designing the
structural frame for a high-rise building,
the public lobby of a theater, or exhibition
spaces for art. Through exhaustive iterations
of drawings and models, Moss explicates
what he finds as an inherent complexity arising from the nuance of human actions. In
the process, he challenges us to rethink the
nature of architecture. Moss's propositions,

Eric Owen Moss, *Umbrella*, Culver City,
California, 1999

built or not, impel us in a particular direction. Architecture is not a confirmation of imposed order and control, but a celebration of our perceptions and our
sense of play. Architecture is an ongoing dialogue between contrasting forms
and the materials whose properties inspire them. Steel bends, wood supports,
cement spreads, and glass is molten. Their life together is complex, as is ours.
Architecture negotiates the existential gaps, and Moss's work gives us a model
of how to do so with grace and exuberance. No irony distances him, or us, from
our experience of space and light and texture, color and movement.

    The strong subtheme running through all of Moss's work is invention.
If nothing can be accepted as given, if architecture celebrates our unfolding
experiences, if architecture, in effect, wakes us up to the complexity of the
world and of ourselves, then the architect must continually invent his designs
from the shifting circumstances of each project. It will not do to have stock
details plugged into one project after another, let alone overall building forms.
Yet it also will not do to create architecture of one-offs that devolve into mere
distractions. Moss understands that something essential must carry over
from project to project, without confining him to a style and stereotyping our
responses. Astutely, he has understood this to be invention. Each project is an
experiment in the sense of research that contributes to a body of knowledge—
his and ours—that can be tapped in many different
ways. His experiments with a wide range of architectural
materials loom particularly large in this domain. The
consequence is that no two of his projects are the same,
yet we can perceive the irrepressibly original Moss in
them all. */

*/ For much (1500+ pages) more,
see Eric Owen Moss, *Construction
Manual: 1988–2008* (Beijing: AADCU,
2009), a new and most thorough
publication of his works, available,
for now, at www.ideabooks.nl.

Slow Manifesto

The Question of Space

Question Site, 2000

Space is essentially a mental construct. We imagine space to be there, even if we experience it as a void, an absence we cannot perceive.

Space is always the implication of objects. For an object to exist, we think, it needs some kind of space. So the first space we can imagine is the space occupied by objects. In order to see an object we must be separate from it. A space must exist between us and the object. Therefore, we imagine a space around the object, and also around ourselves, because, at some stage in our mental development, we realized that we, too, are objects. Space is the medium of our relationships with the world and everything in it, but, for all of that, we do not experience it in a palpable, physical sense. We must think space into existence.

It is worth pausing to consider this assertion. If space is mental and nonmaterial, what does this say about our relationships to the world? And to the idea and reality of architecture?

First, we should consider the probability of the assertion. Isn't space palpable? Isn't it filled with substance—the air we breathe and move through and feel as a tangible presence? Isn't this the way we know space? No, it is not. When we feel the wind blowing, we do not say, "I feel the space moving." The air and the wind are only inhabitants of the space, like us. Space itself is something else. What is it?

Thinking of movies, we must admit that the spaces in which movies are acted out have only minimal physical reality, as projections on a screen.

Nevertheless, they have a full spatial presence that we experience directly and also remember. If this were not the case, we would come away from a movie speaking of our experience of a two-dimensional surface we have seen in a dark room illuminated by moving patterns of light, shadow, and color. But we do not. We speak as though we had been there. This "being there," in the scenography of the movie, is a reality we experience only in our minds. Still, we were there, because space itself is always only mental. On the other hand, we do not believe that we were part of the narrative or were one of the characters acting it out. We identify ourselves with them and the events of their lives, but we do not consider them real. The very fact that our experience of space is essentially mental and not physical makes the "movie space" real. For this reason, we can say that it is the reality of the space that gives the movie's action and the actor's credibility, not the other way around. Even movies with the most unbelievable screenplays and the most inept actors can still leave a strong and entirely credible spatial impression, as countless noir B-movies attest.

Movies were the first "virtual" realities. Before them, paintings and other forms of graphic art worked in a similar way. Giovanni Battista Piranesi's etchings of prisons stay in our minds much more vividly than any similarly grand space—say, the atrium of an enormous contemporary hotel—that we have actually walked through. Surely part of this vividness is due to the superiority of Piranesi's spatial design, but this would matter little if the etching and the atrium were not in some important way the same in our experience. After the movies comes the computer, in all its manifestations. As we stand on the threshold of a world defined in terms of digitally generated realities, we need to consider more carefully than ever before the question of space and the nature of its reality.

Consider the example given by Albert Einstein in his popular book *Relativity*. Here he defines particular space as arising from the simple act of establishing coordinates within general space. So simply drawing a box with conceptually thin—that is, nonphysical—lines is enough to bring a distinct and separate space into being. Let us test his thought. If we think of Austria or Thailand, we take the point. The existence of such spaces is conceptual because the lines of the box, the borders of the nations, drawn between the coordinate points are physical only on maps. Nevertheless, we regard them as real, even when we traverse the actual landscape they circumscribe. When it comes to space, the mental is as potent as the physical. What is the physical, after all, but sensations impacting the neural nets of our brains? Where do the sensations come from? How do we know that what we see is not an artifice of projections onto the brain? Ultimately, we do not. Space, in the end, is what we think it is.

It is easy to fool the senses and therefore the mind. Epics of human history are largely written in terms of places that exist only as idea: motherland, fatherland, homeland, nation, country. The gullibility of human beings to be seduced by what we only think exists is the source of our dreams and fantasies, and also of our inventions—seeing what is not there, as though it were. But that is only half the story. The other half of intelligence is its skepticism. How true are our sensations? Our thoughts? Can we trust them? Is space real, just because we think it is? Are, then, dreams real? And movies? And projects drawn by architects that describe objects that might exist physically but do not?

The question of what is real touches on profound philosophical questions. The most critical of these concerns the limitations of our capability to know through our sense organs and our ability to imagine through our cognitive faculties. For now, we must settle for provisional answers, and the most salient of these seems to be that the limits of the real are isomorphic with the limits of what we can conceive.

November 24, 2009

Libeskind's Machines

Daniel Libeskind, *Memory Machine*, 1985

By the mid-1980s, the reputation of Daniel Libeskind as a leading avant-garde figure in architecture was rapidly rising. This was based on his work as a teacher—he was director and principal teacher at the Cranbrook Academy School of Architecture from 1978 to 1985, establishing it as one of the most creative schools in the world—and on the publication and exhibition of a number of projects that, on their face, seemed to have little to do with architecture. Notable among these were his *Memory Machine*, *Reading Machine*, and *Writing Machine*.

Elaborately constructed and enigmatic in purpose, Libeskind's machines are striking and sumptuous manifestations of ideas that were, at the time he made them, of obsessive interest to academics, critics, and avant-gardists in architecture and out. Principal among these was the idea that architecture must be read—that is, understood—in the same way as a written text.

The chief structural features of written language, grammar and syntax—which organize the ways words are put together into a coherent, meaningful ensemble—clearly relate to architecture. Indeed, so traditional a modernist as Mies van der Rohe was fond of speaking of architecture's "grammar" and declaring that an understanding of it was essential to design. However, when it comes to the meaning of word constructions, leading linguistic and literary theorists believed, by the 1970s and 80s, that written texts do not have a fixed meaning established by what their author intended to say, but rather multiple meanings that readers have to interpret for themselves by using various cultural codes and references. Peter Eisenman and the circle of architects and critics gathered around him applied this to architecture, with the consequence that the "meaning" of architecture—symbolically and in terms of human purposes—was in their view not to be found in either the architects' or their clients' intentions. In short, form does not follow any *a priori* function but has autonomous existence that must, in the end, be read on its own terms. In short, the meaning of architecture is to be found only in architecture itself.

This is a radical position that has not had an impact on most architects who, like it or not, must follow their clients', if not their own, desires and intentions. However, it is possible to imagine that the idea of architecture's autonomy liberated architects to design ever more idiosyncratically expressive forms having little to do with the client-programmed spaces wrapped by them. What began as a radical concept affecting the very core of architecture is compromised, we might say reduced, to commercially marketable and client-acceptable styles—a fate much the same as idealistic modernism suffered in its time.

In any event, the vogue for a linguistic interpretation of architecture has passed, and the avant-garde has moved on, or at least elsewhere. Libeskind's machines, inspired by reading and writing and implicitly interpreting texts as well as memory (treated as text), would be of little interest today if the machines were only didactic illustrations of theory. But they are much more. As objects of design, they have powerful presence as well as convey a refined and highly rigorous aesthetic sensibility. As acts of the disciplined imagination of tectonic possibilities—how many parts might be assembled into a compelling whole—they are highly original, exemplary, and instructive. For example, they show the diverse, even contrasting ways the same material, such as wood, can be used expressively in the same construction and the complexity of joints, from fixed to flexible, enabling the total assemblage. Of course, as handcrafted constructions (a bit too "Renaissance" for comfort, as was Vladimir Tatlin's *Letatlin* flying machine), they are at once nostalgic and visionary, the latter if we believe that technology is not the main issue at stake in architecture.

But the most important legacies of these machines, I believe, are conceptual and of equal or greater value today as when they were made. Their use of analogy to inform the field of architecture is a more potent tool for exploring much-needed new ideas of space and its human purposes than is afforded by the ordinary design process based on history and accepted building typologies. In the past, architects such as Mies found architectural inspiration in works of art,*/ while Le Corbusier produced his own paintings and sculptures to work out complex aesthetic problems in his architecture. Libeskind's machines are in this tradition, though the problems are different. More architects today could benefit from such an analogous method if they set for themselves problems not already solved. This method, like the machines themselves, opens architecture to a wide range of knowledge coming from different fields of thought and work, which is sorely needed in a time such as the present, characterized by increasing diversity in the human situation.

*/ See "Art to Architecture" (March 5, 2009; http://lebbeuswoods.wordpress.com/2009/03/05/art-to-architecture/) [omitted from this volume].

December 2, 2009

Big Tops

Pier Luigi Nervi, airplane hangar, Italy, 1950s. Nervi virtually invented the two-way, reinforced-concrete space frame, using his patented *ferrocemento*.

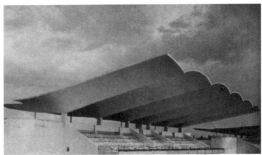

Eduardo Torroja, Zarzuela Hippodrome, Spain, mid-1930s. Torroja was one of the earliest pioneers of thin-shell, reinforced-concrete design and pushed it to its limits.

Roofs are such a basic element of architecture—giving shelter from rain, snow, cold, heat, and extremes of light—we often take them for granted. True, modernist architecture, *à la* Gerrit Rietveld, Mies, Corbusier, and others who followed them, reduced roofs to just another bounding plane in the architectural vocabulary: flat and dull. So be it. However, when it comes to roofing large, open interior spaces, even modernist architects have had to go beyond simplistic abstraction and invent structural systems that can span sometimes great distances without disrupting the spaces beneath them with columns, walls, and other structural supports. Most of the spaces sheltered by big roofs serve straightforwardly pragmatic purposes: warehouses, airplane hangars, markets, sports stadia, pavilions—hardly exalted in the cultural canon Still, they are necessary in a sense that is more than the merely useful.

Following are works of architects/engineers who innovated structural systems, but also methods of analysis, materials, and methods of construction in the design of what some simply call "long span" structures./22 They brought something poetic to the task, something that brings their work into the realm of architecture.

Storm Watch

The Storm, installation at the Arthur A. Houghton Jr. Gallery, Cooper Union, New York, 2001

The realm of architecture is apparently one of stability, but is actually one of restrained force or of forces held in equilibrium. The implications of tectonic stability for inhabitation are immediately apparent, but the epistemological implications are less so. I will touch on them here in only one regard.

In thinking of architecture as at rest, we are adopting a position based on stability and predictability. Also, we are constructing a system of knowledge that privileges these qualities. This underpins our actions and dictates our goals. The unity and symmetry of monumental architecture refers symbolically to a harmonious and balanced universe in which contending forces are reconciled. The traditional role of architecture has been one of reassuring us that things are under our control. But it is quite another thing to think of architecture as in tension.

An architecture in tension suggests a struggling architecture and a humanity with limited control of nature and of itself. The forces in such an architecture are activated, not pacified. For the moment, they seem to be held in check, at least to the extent they can be measured at all. Still, they are straining against the materials holding them. Experience teaches that this is not a stable or predictable situation. Change is inevitable, as the materials age or tire or as they are affected by disturbances within or around them. The forces are, in effect, at war with the materials; they want to overcome them; they want to be free of materiality, to flow into the world's vast oceans of energy, from which they will be reborn again and again in countless cycles of transformation. Such an understanding of architecture conditions our outlook on the world and leads to the construction of a knowledge-system based on concepts and processes of transformation.

The installation of a tension field in Cooper Union was small in size. The room was the size of a large classroom or of a modest laboratory for the testing of materials. At the same time, the installation had no absolute scale. The room was a frame placed around a 1:1 constructed landscape that could just as easily be read as much larger—or much smaller. Forces have magnitude, but no inherent scale. Only the materials—braided steel cables and wood rods (painted to conceal their woodenness)—spoke to both the magnitude and the scale. It was a test model, a mock-up of conditions that had the ambition to address a general, if not universal, condition: a spatial field in increasing tension.

The cables were strung from wall to wall, passing through vertical tubes of steel that allowed for changes of direction until a fluctuating stream of forces were captured in tension. The cables, and the forces contained within them, were not connected. Then wood rods were inserted into the cables, increasing their tension by pulling them together or pushing them apart, putting the rods either in tension or compression. As more rods were added, the tension in the whole field increased. There was a breaking point, never reached, unknown in advance, at which the weakest point in the field would exceed the limit of its capacity to restrain the forces. Because the structure acted as a field and not as a collection of independently stable, "classical" objects, the failure of any element would reduce the tension in the entire structure. The idea of transformation in a tension field is linked with interdependence of the elements in the field and, more accurately, to their interconnectedness. The field changes as an integrated whole, whatever its size or scale. And it performs as a space.

This tension field was a spatial field—that much is obvious. But the nature of its spaces cannot be accounted for by thinking of them as the products of design as we are accustomed to thinking of it. To the contrary, they were constructed in a kind of heuristic game in which I actually designed only a set of standard elements and general rules of their assembly, embodied in a small set of drawings, and left it for collaborators to make. It would have been possible to assemble the elements—cables and rods—in any number of different ways without changing in essence the nature of the field or its spaces. In short, there was no hierarchy in the process of designing or in the placement of elements and their resulting spaces.

But it still mattered in an existential sense, and without an imposed hierarchy to signify degrees of importance, exactly how the elements were assembled.

Different configurations result in different effects. These impact our experiences of the field. They also facilitate our knowledge of it differently. A dense assemblage of rods and cables informs us, in a spatial sense, differently than a dispersed assemblage. Yet the subjects of our knowledge are still "field" and "assembly" and, ultimately, "experience," even though understood from quite different points of view. By way of analogy, the difference would be roughly the same as the idea of "landscape" as understood by a person living in the country and a person living in the city.

In the tension field, unlike the apparently stable field of independent objects dispersed in a designed spatial order, the anti-hierarchical order of spaces, the spatially variable and conceptually indeterminate order of spaces, enables each person—regardless of standpoint—to comprehend that they share with others not only the same planetary surface, but also the same degree of experience. There is a caveat, however. Interconnectedness and global consciousness come with a price. Each person feels the increase in tension produced by the others. The tension field acts as a whole, though without being unified in the classical sense of being designed. Uncertainty as to where the next pressure point will be increases the tension in the system. As the tension increases it feeds back into the entire field. Independent actions often occur, but the idea of pure autonomy is effectively rendered obsolete.

2010

On the Malecón

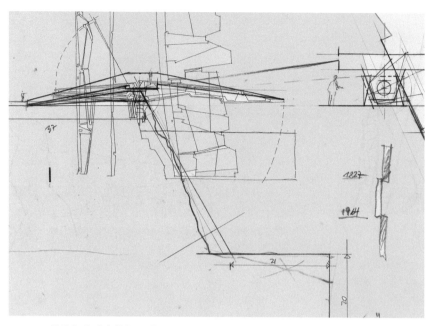

El Malecón de la Habana: Terrace from *Havana Projects*, 1994–95. Section through the six-kilometer-long terrace, cantilevered over the sea—an artificial beach dedicated, in good weather, to public play and recreation

Along the north side of Havana, Cuba, facing the Caribbean and the often-cited ninety miles to the barren Florida Keys, is a long road bordering the sea. This is the Malecón. It is both a lively and forbidding public space—the former because the sea sends waves crashing against a sheer seawall footed on black rocks below, and people come there to walk or sit on the wall to watch and feel and taste the sea; the latter because it is primarily a space for automobiles. Granted, there are not so many cars because of a perennial shortage of gasoline, but this doesn't alter the character of the space: it is a bare, inhospitable roadway separating the city and its people from the pleasures of the warm tropical waters. Granted, as well, there is no natural beach along this stretch and the land itself drops abruptly to some depth beneath the surging water; as a result, the water is too turbulent for swimming. Still, it seems that something could be done to make the Malecón a more hospitable space next to the sea for the people of Havana.

There is another feature of the Malecón to be considered. When hurricanes move across the island or the sea, the sea level rises and the waves become larger and more violent, often flooding the Malecón and its neighborhoods. Every fifty years or so, there is a particularly large storm with winds that drive the sea in a massive storm surge that floods many lower-lying parts of the city, including Old Havana (La Habana Vieja), an area housing poorer people.

The situation is similar to that of the Ninth Ward in New Orleans, which was inundated by a storm surge from a fifty-year storm—Hurricane Katrina—in 2005. The Cuban government has called for engineering proposals to protect against such catastrophic events. However, because of the nation's depressed economy—the result of following Soviet Bloc models as well as the fifty-year trade embargo by the United States—the money to pay for solutions on the scale of, say, The Netherlands Delta Works is neither available nor likely to be in the near future. Havana remains vulnerable.

In spite of the economic barriers to realizing at the present time any large-scale projects, new proposals need to be made. One cannot simply shrug at the impossibility and walk away from the problems. Political situations are changing, and with them the prospects for international cooperation in solving Cuba's urgent human needs, including flood control for Havana.

It seemed to me that the problem of making public space on the Malecón and the construction of a barrier to destructive storm surges could be solved by a single project, which I have proposed and which is shown in schematic form at left. Constructed on the land—instead of in the sea, as other proposals have envisioned—it could be realized as a labor-intensive rather than capital-intensive project. Even so, it would require a determined commitment not only by the government, but also by the people of the city. The problems to be solved are large and extensive and can only be addressed by large and extensive proposals. Halfway measures and symbolic gestures are worse than inadequate—they waste both resources and the hope of actually improving conditions.

In brief, the proposal calls for the construction of a six-kilometer terrace dedicated to public recreation, a type of urban park or abstract beach cantilevered from the Malecón over the sea. Shelter from the sun is built into the layers of each structurally independent terrace segment, which rests on heavy steel hinges such as those used for modern drawbridges. The independent segments can be built one at a time and shaped to the curving line of the roadway so that their ensemble is continuous. Most importantly the segments can be designed to accommodate differing recreational needs along its six-kilometer extent; for example, a set of terrace segments serving one neighborhood could be very open, while another, serving a different neighborhood, could provide more layers of shelter and semi-enclosed spaces. The schematic design shown here only begins to suggest the possible variations.

When the weather turns bad and a passing hurricane raises the sea level and sends a storm surge of water onto the shore, the force of this surge activates a ballast system within the terrace segments and rotates the segments on their hinges into a near-vertical position, creating a strong, high seawall that holds back the surging water. When the storm passes and the water recedes, the segments rotate back into their original positions. The idea is that the sea itself initiates and provides the energy for operating the system—no added mechanical systems to install and maintain, a sustainable system, in the contemporary sense.

Boulez in Space

Mixing the audience with the players in a musical performance is by now a well-known avant-garde tactic, though—like most things avant-garde—it has hardly budged the convention of audience on one side and musicians on the other. In that arrangement, the music is played to or for or at the listeners; moreover, it expresses and enforces social divisions active in the world outside the concert hall, between workers and patrons, between art and "real" life. As has been noted elsewhere, and many times, any arrangement of space is inherently political. However, the political and social origins of any traditional arrangement are often forgotten, which is to say, obscured by habit and nostalgia. We forget that the hierarchies of the societies for which Joseph Haydn and Richard Wagner composed their music are really antithetical to modern ideals of participatory democracy. This does not mean that we should not listen to their works in the spatial arrangements for which they were composed—quite the contrary. What it means is that the new music of our time needs to be performed in spatial arrangements that reflect our most critical experiences and values, those that engage a new level of complexity in relationships between people and between events. The same can also be said of the new architecture of our time.

The spatial designs of Pierre Boulez—a composer, conductor, and critic who sees the necessity of composing new music and also the wisdom of writing critical essays presenting both its musical and social bases—are radical departures from tradition and convention. His works—by nature collaborative and interactive—give form to the anxieties, tensions, and strange, unexpected harmonies that emerge from the discordant mélange of an international community assembling itself from the shards of old societies and the raw forms of new ones. His music is not meant to comfort or distract us, but to give us experiences that aid us in joining the struggle.*/23

*/ *New York Times* article on Boulez: Michael Kimmelman, "Boulez's Gentler Roar," *New York Times*, January 6, 2010, www.nytimes.com/2010/01/10/arts/music/10boulez.html. For Boulez's Répons: http://www.youtube.com/watch?v=nfSfYiGsZMU.

Earthquake (Again)!

In the wake of the earthquake in Port-au-Prince, Haiti, I feel obliged to post this brief essay, written nearly fifteen years ago. When are we going to seriously work on this problem?

Earthquakes are the result of natural, tectonic changes in the solid crust of the earth and, as such, are not inherently catastrophic. Their bad reputation comes from the destruction to human settlements that accompanies them, when buildings collapse under the stress of forces produced by earthquakes.

This destruction is not the "fault" of earthquakes, but rather of the buildings that, even in regions regularly visited by earthquakes, are not designed to work harmoniously with the violent forces periodically released. So buildings collapse, usually with considerable loss of life and injuries. The earthquakes are blamed, as though the purpose of these sublimely unselfconscious phenomena was to damage and destroy the human. "Earthquake Kills Thousands!" "Killer Quake Strikes!" and "Earthquake Levels Town!" are typical aftermath headlines. What they should say is "Falling Buildings Kill Thousands!" "Killer Buildings Strike!" "Inadequately Designed Town Leveled!"

Such headlines will not, of course, appear. If they did, architects, town-planners, engineers, and the entire army of professionals responsible for the design, construction, and maintenance of the affected buildings would be called to account. If that were to happen, they would certainly implicate politicians, developers, banks, and the entire coterie of private and public officials controlling what gets built and where—the financial/economic community that finds it more profitable to rebuild what has been destroyed than to commission the development of architectures that would work with earthquakes and thus survive, even benefit, from them. If this profit-driven community were called to account by public outcry, it would almost certainly turn the blame back on the public itself. After all, corporations and governments are under constant pressure to give the public what it wants, which today means the same products, the same lifestyles, the same buildings and types of buildings to be found anywhere on the planet, regardless of the planet's extremely varied processes of transformation. If all these individuals and social institutions were held responsible for the destruction caused by earthquakes, then the public in earthquake regions would have no choice but to demand radical changes of them. But this would be an expensive revolution, one that all the interests involved could afford only at great cost to their reputations, knowledge and technical expertise, and present economic prosperity.

There is, however, a deeper structure of resistance to investing in the invention of new architectures of and for earthquakes, and this is formed by

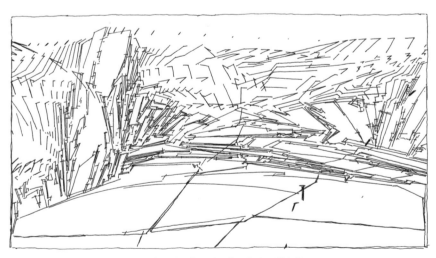

Drawing from *San Francisco Bay Project* (detail), 1995

the most venerable beliefs about the relationship between the human and natural worlds, which are considered to be hostile to one another. The "man versus nature" attitude begins in the founding stories of some of the world's dominant religions. Christianity, Judaism, and Islam share the Biblical account of the expulsion of Adam and Eve from the Garden of Eden, which came as a result of their desire for self-knowledge and, thereby, for independence from the rest of the un-self-aware, wholly interdependent world.

Many philosophers over the past epochs have rationalized this belief, but it was René Descartes who best codified it for the modern era. His philosophy postulates an essential duality of the world, comprised of the human and the Divine, which cannot be bridged. Not coincidentally, he also invented a mathematical system—analytical geometry—that organizes the spatial and temporal properties of the human domain with great efficiency. Cartesian logic and geometry offer a pragmatic usefulness that shows no signs of diminishing, more than three hundred years after their inception and in spite of immense cultural and technological changes to the society they serve. But while Cartesian thought and method succeeded in freeing science, and therefore technology, from the grip of religion per se, they maintained the adversarial Biblical relationship between the domain of the human and the realm of Divine nature.

Nowhere is the fragility of this relationship more clearly demonstrated than in earthquake regions. There, not only has the idea of the Cartesian grid as a symbol of rational efficiency and stability been overturned (literally) by the nature of earthquake forces, but also the civilizational cornerstone of human independence from Nature (a conceit, however transparent, that has propelled the notion of human progress) has been broken to bits. In light of the consistent failure of leading societies such as the United States and Japan to build in ways that work with earthquakes, it is reasonable to begin to reconsider the dominant philosophies, techniques, and goals of building and urban design in earthquake regions.

While today much attention is paid to ideas of "green architecture" and "sustainability," reconsideration by architects and planners of the forms and methods of architecture in seismic regions has hardly begun. What is most needed now are new ideas and approaches that go beyond the defensive reinforcement of existing conceptual and physical structures and open up genuinely new possibilities for architecture integrating Earth's continuing processes of transformation. Once new spatial models that extend the forces of earthquakes into the dynamics of private and social life have been proposed, we can look forward to a post–Biblical reconciliation of the human and the natural. That will be a real beginning.*/

*/ From the New York Times, a sign of hope that attitudes can and are beginning to change: Henry Fountain, "Flawed Building Likely a Big Element," New York Times, January 13, 2010, www.nytimes.com/2010/01/14/world/americas/14construction.html.

Aestheticizing Violence

Architects love to take on the easy problems—the ones already solved—and make them difficult. This way they can have it both ways: operating safely within the boundaries of the known and, at the same time, being daring innovators—but with a minimum of actual risk. For example, the high-rise office tower. Adler & Sullivan solved this problem in 1894 with their Guaranty Building in Buffalo, New York. You can make an office building taller, wider, twist it, sculpt it into all kinds of shapes, or give it a variety of new skins and it will still be essentially the same as Guaranty: a vertical stacking of level floors with grouped stairs and elevators, with public access and service at the ground floor and mechanical services on top. Knowing this, one has even more respect for Mies van der Rohe's Seagram Building, because it tacitly acknowledges the precedent by earnestly recasting it and nothing more. There are other examples, but the point here is different: architects are reluctant to take on the difficult problems—the ones not yet solved—such as the restoration of slums; the reconstruction of buildings and cities damaged by war or devastated by earthquakes, hurricanes, and other natural disasters; and especially the invention of architecture that mitigates the tragic effects of such catastrophes by, in effect, anticipating them.

The reason, I believe, is not the obviously daunting difficulty of such problems, but the risk of being stigmatized by taking them on. Architects who do so—and they are few—are often accused of preying on human misery for their own gain, or at least to advance their careers. Architects are particularly susceptible to this accusation—doctors, for example, who search for a cure for cancer are not. Perhaps it is because architects present themselves as following a "higher cause," meaning a higher "class" of clients and projects. The best architects prefer to be thought of as great artists, not as benefactors of the great numbers of common people, and so ignore the problems that most affect these people. Hence, their problems are unaddressed and remain unsolved.

One of the most common charges leveled at architects who address these unsolved problems is that they are aestheticizing violence. In other words, they make violence, or at least its effects, look good. The violence of poverty. The violence of war. The violence of nature. Not unlike Hollywood action movies, which glamorize violence by making it seem heroic or visually exciting, architectural designs incorporating the effects of violence—in order to transform them into something at least nonviolent—are seen by many as an acceptance of the causes of the violence. I do not believe this is the case. Architects are by nature pragmatists who want to deal with real conditions. Even the most idealistic ground their designs in the actual. So, why would it be surprising that they want to deal with the effects of violence that has already occurred? Perhaps many do—but they are afraid.

It is important to distinguish here between causes and effects. No architect would wish for the violent destruction of human communities just to enhance his or her career, just as no doctor would wish for the creation of cancer just to win a Nobel Prize. But once cancer exists, its destructive effects have to be treated, and—by anticipating them—its cause eliminated or "cured." The few architects who in their work dare to engage destructive forces and these forces' effects in our time must struggle not only with the work but also with the stigma of embarking on it.

January 28, 2010

Bruegel's Presence

Speaking about influences on my work (weren't we?), I have to say that the only architect who moved me as a young man was Mies van der Rohe. Oh, I liked some of the work of other architects, but it was the Mies of the Barcelona Pavilion and Crown Hall at IIT that got my blood flowing. I also have to say that it was painters who had more of an impact on me than architects, and among a handful that did, Pieter Bruegel stands out in my memory. Looking back, I can see very well why this was so, and also what a great influence he ultimately had on my visual imagination.

Pieter Bruegel, *The Fight between Carnival and Lent*, 1559. In this Netherlands town scene, people of all kinds and classes mix casually, unselfconsciously. In the foreground, a somber procession emerging from a church in honor of Lent (when Christians are supposed to sacrifice some pleasure in anticipation of Easter) encounters a band of drunken revelers immersed in their pleasures. The painting is not so much an illustration as an allegory of human diversity and of tolerance of it.

Bruegel lived and worked in Flanders, in the southern part of The Netherlands, in the middle of the sixteenth century. He traveled to Rome as a young man and brought back his experience of the great, revolutionary Renaissance art he saw there. But he remained for all his working life a northern painter—that is, a painter with one foot still firmly in the Middle Ages. What this means is that while he incorporated a measure of Renaissance humanism, he did not adopt with it the lofty idealism embodied in a rebirth of classical knowledge that so inspired Italian artists, but instead remained rooted to the realities of everyday life. His older, near-contemporary Erasmus embodied the skeptical, always questioning intelligence that characterized down-to-earth northerners, and so, in his own way, did Bruegel.

Bruegel's paintings celebrate the informal complexity of the everyday in villages and towns that lacked the spatial and social hierarchies characterizing their medieval counterparts to the south. They had about them a sometimes abrasive melding of classes and of activities that was proto-democratic. Most of his paintings retain a medieval fascination with details and the complicated narrative they create. Their compositions lack any single focal point and are what we would today call "fields" made up of many competing figures and objects, all rendered more or less equally, and requiring the viewer—not the artist—to select what is important to focus on. The themes of the paintings range from the everyday to the allegorical, the mundane to the metaphysical. Even these differences, however, are treated with equanimity, as though they were all in the same measure simply parts of life.

Umberto Eco, the theorist, novelist, and medievalist, has claimed that globalization and the sometimes abrasive melding of peoples and cultures in our time have not yielded a new classical age in the Enlightenment mode, but rather a new medieval age, negotiating between chaos and order, seeking a complex, ever-changing balance of competing forces. The emergence of the Internet, with its anti-hierarchical form, certainly bears out this point of view. Pieter Bruegel's paintings are more alive today than at any time since he made them. In many ways, he was one of us.*/

*/ See this *New York Times* article for a closer look at a newly attributed painting by Pieter Bruegel: Michael Kimmelman, "A Closer Look at 'The Wine of St. Martin's Day,'" *New York Times*, December 13, 2010, www .nytimes.com/interactive/2010/12/13 /arts/design/abroad-the-wine-of-the -feast-of-st-martins-day.html.

February 3, 2010

From New Atlantis II

New Tissue, from *War and Architecture*, 1993

Organizing elements are hidden,
too obvious to notice again.
Scattering rules each apply once.
The structures of spaces interact,
constant engines of chance.

A realm of spaces between
demi-worlds of difference
neither confirms the parts,
nor constitutes a totality,
violent or extreme.

We have deep towers,
standing on earth's inner side,
wherein wars rage against
states of gravity's decay,
at the scale of one.

We have morphological events,
wherein the secrets of change
become visible and plain,
returning to us the pure
mystery of play.

Authenticity

On its face, the concept of authenticity is a simple one. Things or persons are authentic if they emerge from a source of originality. The source might come from a unique way of making, in the case of a thing; or it might come from a unique nature of being, in the case of a person. Because things are made by persons— individuals who employ in some manner the ways of making—the character of things and persons are often closely related. The point is that in any case the source of the authentic will be comprised of unique properties and qualities and not merely those imitated from another source or adopted for effect.

We are all well familiar with the inauthentic, with things that are imitations of something else, and with people who pretend to be what they are not. There are fake Picassos—forgeries of Picasso paintings—just as there are fake Picassos in another sense—persons who pretend to be an original painter by imitating his paintings, sometimes without being aware of doing so. In the case of Giorgio de Chirico, who late in his life imitated his own earlier paintings, there are fake de Chiricos by de Chirico himself. This would also be the case with an architect who makes design sketches for a building he or she has already fully designed. It does not matter what the motive is (often it is to fill out a publication or an exhibition); such sketches are inauthentic, fake, because they were not made in the original struggle to formulate an idea, but rather after the struggle is over.

I realize that by now the ostensibly simple concept of authenticity is beginning to get a bit murky. Is the fake Picasso authentically fake? Is a posturing bore authentically posturing or boring? I suppose so, in a vernacular sort of way. But the idea of the authentically inauthentic is not useful because it reduces the concept to a game of words dependent on the absence of a "source of originality." The source of a fake is the faker, who by definition is not original. Without originality, authenticity does not exist.

In the present age of artistic appropriation, remixes, and what Walter Benjamin called "mechanical reproduction," the concept of authenticity is pushed close to the edge of extinction. Indeed, Benjamin argued for the virtue of the inauthentic, art that was mass-produced by industrial means and wholly without originality. Prime examples would be mechanically copied prints of paintings, movies, and recorded music, as well as the digital images and performances that today flood the Internet. In a literal sense these things are only copies of other, original things that they may strongly resemble (depending on the skillfulness of the copy), but which lack authenticity—that belongs only to the thing copied. However, Benjamin argued for the shattering of art's "aura," inspiring awe and reverence for its originality, in order that art could truly belong to the masses of people and no longer to intellectual and social elites who owned it, controlled it, and used its authenticity to claim and to exercise political power. Benjamin's reasoned objection to the concept of authenticity has greatly influenced intellectuals, theoreticians, and academics right up to the present. But there is more to the story.

Benjamin's viewpoint was radically socialist or communist. He hoped for the advent of an egalitarian society where the people would control the means of production and each would benefit accordingly. In such a society, everyone would have equal access to art—that is, the art made common by mass production. It would be woven into the everyday fabric of living. The Bauhaus had a similar idea and goal. However, Benjamin and Walter Gropius, the Bauhaus founder, not only overestimated the ability of socialism and communism to create such a society, but also underestimated the adaptability of capitalism—its ability to co-opt any idea, including radical egalitarianism, for its own purposes. What Benjamin foresaw without knowing it, and inadvertently contributed to bringing about, was a capitalist society of mass culture that we call "consumer society," where everyone who plays the capitalist game has access to products of every kind, including art. The public museum of today is a retail store of art for consumption by the masses of consumers, as much as movie theaters, television, and the Internet. The irony is, of course, that elites remain in power, still brandishing their control of original art, not least through the museums ("look but don't touch"). Capitalism has succeeded in creating radical egalitarianism of its particular kind and at the same time reinforced the power of ruling elites.

Architecture has become more popular today than ever before. Its popularity does not come from the ways it improves the everyday lives of most people—as modernists like Gropius once hoped it would—but rather because of the "brand names" now associated with its status as a consumer product. For example, in New York City—long the bastion of anonymous, bluntly commercial building boxes—designer buildings are sprouting everywhere.

Tourism, grown to international proportions, has turned the streets of the city into a public museum in which the works of the most renowned architects are displayed. While the masses cannot afford to live or shop in them, their facades—shaped with signature originality—are free for anyone in the streets to see and regard as reverently as they choose, or with whatever awe their brands demand.

Authenticity survives today in a vast landscape of the inauthentic, one largely drained of originality by mass production, mass media, and mass marketing. Authenticity has, as never before, become the luxury of the few.*/

*/ See a related post, dealing with the form of inauthenticity: "Bad Faith" (November 23, 2008).

February 21, 2010

The Edge

At the edge, we perform at our peak, our best. We have no choice, really. Anything less and we fall off the edge, plunging into the unknown. The edge is a limit, in the first place of our knowledge. We have to push ourselves to get to it. The closer we come to the edge, the more we have to use the knowledge we have. At the edge only the hard-core knowledge is useful. All the frills and redundancies, the posturings and pretensions, simply get in the way and in fact will doom us to failure. At the edge it is only the essential and the authentic that count.

Architects rarely work anywhere near the edge. They usually operate well within the boundaries of what they comfortably know and what others know, too. We expect architecture to be stable and sure, indeed with just enough frills and pretensions to make it a little, but not too, different from what we have known perhaps many times before. In this way, architecture can be reassuring and at the same time interesting. The designed spaces we inhabit, architects and their clients believe, should not push us to the edge but instead keep us in a comfort zone where we can live out our lives as fully as possible.

But wait. There is a contradiction here. If our goal is to live as fully as possible, to perform at our peak, our best, to use our most crucial knowledge and to shed all the superficialities that only distract us, then architecture that keeps us in the comfort zone, never testing our knowledge or skills or our will to excel, would seem to be somehow inadequate. The design of spaces we live in should challenge us to be imaginative, inventive, intrepid.

But wait again. Maybe most people prefer comfort to living fully, at the edge. Maybe we can live vicariously to the full through movies, art, sports—that is, by watching others living at the edge, exercising their knowledge and skills to the limit. Throw in the occasional thrill ride at the theme park, or the once-in-a-lifetime car crash, or the inevitable death in the family, and that will do very nicely, thank you. Architecture, in this case, should give us refuge, sanctuary, protection from the extremes, placing us somewhere in a secure existential "middle."

In today's world, living in the middle has become, for many people, difficult. Living at the edge because of war, natural disasters, and loss of homes, jobs, and identities, they do not have the advantage of being actors, artists, or athletes trained to push themselves to the limits of their knowledge and skill and to perform at their best on the edge. Only those used to living in poverty, including slum dwellers, learn somehow to live there, but their daily struggles for survival yield an abject victory at best. For the rest, the indignities of loss mount as they wait to be rescued. We do not often hear the stories of those for whom rescue never comes.

Philippe Petit's walk on a wire between the Twin Towers of the World Trade Center, in August of 1974, tells us a lot about architecture and the edge. He and his team, who illegally penetrated the buildings' security systems and rigged the wire, conceived the two towers as anchor points, stable and sure. Architecture, we believe, endures. Our lives continually moving within and around it are fleeting, ephemeral. It is a very great, but also instructive, irony that, in this case, the architecture did not endure. The towers were brought down by illegal "interventions" different from Petit's only in their intent to do harm, and to prove the instability of architecture. Both proved the vulnerability of presumably secure systems—especially the social ones symbolized by architecture—and shifted the focus of public perception and debate to what might be called "the endurance of ephemerality" in contemporary worlds driven so often to the edge.

High Houses

The *High Houses* are proposed as part of the reconstruction of Sarajevo after the siege of the city that lasted from 1992 though late 1995. Their site is the badly damaged old tobacco factory in the Marijin dvor section near the city center.

The concept of the project is simple. The houses rise up high into the airspace once occupied by falling mortar and artillery shells fired by the city's besiegers in the surrounding mountains. By occupying the airspace, the *High Houses* reclaim it for the people of the city. Balancing on scavenged steel beams welded end to end, they are spaces of a new beginning for Sarajevo, one that challenges—in physical terms—the city's past and present, aiming at a future uniquely Sarajevan. Stabilized by steel cables anchored to the site, the houses, poised like catapults, fulfill the paradoxical desire to fly and at the same time are rooted in their place of origin.

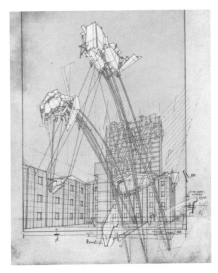

High Houses, from *War and Architecture*, 1993

These houses are not for everyone. Indeed, probably only a few could master their challenges. Yet each mastery would manifest a spirit of courage and inventive skill in the name of all who must reinvent a city transformed by destruction.

March 9, 2010

ANTI: Journey to Architecture

Raimund Abraham and I were colleagues for more than twenty years. We taught at Cooper Union and met many times on reviews of students' work, when we sometimes clashed, which was inevitable, given our different philosophies about architecture. We even co-taught two design studios, thanks to the benevolent mischievousness of our dean, John Hejduk, who loved to stir things up for the students and faculty, keeping everyone on their toes. Both studios were disappointing in terms of the resulting projects, neither for lack of collegial effort on our part nor on the part of the students, but I suppose you can stretch the dialectic just so far. The students survived the experiment and moved on—a testament to their resilience and intelligence, and in some strange way the experiences brought Abraham and me closer together. Gradually but surely, and almost because of our differences, we became friends.

Now maybe it is a "male thing," or just the peculiar natures of Abraham and me, but friendship is ultimately founded on mutual respect. In our case, respect had to do with our work in architecture. Abraham used to say to me, "There are only a few of us left." It would be easy to dismiss this as an old man's sentiment about the dying off of one's generation and the things it valued most, except that Abraham was not an old man. His mind and spirit were young. Being a teacher and working with young and aspiring people, always going with them toward the horizon of their dreams and hopes, keeps a man young, whatever his age. But there is more. Abraham was always pushing himself in his projects, always testing his assumptions, his beliefs. So, what he meant by his remark is that so few architects who reach maturity in their work can overcome the seduction of success, if they achieve it, and stay true to their youthful ideals whatever the cost, even if that cost is their success. And he was right.

In the summer of 2007, Abraham and I met, as we occasionally did, for lunch at the B Bar on the Bowery. Without preamble, he said that we should go to La Tourette for a week, stay in the monks' cells, meet daily, and discuss architecture. Not so much the state of architecture generally, but our own work and the quite different, even conflicting ideas that drove it. It was a surprising proposal and a daunting prospect, because I knew from past encounters that Abraham was extraordinarily quick, insightful, and articulate. A most formidable adversary, if that is what he was to be. Still, and for reasons I cannot say or do not know, I agreed.

So in October of that year, we met at JFK Airport, air tickets in hand, and set off on our journey. It was a wild trip, poorly planned, no doubt intentionally so by both of us, that took us by car from Zurich to Ronchamp, Besançon and the Royal Salt Works by Ledoux, to Lyon and Eveux-sur-L'Abresle and La Tourette, to Firminy and back across France and Switzerland to Zurich, with many unexpected incidents and adventures along the way. At the heart of the seven days we spent together were many discussions, dialogues, and plain disputes about the nature of architecture, carried on from a morning cafe where we were accosted by two drunken prostitutes, to a cold dark monk's cell in Le Corbusier's monastery. When we returned to New York, we met and continued our discourse, as Abraham preferred to call it. While we never concluded our talks, we both understood that there was no conclusion, but only continued journeys into the realm of ideas.

At the time of Abraham's death, we were working on a book about our journey and the discussions that occurred along the way. It is my goal—no, my mission—to see the book completed and published./24

April 8, 2010

Slums of New York

"Social housing," or what we in the United States call "public housing," means government-supported living spaces for those unable to pay free-market rates for them, and it is rooted in a humanistic idea of society. There are particular human rights that are not merely the privilege of the well-off and the well connected, but are the basic rights of all people, by virtue of their being human. One of these is the right to a place within their community as secure as possible from harm.

The history of this idea goes back to human beginnings. It seems, from what archaeologists have discovered about the remotest human ancestors, that a distinguishing characteristic of humans, as opposed to other animals, is their impulse to care for each other. Most animal species isolate and abandon their wounded or weak members, leaving them as prey to predators who attack the weak first. Excavated prehistoric human skeletons showing evidence of injuries or wounds also show evidence of attempts to treat them, with the obvious intent of restoring an injured person's faculties and capacities.

Compassion—the feeling of another's suffering as though it were one's own—is not a merely sentimental add-on to the human psyche, but rather a part of basic survival instinct. Individuals survive only if their community survives, and the community survives only by the concerted effort of all its members. This is another way of saying that I will do well only if you do well. Some theorists have called this "enlightened self-interest," and it works on both practical and metaphysical levels. As social creatures, we need each other emotionally. We also need each other to assemble the diverse skills needed to perform the complex tasks that are distinctly human, such as making science and art, commerce and trade, farming and industrial production. If we are to succeed in these ventures, we must take care of our own. Not the least part of this caring is the securing of a physical place for each person within the communal structure—the landscape of the city—that enables all to live with the dignity they need and deserve.

Jacob Riis was an immigrant in New York City, in the latter part of the nineteenth century, whose distress over the desperate living conditions endured by the poor took a proactive form. Using the then-latest camera techniques, especially the flash, he photographed for the first time the dark and squalid interiors of New York's tenements, exposing to a wide public an appalling degradation of human life. The publication of these photos in newspapers and books in the 1890s, combined with a campaign of public lectures by him and a few colleagues, raised public consciousness of the inhumanity hidden from view at the heart of the prosperous city. They contributed eventually to the public housing movement, wherein the taxes paid by the well-off would support those struggling for survival at the outermost fringes of society.

The poor shown in Riis's photographs are not loafers and indigents, but working members of their community. They provide essential—if menial—services, working to make better futures for their children, fulfilling the "American dream" that brought them to this fabled land of opportunity. Crowded together in small, dark rooms—where they slept, ate, shared communal bathrooms, and also did laundry for others, repaired clothing and household utensils, or simply found respite from hard manual labor—the people of the tenements evoke respect as much as pathos. They are the durable substance of an America just being born from waves of immigrants who had come to make a better way of life. The manner in which they dress shows their inherent self-respect and their aspirations. Their faces betray not a hint of self-pity. They bear the exploitative rents imposed by their landlords with a calm reserve reflecting their faith in the future.

Public housing in America began during the Great Depression of the 1930s and really took off after World War II, when a super-prosperous America—the last-standing great industrial power—decided to make good on the promises of its elected politicians. Following the design principles espoused by modernist architects such as Le Corbusier and Aldo Van Eyck, who placed their hope in enlightened government, tax-financed public housing "projects" were rapidly built in most American cities.

But then something happened. The super-prosperity ended and new enemies and threats to the community arose in the American psyche. The will to maintain existing public housing, not to mention improve it, subsided, and decay and public disillusionment set in. The root cause of America's slums— economic disparity between the rich and the poor, which had been addressed by successive governments from the 1930s through the 1960s—was increasingly ignored and, finally, exacerbated under the triumphant banner of "liberal democracy" and the "free market system." Today, public housing is barely mentioned. Schools of architecture do not study it because there is no longer the client—government—for its realization. The design and construction of new housing stock is left in the hands of real estate developers, who see no profit in building living spaces for those unable to pay market-rate rents.

Degrading living conditions still exist for very many in New York today, ironically behind the facades of the very public housing projects once considered an important part of the solution to the problem. It is not only that there is no contemporary Jacob Riis to expose them, but more so that there is no longer an America to be shocked into action by their exposure.

April 13, 2010

Terrible Beauty

Francisco Goya witnessed the horrors of Spain's war with France at the beginning of the nineteenth century and could not stay silent. Instead of creating propagandistic art, extolling glorious military heroism, he focused on the atrocities of the armies committed against ordinary people. He knew that when soldiers get into a killing craze, they murder and rape indiscriminately, often just for the hell of it. If there were an Iraqi or Afghan Goya working today, he or she would not make journalistic photos of the slaughter of people who just happen to be there, but would draw and paint it, becoming selective, "aestheticizing" the atrocities, in order to elevate them to a serious level of reflection. The artist does not merely present us with raw material, which is always difficult to confront and understand—indeed, it is easier to dismiss it with only a shudder—but instead creates indelible images that cannot be put out of the mind. For all the risks of making human depravity "look good," the human conscience needs such images in order to burrow deeply into its meanings and implications. Jesus of Nazareth nailed to a wooden cross. Goya's nameless victims of torture and dismemberment. Contemplating these images, we can never fall into a simplistic idea of our human condition./25

April 18, 2010

Darkness Ascending

Over at BLDGBLOG, Geoff Manaugh writes of the ash cloud spreading from the erupting Icelandic volcano across Europe, and undoubtedly beyond, in terms of a science-fiction scenario come true.*/ He is certainly right about that, and it does not take much imagination to realize, as the volcano continues to erupt and the ash cloud continues to expand, that more of Europe, the Middle East, and northern Africa might be affected. Air travel will shut down, no one can say for how long, and with it the vital movement of people and goods. This is more than an inconvenience. After only three days it is already a disaster for travelers from

*/ Geoff Manaugh, "Continent-Scale Weather Systems Made of Glass," BLDGBLOG, April 17, 2010, http://bldg-blog.blogspot.com/2010/04/continent-scale-weather-systems-made-of.html.

all parts of the globe, their families, their businesses, and for airlines and the recovering European economy. Worse yet, it is another blow to human pride—following on a spate of recent earthquakes—and our sense of control, if not over nature, exactly, then at least over our own affairs. The ash cloud shows us how fragile our technological systems, and therefore our present civilization, are particularly when confronted by nature's altogether natural convulsions.

We cannot stop the volcano's eruption or the resulting ash cloud, its expansion, or devastating effects. We can only hope that it will all pass soon—which it may or may not—and we can get back to normal. Perhaps, this situation tells us, we should also be rethinking our idea of the normal. Who can say whether our increasing global dependency on technologies that are increasingly vulnerable to nature's inevitable transformations will not become the new normal? If that is to be the case, then we had better consider a radically new relationship to them.*/

*/ What we are not hearing about in the mainstream media is the extent of fallout of ash and other particles from the apparently thinning cloud. An article on the human and economic impact in Kenya: Jeffrey Gettleman, "With Flights Grounded, Kenya's Produce Wilts," *New York Times*, April 19, 2010, www.nytimes .com/2010/04/20/world/africa /20kenya.html.

April 21, 2010

As It Is: Interview with Lebbeus Woods 1

Lebbeus Woods in collaboration with Alexis Rochas, *The Fall*, installation at Fondation Cartier, Paris, 2002

SEBASTIANO OLIVOTTO: In the Fondation Cartier exhibition *Unknown Quantity*, you were invited by the philosopher Paul Virilio to create an installation, *The Fall*. What is the basic idea of this work?

LEBBEUS WOODS: The exploration of a space of radical transformation. Paul Virilio and I, in our different ways, share an intense interest in the changes brought about by technological innovation, by cultural and social upheavals, by natural catastrophes like earthquakes and the social and architectural responses to them. I see these extreme cases as the avant-garde of a coming normality, one that we must engage creatively now, inventing new languages, rules, and methods if we are to preserve what is essential to our humanity—that is, compassion, reason, independence of thought, and action. Paul, in this exhibition, confronts the accident as an integral part of progress. He wants to face its terrors as a way of transcending them. I respect that. For my part, I want to face the consequences of destruction in order to employ them in the service of constructive aspirations. This means engaging the consequences of destruction—whether from war, earthquake, neglect, or abandonment—head-on, attempting neither to erase nor to memorialize them, but rather to use them as the starting points for a new sensibility, a new basis for creative action. *The Fall* uses a hypothesis, not an actuality, in this way.

SO: You started your works investigating how objects emerge from chaos and turbulence.

LW: I must admit that monumentality and permanence were givens in my education in architecture, even in the late modernist period that was in the backwaters of modernism's social and political and technological turbulence. I've come to believe, from that experience and a lot of reflection, that modernism was a failed movement because it did not deliver on its promises of facilitating social change through a new architecture. Instead, it was classicism dressed up in new clothes. The essence of the modern condition—the contemporary condition—is transience. Things pass, they evolve, and quickly. There is hardly time to absorb a new mode, a new technique, a new place, a new situation, before it is made obsolete by something newer, which we must adapt to without having the time to do so. This kind of transience, which used to be called "revolutionary" and is now hardly noticed, demands of us an adaptiveness, a creativity that uses entirely different rules than history—classicism—can provide. Classicism and the monumental are still very much with us today. The Guggenheim Bilbao is a classical monument. The architecture of transience, the architecture of our true modernity, has barely been imagined, let alone attempted in construction.

As a footnote, let me say that we must not equate transience with flexibility. Architecture should never be flexible. Rather it should be firmly and unconditionally what it is. Given the abstract nature of its shaping of spaces for living, it can and should be open for interpretation by different people, for whatever reasons they might have. This is a characteristic I emphasize. Also, architecture cannot present a one-size-fits-all set of conditions. Rather, it should be definite, precise, and unequivocal so that people can respond to it in whatever way they choose. Only by being singular, original, and authentic can architecture offer to people spaces in which they are encouraged to be the same.

SO: We met in Berlin at the opening of the 7 *Hills* exhibition, one of the most important exhibitions in the history of that city. On that occasion you proposed a steel beam jungle in which some artworks found their place. Now, looking at *The Fall*, it seems to me that the jungle moved from the perimeter of the room to the center to be the real protagonist of the space and the only interlocutor with the public.

LW: In the 7 *Hills* exhibition, I worked with Dr. Thomas Medicus, a historian and curator of the "hill" entitled "Civilization." We both agreed that civilization could not be presented as the orderly progression most historians would have us believe it to be, but only as a paradoxical, nonlinear accumulation that is redundant, excessive, and mythological. What you describe as a "steel beam jungle," I thought of as a cabinet, a collection displaying the accumulated artifacts of random centuries. I also thought of it as a labyrinth, a complex circuit of spatial frames in which it is easy to become lost or confused. Confusion, in our Western tradition, is the first step in the process of learning. The artifacts of many epochs were juxtaposed, blurring comfortable timelines. Architecture here was neither rhetorical nor didactic—it conveyed no ideology—but was instead heuristic: its structure liberated unexpected associations between the artifacts of civilization, making possible multiple interpretations of its lineage.

The installation in Paris had quite a different ambition, even though the means of creating space had something in common with the installation in Berlin. There were no artifacts, for one. But the biggest difference was a higher degree of abstraction in Paris—a more purely tectonic realization. This brought it closer to architecture that I consider a constructed idea of itself.

SO: Was your aim, in these two installations, to show that architecture is no longer in the service of art, but only in the service of architecture itself, as the most comprehensive form of art?

LW: I never thought architecture was in the service of art. Architecture serves ideas, hopefully ideas big enough to embrace many aspects of life. Architecture's comprehensiveness, though, is not to be seen directly. It's not a collage of various disciplines or forms of knowledge, as postmodernism would have it. Instead, it's synthetic, abstract. And by this I don't mean it is minimalist, a reduction. It must create a complexity that offers highly individual interpretations and uses. Programmatically speaking, it can only do this if it is, in the first place, "about" itself.

SO: This attitude asserts, tacitly or not, that the real art is to be created in the relationship between space and the spectator's body movement. Even the Venice Biennale of Architecture and the larger Biennale of art seem, in the last editions, to be the same.

LW: I would state it differently. Architecture creates a field of potentials, defined by spatial limits and also by its own imbedded methodology, within which people may choose to act or not. Traditional architecture tries to choreograph people's movements, even their thoughts and feelings. The architecture I envision is more anarchic. For some years I called it "freespace," free of predetermined purposes and meanings. The difficulty of occupying such spaces confronts the crisis of contemporary existence, namely the necessity to invent oneself and meaning in the face of world-destroying changes.

April 22, 2010

As It Is: Interview with Lebbeus Woods 2

SEBASTIANO OLIVOTTO: Is the result of the metaphorical or actual fall an enfeeblement of the traditional arts or instead the evolution of architecture as an art in itself rather than an extension of technology?

LEBBEUS WOODS: Architecture must find its own way. To call it an "art" confuses the issues that are crucial to its formulation today—or, I should say, its reformulation. As an architect, I can learn something from everything, including the traditional arts and various technologies, high and low. But this knowledge cannot in itself inspire the making of a new architecture.

SO: One of your early works was *Einstein Tomb.**/ A flying architecture, freedom from gravity, and the relativity of time and space were the main themes of that work. With *The Fall* installation the theme is gravity and present reality.

LW: The way you put it brings to mind the fate of Icarus! And it's true that my ideas have come closer to earth over the past twenty years. The Einstein project came at a moment of what I would call "philosophical idealism," when I was looking to science and mythology for ideas that could inform architecture. Since then, my skepticism and existentialism reasserted themselves. The *Aerial Paris* project of some years ago shows what an existentialist architecture that flies might be.

SO: Your work has also evolved from considering architecture as a volume comprised of architectural elements to architecture as a void between vectors or lines. It seems to me that your composition has matured in an unusual and maybe inverse trajectory, in which you obtain space no more through addition but through subtraction.

LW: Yes and no. Yes, my architectural means have changed. No, I still consider architecture as a construction made up of parts.

SO: It also seems that with this installation in Paris you wanted to create a space that is the direct translation of two-dimensional drawings. If we consider the tube you used in this installation as a metaphor of the drawings' lines, we can affirm that your idea is to use architecture to represent the drawings and not the contrary, as is usually done.

LW: Wouldn't it be wonderful if we could draw actual space, and not only its representation! In a way, that's exactly what we—I and my collaborator on this

*/ See "The Vagrant Light of Stars" (September 27, 2009; http://lebbeuswoods.wordpress.com /2009/09/27/the-vagrant-light-of -stars/) [omitted from this volume].

project, Alexis Rochas—did in Paris. We created a spontaneous architecture, one that worked directly with existing conditions. It is idiosyncratic and so complex that it could never be built again in the same way. Its coherence, justifying my claim that it is in fact a system of order, comes from the design not of the space itself, but of the elements (aluminum grids and tubes), the language by which the grids are made and the tubes are bent, and, not least, the rules governing their placement. Spontaneity only works within clear limitations—like the improvisations in baroque music and jazz.

so: This seems to be very innovative and to suggest that architecture needs to be freed of its stereotypes and of elements like walls, etc.

lw: Not all architecture. Just this architecture, which is experimental, trying out new ways and means. And, of course, it is not "architecture freed of itself," just of certain historically certified notions, such as typology—forms of preconception that sponsor the already known and the too-often rehearsed.

so: Doesn't such an architecture run the risk of becoming formalistic, that is, socially and culturally sterile?

lw: Yes, it's a risk. When you take architecture away from the narratives of history, from the signs and symbols giving social existence agreed-upon meanings, you are putting a big responsibility on individuals to give it meaning. The architect makes the first move by investing space with his or her understanding of the conditions and demands of reality. As I see it, these conditions and demands call for a high degree of individual initiative because social life has become so fluid that it can no longer be symbolized in static form.

so: You have investigated complex urban realities, such as those in Sarajevo and Havana, borderline and peripheral situations. You affirm that there is a constant relation between periphery and center. Is what happens on the periphery a consequence of central phenomena, or vice versa?

lw: Huge question. I'll try to focus it on the understanding I came to after visiting the places you mention and their impact on my ideas about architecture. We are conditioned to think of the center of a culture—a capital city, for example, dominating the periphery of its sphere of influence. The center radiates and the periphery absorbs its energy and is transformed by it. This model works well so long as the center is the place of innovation in the culture—that it is the source of growth and change. Often it is. But in recent years, centers have become culturally—socially and politically—more stagnant, taking on the roles of museums of culture, places where the past is more important than the future. Perhaps this is the result of tourism and its vast economy or the general cyclical evolution of things. The periphery—towns, countries, and cultures that are still in many ways dependent on a center—has experienced sudden, often violent and dramatic changes in ways the more controlled centers have not. Communication technologies such as television and the Internet, made global through satellite networks, have elevated the importance of these peripheral events because they can be seen everywhere. As a result, peripheries become centers.

The events occurring in places like Sarajevo—and now Baghdad— are terrible and challenging to the status quo maintained in the big centers. They change the way we see the world. As a result the concepts of center and periphery no longer have fixed meanings but are part of a fluid condition that is unpredictable and, in a sense, uncontrollable. Big centers like the US, trying to hold onto its past and the power it has had, can only confront this new condition with a violence greater, it hopes, than those of its enemies. In doing so, it is trying to force the peripheries back into their former, less influential role. This is a policy doomed to fail. The balance has already shifted, due to technological change and its consequences, past the point of no return.

Thinking of architecture in relation to this phenomenon, it is surprising to me that the building type of greatest interest today is the museum. It is as though architects are turning their backs on the vital questions in order to live in a fantasy world of new shapes that cover up stagnant, outmoded ideas, thereby perpetuating them. Obviously, the old centers are where there is money to build. That's where the clients are, and they have room for architecture only when it advertises a status quo. In Paris, my client was a philosopher, not a board of trustees, and a philosopher whose ideas take fully into account the new dynamics of center and periphery, of accident and design. That's why I was able to experiment as I did.

so: You were a journalist during the Sarajevo siege. How did the experience of observing this crisis change your way of thinking about architecture?

lw: In the winter of 1993, Sarajevo was surrounded and under murderous attack by Bosnian Serb forces. The only way to get through their lines was to fly into the airport on UN relief flights. The only way for me to get on one of those flights from Ancona, Italy, was to be, or pretend to be, a journalist. My real purpose in going was to meet with colleagues I knew in Sarajevo, to bring moral support from outside, and to begin discussions about rebuilding the city, when that time finally came. I took with me forty copies of the pamphlet *War and Architecture*, which presented my strategies for the reconstruction of war-damaged buildings and the reasoning behind them. Also, I went to arrange a workshop for students and architects in Sarajevo that would bring creative architects there to deal with the difficult questions that would eventually have to be dealt with. That workshop happened the following March, with Thom Mayne, Ekkehard Rehfeld, and myself attending./26

My experiences in Sarajevo fortified a conviction that architecture must address seemingly intractable problems like these, even though there are no clients per se, and no money. First of all, because buildings were damaged or lost, and this directly impacts people's lives. It's not hypothetical. They have to be repaired, rebuilt. Secondly, the attack on Sarajevo was an attack on civilization. The aggressors wanted to destroy its urbanity, its tolerance, its complexity, its cosmopolitan spirit. It was an attack on the idea of the city and therefore on cities everywhere. It was an attack on London, Buenos Aires, New York. If we, as architects, ignored it, we would be ill equipped to deal with the same sort of attack when it fell upon our city.

so: In some of the works related to war and the irreversible damage it causes, you used the "scar" and "scab" concepts. Is this architecture as surgery?

lw: No, I don't think so. It is just architecture doing what it is supposed to do—dealing with human conditions and problems. It is trying to formulate space with the potential to enable new ways of thinking and living, those result-ing from the trauma of war.

so: They also look like temporary structures. In your drawings, though, the materials look aged. Is that meant to suggest permanence to the work, or does it suggest that these architectures are the result of an assemblage and rein-terpretation of ready-made objects, even fragments and waste of the war itself?

lw: Both. The permanent is only an extended form of the temporary. And, if you believe in the laws of the conservation of matter and energy, even the new is only the old in another form. It is of crucial interest exactly what this "other" form is.

so: In a time of global crisis like the present, what is the role of art? What is the value of architecture? Is it destined to disappear, leaving the scene to the standard and the real estate value, or do you think that creativity can stimulate the beginning of a new movement of capital toward a new economic welfare for many?

lw: I wish I could believe that architecture will be instrumental in mak-ing this kind of reform, but I don't. Money and power will serve themselves and have very little use at the present time for the kinds of ideas we've been discussing. But exactly for that reason, exactly because the global situation is so turbulent and uncertain, it's important that some architects devote themselves to ideas they believe make architecture responsive to the highest aspirations—their own and those of others as they understand them to be. I see little hope for the moment that this kind of work will make any significant impact on the way most people think and work, but it will keep the ideas alive, and also the hope.

May 17, 2010

Just Change

Change, and in particular transformation—one form changing into another—is not simply a matter of the alteration of an existing form to create a new one. Rather, change creates what we could call a "third form"—really a third state that is the state of changing. We are so accustomed to thinking in dialectical, binary terms, employing either/or reasoning, that we overlook or consciously avoid the in-between state of change, which is really the state we continuously inhabit. Our fixation on goals—forms that for whatever reasons we desire—induces us to pass over the so-called "intermediate state," the state of transition, the actual state of change, in our rush to get to the desired form. When we get there, of course, we find that our goal, once attained, no longer holds our interest, so we set a new goal. In other words, we keep changing, but without ever embracing the state—and the forms—of changing itself.

As long as we can keep up with changes, moving from goal to goal, this does not matter so much. In fact human civilization has worked for thousands of years without much thought being given to the states of changing. However, when change starts to get ahead of us—that is, when we are not able to absorb one change fully before the next change comes—our goal-fixated system starts to break down. This is because we are more and more caught in the state of changing, and less and less able to reach our desired goals, even if only long enough to get bored with them. At a certain point, the only attainable goal is to live within the state of change itself, like refugees, gypsies, or nomads. It seems likely that in the future, if the pace of change—social, political, economic, cultural—continues to increase, this condition will become common in all social classes.

In such a world, the design and construction of permanent buildings will become less important than it is today, and architects will turn their attention to the development of concepts and techniques of building temporary living spaces. At their most primitive, these will involve portable structures such as tents. With increasing sophistication they will involve site-specific constructions that are created and, just as importantly, disappear as needed or desired.

May 28, 2010

Walls of Change

Walls are meant to separate, that is true. After all, it is an essential mission of the architect to define space, which means to construct limits, edges, boundaries that carve out particular pieces of undifferentiated space for human purposes. Walls of many different shapes and materials are prime means at the architect's disposal, and we are used to thinking of them as dividers between one side and another. Most often these two sides are different, even opposing—cold/warm, dark/light, noisy/quiet, public/private—and the separating walls secure people or things on one side from people or things on the other. On rare occasions such walls reverse their roles and bring people together. Think of the Berlin Wall on November 9, 1989, when East and West Germans swarmed around and on the wall, effectively bringing the political division of Germany to an end. Or, in a more hypothetical example, think of the Israeli "security fence" as the site for my proposed Wall Game bringing Israelis and Palestinians together in constructive play. */

At yet other times, walls that separate and divide can become armatures for change—that is, for the transformation of conditions on one side or both. Commonplace examples come to mind. Consider the building wall on a public street covered with graffiti—at once an aesthetic and political presence that impacts all who see it. Or, a simpler example, the interior wall of a private house, where the owners hang paintings, photographs, or a flat-screen TV, changing the mood, evoking nostalgia, or delivering news that subtly or abruptly changes their views of the world. In such cases the wall becomes more than a spatial divider, but rather an instrument of change.

In Havana some years ago, it was proposed that a series of walls be constructed within and around Old Havana (La Habana Vieja). This section of the modern

*/ See "Wall Games" (November 9, 2009; http://lebbeuswoods .wordpress.com/2009/11/09/wall -games/) [omitted from this volume].

city dates back to the beginning of the New World in the sixteenth century and still has buildings from that period as well as succeeding centuries, up to the present. Many are in a state of decay from lack of upkeep and restoration, simply because the communist government does not have the funds for these, and the only private development is by foreign investors building luxury hotels and other projects for foreign tourism. At the time of my proposal, the old city was populated by an economic and racial underclass that foreign capital had no interest in helping, so that any effort to save this unique city-within-a-city would have to be from the ground up—not counting on much top-down funding by government or investors.

Ideally, the proposed walls would contain some infrastructural purposes: water purification, at the least; the generation of electricity, like an urban battery, at the most. This means that these would be hi-tech walls into which individual dwellings would plug, as self-sustaining urban units. A good deal of clever engineering and sophistication in construction would be required to build them. Professionals, whether public or private, would have to be involved in the design and the supervision of construction. Their services could be donated to the project of saving this endangered district, or underwritten by international grants. The point is, the proposed urban walls would act as generators—or, more precisely, as re-generators—of the old city.

The decaying of the old city takes the form of collapsing or deteriorating buildings that leave voids to be filled with new construction one at a time, as needed. The building methods would be somewhat spontaneous, employing the construction skills of the builders—teams of inhabitants whose mastery of techniques and the assembly of materials would improve with time. Specialized teams would build the massive new infrastructural walls, the armatures of change. All together, they would form a community devoted to constructing their own environment. Its economy would be based on in-kind trading of goods and services and would eventually extend beyond the newly walled old city into greater Havana itself.

A final note. The new social circumstances of this community, as well as the necessity to invent new building techniques to deal with voided spaces in existing buildings and the new infrastructural walls, suggest that the spaces they build and choose to inhabit will embody new relationships within and without. In short, they could constitute a new urban architecture, unique to its place and time. For this reason, the drawing of the proposed project shown here is to be understood only as an aid to thinking and not as a prescription. What would emerge in reality would be far more complex, subtle, and new.

La Habana Vieja: Walls (detail), from *Havana Projects*, 1994–95

Einstein Tomb @ 30

Einstein Tomb, 1980. The Einstein Tomb in lunar orbit, just before the light-launch into deep space.

It has been thirty years since the summer of 1980 when the *Einstein Tomb* was launched on a beam of light into deep space, never to be seen again.

Its vanishing was as it should be, because Albert Einstein, the inventor of the twin theories of relativity (one for the electromagnetic/human scale, the other for the gravitational/cosmic scale) wanted no site for the veneration of his memory. To insure this, he instructed that his body should be cremated (which it was) and his ashes scattered over the Atlantic Ocean, the vast fluid domain separating his two homes in Europe and America (which they were).

Still, we—the heirs of his memory and ideas—are entitled to honor them both in some tangible form. The tricky part is to do this in a way that also honors his humble wish to be only a memory and not a venerated celebrity, secular saint, or demigod. Perhaps he, not being an overtly religious man (though he sometimes said "God does not play dice with the universe" and "The Old One is not malicious"), was remembering the Old Testament commandment, "Make no graven images." In any event, the only solution, it seems, was to make a tomb, then send/take it away. This was/is the *Einstein Tomb*.

Of course, it is more a memorial than a tomb, as it contains none of his earthly remains. And just as Étienne–Louis Boullée intended in his *Cenotaph for Newton*, it demonstrates its author's interpretations of its subject's particular ideas about time and space. Both Newton and Einstein changed our ways of thinking about time and space, and consequently everything that happens in them, everyday life included. Newton gave us the mechanistic, deterministic universe—if we know the active forces we can precisely predict their outcome. Einstein gave us the counterintuitive universe—things are ultimately *not* as they appear, but instead follow laws not readily apparent, though still immutable. His thought gave us elastic time and space, dependent on our relative point of view, and such systems as quantum theory, which have resulted (among many ways) in solid-state physics and microchip (computer and communications) technologies. His ideas have radically impacted our world.

In a filmstrip of *Einstein Tomb*, we see it being assembled in the low-gravity lunar orbit./27 This microcosmic scene occurs at a moment when the moon, the Earth, and the sun align—a moment of mythic or perhaps especially portentous energy. A foreign object intrudes and reveals itself to be a rectangular solid, akin to the monolith described by Arthur C. Clarke and Stanley Kubrick in *2001*. Soon, however, it is joined by another rectangular solid and these come together in a cruciform. A religious symbol? But no, it is more a plus sign formed by the intersection of two minus signs. At some point, this cross can be seen to expand on two opposing ends—skyscrapers, perhaps? Is this a city? Then suddenly a flash of light on the moon seemingly pierces the cruciform, but actually drives it into space. Because the *Einstein Tomb* is a massless idea, it can travel at the speed of light far into the universe. In this way it will test Einstein's theory of gravitation, which predicts that this space and time will, paradoxically, meet itself again, and again.

> This vessel, this tomb
> containing nothing
> wandering on a random pulse of light
> has always existed. Tomorrow,
> or the day after tomorrow, it will appear
> among the fixed and stable constellations
> of night. Even now it approaches
> from (limitless) possibility.
> All random journeys
> all the immortal corridors
> begin and end in the vaulted space
> of Earth's night,
> under the vagrant light of stars.

The Cube

When the Cube arrives, it will change every-thing. The Cube is so simple, therefore so complex. Simple things are never what they appear to be. However, their seeming sim-plicity is not a deception but rather a way of being everywhere and hardly being noticed. The change comes later, and slowly at first.

The Cube, from *NYC Night*, 2010

Many expect the Cube to arrive at night, when it will be difficult to see. There will be no public announcements, no welcome ceremo-nies. More importantly, there will be no defenses thrown up against it. Quietly, but surely, it will come.

There are several fine books written a while ago about its advent. The one penned by the well-known anthropologist (I do not think it wise to mention names, but you know who I mean, the professor who received a Nobel earlier this year) laid out the case in unequivocal scientific language: "There is noth-ing mystical about the Cube," he writes. "To the contrary, it is a direct result of many lines of rigorous research coming together. It is the perfect synthesis of scholarly fieldwork, communications technology, and epistemology—in many ways, really, a culmination of a wide range of scientific endeavor."

Another book, reviewed in much of the popular press (including online), is authored by a theologian at the most famous Ivy League Divinity School. She asserts, "We must play down the Messianic aspect of the Cube, because that will only breed hatred and fear. Instead, we should consider it a part of Nature, like a lunar eclipse."

The highly illustrated volume written by the architect widely celebrated for innovative projects concludes with the implication that the Cube is based on one of her designs. "It represents a radical shift," she writes, "not only in ideas about architecture, but also in city planning. Like modernism in its time, it will change everything."

These widely read and talked-about books, together with dozens of arti-cles in newspapers and magazines, as well as incessant commentary on cable news channels and countless blogs, created for a while an almost unbearable sense of anticipation of the coming of the Cube. When it did not come, though, the attention of the mass media, as well as the public, shifted elsewhere. Even the academics and scholars moved on.

Still, in the thoughts and dreams of many regular people, the Cube lin-gers as an idea, a possibility, and a hope for the future. I am one of those and consider myself lucky to believe that when the Cube arrives—which it will, it must, really—it will change everything, forever.

Terrible Beauty 2: The Ineffable

When was the last time you heard the word "ineffable" in a discussion about architecture? Never? Well, I'm not surprised. Ineffable means "unspeakable"—that which cannot be said—so I can understand why people do not speak of it. And yet, the ineffable is an important concept and even more so a momentous and profoundly disturbing experience when we encounter it, which most of us will, at one time or another, in the unfolding of our lives.

The ineffable is sometimes called "the beauty beyond expression," having to do with the apprehension of the divine or with some essence of existence hidden from us in normal situations. The ineffable is revealed only when the curtain of normalcy around us is pulled away and we are confronted with a very different world than we imagined we inhabit. This is often a frightening experience, even terrifying, because we're not sure what to do next or what to think. A car accident, a tornado, the loss of someone we love and need—traumatic experiences that shake us out of our accustomed, taken-for-granted reality, and we are left to struggle for understanding. Only thrill seekers who enjoy the adrenalin-rush of fear seek out such experiences. The rest of us try to keep things as they are, paying the price of boredom, if necessary, to keep ourselves in the comfort range of the familiar. The ineffable is well out of our comfort range.

For this reason, the ineffable is not a topic, let alone a goal, of architectural design. We can say that in fact design is the enemy of and a defense against the ineffable. As soon as we design, we start to control, to set up the defining boundaries and limits, and we squeeze out the ineffable, which is something that emerges when systems fail, when the limits are transgressed, and when things fall apart. We like to set up things so we feel we are in control. Our environment is designed to reassure us that everything is OK. That is what politicians do, telling us, "Everything is OK, don't worry about Iraq, it's going to be OK; don't worry about pollution, we are going to take care of it." Architects are a big part of this game of reassurance. We design endless variations of the normal and the familiar, sometimes dressing it up to look different. But inside—when we inhabit it—we find that we can behave and think normally. Our perception of the world is not affected or changed.

I grow weary when I hear the optimistic talk of architects proclaiming, like salespersons, that architecture will make living easier, more pleasurable, safer, more secure. Our habits—optimistic talk being one of them—only serve to reassure us that everything is OK, even if it is not. We don't want to feel uncomfortable; we don't want to have to move in a way that we are not habitually used to moving. But it is only when we are shaken out of our habits that we are able to change and to grow. What if to make things better, to enable people to cope creatively with the traumas of change, we have to make things more difficult, more risky, less secure? How often have architects dared to do that?/28

Loss is inevitable in the story of each person. Losing your wallet, losing your job, losing your home, your family, your city—the degree of loss escalates from the inconvenient to the inconceivable, and with it the experience of the ineffable. Loss, however, is necessary in order for us to change, not only in our habits, but also in our understandings and beliefs. As long as we cling comfortably to what we are and know, we cannot learn or create. If design is to be a creative act, it must take on the most difficult situations in our lives. It must offer more than comfort and reassurance. It must confront the unspeakable—the ineffable—and become a means by which we can transcend it. This means that we—as individuals and as architects—must, as the existentialist poet Nikos Kazantzakis once put it, "build the affirmative structure of our lives over an abyss of nothingness." A heroic— probably too heroic—task, it is true. Except for those who have no choice.

August 8, 2010

Eight Diagrams of the Future

Who says we cannot know the future? We can, but it is always a matter of interpretation, that is, of imagination. If that seems obvious, I should point out something not so obvious: that knowing the present is also always an act of imagination. We gather the facts, at least the ones available or the ones we want, and describe what is happening around and within us. It is always an act of invention. If—following the conventions of our social group—enough people agree, then we have an accurate description of reality, the truth that Voltaire called (referring to history), "the lie commonly agreed upon."

We can know the future to exactly the same extent that we can know the past or imagine the present. They are not interchangeable but do share the quality—owing to the structure of the human brain—of having been invented or, if you prefer, constructed.[*]/ The imagination needs some material to work with—bits and pieces are all we have. The more open to imagination they are, the more they can be interpreted, and therefore the "truer" they are.

I am putting forward eight diagrams—the very best, most accurately constructed diagrams of the future I am capable of devising—in order to help us know what it might be. Such knowledge may serve us well. Or it may not. Knowledge always cuts both ways.

To some of you, this might seem a variation on the Rorschach test, that is, an essentially psychological exercise. To others, it might seem like the mystical reading of tea leaves or the entrails of a ritually sacrificed goat. Fair enough. But I should note that in both of those situations, the material is created acciden- tally or—if you prefer—randomly. The eight diagrams here are the products of conscious design.

Another reference comes to mind, though it, too, may be only distantly related to the eight diagrams: *The*

[*]/ See "Constructing a Reality" (July 17, 2010; http://lebbeuswoods.wordpress .com/2010/07/17/constructing-a-reality/) [omitted from this volume].

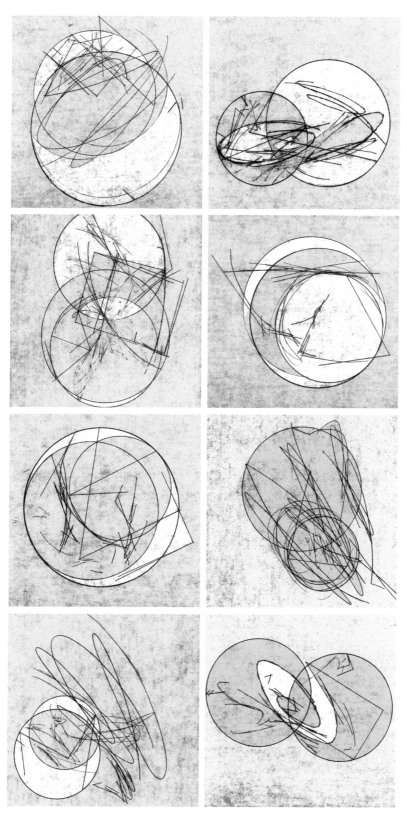

Diagram of the Future 1–8, c. 2010

Glass Bead Game devised by writer Hermann Hesse. In Hesse's novel, (quoting Wikipedia) the exact nature of the game "remains elusive and [its] devotees occupy a special school....The rules of the game are only alluded to—they are so sophisticated that they are not easy to imagine. Playing the game well requires years of hard study of music, mathematics, and cultural history. The game is essentially an abstract synthesis of all arts and sciences. It proceeds by players making deep connections between seemingly unrelated topics." */

The last sentences in this paragraph from the Wikipedia entry will appeal to anyone interested in a future formed by "a synthesis of all arts and sciences...proceed[ing] by players making deep connections between seemingly unrelated topics." Or is this nothing more than elitist propaganda, a distant echo of Plato's "philosopher kings" in *The Republic*? To counter that judgment, perhaps we can substitute "all people" for "players"— isn't universal education, hence universal participation, the goal, indeed the necessity, of political and social democracy? But will democracy be in the future at all?

*/ "The Glass Bead Game," *Wikipedia*, last modified October 13, 2014, http://en.wikipedia.org/wiki /The_Glass_Bead_Game.

August 12, 2010

The Experimental

The task of the experimental architect is to take us to places and spaces we haven't been before. That is more difficult than it sounds, particularly in this age of computer-based hyper-rendering that can look back over, and exploit ad infinitum, a long history of imaginative and speculative architectural design. This is also an age when many social problems—such as the rapid growth of urban slums and the need of low-cost housing for what used to be called the "working class"—remain not only unsolved but also unaddressed. So, we might ask, why should we even care to make, let alone support with our interest, more or less abstract speculations about new and unfamiliar kinds of spaces?

This question evokes the common argument against the exploration of outer space—to the moon, Mars, and beyond. With so many problems here on Earth, why should we devote precious financial and intellectual resources to off-planet exploration? What's to be gained, in terms of our terrestrial concerns? Better that we devote ourselves to "real-world" problems. It's a hard argument to counter. Indeed, it's clear that we should put the problems of our home planet first. Then, when we have those solved or at least have them on the right track, we can turn our attention to the stars.

This, in turn, is something like the argument against government funding of art. We understand that paintings, sculptures, poetry, and the like are luxury goods—only the well-off can afford to take the time for them. Most of us are working too hard to make ends meet to afford the luxury of time, and price of tickets, to go to museums and concerts where art is displayed in plush settings. Better that the taxpayers' money go to solving urgent problems like poverty and substandard education for our children. Well, yes.

The problem with these arguments is twofold. First, if we have to wait until the world is made right before we can afford the satisfaction of beauty (in whatever terms), we will never have it, because the world will never be made right enough. Second—and this is the more subtle point—it may be that the apprehension of beauty in art, music, poetry, and even architecture is necessary to solve the grittier real-world problems. The experience of beauty—especially difficult or "terrible" beauty—is one that gives us a sense of personal connection to a wider world. */ No doubt this sense of belonging to a world inhabited by a complex multiplicity of people and things inspires us and gives us the desire to concretize our relationships beyond the fleeting moments given by music and art and, say, an experimental architectural drawing. Without art to broaden our world view we might well stay mired in our narrow personal problems, isolated and apathetic.

If this seems esoteric, then we should consider the spin-off effects of many forms of research and experimental projects. The Apollo program that put men on the moon in the late1960s is a good example. A decade or so before the first moon landing in 1969, the very idea of rockets and the exploration of the moon and other planets was the stuff of pulp science fiction. However, a handful of serious scientists, led by Willy Ley and Wernher von Braun, began to speculate on practical ways to go to the moon in the early 1950s, long before the vicissitudes of Cold War competition with the USSR spurred the US government to actually make it happen. The Apollo and the other programs that led up to it were very expensive, and there were many who questioned their value, though criticism was muted in the general atmosphere of patriotic fervor. Americans were inspired by visions of manifest destiny, that it was they who were destined to conquer a new frontier in the name of all mankind. (Interestingly, the 1960s was also a period of political and social upheaval and change, giving us another, malevolent upsurge of manifest destiny, the Vietnam War, but also the enactment of revolutionary civil rights laws.)

In the end, as we know, the moon was "conquered," not once but numerous times. With "mission accomplished," and home-world problems pushing to the forefront, the desire to continue planetary exploration faded, and the rockets and technologies supporting the moon flights languished and fell into obsolescence. While it is hard to argue with critics who say that nothing much was accomplished by the act of landing men on the moon, there is plenty of evidence that the technological spin-offs of the space programs have been significant, impacting society particularly in the development of telecommunications, computers, and satellites.

There is a more critical reason for experimental projects of different kinds than the practical benefits that may—or may not—result from them. The truth is that most experiments lead nowhere and, judged from a strict cost-benefit viewpoint, are a waste. However, learning and invention are notoriously inefficient, requiring many failed attempts and dead-ended explorations to find one that is fertile enough to open out onto a rich new landscape of possibilities. If a society is unwilling to tolerate such waste it will stagnate. In today's

*/ See "Terrible Beauty 2: The Ineffable" (July 24, 2010).

world, which is under tremendous pressures of change, a vital and growing society not only tolerates but also actively supports experimentation as the only way to transform the difficulties created by change into creative opportunities to enhance and deepen human experience. This is doubly true for the field of architecture that, charged with continuously remaking the world, is at the forefront of this struggle.

August 22, 2010

By Hand

It is very difficult to imagine, in this age of word processing, that there was a time when people wrote anything and everything by hand. Yet it is so. All the great works of Western thought—coming from Aristotle to Shakespeare to Locke to Einstein—were formulated by putting a hand-held stylus to parchment or, later, to paper. The keyword here is "formulated," because the act of writing is the act of thinking. We cannot think everything out in the mind and then simply copy it down in written form. Without the act of writing, thoughts remain unformed and incomplete. So—as Marshall McLuhan noted—the way we write is part of the content of what we write—"the medium is the message" or at least a part of it.

This is a reality shaped by nuance. After all, does not the word "air" have the same meaning regardless of whether it is written by hand or word processor or, for that matter, set in lead type on a linotype press or on a modern digital press and printed on a book page? Yes, air means air, in whatever medium it appears. If we are only interested in getting the conventional meaning of a word, it matters little how it appears to us, and we can believe that nothing of consequence is lost in the translation from handwriting to printing. If we consider, though, how different typefaces affect the meaning of a word, say, AIR instead of *air*, we have to grant that the meaning is subtly affected by the form in which it appears, especially in relation to its context. If that is the case, then the handwritten word is subtly different from the typeset word—perhaps because of the imprint of the author's personality or, even more subtly, the effect of different shapes or colors on our understanding of the precise meanings of words.

As we know, though, the impulse of Western civilization is towards standardization, in the same spirit as industrialization, mass production, and consumerist conformity, which through franchises and global advertising present the same products to people everywhere, however different they may be or aspire to be. Their acceptance of (buying and living with) the product or the meaning of the word (read in standardized, typeset form) enforces a homogeneity of understanding, a social bond that transcends individual idiosyncrasies in favor of commonality and community. It is difficult to read handwritten, idiosyncratic forms of text, and indeed they cry out for a common, accessible form that we can share and discuss and—in some practical, cultural way—use./29

Slow Manifesto

Still, we must wonder, what do we lose in the process of homogenization and standardization? Is it anything important for us to know, to experience? Also, in this age of digitalization, which can present us with the idiosyncratic as easily as the standardized and the mass produced, do we any more need to sacrifice the personal nuance to achieve accessibility and common clarity? Can we not have both?

September 7, 2010

Gesamtkunstwerk

The idea of *Gesamtkunstwerk*—a German word for "total artwork"—has long since gone the way of all nineteenth-century Romantic ideals, onto the trash heap of history. It began with the belief that art really mattered in human society, morally and politically. This belief was rooted in the great value the ruling classes had always given to art as a symbol of their wealth and power, but also to its place in religions important to European history. It was only natural, therefore, that at the beginning of the modern age many believed that newly emerging industrialized democracies, both capitalist and socialist, needed not only their own new forms of art, but also new forms of integrating the arts, as had been done in the great cultures of the past. Architecture, painting, and sculpture had indeed been brought together in the import-

From *Architecture-Sculpture-Painting*, 1979

ant buildings of most ancient civilizations, such as Egyptian and Greek temples, as well as in medieval cathedrals, Renaissance palaces, and baroque churches, and were combined there with music and both religious and secular rituals and performances. Total artworks. The most notable modernist attempts to accomplish the same were by the Bauhaus members and the Russian Constructivists, though each were defeated by political forces—but that is another story.

Today, art is a commodity separated from itself, so to speak, in order to break it down into salable units. Modernism never found its *Gesamtkunstwerk*.

At a certain stage of my life, I fervently believed that architecture could sponsor a reunification of the arts, in the service of both public and private life, even though it would have to do so very much against all tendencies and trends. Vestiges of this have remained throughout the succeeding years—in *System Wien*, for example*/—but never in such an ambitious and hopeful a form as these drawings. Auf Wiedersehen, old friend!

*/ See "Architecture of Energy" (June 5, 2009).

Building Landscapes

DMZ, from *Terra Nova*, 1988

We all know that architects design buildings, those discrete objects that sit on a site somewhere in a town or a city or the suburbs or the countryside. We also know that architects, at least most of them, make an effort to design their buildings with some sensitivity to the particulars of their sites and even to a broader landscape commonly known as "the context." But in our contemporary urban world, with its aggregates of buildings that become in themselves artificial landscapes and contexts—entirely displacing the natural—the architect's role would seem to inevitably expand beyond designing built single objects. Also, in our contemporary world of environmental and global ecological concerns, it is clear that even the design of single buildings has broad consequences and must be framed in those terms by their designers, indeed by all involved in their realization. It is up to architects, with their presumably wider perspective, to take the lead.

A few architects have explored the possibilities of fusing buildings and landscapes, creating what Thom Mayne has called "hybrid landscapes." While such are not in themselves inherently ecological, this approach indicates a sensibility that could lead in that direction. At the very least, it manifests a different attitude toward architecture, one that plays down a heroic conquest of nature and looks for modes of coexistence with it. As in all cases of coexistence, neither presence is sacrificed at the expense of the other; rather, each impacts the other in creating—hopefully—a balance, even a new form of harmony.

Terrible Beauty 3: I Am Become Death

The detonation of nuclear fission and fusion—atomic—bombs, still the most feared WMD's, inspires many metaphors, including "hell on earth," "a sun brought down to earth," and the lines from the *Bhagavad Gita* quoted by the head of the Manhattan Project, J. Robert Oppenheimer, as he witnessed the first test of an atomic bomb in New Mexico, in 1945, "Now I am become Death, the destroyer of worlds."

Two atomic bombs have been used on cities—Hiroshima and Nagasaki, Japan, in August 1945—though tens of thousands of nuclear fission and fusion bombs exist in the world today, in the hands of national governments that have so far been moved for various reasons not to use them in war or as an instrument of national policy. Yet they are here, a button push away from fulfilling their terrible purpose of creating unimaginable destruction and suffering. As emerging national states and their often-autocratic leaders jockey for position and power in global society, the possession of nuclear weapons gives them leverage in being taken seriously. We hope that these weapons will never be used, but cannot be naive—we must also live with the prospect that they could be. */

*/ A recent *New York Times* article: William J. Broad, "The Hidden Travels of the Bomb," *New York Times*, December 8, 2008, http://www.nytimes.com/2008/12/09/science/09bomb.html. Related reference on this blog: "Big Bang: 'Doctor Atomic'" (November 13, 2008; http://lebbeuswoods.wordpress.com/2008/11/13/big-bang/) [omitted from this volume].

Gehry's Skyscraper

Frank Gehry certainly knows how to breathe new life into an old idea. He also knows how to create dramatic forms that create an impression of being daringly innovative even while he meets the demands of clients for more or less conventional spaces serving entirely conventional purposes. He is the undisputed master in our time of architectural styling. His new seventy-six storey residential tower in Lower Manhattan is stunning confirmation.

The importance of styling should be neither over- nor underestimated. Changing the appearance of a product without significantly altering the way it works or other aspects of its content is indeed superficial—literally. Yet today, appearance is an important part of any product's content. This is increasingly so in a time that is characterized by continual change and that extensively uses mass media to present products to potential consumers. A new style signals a new development in the ways people live, or that producers hope people will want to live. Also, a new style alters people's sensibilities about many important things that cannot be directly experienced or expressed—for example, their community's priorities and values.

The blocky, gridded facades of tall buildings of the 1950s testify to the ideal of a rational and predictable social order based on conformity to presumably universal norms. Gehry's skyscraper, with interiors (the living units) that conform to accepted rational norms, gives the appearance of being idiosyncratic, unique, and transformative rather than stable. Its facades appear to be bent, folded, or wrinkled as though by accident—even though these "accidents" are not accidental at all, but rather the result of careful design and highly controlled and sophisticated construction technology. In our present media-dominated, image-conscious society, it is not the causes that are most important, but the effects.

This is hardly a new phenomenon. In the early twentieth century, product advertising through all forms of communications media was designed to appeal to the emotions rather than the rational intellect. Since then, the image of a product has taken precedence in people's perceptions and choices. In the 1920s, the design of the crystal set radio—one of the first mass-media products—reflected the straightforward, "functional" appeal of a new technology. By 1950, the same radio—technically—was wrapped in a new cover reflecting the streamlined, speeded-up character of modern life and also its increasing concern with appearances and the symbolic impact of form. The crystal set of the 1920s is, in a sense, innocent, while its sleek, stylish descendent is unashamedly self-conscious.

October 16, 2010

Mies Is More

Is this what Mies van der Rohe meant by his remark, "Less is more"? A minimal architecture enables a maximum variety of living within. The spare and relatively neutral frame that such an architecture places around space not only allows without conflict all manner of furniture, bric-a-brac, appliances, and artworks, as well as human activities, to exist within it, but also actively invites them in order to relieve its own plainness and sameness. Heavily ornamented or aggressively shaped walls, floors, and ceilings defining spaces demand not only attention but also respect for what they express in themselves. If they are not respected, by juxtaposing against them aggressively different things, then the result will be aesthetically uneasy and perhaps unpleasant, depending on one's tolerance of or taste for conflict.

The neutrality of modern architecture—such as that of Mies, Gerrit Rietveld, Le Corbusier, and later works by Walter Gropius, Marcel Breuer, and Gordon Bunshaft—was argued as its great virtue because it did not (or so the argument goes) impose aesthetic values on an open, free, democratic society. Many modernist architects were, in fact, socialists, or flirted with democratic-socialist ideals, who placed on the exterior, public space

Corine Vermeulen, *Richard and Beverly*, from the series *Thanks for the View, Mr. Mies*, Detroit, 2009

Corine Vermeulen, *Christian and Michele*, from the series *Thanks for the View, Mr. Mies*, Detroit, 2009

of architecture an emphasis on the broader social good over individual self-expression and other forms of self-interest. This was a position challenged by postmodernist architects who proposed designs more in keeping with capitalist, free-market ideals of "anything goes," juxtaposing—collaging—widely and sometimes wildly disparate things. In this way, the aesthetic sensibilities of our time evolved.

But in the days when Mies designed the row housing for Detroit's Lafayette Park middle-class housing development, architectural neutrality still seemed to hold the promise of great social freedom. Seeing this series of recent interior photographs in identical units in this development is convincing testimony that at least here the promise was kept.*/

*/ The photos here appear in a recent *New York Times* article, authored by Danielle Aubert, Lana Cavar, and Natasha Chandani of Placement: "Living With Mies," *New York Times*, October 4, 2010, http://opinionator. blogs.nytimes.com /2010/10/14/living-with-mies/.

October 22, 2010

A Moment of Silence

How can we not, each of us, take a moment of silence in memory of the tens of thousands of Iraqi civilians—men, women, and children, each with the unique stamp of his or her humanity—killed and still being killed in the violence unleashed by the United States invasion in 2003.†/ A moment of silence.

†/ See Sabrina Tavernise and Andrew W. Lehren, "A Grim Portrait of Civilian Deaths in Iraq," *New York Times*, October 22, 2010, www .nytimes.com/2010/10/23/world /middleeast/23casualties.html.

Thom Mayne's Mind

Thom Mayne, *Bubbles* (detail), 2011

What's on Thom Mayne's mind these days? Better yet, what's in it? The reason this matters is that he is one of a handful of architects working today who is building projects that are powerful visually and experientially and are at the same time challenging in terms of the ideas that shape them. There is something to be learned from what he thinks and the way he thinks.

In his mid-sixties now and at what would seem the height of his career, Mayne is clearly restless. At the same moment when his large-scale commissions are in various stages of design or construction, he has embarked on an exploratory project—a series of physical models—that challenges the architecture he has created up to now, raising new questions about the nature of architectural form and its meanings.

Mayne is best known for his masterly, adventurous deployment of a technological architectural language in the service of complex programs of use that, more recently, also aim for ecological sustainability. There has never been any doubt about the importance he places on form and its transformations, as the name of his office—Morphosis—more than suggests. Whatever architecture may be, Mayne seems to think, it must come together in tectonic, constructed form that coherently takes a place in the sometimes-colliding worlds of the natural and the human. His new model studies push far beyond his previous work, coupling his growing interest in architecture-as-landscape with evocations of innovative technologies of building and, perhaps more importantly, designing built space.*/

*/ See "Building Landscapes" (September 13, 2010).

It is pure speculation on my part, but it seems, looking at this series of model studies, that Mayne is thinking something like this: the new, computer-controlled techniques of designing and building will liberate us from the older type of mass-produced architectural components and therefore the high-tech vocabulary that has, up to now, heavily influenced the formal qualities of modern architecture. Increasingly, all manner of forms will be designed and actually constructed. But why? For the sake of novelty? To create the illusion of progress by wrapping the same old ideas in new skins?*/ Or to serve genuinely new ways of living in relation to ourselves and the earth?

Mayne's morphological approach in his series of models creates spaces that can only be inhabited in new ways. In other words, new ways of living must be invented. This architecture calls for hopeful beginnings. Further, its fusion of buildings and landscapes indicates an alternative to traditional, prescriptive planning practices, one that is based on an integration of the artificial and the natural. Further still, the model's differences from one another point to communities of diversity, dominated by no single style or approach. Their freer aesthetic enables a freer ethic. Architecture will no longer be an instrument enforcing an institutional, mass-social ideology, but will become a vehicle for both the inward and outward expansion of human possibilities. People are infinitely various, though they share common human traits, and they need not be coerced or seduced into being stereotypes. The architecture they inhabit should be equally free of deterministic typologies, emerging instead from each person's or their community's shared and ever-changing necessities of body and spirit.

In my view, Mayne's is a brave vision, all the more so because it raises more questions than it gives answers. Not the least of these concerns is the role of the architect in a continually emerging world. What is an architect to do, confronted with so many variables, possibilities, and unknowns? Fall back to the safety of the familiar, the known typologies, the already successful formulas certified by history? Or adopt an "anything goes" attitude? These are equally depressing prospects, I would say. Mayne's courage in creating undiluted architectural worlds is all the more admirable because he could easily go on creative cruise control at this high point in his life, but that is simply not in his character. It seems that his curiosity, his need to push beyond what he knows, and his stubborn faith in architecture as an instrument of thought as well as action propel him only forward. These models are risky and problematic. They are certain to attract criticism for being unresolved, unexplained, and unjustified by tendentious arguments. They may well come to nothing, in terms of applicability to the practice of architecture or to the future of society. No matter, I say. They open unexpected doors. They excite the imagination. They inspire.

*/ See "Gehry's Skyscraper" (October 11, 2010).

Da Vinci's Blobs

Blobs were all the rage in architecture a few years back—does anyone recall? That fashion has passed, replaced by parametrics. These two trends share the characteristic of being inspired by the ease with which digital computers can generate complex shapes. Perhaps, in the case of blobs, we should say "nonshapes," given that these particular forms have, shall we say, *fluid* boundaries, evoking indeterminacy and something in continual flux. Hence the generic name, which may have its roots in the science fiction movie *The Blob* about an alien life-form that oozed its omnivorous way through a small American town in the 1950s. In any event, and putting aside the omnivorousness of digital computation, blobs have more of a history than was generally acknowledged at the height of their popularity. That history reaches back to precomputer days—the inflatables of the 1960s, pushed to prominence by Haus-Rucker-Co, Coop Himmelb(l)au, and Archigram, and much, much further back to, well, the Italian Renaissance.

Leonardo da Vinci, *Tempest over Horsemen and Trees with Enormous Waves*, c. 1514. For this study, which is more of water and wind than of storm, da Vinci used sharpened chalk and pen and ink.

Now, it is true that no Renaissance architect proposed blob buildings. But it was a time when artists—most notably Leonardo da Vinci—were taking an intense interest in the exact workings of nature. Da Vinci, as well as Michelangelo Buonarroti, dissected cadavers in order to understand the human body's musculature and skeletal structure, the better to paint its form and movement convincingly. Da Vinci, and later, Albrecht Dürer, studied plants in vivid detail, satisfying their innate curiosity, no doubt, but again with the aim of painting them as living things and not as mere props. In their art, they had the great ambition to project an entire living world in which the human and the natural were codependent and unified not through mere symbolism, but by a richness of differences and diversity. Da Vinci's paintings were philosophical in a sense that paintings before his had never been, manifesting what we today call "humanist" philosophy, which gives human beings the central role because of their ability to understand all other things. His paintings are, in an exquisitely inspired way, encyclopedic.

For da Vinci, drawing was the prime means of analyzing the phenomena of the living world. Painting was the synthesis. "Analyzing," in the way I use it here, is not taking apart something observed or experienced, nor is "synthesis" putting parts back together. Da Vinci's method of analysis was by *analogy*. Rather than pick apart a phenomenon, separating what he perceived as its components, he created in a drawing a parallel world, an analog to reality. Working with analogs, he could emphasize the features of phenomena he considered most important. Da Vinci's blobs—drawn masses of turbulent water or stormy air—are prime examples of his analogical method of analysis.

Looking at a rapidly flowing stream or a thunderstorm leaves a strong visual impression, but many aspects of what is actually happening remain hidden from or are simply beyond the reach of observation, either by the naked eye or instruments. They have to be inferred from what can be observed, and this is a matter of interpretation, of imagination. This is the method Albert Einstein used in developing his theories of relativity, because he could not directly observe objects moving close to the speed of light or the movements of stars in interstellar space. In science this is called "making a hypothesis," and the application of this method took modern physics far beyond empiricism, which was based strictly on what could be observed. (Isaac Newton had proudly claimed, "I make no hypotheses.") Da Vinci, in this way as in others, anticipated future developments—he created hypothetical worlds that revealed the hidden structures of nature. These, in turn, helped him create paintings of great originality that are imbued with a lasting aura of conceptual power.

Ironically, da Vinci was—as an architect—derivative of other architects of his time, such as Filarete. It never occurred to him to propose his ethereal fluid blobs as habitable structures as, most notably in our time, Yves Klein did with his Air Architecture and, most recently, Diller + Scofidio with their Blur Building.*/ Interestingly enough, though, da Vinci drew his storms engulfing landscapes, villages, and their inhabitants, inadvertently imagining an architecture of radical transformation, close to the spirit of our own times./30

In some ways, da Vinci's drawings are warnings, yet they are not without hope. Human beings cannot control nature, whose power can destroy them. But through their understanding of it, they can adapt themselves when necessary. His understanding of the changing forces liberated by fluid dynamics anticipated key developments in modern science and art. Arguably, he was the first architect of their indeterminate form.

*/ See "Diller & Scofidio: The Blur Building," Designboom, www .designboom.com/eng/funclub /dillerscofidio.html.

Slipstreaming

The characteristic of fluids that most interested Leonardo da Vinci was turbulence. He lived in a politically turbulent age. He had a turbulent, restless mind. The world he lived in felt most strongly the cultural turbulence of new discoveries and new ideas, and he was driven by the desire to be part of what we look back on as the rebirth of an intellectual freedom that Europe had not seen since the collapse of the Roman Empire more than a millennium before. The effect of this freedom on the intellectually repressive, dogmatic stasis of the Middle Ages was like the turbulence of a waterfall on a placid pond, or of a thunderstorm breaking suddenly in calm skies. Da Vinci's drawings capture the drama of such violent events but were not mere illustrations of them.[*] Rather, their rigorous analyses of how the complex interplay of forces actually worked were events in themselves, the first stirrings of scientific and technological imagination that would, over the next few centuries, transform the world.

Flow, from *Slipstreaming*, c. 2005

The turbulence that most interests us today is of a different order than that which fascinated da Vinci and characterized his time. It is the turbulence called a "slipstream," created by a body—either fluid or solid—moving rapidly within a larger fluid body, which may itself be moving or at rest. The historically recent advent of propulsion systems capable of moving aircraft, boats, cars, and pulses of gas, fluids, or solids at high speed has resulted in the creation of a new type of turbulent space in their wake.

The slipstream is a highly dynamic space active with forces that impel a direction. The slipstream itself moves, together with the moving body that continuously creates it. Its boundaries are variable, depending on the velocity and shape of that moving body, and also the characteristics—density, viscosity, and the like—of the fluid through which it moves. All of this can be described precisely with mathematics. However, these descriptions cannot bring us to full analytical understanding. We need other perspectives, and for that we must turn to the analog.

The analog emphasizes some aspects of a slipstream space while it ignores others. In effect, it creates a fictional construct based on facts, or at least selected ones. However, it is important to realize that every description—even the most rigorous scientific one, backed up by mathematics—is fictional. Every theory that has been widely accepted enough to become a law is an invention by human beings who emphasize what they consider the most salient characteristics of phenomena. In a sense, all of science is an analog of nature, of the reality of the world. Its relative success or failure depends not on absolute truth—who possesses such?—but on human consensus. How many colleagues are willing to endorse your fiction? That will of course depend on how well it fits into their fictions or theoretical constructs, and therefore how useful it is in a particular scientific context. Rarely, someone invents a new theory—such as Copernicus's theory of the solar system or Newton's theory of gravity—that forces everyone to change their theories.

[*] See "Da Vinci's Blobs" (December 3, 2010).

Slipstream space can be inhabited by people and sometimes is. Auto racers get extra speed while spending less fuel by following fast cars in front of them, as do drivers of eighteen-wheelers, whose boxy trailers create exceptionally violent turbulence and powerful slipstreams, which is why you will often see, on the highway, two or more of these trucks following each other in a tightly spaced line. Separated from the slipstream space by their vehicles' enclosures, these drivers do not experience the space directly, but only through the instruments of their machines. Modern technological living provides many such indirectly experienced spaces, perhaps most prominently cyberspace. Its virtuality is, on an experiential level, analogical and in exactly the terms of selectiveness described here. Virtual and analog experiences emphasize some characteristics of a phenomenon while ignoring others. That is the price to be paid for vastly expanding the boundaries of our experience and for exploring the imaginary in the real.

December 31, 2010

Killer Buildings

The reason we so often stand mute before images showing the New Delhi building collapse, the Deepwater Horizon oil rig explosion, the Shanghai high-rise apartment building fire, and the like is because "they speak for themselves." But do they? Certainly, we are hesitant to speak for fear of uttering clichés in the presence of human tragedy. We have an innate sense that we must not profane what is nothing less than a sacred site—a place where human beings have been killed. Yes, "killed" and not "died" in the natural course of their lives. What has killed them, and why?

The most obvious answer is that the building killed them. Suddenly, unexpectedly, the building collapsed, crushing those who lived within under its immense weight. So the building has a particular kind of volition. It can independently decide to collapse—no person needs to command it to do so. Who would? But, actually, it has been programmed by people to collapse under certain conditions.

In the first place, architects and structural engineers have established the building's materials and their elastic limits—the points at which the materials will fail. In the second place, the building's constructors activate the material's limits, which will inevitably deviate from those anticipated by the designers. Buildings may be thought of as low-tech cyborgs, encoded with instructions about how to live and when to die. But that brings us to the third place. All buildings have their own intimate relationships with conditions around them and thus a small degree of independent life. When confronted by certain conditions, they can self-destruct without warning, taking their inhabitants with them.

Shapeless clouds of smoke disturb a city's geometric order. The geometry is predictable and reassuring. The smoke obscures the geometry, challenges the order, and is unsettling, even alarming. Mathematicians and poets may tell us that the smoke is only the form of a different order, but we are not reassured. Instead, such descriptions only confirm our fears of disorder and the looming emotional chaos of loss.

As the smoke diminishes, we see that only a single building—a single example of the order we depend on—is burning. Standing almost alone in a vast geometric landscape, the fire that consumes it is within containable, acceptable limits—at least those of the designing architects and engineers, but also of our abilities to tolerate threats to the stability of our immediate world. Then, we recoil in horror at that thought—there may be people still inside—maybe all could not escape. Knowing how tall the building is, the probable shutdown of elevators, the possible blockage of stairwells by smoke and debris, if not flames . . .

From the black vultures circling the tower—the news helicopters that can take but not give—we can look into the building's high windows and see the burning interiors of apartments, their once useful furniture absurdly ablaze. People lived in these spaces, high above the city. Squinting our eyes, we easily imagine those who may have died and wildly fear seeing any who have not. It is only then we ask why such houses—which, in a major catastrophe, offer little chance of escape or rescue—are built at all. It would be comforting, in a strange sense, if the answer would be that the risk is the price people gladly pay for such privileged perches in the sky. But we know this is not true.

People live and work in towers because they're given no choice. Land in the city is expensive. Also, land only slowly becomes available for new buildings, so the only answer for those who build offices and houses is to stack them as high as they can. Or at least that is the only answer that architects and planners have so far been able to devise. Until other concepts are invented, towers will continue to rise. When night comes over this city, searchlights are turned onto the tower, transforming it into a dazzling spectacle whose uncanny beauty mocks its terrible reality. */31

*/ Article on the Deepwater Horizon fire: David Barstow, David Rohde, and Stephanie Saul, "Deepwater Horizon's Final Hours," New York Times, December 25, 2010, www.nytimes.com/2010/12/26/us/26spill.html. Early article on the Shanghai tower fire: David Barboza, "Workers Detained as Toll Hits 53 in Shanghai Fire," New York Times, November 15, 2010, www.nytimes.com/2010/11/16/world/asia/16shanghai.html. Follow-up article on the Shanghai tower fire: Michael Wines and David Barboza, "Fire Trips Alarms About China's Building Boom; Censors Respond," New York Times, November 16, 2010, www.nytimes.com/2010/11/17/world/asia/17shanghai.html. Article on the New Delhi building collapse: Lydia Polgreen and Saimah Khwaja, "Delhi Building Collapse Tied to Bad Construction," New York Times, November 16, 2010, www.nytimes.com/2010/11/17/world/asia/17india.html.

Slow Manifesto

2011

The Dreams that Stuff Is Made Of

Drawings from *Conflict Space*, 2006. A corner of Woods's large-drawing room, cleaned up to display the drawings

A while ago, Thom Mayne and I were talking about our recent projects, some of which have nothing explicitly to do with buildings. This is the exception for Mayne but the norm for me these days, and at least part of our discussion was about why we would want to make work that looked to most people more like art than architecture. Interestingly, we both claimed the projects in question—Mayne's series of large physical models and my series of large drawings—addressed spatial and tectonic issues most relevant to the design of habitable space.[*] I suspect that we will have a hard time convincing our more skeptical colleagues about this—so be it. Experimentation and research don't aim for immediate acceptance, but rather for opening new ways of thinking and working, for their authors as well as anyone who might creatively interpret the outcome, which is the only justification for their publication.

    To regular readers I say, don't worry, I'm not going to trot out the arguments for experimentation that I've made in many posts and indeed quite recently.[†] Instead, I'd like to address some specifics of the *Conflict Space* series of drawings, shown here. This is partly in answer to recent requests by readers for me to discuss how I draw. While I remain skeptical of putting too much emphasis on drawing, for fear of distracting from its content, the way a drawing is constructed is, as in a building, part of its content.

[*] See "Thom Mayne's Mind" (November 25, 2010).

[†] See "The Experimental" (August 12, 2010).

The impulse to make these large drawings—they are, with one exception, 74 inches high by 120 inches wide (188 by 305 centimeters)—came first from my desire to make drawings at the scale of a room, that is, at an architectural scale. The reason for this is rather simple: to see if one could physically and not only mentally inhabit the space of a drawing. The second driving force was to see if drawing at that scale would produce something different than I'd imagined or drawn before.

Regarding the question of scale, I would say that the drawings in this series, experienced in the flesh, do invite our physical participation in the drawn spaces. This can be attributed in part to their size but also to the fact that their presence is quite tactile. That is, one sees that the drawing's surfaces, lines, and textures are made by a hand on actual, not simulated or virtual, material. The same effect could not be achieved through a blow-up of a smaller drawing. Secondly, drawing at this larger scale did inspire a different way of making marks and thus a type of space I had not drawn before, one emerging from the subtle variety and scale of marks only in drawings large enough to permit such a range, from the light to the heavy, the thick to the thin. Of course, viewing them on a computer screen negates these very qualities. This is similar to the experience of seeing an actual building and then photos of it. Following this thought leads us in the direction of considering representation as reality, which is not where I want to go in this post. Rather, I want to stay focused on the drawings and how they came to be what they are.

At the outset, I decided to work within strict, clearly defined limits. I wanted to restrict myself severely in order to see what could be accomplished with a minimum of means. I won't deny that this was in part a reaction to the surfeit of means I had employed in the past (tone, color, shading) accomplished through a variety of media (graphite and color pencils, pastels, ink), not to mention the rendering capabilities of digital computers, which enable a truly infinite range of possibilities. I wanted to put all that aside, to free myself of it and also to free architecture—always the subject of my drawings—of an excess that increasingly seems to me to be suffocating its true spirit.

Architecture does begin with the plow, the brick, and acts of making. In different epochs, the uses of these three are inspired by different ideals. In our own, the plow, the brick, and the making must serve our complexity and diversity, the thousand subtle variations on a thousand human themes, even as they remain plow, brick, and making. Architecture has become the most difficult and daunting of arts.

Such were the thoughts in mind as I prepared to draw. I chose as a ground a fine linen canvas that I prepared with black (actually very dark gray) acrylic paint. The result was a matte surface, perfect for receiving any drawing medium. For mine I chose an artists' quality, water-based white crayon because of its opacity and also its ability to be manually sharpened to a fine point by a hand-held sharpener. I would make white marks on a black field. The reason was, I admit, counterintuitive. Our cultural habits prejudice black lines on a white field as being the most evocative of space. White lines on a dark field are abstract, even flat and two-dimensional. Regardless, I reasoned that the drawing of a line is in itself positive, an assertion of edge and boundary that will overcome spatial "reading" habits—my first big gamble.

The second gamble was that I would use only straight lines drawn with a specially made straightedge that enabled me to hold it firmly against the vertical surface of the primed canvas. The straight line is a spatial vector, conveying direction and magnitude of energy, not just symbolically, but also in the physical, intellectual, and emotional energy it takes to draw the line exactly as it is. Moreover, any curve can be created with straight lines, the smoothest with a mathematically infinite number. With straight lines, the boundaries of any form can be established.

Using this approach, the drawings aim to evoke in two dimensions three-dimensional figures that overlap and interpenetrate one another in spaces at once ambiguous and precise. In one sense, this echoes the goal of early modernism to achieve spatial continuity and social universality. But it differs radically from it in that here a universal visual language of vectors yields the idiosyncratic and discontinuous. This is important to an era such as the present one in which individuals are locked in a decisive struggle for their identities with the leveling forces of commercialized mass culture. Modernism, in its day, sought to reinforce a then-emerging demand for social justice and challenged a rigid class system by establishing an egalitarian environment. Today, the "egalitarian environment" of consumerism does little to support social justice in any form. These drawings aspire to finding, in spatial terms, what I have elsewhere called "the differences in radical similarities."*/ Too grandiose? No doubt. But such are the dreams that provide the energy to drive such projects.†/

*/ See "Same Difference" (January 13, 2009; http://lebbeuswoods .wordpress.com/2009/01/13/same -difference/) [omitted from this volume].

†/ PS Thom Mayne and I have agreed to carry forward our discussion of his exploratory models. Keep an eye out for future posts. [The post "Talking with Thom Mayne" (April 23, 2011; http://lebbeuswoods.wordpress .com/2012/04/23/talking-with-thom -mayne/) has been omitted from this volume.]

February 1, 2011

Inventing Discovery

A stone stela was discovered on a tiny rock island off the coast of Nova Scotia, Canada. When the apparently ancient artifact was cut open, a mechanical, geometric object was reportedly found inside. But was its presence invented? Why is it important to know? Can we ever know, for sure?

Heinz von Foerster, one of the founders of the transdisciplinary field of cybernetics, told me a story about one of his PhD advisees. This young man had written what von Foerster considered a brilliant dissertation in the field of physics, and all that remained for him to get his doctorate degree was to present it to his faculty committee for their approval. In the course of his lucid presentation, he said, "When Isaac Newton invented gravity..." One of his professors interrupted him, saying, "You mean, when Isaac Newton *discovered* gravity." The young candidate replied, "No, professor. When Newton invented gravity." He failed the examination. After being given pause to reflect on his error, he again met with his faculty committee, and again said, "When Isaac Newton invented gravity..." Again he failed. Frustrated and fearful, he went to see von Foerster for advice on what to do. Von Foerster told him, "The next time you get to the part about Newton, simply say, "When Isaac Newton *discovered* gravity..." Next time, the young candidate said exactly that and passed "with distinction."

The point von Foerster wanted to make with this story is that the idea of knowledge generally accepted by professors of science and just about everyone else is that the truth—reality—is "out there" and it is our task to find, to discover it. In other words, reality exists independent of us. While von Foerster and a number of cognitive scientists would not argue with this idea, they would say that it is irrelevant because the closed nature of the human nervous system makes perceiving any reality independent of it impossible. When we look out at the world, what we perceive are our perceptions, neither more nor less.*/

Hence, Isaac Newton did not discover gravity, a set of phenomena affecting our nervous system and thus our perceptions; he invented it as a description of these phenomena that, as it turns out, has been agreed upon by a majority of knowledgeable people. Before Newton proposed his theory of gravity, people had other theories explaining the physical attraction of bodies to each other. Most knowledgeable people agreed with them. After Newton, Albert Einstein invented a new description/theory of gravity that most knowledgeable persons have come to agree with and accept as true. Eventually there will be a theory that replaces Einstein's and most knowledgeable people... and so on.

Does reality change with the coming of a new theory describing it and people's belief in it? Or are the theories simply wrong? Will there one day be a correct description of the reality that is out there, waiting to be discovered? Modern science does not attempt to answer this question, because it does not consider it relevant to understanding. What is relevant is inventing descriptions that lead to deeper knowledge of how we interact with the phenomena affecting us, including an understanding of understanding. What, after all, is knowledge?

As for the stela on the tiny rock island, we can at least be sure that if enough knowledgeable people believe what was found when it was opened is real, then it is.

*/ What we perceive are our perceptions. See "Constructing a Reality" (July 17, 2010; http://lebbeuswoods.wordpress .com/2010/07/17/constructing-a-reality/) [omitted from this volume].

February 12, 2011

Ode to Joy

Human solidarity is a powerful and rare event. When it occurs in the cause of freedom—which is really the cause of human creative potential—it is inspiring and terrifying. It inspires those who believe in people's goodness and need for each other; it terrifies those who believe that people must be controlled, for their own good and for the good of the controllers. People's solidarity lasts only

when it is protected by institutions that they alone create. Indeed, that is the first creative task to be accomplished, and therein lies the rub.

But let us not dwell on the future. Rather, let us
join the Egyptians in Cairo's Tahrir Square last night,
for this moment of their freedom, in their joy and exultation. Long may it last! */₃₂

*/ See the *New York Times* interactive graphic: Stephen Farrell et al.,
"18 Days at the Center of Egypt's
Revolution," *New York Times*,
February 12, 2011, www.nytimes
.com/interactive/2011/02/12/world
/middleeast/0212-egypt-tahrir-18
-days-graphic.html.

February 15, 2011

A Space of Light

The Light Pavilion is designed to be an experimental space—that is, one that gives us the
opportunity to experience a type of space
we haven't experienced before. Whether it
will be a pleasant or unpleasant experience,
exciting or dull, uplifting or merely frightening, inspiring or depressing, worthwhile or a
waste of time is not determined in advance by
the fulfillment of our familiar expectations,
because we can have none, never having
encountered such a space before. We shall
simply have to go into the space and pass
through it, perhaps more than once. That is
the most crucial aspect of its experimental
nature, and we—its transient inhabitants—
are experimentalists in full partnership with
the space's designers. Each of our experiences will be unique, personal.

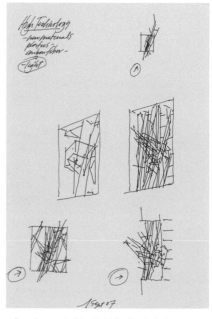

Development of the Light Pavilion's design, 2007

Set within a better-known three-
dimensional geometry and framed by it, the
Light Pavilion exerts its differences. Most apparently, the elements defining it
do not follow the known, rectilinear geometry of its architectural setting. The
columns supporting stairs and viewing platforms obey a geometry defined by
dynamic movement. Their deviation from the rectilinear grid releases its spaces
from static stability and sets them in motion, encouraging visitors to explore.

The structural columns articulating the pavilion's interior spaces are illuminated from within. In the twilight and night hours they glow, creating a luminous
space into which the solid architectural elements appear to merge. This quality is
amplified by the mirrored surfaces enclosing the pavilion, which visually extend
its spaces infinitely. We might speculate that this new type of space stands
somewhere between traditional architecture and the virtual environments of
cyberspace, a domain we increasingly occupy in our homes and workplaces.
But the Light Pavilion emphasizes the physical over the mental or the virtual.

Slow Manifesto

Lebbeus Woods in collaboration with Christoph a. Kumpusch, Light Pavilion, Chengdu, China, 2012.
Top: View from the central plaza. Bottom: View from within the pavilion

From distances across the city, the pavilion is a beacon of light for the Raffles City complex. From within the buildings, and especially from the large public plaza between them, the glowing structure radiates subtly changing color to symbolize different holidays and times of day, month, and year.

The space has been designed to expand the scope and depth of our experiences. That is its sole purpose, its only function. If one needed to give a reason to skeptics for creating such experimental spaces in the context of this large urban development project, it would be this: our rapidly changing world constantly confronts us with new challenges to our abilities to understand and to act, encouraging us to encounter new dimensions of experience.

Text by Lebbeus Woods and Christoph a. Kumpusch

A Lone Shaper of Worlds

At eighty years old, George Kokines is a man—and a painter—of remarkable vitality, humbling many younger than he. Part of his vitality is due to his rugged Greek character. But the more important part is his dedication to painting. For George (yes, we're friends), painting is more than a means of express- ing thoughts and feelings; it is a way of living. What that means is that the act of painting, which is as physical as mental, is a condenser of his life and experiences. To be a painter, one must first have a life, rich with experiences.

George Kokines, *September 11*, installation at Elgin Academy, Chicago, 2010

The story of my knowing George is worth telling. Some years ago, I hung out three or four days a week at a bar called Fanelli's Cafe. In those days (no longer) it was a fashionably unfashionable spot in New York's SoHo, at the end of the neighborhood's tenure as a bohemian nexus for artists and galleries. Dark and vaguely sinister, the long room with the long bar was populated in the morning hours (when I preferred to be there) with a motley crew of regu- lars—painters and hangers on, writers, filmmakers, agents, and regular guys (it was mostly male) who had discovered that interesting conversations would occasionally occur and that they were free to jump in. Crucial to the atmo- sphere of the place were the bartenders. They not only dispensed the needed medication, or fuel for talking, needed by the regulars, but also set the gen- eral mood of the bar. One of the morning bartenders (they opened at 10) was Larry, a droll comedian who never cracked a smile as he made outrageously funny quips about the customers. Another was George, quiet, efficient, and not aiming to please.

The bar was rather empty in the morning and I always took a seat at the far end, away from the heavily imbibing regulars, sipping my drink and working in one of my small sketchbooks. When George was on duty, we would get into conversations about this and that, and increasingly about art. He learned I was an architect and I that he was a painter. I learned that he tended bar to earn money to keep his studio and continue painting—a very honorable path for a serious painter. He learned that I didn't "do buildings," but taught and made speculative projects. Between his pouring drinks and my drawing in a sketch- book, we talked about many ideas and experiences, both trivial and profound.

By September 11, 2001, I had long since stopped being a regular at Fanelli's, but George and I kept in touch. I went to his studio and saw the large "cement" paintings he was working on as well as smaller canvases in oils. He came to my loft-like apartment, where I was working on drawings and mod- els for *The Fall* installation and was also holding a workshop for international students called "Gr(o)und." George experienced the destruction of the World

Trade Center towers first hand—his studio was two blocks away. The military forced him and all residents of the neighborhood to evacuate. Some years later, after George had returned to Chicago, the city of his highly successful early career, the mural-sized painting *September 11* emerged, slowly and laboriously and, I'm sure, painfully. Looking at the video of its emergence, we are struck not only by the painter's trial-and-error method, but more so by its seemingly inexorable move towards a final, unequivocal synthesis.[*]/ The world of abstraction he takes us into is at once personal and universal—or, it is better to say, universal precisely because it is intimately personal. That indeed is the meaning of *September 11*, the mural and the day.

[*]/ See "September 11: An Installation by George Kokines," posted December 22, 2010, www.youtube.com/watch?v=VI8VIpxBB18.

February 27, 2011

Rethinking Roche

I was very happy to see the recent article "Turning a Rearview Mirror on Kevin Roche" reappraising the early work of Kevin Roche, an architect who—along with his partner John Dinkeloo—I worked for from 1964 to 1968.[†]/ During those four intensive years, I had the good fortune to have worked primarily on the Ford Foundation Building in New York. I was in the production team—first in design development and construction drawings (all by hand in those days), then in coordination with the engineers, and finally in construction coordination and supervision in the field. I have many stories to tell about what I call my "PhD in architecture" but will save them for another occasion. What concerns me here is the critical appraisal of this building, then and now.

Let's start with then. In the late 1960s and early 70s this building—completed in 1968—was savaged by the influential postmodernist critic and historian Vincent Scully, an avid follower of the then-new theories of Robert Venturi and Denise Scott Brown. He named architects such as Paul Rudolph, John Johansen, and Kevin Roche as villains, denigrating them as proponents of modernism and as enemies of a new, supposedly populist architecture practiced by Venturi, of course, and his legions of followers. The Ford Foundation Building—arguably Roche's masterpiece—was labeled by Scully as "elitist" and "fascist."

This building, which has worn well over the past forty years, made a superficially easy target for critics with populist theories to sell. Monumental in feel, although a mere thirteen stories high, it presents a one-story facade on Forty-Second Street—very "fascistic." Looking beyond the clear glass surface, however, we see a thirteen-story, landscaped garden that is a visual amenity to the street and sidewalk, a lush interior landscape that was (in those pre-terrorism days of 1968) entirely open to the public. People could enter, walk through, or sit for a while, enjoying a breather—literally—from the traffic, dust, and noise of the bustling city. It was a genuinely populist piece of urbanism, much more so than the pandering,

[†]/ See Nicolai Ouroussoff, "Turning a Rearview Mirror on Kevin Roche," *New York Times*, February 22, 2011, www.nytimes.com/2011/02/23/arts/design/23roche.html.

tongue-in-cheek kitsch of then more critically celebrated works such as Charles Moore's Piazza d'Italia in New Orleans. As a footnote, I should add that the Ford Foundation Garden was the first construction anywhere of a large-scale public atrium, one that inspired John Portman's more commercial Hyatt Hotel atria and many others of the decades to come.

In addition to their attack on the architecture, the critics intoned that we had to understand that this was the headquarters of the Ford Foundation, an "elitist" institution if ever there was one, flush with its billions in Ford stocks. But looking past the surface again, we learn that this foundation was dedicated to promoting better education throughout the world by building schools, often in poor and developing countries, and financing them and their programs to fit local needs. No expensive art. No operas. No exclusive private schools. At the end of each year, the foundation was required by law to spend all its earnings, and this foundation's self-appointed mission was public education. Elitist indeed.

What the critics really hated, but didn't have the honesty to say, was the building's style. It didn't conform to the fashionable collage style of the day, with its ironic historical allusions, its vaguely surreal pastiche of contrasting parts. It was too old-fashioned, too modernist. Actually, what Kevin Roche had created in this building was a new, humanized modernism, richer in materials and form, and infused with innovations. These included the garden, interior climate control, and efficient integration of mechanical, structural, and architectural systems. It was a building for a rich institution, no doubt, but many of its features had the potential to be applied anywhere. In truth, the critics resented its brusque elegance and beauty at the very moment they wanted to celebrate postmodernism's self-conscious ugliness. A glance back at the most praised works of the 1970s and 80s, will, I believe, confirm this assessment.

There is much more to be said about the Ford Foundation Building that I hope will emerge from the present reappraisal of this and other early works of Kevin Roche and John Dinkeloo. In closing, I'll simply add a note about their Oakland Museum project, designed and built at about the same time as the Ford Foundation Building. With its galleries slid beneath, and opening onto, gently cascading landscaped terraces, Roche's idea of the public garden in the city was taken fully into the open. Here is humanistic modernism at its most vibrant, a typology that was also proto-green in its concern for bringing nature into the city's relentless artificiality.

March 4, 2011

Mystery of the Normal

Ross Racine's computer drawings of imaginary or perhaps ideal suburbs strike me as profound, in a trivial sort of way. The trivial part is the obviousness of their contrivance—they have a jokey, one-liner sort of message alluding to the absurdity of tract layouts that aim for interest even as they invoke the boredom of predictability. The profound part is their revelation of a human mystery to

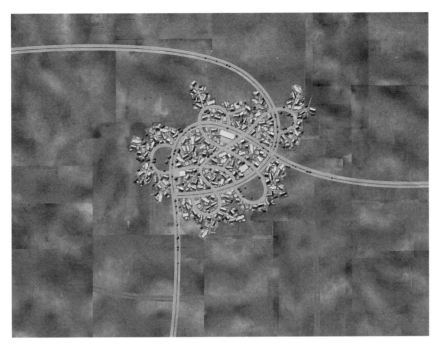

Ross Racine, *Hickoryglen Estates*, 2008

be found precisely in the obvious, where no one would expect to find it. I'll try to explain.

Artists and poets have struggled over the centuries to make works that startle us with their originality and, in effect, wake us up to the depth of human feelings in our own uniqueness and individuality. The artist's and the poet's originality connects with our own, invoking the feeling that to be human is to be unique. The artist is a mirror of ourselves, inspiring us not to be artists but individuals, shaping our lives much the same as an artist shapes a block of marble or a blank canvas.

But the raw fact is, most of us are not unique. Our lives, except for the smallest details, pretty much resemble the lives of others, particularly those in our social group, whatever it might be, defined by economic class, race, educational background, and much more. The truth is that we are intensely social creatures and our social context often overwhelms our individual traits and aspirations. This would seem to be the message imbedded in Racine's drawings of suburbs.

Still, the mystery of these diagrams (for that is what they are) is found precisely in what is missing from them: the machinations of human desire and hope, which varies—if ever so slightly—from person to person. Because each human creature is different from all others—think of DNA and each life's story—the ordinary and the normal are ultimately revealed to be paradigms that lead us away from the actuality of the human condition. Racine's drawings, through the extremity of their normality, bring us back. For this reason, they have a profoundly powerful, unforgettable effect. */

*/ See "Aerials," posted January 20, 2011, www.bauzeitgeist.blogspot .com/2011/01/aerials.html, for the context of a critical discussion.

Magic Marker

The 1962 science fiction film, *La Jetée*, by Chris Marker, ranks very near the top in films, inviting comparison with early classics such as *Nosferatu* and *Faust*, as well as later tours de force like *Beauty and the Beast* and *Alphaville*, even though it is only twenty-eight minutes long. Without question, it puts to shame contemporary films of its genre and most especially its remake, *Twelve Monkeys*, which had an all-star cast, a vastly bigger budget and the slickest special effects money can buy. How could this be, given *La Jetée*'s black-and-white format and the fact that it is made entirely (almost) from still photographs? Its actors are little known and we never hear them speak, instead hearing only music and a narrator's voice superimposed on the still images. The story is rather conventional, a tale from a post–World War III world, in which the hero must travel into the past and the future in search of energy sources and food for a ruined, radioactive city. And yes, there is a man–woman love interest that, in Romeo and Juliet style, is in the end tragically thwarted by fate. How did Marker turn such mundane ingredients into a masterpiece, a work of art of the highest order? The answer, I believe, is of value to artists in every medium, including the stubbornly resistant-to-art field of architecture.

Let me sum up the answer in a simple phrase: the power of evocation. For everything that is not shown, the filmmaker counts on the power of his viewers' imaginations. This approach depends on the discretion of the artist, his ability to know what to put in and what to leave out. The omissions are as important, or perhaps more important, than what is put in. Only the voids—what is not there—can be fully filled by our imaginations. It's an extremely delicate game of balance, one that varies from scene to scene, sequence to sequence. The film evokes a sense of continuity, a wholeness, that is not actually there. In this way, the viewers are active collaborators with the filmmaker and not merely passive spectators. The film is completed each time and only when it is viewed.

What makes this game work is the film's verisimilitude, its accurate construction of a parallel with our actual experience. If we use architecture as an example, we begin by realizing that architecture is still, not itself moving, and thus lacks—in our perceptions at least—continuity. Walking through a building is much like the film, a sequence of still views that rely on a turn of the head to evoke movement. In that instant of turning we effectively perceive a blur at best, which our brains don't register, much as they don't register the background noise we live with. In this way turning our heads becomes a quick cut from one image to the next, much the same as the film. It is telling to note that Marker does not use dissolves. Rather, he stays close to the way we actually see, discontinuously.

So much for what is left out. What is left in *La Jetée* is a set of photographic images of characters and places that are visually striking but at the same time informal. Rather than aiming to be stand-alone works of art, the stills are like frames from a motion picture—a movie—that does not exist. This is another instance of incompletion, of making evocative voids to be filled by imagination, but something more. The stills, which stay on the screen for minutes, not seconds, invite us to go into each image in a way we cannot when watching a movie, discovering details and studying the actor's expressions, appearance, gestures, in depth. The effect is highly emotional, yet in a contemplative, even intellectual way. This paradoxical quality enhances the evocative power of *La Jetée*.

How might Marker's approach inform the plastic arts and especially architecture? It cannot be through the design of intentionally incomplete buildings—though every architect knows the excitement of seeing a building still in construction, or another that has slowly, gracefully become a ruin. This kind of self-conscious literalism is fit only for theme parks and B-movies. The *La Jetée* approach in architecture must be as abstract as architecture itself. So, the creation of spaces of the imagination can only be found, it would seem, in an architecture of fragments, loosely joined like neurons in the brain, separated by synapses that can only be bridged by an electrical charge of thought. The key to such an architecture would be the potency of its fragments and thus its capability to inspire leaps of imagination that join them into a whole within the mind. Exactly how such an architecture would appear to us we cannot know at present, as its emergence is still in the future.*/

*/ *La Jetée* can be seen in its entirety at several online sites.

April 26, 2011

Zvi Hecker's Sense of Place

Zvi Hecker and Rafi Segal, Palmach Museum of History, Tel Aviv, Israel, 2000

Most of Zvi Hecker's architecture achieves a rare combination of originality and modesty. Its originality is not in the introduction of novel forms, but rather in the ways it brings together already familiar forms in relationship to particular sites and programs. The modesty of his buildings is a result of this kind of originality and the social character it lends them: they read like distillations of some of a society's best ideas about the design of space, reinvented in ways that makes them new. In this sense, Hecker's is an ideal architecture, celebrating both the individual and the community of which he is a part, and realizing their mutual interdependence.

Not to harp on this point, but it seems to me that this is what architecture, at its best, is about. You find a similar quality in the work of Mies van der Rohe, though in his case he invented the forms that became the social norm. Also the work of Aldo van Eyck and Jacob Bakema. Architecture as an idea cannot be limited to one-off masterpieces but should create an inspiring fabric of spaces and ways of living, a tapestry of human invention and aspiration. It is possible to imagine a vibrant urban tapestry—a city—with many Zvi Hecker buildings, while it is not possible to imagine the same with the singular buildings of, say, Zaha Hadid.

The Palmach Museum of History in Tel Aviv, Israel, designed by Hecker in collaboration with Rafi Segal, offers an excellent example of exactly this. In 1998, Hecker wrote, "The Palmach Museum of History is essentially a landscape. It is a landscape of the dreams that have made Israel a reality. The form of this landscape is homage to the ideals that Palmach stood and fought for. They are also the invisible foundations that carry the load built in fifty years of Israel's independence."

Typically, Hecker invokes an ideal of social meaning, inferring the way—creating a landscape—architecture can bring it palpably into reality. Constructed of common local stone, tile, and far-from-perfect poured-in-place concrete, the museum offers us dynamic forms and roughly textured spaces appropriate to a history of struggle and conflict, and to a victory of hope over despair.

May 1, 2011

Slums: To the Stars

A lot of attention is being paid to squatters taking over an unfinished skyscraper in Caracas, Venezuela, and rightly so.[*] It is both a morality tale from which we can draw many harsh lessons about our contemporary global society and a prophesy of the future. Surely, with vacant land running out in the vast cities to which migrants from rural areas are now flocking by the millions and in every part of the world, it is inevitable that slums will occupy abandoned, unfinished, or unleased skyscrapers.

The harshest lesson of this phenomenon is that slums are radically out of the control of governments and private institutions, yet we have no choice but to look to these institutions to treat the existence and the effects of this human scourge. Without some measure of controlling or at least slowing the spread of poverty and slums, it is conceivable that in the next few decades they will begin to overwhelm organized society and eventually push it to the brink of a new Dark Age. In such an age, it will not only be public services that

[*] See Jesús Fuenmayor, "The Tower of David," *Domus* (April 28, 2011), www.domusweb.it/en/architecture /the-tower-of-david/.

will begin to collapse from overuse, much of it illegal, but also social systems of every kind, from education to art. The financial burden of paying for the problems created by a vast population that pays no taxes will make many of civilized society's essential activities unsustainable.

This is a grim and frightening prospect indeed and one that is already beginning to happen. The takeover of the Caracas skyscraper is not just an oddity. Rather, it is a first drop of rain in a coming storm caused when the global financial system falters, even a little, and a financier-developer must abandon a project for lack of funds. A crack has opened up and it is immediately filled by people desperate to find shelter and establish a community, people who have every right to both but have been excluded from those provided by established society. These people have no choice but look for cracks in the social edifice and, when they find them, move quickly and decisively. As mainstream society falters more under the increasing weight of the impoverished and excluded, more cracks will appear and be filled. It will be an incremental process, but inexorable. Unless, that is, the powers that be in our present society begin to address the root causes of poverty.

Another lesson to be learned from the Caracas story is that all those who have been hoping for a social revolution to emerge from the dispossessed squatters and slum dwellers—the poor—had better think again. What these people want is not a new, egalitarian society founded on ideals of social justice, but only what most others already have—a consumer society with all the bells and whistles and toys. Clearly, the Caracas tower is not a breeding ground for radical social change. It is an unintended parody of the society that created the squatters' dire situation to begin with.

May 8, 2011

Drawings, Stories 2[*/]

The engineer explained it to me this way: "When we fully understood, at the end of the century, that building solid buildings was inherently unsustainable—due to the laws of thermodynamics as well as factors such as the quality of materials, details of joining them together, and other aspects of design—the push was on to find an entirely new way to construct buildings. This at first sounded to everyone like something impossible. What about all those thousands of years of architectural history and culture? You can't just push them aside and install some 'new way' in their place.

"But the fact is, we didn't have any choice. The planet was becoming unlivable at a much faster rate than anyone had predicted or imagined was possible. That was the time when the 'exponents' in ecology were discovered. Climate change, air and water pollution, melting of the ice caps and rising of the sea levels, as well as ozone layer depletion that exposed all living things to dangerous levels of cosmic-ray bombardment, and the destruction of

[*/] This is the first in a series of three posts presenting drawings and stories behind them. [All are included in this volume.]

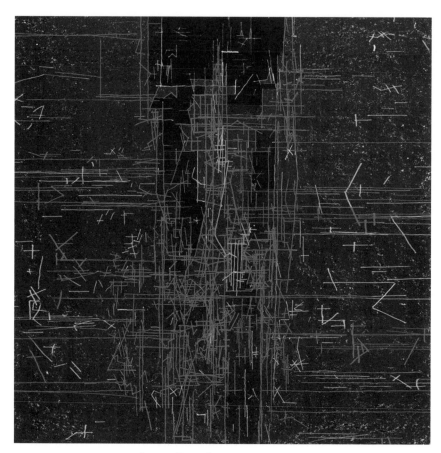

From *100 Towers Project, 11A-SQ-3*, 2007–11

agriculture were not linear processes as had long been thought, taking centuries to become critical. Instead they were accelerating exponentially, which we finally understood as the result of feedback mechanisms operating deep within interdependent ecosystems. Anyway, the search for new ways of doing many things, including the construction of buildings, was put on an emergency basis. And naturally—or luckily, depending on the level of your faith in human ingenuity—new ways were found.

"It is true that the existence of human beings—eleven billion of them—is not essential to the well-being of the planet. Indeed, quite the opposite, when we own up to the human causes of the planet's life-threatening problems. Still, people made up their minds to stay on and conduct their lives pretty much as they always had, with some serious behavior modifications. A new way of constructing buildings, for one, was discovered, or invented, within a few years. Within a few more years, it had all but replaced the long-held traditions of making solid buildings.

"The key was not the discovery of some entirely new principle, but rather the radical reinterpretation of a long-known one: the equivalency of matter and energy. What Albert Einstein had formulated so precisely in the early twentieth century, the science consortiums in the early part of this century reformulated in terms of free-energy forms. The most important of these for constructing buildings was not the field, but the vector, based on a kind of string theory of electromagnetism that binds primarily visible light particles in a continuously regenerative way. A building built of these vectors in effect recreates itself nanosecond to nanosecond, working with and against other particles (and their respective forces, such as gravitons and gravity) as the Law of Continuity requires. In short, a building's enclosing surfaces are constructed of light, an infinitely renewable resource that is *simultaneously* matter and energy. As it turned out, the technology for constructing in this new way was fairly simple, though it developed rather slowly from massive, unsustainable machines to the compact ones used today, which are made using much the same methods of construction as they enable."

May 10, 2011

Drawings, Stories 3

The cognitive scientist explained it to me this way: "For a few thousand years, architecture had been the conscious communication of a few important ideas within a particular human community. Chief among these ideas was *stability*. People considered their existence as fragile within a natural world that was basically hostile to them. In order to survive and, beyond that, to flourish on the planet, people had to struggle against the effects of nature, one of which was their own inevitable mortality that most often came about as a result of 'natural causes.'

"The cognitive processes that produced these ideas have their roots in the emergence of the human brain and its own self-reflectivity, which occurred millions of years earlier than the invention of architecture and indeed human society and the very idea of individuality. The neural structure of the human brain evolved differently from that of the animal brain, becoming larger and more complex. The brain's complexity led to the invention of diverse defenses, one of which was architecture, against natural forces and their effects. Architecture—the conception of enclosed spaces for living—made possible a balance between human fragility and natural hostility, a stability that encouraged and assured the establishment of both human society and individuality.

"The structure of the human brain is the key to understanding the evolution of the human mode of existence. It is crucial, as we learned in the twentieth century, that the human brain is two-tiered. It is, like all brains, comprised of neural nets that function according to principles of electromagnetism—neurons processing electrons. The nets are biological computers computing what we broadly call 'thoughts.' On the first tier, the human brain computes rules of behavior and, on the second tier, rules of the rules. The latter enable us to change our behavior as our changing circumstances require, making us adaptable—our supremely and particularly human trait. This means that we can change ourselves as well as change our environment, say, through making buildings.

From *100 Towers Project*, 1C-SQ-1, 2007–11

"When the severe environmental crisis struck our planet at the end of the last century, it became urgently necessary to change not only our behavior, but also the rules by which we govern our behavior. In short, we had to engage in second-tier, or second-order, thinking. It was only by doing this that we as individuals and as a global community were able to break out of our old, dysfunctional ways of thinking and living and invent, for example, new modes of constructing buildings. It was equally important that we also change our ways of living in them. Indeed, it would make no sense to build new kinds of buildings if we were unable to adapt ourselves to them. This had to happen on an individual level and not only a societal level, and within a generation or two at most.

"Was it coincidence that the new way of building mirrored, in effect, the neural structure of the human brain by creating a continually regenerating network form that resembles the structures of both matter and energy? Or, could it be a sign that attitudes toward nature are now less defensive than they were and more conciliatory? Debate continues on these questions up to the present moment, no doubt because the process of invention left little time for philosophical considerations. However, it seems certain that changes to the neural structure of the brain will result in a few generations. Our idea of what is human will necessarily evolve."

Slow Manifesto

Ai Weiwei Is Released!

The terms of Ai's release are stringent, but the important thing is that he is free. We should celebrate that, whatever the terms, and hope the best for his future.*/33

*/ See Edward Wong, "Dissident Chinese Artist Is Released," *New York Times,* June 22, 2011, www .nytimes.com/2011/06/23/world /asia/23artist.html.

Drawings, Stories 4

This is what the urban dweller said to me: "Sure, the new ways of building created new kinds of cities. Instead of streets and sidewalks to get around, we were forced to move endlessly in three dimensions to get from building to building, from one part of the city to the next. For most of us it was not a better way of living, just different, uncomfortably different. The city slowly became what they called a 'network,' something like a complicated organization chart, but built in real space. That's not entirely accurate, because organization charts usually have the most important places clearly marked, if you know what I mean, and less important spaces related to them, so there is some kind of order to guide you where to go, or where it was important to be, or at least how to find your way home—'I live three blocks north of the Capitol Building,' or, 'You can find me at the end of Harmony Street,' and things like that.

"The new city had no order like a grid, and it didn't help that buildings would change faster than in the old days. There are parts of the city built in the old ways, from materials, not energy, so we have been able to go there over the years and see them slowly decay in the rain, wind, and sunlight. We see the old signposts, with street and building names, and they only remind us of a world we lost, or was lost for us by the great minds that engineered the new ways of building.

"They say that it was necessary to save the planet from us, and to save us from what pop poets are calling 'the planet's revenge.' The great minds tell us that it's all for the better. Living in a network rather than a neighborhood will make us, eventually, smarter, more independent, more secure. They say that the old ways made us dependent on the people in charge of everything—the politicians and CEO's, the bosses. Now we've been liberated, and we're free to shape our own worlds, not just as fantasy but also as reality.

"The only problem is that you're not really free if you have to do something. And the other problem is that we all have to live together. Because there are no supervisors to tell us how to bring our fantasies together and shape a reality, we have to spend most of our time and energy talking—excuse me, networking—with others about how to do it. Yes, I know about the newest

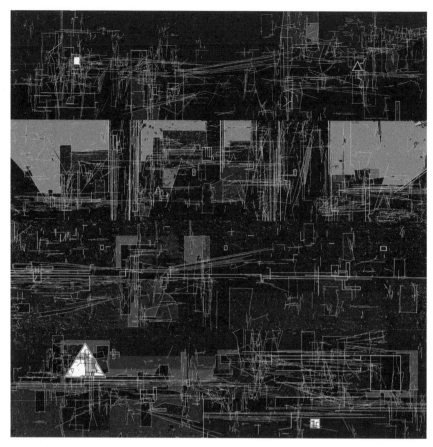

From *4SIMLANDscapes*, 2010

negotiation machines and how to use them, and about the architects who translate their results into the actual spaces of the city, my house for example. But it's
very difficult and demanding. They say the next generation will find it all very
easy and natural, but there are times when I wish I could say 'I live at the end of
Harmony Street,' or had a boss at my work to tell me what to do. But the streets
and the bosses, which were somehow linked, are long gone."

June 25, 2011

RIEA: The Backstory

Heinz von Foerster once told me, "You are an epistemologist." His opinion, in
this case and others, meant a lot to me. On the other hand, I wasn't sure what
an epistemologist was. I did know that it was someone interested in knowledge
and the nature of knowledge. What is knowledge? How do we know it or anything else? These are the questions an epistemologist asks. But, what good are
the answers? How do we know the answers are true? More questions for the
epistemologist.

It seems that the answers form a kind of circular riddle: I know because I know; I think, therefore I am. Oh, yes, René Descartes and all those long-ago ponderers who wanted to understand understanding and place the human being squarely at the center of the world-labyrinth. Theseus was not an epistemologist, because Ariadne gave him the answer to the problem he had to solve—how to escape from the labyrinth, that is, how to solve its spatial riddle. Ariadne was an epistemologist, because she figured out the *method* of understanding how to escape from Minos's diabolical trap.

The first conference of RIEA, Oneonta, New York, 1988. Seated around the table, counterclockwise from left rear: Gordon Gilbert, Michael Webb, Hani Rashid, Michael Sorkin, Lebbeus Woods, Ken Kaplan, Ted Krueger, Peter Cook, and Neil Denari

Epistemologists are concerned not only with the answers to a question, but also with how you get to the answers and, once there, how you know they are true. We learn little from a raw answer to a given problem, because every problem is different in its details. But we learn much from the method of finding an answer, because it anticipates variables in similar problems.

Nearly twenty-three years ago, when Olive Brown and I founded the Research Institute for Experimental Architecture (RIEA), we had foremost in mind an epistemological approach to architecture. Architecture is, before anything else, a field of knowledge. Olive, a psychologist, and I were married at the time, and she had a strong commitment to the idea of experimental architecture. She was instrumental in fund-raising and organizing the institute's events.

The founding event was a two-day meeting of experimental architects in upstate Oneonta, New York. We rented a cottage and a barn on an old rural estate and thought it perfect as the place for what later came to be called the first conference of RIEA. Motels in the local villages provided shelter for a select few invited architects coming from New York, Los Angeles, London— architects who had not built much if anything, but who had made groundbreaking conceptual projects.

The idea of the meeting was to sort out what experimental architecture might be. Were their ideas we had in common? Did we share any principles that guided the topics of our experimental projects? Did it make sense to somehow collaborate, or was it better if we remained solo workers, pursuing our separate, idiosyncratic paths? And of course, did it make sense to establish an institute of experimental architecture? Would institutionalizing the idea of experimentation stiffen or even kill the free spirit considered necessary for experimenting?

In science, there are many institutes for research and experimentation. If the development of science were left up to lone and isolated individuals, it would not get very far. Today, in science, there are still solo innovators, but their ideas must be taken up and tested by others to be considered valid, true, and even useful. Scientists dedicated to exploration know that they need each other and must share information about concepts and techniques with one another, often through the auspices of institutes.

At this stage, architects do not. They model themselves on the traditional figure of the artist as an inspired loner. The main task of the artist is to produce uniquely original, inimitable masterpieces, not contributions to a body of knowledge. Even when the gifted artist is backed up by a production team, the goal is the same. The founding idea of RIEA was to challenge that model, to create a collaborative spirit that could advance architecture by together meeting many challenges that could not be met by inspired loners.

RIEA still exists.*/ Olive Brown and I are no longer married, or active in it. The founding questions still remain, largely unanswered. The challenges are being addressed by a new generation of highly dedicated, collaborating architects. Still, they remain largely unmet. It was a much more difficult task than I ever imagined. Yet, the potential remains.

*/ See RIEA, www.riea.ch/.

June 28, 2011

Steven Holl's Horizontal Skyscraper

Steven Holl and I have been close friends for many years, and he commissioned me to design the Light Pavilion in his mixed-use project, Raffles City, in Chengdu, China./34 I mention this in the spirit of full disclosure. Still, I do not believe these factors have clouded my critical judgment about Holl's Vanke Center project in Shenzhen, China, though you have to decide this for yourselves. In past posts I have not hesitated to express my critical judgments of several prominent architects with whom I've been close for many years in quite different ways than those written below. †/

As he did with his Linked Hybrid towers in Beijing, Steven Holl—in his Shenzhen Horizontal Skyscraper—shows that he is the master of the large-scale, multi-use building. These projects are new building types, as their metaphoric titles proclaim, in sharp and challenging contrast to the usual developer typologies. In Shenzhen, the large buildings hover above what is to be a large, open garden, freeing—to a remarkable degree—the ground plane for public use. This concern for making open space for people to enjoy is a primary goal of Holl's urban designs and sets them apart. The architectural forms are straightforward, even modest by today's flashy standards, but their presence on the landscape is extraordinary. In Shenzhen, it took some special engineering to make the long buildings span between a small number of vertical cores, creating a new type of public

†/ The following commentary is an expanded version of one that appeared in a previous post, "Steven Holl in Shenzhen" (July 10, 2009; http://lebbeuswoods.wordpress.com/2009/07/10/steven-holl-in-shenzhen/) [omitted from this volume]. It attempts to give a summary historical background for the Horizontal Skyscraper project.

Steven Holl, Horizontal Skyscraper—Vanke Center, Shenzhen, China, 2009

space, but Holl's team achieved this, and within the developer's budget. Now completed, this project will hopefully become a model for others—not to be literally copied, but to show the decisive effect imagination and innovation can have. In a world where the number of large-scale commercial projects is certain to increase, and steadily, it offers inspiration and hope that architecture can make a difference after all.

The architect Henri Ciriani once remarked that modern architecture allowed people, for the first time in history, to not only walk around, on, and through buildings, but under them. Lighter building materials and stronger structural systems—but most all a desire to be free of gravity, or rather to overcome it—made the levitation of large building masses possible and inevitable. The advent of airplanes—heavier-than-air inhabitations—was a great stimulus to human imagination. It not only showed that buildings could fly—in a particular sense—but also created a new concept of space, one fully three dimensional, in which the ideas of over, on, and under gained a new significance. It was the hubris of modernism to believe that man had finally conquered nature. Overcoming gravity was the final, decisive battle to be won. El Lissitzky's horizontal skyscrapers led the way in architecture. Le Corbusier's buildings lifted high on columns freed the ground for human use and also liberated it from the domination of gravity. Over the decades since these revolutionary works, many buildings have been designed and built to be inhabited raised masses, but it was not until the design and construction of Holl's Shenzhen project that the concept has been realized with the boldness and idealism envisioned by early modernists.

The Horizontal Skyscraper project does not emerge from Holl's knowledge of history or a desire to continue the modernist project, as some architects have proclaimed for their work, but from his own deep interest in phenomenology and the nature of human experience. His published books are filled with references to and speculations on light, density, fluidity, gravity, and many other phenomena and their impact on human perception, cognition, and, ultimately, the design of architecture as a primary source of human experience. His thoughts and conclusions have taken their most potent form in his projects. The earliest precursor to the Horizontal Skyscraper is the Gymnasium Bridge in New York, designed in the late 1970s. The building is bridge-like only in its spanning of the Harlem River; it is significant not as a means of transit but rather for its cultural connection between the South Bronx and Manhattan through the activities and events it houses. Ten years later, Holl designed a competition-winning addition to the American Library in Berlin with a portion of the building raised high on piloti and connected to other portions by a translucent, inhabited bridge. Most important, though, was his design for the Retaining Bar buildings in his Phoenix Edge of the City project, in which slender vertical housing blocks turn sharply horizontal, creating in effect a porous urban wall within which public space is more "under" than "on." These explorations reach their culmination in the Shenzhen Horizontal Skyscraper. With its realization, the hopeful prospect of new kinds of urban space and experience has been fully opened.*/

*/ Nicolai Ouroussoff has written a review of the Horizontal Skyscraper project in the *New York Times*. It addresses its urban and cultural, as well as its architectural, aspects and is, in my opinion, well worth reading. See Nicolai Ouroussoff, "Turning Design on Its Side," *New York Times*, June 27, 2011, www.nytimes.com /2011/06/28/arts/design/steven-holls -design-for-the-vanke-center-in-china -review.html.

July 19, 2011

Wild Buildings

On the coasts circumventing the Mediterranean Sea, a type of construction has proliferated in the last thirty years or so that is usually referred to as "wild building." What is wild about it is not the buildings' designs, which are utterly conventional, but rather their lack of legal status in the towns and cities to which they are loosely attached.

Usually built in unplanned, shapeless clusters, they are like squatter communities in the same sense as slums anywhere, except they are not like typical slums. The first big and most noticeable difference is the materiality of the buildings; they are constructed of reinforced concrete with clay tile infill—very durable and permanent. The second difference is that the people who build and inhabit these structures are not poor, but rich enough to commission such sturdy construction. In fact, they are most often people who have moved from rural areas, where they lived quite well as farmers, often benefiting from government subsidies as well as the profitability of their crops and livestock.

What makes the comparison with slums at all appropriate is that, when the new settlers migrate with their families to the city, they do so for the same reasons as all slum dwellers: to improve their economic prospects. In these cases, though, they aren't looking for low-pay factory or service jobs. They have enough money to open profitable businesses that they plan to keep in their families for generations.

Another point of comparison is that they build on land not legally zoned by the city for residential construction, but only for agricultural purposes. When they begin to build, inspectors and zoning officials tell the owners that they cannot continue, and levy fines. Once paid, the construction continues.

Yet another similarity with slums everywhere is that these wild communities are not provided any services—electricity, water, sanitation—by the city. To obtain these, the owner-residents have to find ways to generate their own or, more commonly, they simply tap into nearby city services and illegally take what they need. Once again, fines are levied and paid.

"Family" is the keyword in these "wild" communities. The buildings are constructed one floor at a time. The founding generation of a family builds the first floor of the house, extending the concrete columns, with the reinforcing bars, above, ready to receive the next floor. The eldest son or daughter of the family will add this next floor, when he or she marries and founds the next generation. The structure of the house is engineered (in most cases by ad hoc methods) to receive several floors over the coming generations.

This is a city, or at least a community, that grows from the inside out, according to rules that are informal at best. Without glamorizing it, we might say it is an architecture, and an urbanism, setting an example of ad hoc growth informing a future sure to be governed by uncertainty.

July 21, 2011

Blooms(birth)day Bash

It's rare that I will post something that seems more appropriate for the gossip pages of a local tabloid, but the Blooms(birth)day party held in our house on June 16 will be the exception. Not only was it a fun party, but also the honorees—Leopold Bloom, Diane Lewis, and I—lent a unique atmosphere to the event. Bloom, the Joycean character who lived a lifetime in a single day—June 16—reinventing not only Dublin but also, perhaps, the world thereafter, was commemorated by our guests'

At the bar, left to right: Steven Holl, Aleksandra Wagner, Chris Mann, and Lebbeus Woods; in the background: Penny Bittone

celebratory mood, as well as readings by the gifted actor, Penny Bittone. Penny moved unannounced from room to room, taking devotees of *Ulysses* with him. Diane, whose birthday it was, was surrounded by friends and was in top form. I, whose birthday it wasn't (but was being belatedly noted) enjoyed Lebanese food and took in the very animated landscape, a hermit briefly out of his lair.

My wife Aleksandra and I are party-givers, it is true, and this was one of our best. For this reason I thought I'd share it with you.

Lauretta Vinciarelli (1943–2011)

Lauretta Vinciarelli, *Per Sal e Ron*, 1993

Lauretta Vinciarelli has died, and her passing is a serious body blow to architecture. We have lost not only one of our most rousing architectural draftsmen (sic) but also one of the rare visionaries of architectural space. Her exquisite watercolor paintings have presented to us new spaces of the almost–familiar—for example, several series of what might be causeways or catacombs that strike us as monuments of our time more convincing than the slick museums and corporate edifices that our most prominent architects favor. From a large body of work embracing many themes, it is these that I focus on here.

Vinciarelli, a daughter of Rome's environs, never lost her belief in classical order and beauty, yet at the same time had the social conscience of Rome's leftist perspectives, which elevated everyday life to a higher level of architecture and art. The largely hidden spaces she designed and painted so masterfully, often flooded with the water of uncontrolled or intentional flows, speak of unconscious worlds, devoid of people yet clearly intended for them, spaces we might guess for those who somehow sustain an unseen world beyond. They evoke the levels of emotion and thought that support a type of civil life founded on precise and orderly infrastructure.

For all their calm and studied precision, Vinciarelli's spaces are disquieting. The harmony and grace of their austere forms and composition speak of self–possession and control, but also of melancholy. These are utopias, we might fear, too perfect for us mere mortals to endure and are thus lonely places. In her paintings, we never step back to see an overall picture, but are always within, remaining free to hope that her world of beauty and harmonious order might, in different ways, extend beyond the limits of the frame to a wider constructed landscape. Vinciarelli gives us a spatial and, indeed, an ethical foundation for such a world. Hers is an architecture of insinuation and suggestion. The dark side of her vision is not in shadows and the like, but rather in the possibility, even the likelihood, that her ideals—and perhaps all ideals—will be thwarted by the enemies of beauty or will simply remain unfulfilled. This brings us directly to the political issues raised by her work.

The spaces she has designed and rendered do not seem to be the work of a single architect, though they are. Instead, they have the character of collective constructions, the products of a culture, even an entire civilization. In them we cannot find the self-aggrandizing, egoistic insistence on a signature style that separates their architect from others, but rather a profound modesty such as we find in medieval Italian towns built by anonymous craftsmen and artists. Or, we might say, in a socialist dream of free collaboration between the most dedicated and gifted of architects and builders working unselfishly together. Whether Vinciarelli ever wrote or spoke about her work in these or similar terms, I cannot say. But the collective character of her designs is nevertheless one of their most striking features.

This is not so with the watercolor paintings themselves—they are only hers. Like all great draftsmen (sic again, because I reject neutered terms like "draftspersons" or, even more, "draftswomen," because it separates her from the great history of architectural drawing that has been made, like it or not, mostly by men), Vinciarelli invented her own techniques. This is important to recognize and consider because the way she draws is inseparable from what she draws. The texture and reflectivity of surfaces, the nuanced chiaroscuro, and especially the color that animates the spaces were painstakingly achieved by applying gossamer layers of pigment until the desired densities and luminosity were achieved. Though this technique was used by the "old masters," her application of it to watercolor painting is unique. There was no way to erase or undo what had been laid down. She could only go forward, with absolute commitment to her vision. This is what she did in her architecture, her paintings, and her life. */

*/ The image here is taken from an excellent monograph on Lauretta Vinciarelli's work. See Brooke Hodge, ed., *Not Architecture but Evidence that It Exists: Lauretta Vinciarelli: Watercolors* (New York: Princeton Architectural Press, 1998). We can only hope that more complete editions of her work will emerge in the future.

August 17, 2011

Real Paper Architecture

When rummaging though her extensive library, Aleksandra Wagner discovered a pattern book of the old city of Prague. Similar to a dressmaker's pattern book, it is meant to be cut up, very precisely, and assembled into a three-dimensional

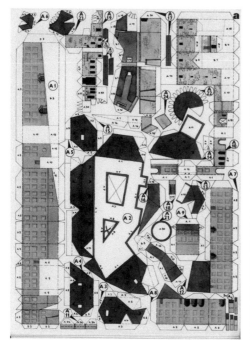

Pages from Pavel Blecha and Richard Vyškovský, *Prague Castle: Paper Models*, 1975

paper model. Designed and printed in the early 1970s in Czechoslovakia, it is remarkable in several ways:

First: in that pre-computer era, all measurements of the actual architecture had to be made by hand—a formidable task in itself.

Second: the patterns of the scale buildings had to be calculated and drawn by hand. In engineering school, these patterns are called "developments" and must take into account the actual dimensions of walls, roofs, and all other architectural surfaces, and therefore are not simply orthographic projections of plans and elevations of the buildings.

Third: the several pages of written instructions on the model's assembly would seem to have been as difficult to compose as they will be to follow.

Fourth: in that pre-laser-cutting era, the authors had a very high regard for a model maker's manual skills, not to mention surplus of time and determination.

It is also worth mentioning that the book's pattern pages have the visual allure of abstract paintings, enhanced by the knowledge that the shapes were arranged not for their composition but for efficient use of the paper they are printed on. Perhaps they can be thought of as "functional" art. If so, then they have more relationship to architecture than the representations that can be made from them.

Slow Manifesto

September 11, 2001–2011

WE SAW IT COMING: For anyone who saw the burning twin towers in Sarajevo, which were attacked in the summer of 1992 by terrorists bent on undermining the morale of the people of that cosmopolitan city, the attacks on the twin towers of the World Trade Center in New York nine years later, with the same goals in mind, came as no great surprise. The fall of the Iron Curtain and the end of the Cold War had produced a new type of global struggle based not on vast armies clashing in the field, but on small-scale insurgencies attacking the centers of their enemies' power, disrupting them and thereby undermining their self-confidence and ability to dominate others. This new type of warfare was called "terrorism." Its main weapon is creating fear in the enemy, both government and ordinary citizens, leading not to armistices, treaties, and other official instruments of reconciliation between legally recognized states, but to de facto victories, in which the insurgents hope to win economic or political concessions that strengthen them in their own domain or globally, in the sense that they are ever more feared and hence ever more powerful and influential.

One significant new feature of this new type of conflict is that opposing sides are not drawn along sociopolitical lines—one communist and one capitalist—as in the Cold War rivalry between two superpowers, but rather along religious ones. This is a throwback to the Middle Ages and not modern at all, except in terms of weaponry and techniques of command and control. The conflict now is primarily between Christians and Muslims. The attack on Sarajevo was carried out by a Christian insurgency against a Muslim majority. The attack on the World Trade Center in New York was carried out by a Muslim insurgency against a Christian majority. Both had the goal of degrading a way of life. Both attacks were attacks on the idea of the city itself.

On March 5, 1994, a conference was convened in the Great Hall of Cooper Union in New York City. It was titled "Sarajevo/New York: The City Under Siege." Many of the most astute observers and analysts of the ongoing attack on Sarajevo and its consequences for cities everywhere participated. The conference's aim was to make New Yorkers aware of not only the urgent needs of Sarajevans but also the possibility that "it could happen here." How many people left at the end of that day with the idea that New York City could be attacked I cannot say. But some of us saw it coming and many—if they understood at all what was happening an ocean away—should have.

A GREAT MIND IS A TERRIBLE THING TO WASTE: Fierce debates swirled around the World Trade Center site after its towers fell, focusing on how, or even if, the site should be rebuilt. Some of the most brilliant and creative architects of our time entered the debate, often with specific design proposals. Any number of these—if they had been used as a point of departure—could have turned tragedy into triumph by radically reforming the devastated site into a new kind of public urban space. The design scheme finally selected—by Daniel Libeskind, an architect of great renown for his evocative conceptual designs and the Jewish Museum in Berlin—was the least innovative of all, and the least demanding of politicians and developers, accounting, no doubt, for its digestibility. Amounting to nothing more than a conventional grouping of conventional skyscrapers, dominated by a so-called "Liberty Tower" 1,776 feet tall, it was meant to symbolize an American resilience in some way that was never entirely clear. A reminder of the Declaration of Independence of the United States from the British monarchy on July 4, 1776, seems oddly detached from the Al Qaeda attacks, the reasons for them, or any serious vision of what might be the best response—but it was hailed at the time by many as a brilliant idea.

In any event, even Libeskind's uninspiring proposal was eventually hijacked by politicians and developers, who handed it over to David Childs of Skidmore, Owings & Merrill (SOM), and he oversaw its further descent into an indifferent conventionality. The chance to create a great new work of architecture and public space—the best memorial to human courage and resilience in the face of terrible loss—had itself been lost.

NEW YORK, NEW YORK: It is often said that New York is a center of global culture. The only culture that it is truly the center of is the culture of buying and selling, and of someone, usually a wealthy elite, making money in the process. In New York, and increasingly elsewhere, the culture of profit is the one around which all other subcultures revolve. Of course, art and music and literature and dance all flourish in New York because there is the possibility to buy and sell them in one form or another—they make money. Without that money the cultures of beauty and inspiration would simply wither away, or so we are told. What we are not told by corporations and individual patrons, who assure us that capitalism is the great sponsor of the arts, is that only the arts that fit into the mainstream are bought and sold. The mainstream can tolerate and even requires a certain amount of naughty avant-garde artworks that shock, criticize, provoke, and attack corporate assumptions in order to claim legitimacy in historical terms. But there are precise limits to what can be done and promoted for profit, and they are tightly drawn. Any serious, unironic invocation of socialism will be ignored by the marketplace. Or any serious invocation of actual revolution, under the aegis of any ideology. Or any serious invocation of a future that does not include capitalism as its centerpiece. The list is long, but little discussed in public—that, too, it is avoided by artists and critics who adopted long ago a self-censoring caution lest they be considered terrorist sympathizers or otherwise unfit for the marketplace.

New York is a city with few innovative contemporary buildings. Famous names are trotted in for the occasional extra-marketable building, but none are invited to make ambitious urban proposals that could affect the future of the city and the way most people actually live. Most notably absent are world-famous American architects like Eric Owen Moss and Steven Holl, who lives in the city. Thom Mayne and his firm Morphosis have built a radical building for

Cooper Union, a progressive university that insists its students attend for free. The rest of the city is the product of real estate speculation, of profit and loss—the model that cities around the world seem eager to follow.

The message sent by New York, a focus of global attention on this September 11, is simple: *Business as usual.**/

*/ For publication of this article in another venue, see Lebbeus Woods, "We Saw it Coming," *Domus* (September 7, 2011), www.domusweb .it/en/architecture/2011/09/07/we -saw-it-coming.html.

September 13, 2011

Exuberant Space

Filip Dujardin, *Untitled*, from the series *Fictions*, 2007. This photomontage has been widely published on the Internet for some time, but never with commentary that addresses issues I mention here, important to contemporary discourse.

What at first glance seem like absurdist montages of buildings by photographer Filip Dujardin, good for amusement only, actually raise some important questions.†/ It doesn't take long to realize that these images are actually design "drawings," made with photographs, making architectural proposals that invite us to think seriously about them.

†/ See Filip Dujardin, www .filipdujardin.be.

The most obvious question that arises is about the buildings' unusual forms. What, might we imagine, is the purpose of the buildings that demands their highly sculptural forms, assembled from what are clearly parts of ordinary buildings? A clue is found in the last century's modernist architecture, whose new materials and structural systems had the capability of effectively floating and flying buildings, free of the gravity that for centuries had bound them so closely to the earth. Cantilevers and long spans were not only a conquest of natural forces but also a liberation of the human spirit from a servitude to them, putting human beings—through advanced technology—more fully on their own and more responsible for their own well-being. In this way, modern architecture had far-reaching ethical, even spiritual, consequences. But that wasn't the only reason structurally daring buildings were proposed and sometimes built—it was also for the sheer, playful fun of it and the exuberant enjoyment of space.

I don't imagine Dujardin's designs will have any weighty consequences. For one thing, they don't exemplify any new concepts. Rather, they are themselves consequences of principles that modernism introduced a century ago. They do, however, breathe some new life into those old ideas that many have pronounced dead. Looking at some of Steven Holl's later projects, such as the Horizontal Skyscraper and the Edge of the City project for Phoenix—as well as Dujardin's designs—it is clear that those old ideas are very much alive.[*]

So enjoy. Guilt free.

*/ See "Steven Holl's Horizontal Skyscraper" (June 28, 2011) [included in this volume] and "Visionary Architecture" (December 11, 2008; http://lebbeuswoods.wordpress .com/2008/12/11/visionary -architecture/) [omitted from this volume].

October 12, 2011

Corridor of Recollection

Corridor in the Heinz Architectural Center of the Carnegie Museum of Art, part of the exhibition *Lebbeus Woods: Experimental Architecture*, curated by Tracy Myers, Pittsburgh, 2004

The idea of the *Lebbeus Woods: Experimental Architecture* exhibition was not only to show a number of experimental projects, but also to make their installation an experiment by displaying two-dimensional images in a way that reforms an existing space. To this end, digital prints ten feet high and four to twenty feet long were mounted to rigid panels, placed at varying angles to the walls and each other, and supported by bent aluminum tubes. Together, these elements modulated the corridor space in ways that subtly interact with the illusory spaces of the mounted project images. A series of floor plates with etched keywords replaced the usual wall-mounted introductory text. The goal was to create an environment that not only proclaimed something new, but also fulfilled its promise, even in a modest way.

Exhibitions are temporary. The one shown here is long gone. The architecture (and I claim this installation for its domain, though many would disagree) of transience seems to me to speak of our contemporary ways of living more precisely and more poignantly than many a grand monument designed to enshrine the ideas of the permanent and enduring. It is not, though, a matter of either/or—the human world needs both. Still, little talent is devoted to the transient architecture, simply because it does not memorialize its architects. So be it.

A corridor links two perhaps very different spaces. It is in effect a space of transition between them. Transition. Transience. A pause. A place of reflection on what we are leaving and what we are coming to. These are the very essence of the exploratory, the speculative, and the experimental. */

*/ Note: The very fine booklet produced by the Carnegie Museum of Art for this exhibition is still available, but, because of its rarity, at an absurd price. It does not include documentation of the exhibition itself. See Tracy Myers, ed., *Lebbeus Woods: Experimental Architecture* (Pittsburgh: Carnegie Museum of Art, 2004).

November 28, 2011

Return of the Manifesto

First, a little story. In 1994, when I attended an architecture conference in Havana organized by the Museum of Applied Art (MAK) in Vienna, the director of the museum, Peter Noever, asked the participants to write their personal manifestos of architecture in order to shake up the discussions a bit. I was the only one who did. The others, including Thom Mayne, Eric Owen Moss, Carme Pinós, and Wolf D. Prix, ignored the request. It was only when Noever insisted that several of us got together to hammer out something over some mojitos. It was quickly obvious that there was little enthusiasm for manifestos, even under the influence, and when Prix started reciting the lyrics to Bob Dylan's "Desolation Row": "They're selling postcards of the hanging. They're painting the passports brown. The beauty parlor is filled with sailors. The circus is in town..." we knew the project was hopeless.

The assembled company at this conference, set in a fabled country that had run out of patience with ideological rhetoric, knew that the manifesto as a genre was dead. No one wanted manifestos. Nobody believed in them. So, what was their point? That was seventeen years ago.

After a long period of often frivolous form making and unprincipled egoism in architecture, which have played into the hands of the most venal interests of real estate developers and marketers, some architects are looking for more substantial ideas to serve, more meaningful goals to strive for, and the manifesto has come back. It is probably a temporary aberration, owing to an unsustainable idealism that lurks within statements of principle. But even their brief resurgence can help to regenerate—at least for a while—our beloved, beleaguered field.

Of half a dozen new manifesto compendia, the one that seems to have attracted the most critical attention is titled *Urban Future Manifestos*, collected and edited by—guess who?—Peter Noever, in collaboration with Kimberli Meyer.[*]/ Persistence, it seems, sometimes pays off.

[*]/ See John Southern, "Urban Future Manifestos" *Domus* (November 25, 2011), www.domusweb.it/en /reviews/2011/11/25/urban-future -manifestos.html [a review of Peter Noever and Kimberli Meyer, eds., *Urban Future Manifestos* (Ostfildern, Germany: Hatje Cantz Verlag, 2010)].

December 2, 2011

War and Architecture: The Sarajevo Window

Some twenty years go, I wrote, "Architecture and war are not incompatible. Architecture is war. War is architecture. I am at war with my time, with history, with all authority that resides in fixed and frightened forms. I am one of millions who do not fit in, who have no home, no family, no doctrine, no firm place to call my own, no known beginning or end, no 'sacred and primordial site.' I declare war on all icons and finalities, on all histories that would chain me with my own falseness, my own pitiful fears. I know only moments, and lifetimes that are as moments, and forms that appear with infinite strength, then 'melt into air.' I am an architect, a constructor of worlds, a sensualist who worships the flesh, the melody, a silhouette against the darkening sky. I cannot know your name. Nor can you know mine. Tomorrow, we begin together the construction of a city."

This manifesto was read aloud on the steps of the burned-out Olympic Museum in Sarajevo on November 26, 1993, in full view of Serbian snipers and artillery gunners. Happily, no fire rained down on the assembled audience, in which I was included among many others. Coming to the last line, one of the two gifted actor-readers objected, "Why wait until tomorrow?" Typical Sarajevan humor, candor, and bravado in the face of overwhelming odds.

Over the two decades since this manifesto was written, I have had much time to consider the words I wrote and what I meant by them. At that time, I was responding to an urgent situation in Sarajevo, Bosnia—a city under a sustained terrorist attack that, in the West, was considered a siege, as though it were part of a normal war, which it was not. Snipers had turned streets into lethal shooting galleries and artillery gunners had turned ordinary buildings where people worked and lived into incendiary death traps. It was clear that architecture was part of the problem—the killing of thousands of innocent men, women, and children—and I felt strongly that as long as the attacks continued (it turned out they continued for more than three years) architecture also had to be part of the solution.

Without the help of architects, people had built temporary walls as shields against snipers and thrown up all sorts of improvised repairs to their homes and workplaces. I reasoned that these makeshift structures, though more or less effective for their purposes, created a degraded environment, which was exactly the goal of the terrorists. To survive, and to frustrate the enemies of their refined culture, people need a sense of order in their world, one that is consciously created or designed. Sarajevans nobly showed this need by the way they dressed, in spite of the lack of water, heat, or lighting, somehow always in clean, pressed clothing, the women elegantly coifed and made up, incongruously strolling in the parts of the city center that were screened from snipers if not from mortars and cannons in the hills above, like players from an Alain Resnais film. Inspired by this and a dash of Michelangelo's designs for the fortifications of Florence, I set out to consider how to repair damaged houses and offices in ways that embodied the élan of their inhabitants, as well as kept out the rain, snow, and cold. These were extremely modest designs, made from scavenged metal, wood, and even cardboard.

One principle I adopted in the beginning was that such found materials would be reshaped, piece by piece. More than anything, I wanted this small-scale architecture to avoid becoming junk sculpture, or a collage of detritus. Intention is important, even at the smallest scale, and the intention in Sarajevo was to consciously reshape its world, turning ruins and battered remnants into a new kind of architecture, a uniquely *Sarajevan* architecture, something of which the city's people could be proud. The goal was also to establish some basic rules of reconstruction, keeping in mind the enormous task of rebuilding the damaged city that would begin when the terrorists were defeated and people could turn their energy to building the new city and a new way of civic life.

December 15, 2011

War and Architecture: Three Principles[*]

I am revisiting the work I did some fifteen years ago for an unhappy reason. Originally intended to address the destruction of buildings in Sarajevo, Bosnia—which I and many others hoped would prove to be an isolated catastrophe—it has instead turned out to be only the beginning of a new trend resulting from globalization:

[*] Note to the readers: I wish to apologize for what must seem a blatant self-promotion in this post, but it is not possible to separate the personal from the conceptual, because the two stories are here so fully intertwined. As I said in an earlier post ["War and Architecture: The Sarajevo Window" (December 2, 2011)], the ideas developed in this work have such currency in the present that, I believe, it is a necessary risk to take. I can only ask for the readers' generous forbearance.

Sarajevo, from *War and Architecture*, 1993. A typical Sarajevo residential block, badly damaged in places, reconstructed with new types of spaces for residents' use. The principle here is that reconstruction integrates people's experiences of the destruction into needed social changes, as well as architectural ones.

a proliferation of regional, often insurgent-driven wars that have resulted in the piece-by-piece destruction of cities and the killing of their inhabitants that characterized the torturous three-year attack on Sarajevo.*/

In going over what I wrote about this work at the time—in 1993—I find it inadequate in its explanation of what inspired the designs, drawings, and models and what I hoped to achieve by making them. No wonder, I say in hindsight, that the work was accused of "aestheticizing violence" and merely being exploitative of a tragic human condition. I failed to put it in the broader human context that it needed to be understood as an architectural proposal serving rational and needed purposes. I hope to correct—to the extent I can here—this failure.

Because of my work concerned with the Sarajevo crisis long ago, people have often asked what I was working on for Baghdad, or Kabul, or Tripoli, or a growing list of cities that have shared its fate. My answer is always the same: *nothing*. While each is different, the destruction they have suffered is so similar to that suffered by Sarajevo that the principles I established there apply as well to the more recent catastrophes. This is a crucial point. My "war and architecture" work was not aimed at proposing the reconstruction of particular buildings—that should be the work of local architects—but at deriving guiding principles. The specific buildings I addressed with my designs were meant as demonstrations of how these principles might work in particular cases, rather than as actual building proposals. Again, I strongly believe that reconstructions should be designed by local architects who understand the local conditions far, far better than I ever could. I did and still do feel, equally strongly, that I and other "conceptualists" can make a contribution to reconstruction

*/ For more on the torturous three-year attack on Sarajevo, see "September 11, 2001–2011" (September 8, 2011).

on the level of *principle*, because we can more readily have a broader view, not having directly suffered the trauma of our city's destruction and its lingering emotional and intellectual effects.

So, to the principles. Before attempting to address the reconstruction prospects forced upon us by the destruction of Sarajevo, I studied the history of modern cities attacked in World War II. There is a massive literature on this heart-wrenching but crucial moment in human history. However, there is a small literature on the rebuilding of the damaged cities—many of which were severely damaged—and even less about the actual concepts that guided their reconstruction. From my studies, I can see only two guiding principles shared by the majority of postwar reconstruction projects.

The first principle: restore what has been lost to its prewar condition. The idea is to restore "normalcy," where the normal is the way of living lost as a result of the war. The idea considers the war as only an interruption of an ongoing flow of the normal.

The second principle: demolish the damaged and destroyed buildings and build something entirely new. This "new" could be something radically different from what existed before, or only an updated version of the lost prewar normal. Its application is very expensive financially, at the least.

Both of these concepts reflect the desires of most city inhabitants to "get back to normal" and forget the trauma they suffered as a result of the violence and destruction. Yet, both concepts ignore the effects of the war and destruction on the people who suffered through them—not only the personal psychological effects, but also those forcing changes to people's social, political, and economic relationships. Before the war, Sarajevo was the capital of Bosnia and Herzegovina, one of the states in the Socialist Federal Republic of Yugoslavia. After the war, it was the capital of an independent country and no longer socialist. The impact of this change alone on people's everyday lives has been enormous, and particularly so in the ways they perceive each other and themselves. In this sense, it is not possible to get back to normal. The prewar normal no longer exists, having been irrevocably destroyed. Still, this does not mean that many—even most—people will not desire to do so. In such a society, wise leaders are needed to persuade people that something new must be created—a new normal that modifies or in some ways replaces the lost one, and, further, that it can only be created with their consent and creative participation. In effect, a new principle of reconstruction needs to be established.

We'll call it the third principle: the postwar city must create the new from the damaged old. Many of the buildings in war-damaged cities are relatively salvageable, and because the finances of individuals and remaining institutions have been depleted by war and its privations, that salvageable building stock must be used to build the "new" city. And because the new ways of living will not be the same as the old, the reconstruction of old buildings must enable new ways and ideas of living. The familiar old must be transformed, by conscious intention and design, into the unfamiliar new.

It is worth mentioning that the most-needed buildings are the so-called ordinary ones—apartments and office buildings, primarily. Symbolic structures—

such as churches, synagogues, mosques, and those buildings of historical significance that are key to the cultural memory of the city and its people—must also be salvaged and repaired. With these latter buildings, the first principle—restoration to the prewar state—is almost always justified, whatever the cost, which is always high. However, the application of this principle to ordinary buildings makes no sense, because there is nothing especially memorable to restore. To the contrary, the apartment and office blocks that survive destruction must provide the day-to-day spaces for new ways of living to be enabled by their "radical reconstruction."/35 I think it is possible, and just, to project the third principle into the reconstruction of today's war-damaged cities.

2012

Origins

Site of the Arnold Engineering Development Center (AEDC) near Tullahoma, Tennessee, c. 1950, showing the
Elk River Dam and Woods Reservoir, named in memory of Colonel Lebbeus B. Woods III—my father—
officer in command of its construction, whose portrait photo c. 1950 is inset.

I am the son of a distinguished Air Force officer and bear his name. He died in 1953, at the age of fifty-two, from a rare form of blood cancer caused by his involvement with the development and testing of the atomic bomb, though his service record blandly states his cause of death simply as "a result of service."

He was born to parents who were schoolteachers in the wilds of South Dakota, on a large Sioux reservation. After joining the US Army in 1918, he took the highly competitive exams to enter West Point and, with only his equivalent of an eighth-grade education, got in. Graduating as an officer in 1925, he resigned his commission to become a civil engineer for the Pennsylvania Railroad, designing and directing the construction of railway bridges until the outbreak of World War II, in 1942.

He continued his engineering work in the army, building airfields, bridges, and other necessary facilities in England and Europe as the Allies steadily advanced against the Axis forces. In 1944 he was assigned to the Manhattan Project in Los Alamos, New Mexico, to construct the buildings and other structures needed by Robert Oppenheimer, Edward Teller, and other scientists to develop the atomic bomb. His first exposure to radiation was the bomb's test at the Trinity site in New Mexico; his second, in 1948, was at the

Bikini Atoll in the Pacific. Five years later, he died a painful death—as had hundreds of thousands of others, both Americans and Japanese.

In that brief period, he accomplished a final mission: the building of the Arnold Engineering Development Center (AEDC), a sprawling experimental facility in southern Tennessee that, since its completion in 1953, has been vital to the invention and development of air- and spacecraft and their jet or rocket propulsion systems. AEDC has been instrumental not only for the military but

The Transonic Circuit—a wind tunnel for testing air- and spacecraft in dense atmospheres at extremely high speeds—at the AEDC, c. 1950

also for NASA projects such as the Space Shuttle. A large manmade lake, made to supply enormous quantities of water needed by AEDC but also famous for its ecologically protected woodlands and wildlife, is named in his memory.

I was born into and spent my early years during a time of war, first a hot one and then "cold," but my childhood experiences unfolded—oddly enough—in a milieu of creative engineering, problem solving, and construction. Patriotism was a given, so there was no ideological contention at home. My parents were both FDR Democrats, so there was little political debate. What was important was getting the job done for good reasons. Up to age thirteen, I spent my free time reading, drawing, and hanging out around jet aircraft and their pilots. I and a few other officers' children used to sneak down to the flight line to watch jet fighters and bombers take off and land, then have Cokes in the flight line café where the pilots went for coffee, still dressed in their flight gear. Once, at the air base in Ohio that was my father's last command, I climbed some fences and wandered for hours in a vast field of derelict fighters and bombers, exploring them inside and out, until military police showed up and took me into custody. It seems that some of these planes had been used in the Bikini atomic tests, and it took hours of medical exams, interrogation, and my father's high rank for me to return home to the officers' quarter of the base.

I also grew up around a certain kind of architecture, though I'm certain I didn't call it that or have much of an idea of what the term meant. I suppose that I would now call it "functional" architecture, because its uses dominated the genesis of its form. Still, it had a self-conscious aesthetic and a design intent that included its visual qualities and the emotions they evoked. The building forms and their meanings are in a way romantic and fantastical: wind tunnels, transonic circuits, gas dynamics laboratories—a kind of architecture for opening up and exploring new worlds. Even the more conventional industrial forms of steam plants and other support buildings reflect traces of the glow of a great adventure, experienced in this context of immensely consequential invention. All of it stayed with me, though was not to emerge—radically transformed—until many years later. */

*/ Related posts: "Big Bang: 'Doctor Atomic'" (November 13, 2008; http://lebbeuswoods.wordpress.com /2008/11/13/big-bang/) [omitted from this volume] and "Terrible Beauty 3: 'I Am Become Death'" (September 14, 2010) [included in this volume].

Kiss Me Deadly

Spoiler alert: the following reveals the surprise ending to the 1955 movie *Kiss Me Deadly*.

Ten years after the United States dropped atomic bombs on the Japanese cities of Hiroshima and Nagasaki in August 1945, the American public had little understanding about what made these bombs different from so-called normal bombs, other than the demonstrated fact that their destructive power was much greater. Americans' lack of understanding that the true difference was qualitative, as much or more than quantitative, created an atmosphere of acceptance for nuclear weapons—Americans had no problem with bigger bombs that brought about more destruction so long as they had more of them than their enemies. If they had understood, though, that atomic—nuclear—bombs had aftereffects in some ways more devastating than their explosive power, the public might have been less enthusiastic about building ever-more-powerful weapons.

If they had known, for example, that a powerful bomb—many times more devastating than the Hiroshima bomb—would not only obliterate a city in a stroke, but also poison the earth on which it had rested, making it uninhabitable for perhaps twenty thousand years, then plans for rebuilding and restoring a society would have been seen for what they are: dangerous fantasies justifying using the bombs in the first place. This understanding, fortunately, is what eventually happened, thanks to the educating efforts of many individuals who took it upon themselves to wake people up to the real dangers of nuclear weapons. The us government deserves no credit in this regard and, in fact, played down the dangers so that it could leave open its options for future use of nuclear weapons.

One example of this educating effort is the 1955 film *Kiss Me Deadly*, a Robert Aldrich production based on a novel by then-popular writer Mickey Spillane. With a good script, it's a well-directed and well-acted crime thriller (despite its lurid advertising) involving the hunt for "a great whatsit" that costs many people their lives at the hands of a shadowy international conspiracy trying to get hold of it. This whatsit is small enough to be hidden easily and contains something very precious.

"Diamonds, rubies, perhaps?" asks the mastermind of the conspiracy, but only rhetorically, as he already knows what it is. "Even narcotics?" The whatsit turns out to be a cubic leather case that contains a metal box. Mike Hammer—the archetypal Spillane private detective—is the first to find the coveted box hidden at the bottom of a gym locker. Eventually it winds up in the hands of the mastermind and a woman he used to get the box away from Mike. "What's in it?" she asks. The foreign-accented conspirator, who has a penchant for quoting parables and adages, answers with the story of Pandora's Box: that when opened it "let loose all the evils in the world."

"I don't care about the evil—what's in the box?"

"Did you ever hear of Lot's wife?" he replies obliquely, telling the story of the woman killed by her curiosity.

Unsatisfied with the Biblical reference, she persists. He then tells her that it contains "the head of the Medusa, and whoever looks upon it will be turned not into a pillar of salt, but of brimstone and ashes."

Out of patience, she shoots him, taking the box for herself. With his dying breath, he begs her—"like Cerberus barking with all his heads at the gates of Hell"—not to open the box.

But she does.

The intense light streaming from the box emits a sound more sinister and terrifying than any I have heard in cinema. It ranks as one of the art form's greatest special effects, lending the iridescent substance in the box a quality at once utterly alien and familiar, like hellish, primeval screams long suppressed within ourselves. As the woman is incinerated by what is clearly some form of radiation, we feel deeply the meaning of the ancient parables of annihilation and are confronted by the dreadful reality of the manmade radioactive material we know is at the core of every nuclear weapon: it doesn't need to explode to kill us or to destroy the world.

January 20, 2012

Yendo's Exprosthesis

In his latest projects, Masahiko Yendo presents us with some of the strangest designed objects I have ever seen. To confound their mystery (I cannot think of a better word) he describes them in terms that suggest they serve highly rational purposes. The objects—some of which appear to be dwelling places for human beings and others instruments for human use—are fraught with decay and detritus-like character, raising many questions. Are they designs for things yet to be built? Or are they readymades or found objects that are being adapted for reuse? Or are they artifacts from the past that we are discovering in a museum collection of things belonging to a lost or forgotten civilization?

Of these and other interpretations, I imagine them as objects yet to be made in a coming world, one in which people have no choice but to work with whatever materi-

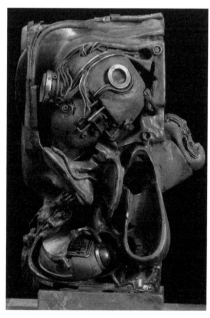

Masahiko Yendo, *Exprosthesis*, c. 2008

als can be scavenged, simply because the manufacture of new materials, even for entirely new purposes, no longer sufficiently occurs. I admit that this is rather trite and shop-worn scenario—the stuff of pulp science fiction—but that doesn't make it less vivid or even less valid. Just from reading the daily newspapers and the spate of new books on various global crises—including the population explosion and a growing scarcity of resources, including food—anyone can imagine a coming world in which the overcrowding of cities and the careless squandering of natural and human resources forces the kind of unexpected recycling that Yendo's work depicts.

So what? we might say. There are plenty of Jeremiads and Cassandra-like predictions out there—who needs another? In my view, Yendo's designed objects are much more than a warning. While they are not the solution to a problem whose causes lie far beyond the realm of architecture, they effectively strive to go around the problem, rather then engage it head-on, by addressing not its causes but its effects.

This is a classic problem-solving tactic. Albert Einstein employed it in his postulation of the theory of special relativity. The big debate at the end of the nineteenth century was about the nature of the "aether," an elemental sub-stance that was believed to pervade all of space, enabling everything from the movement of elemental particles like light to that of the planets. Physicists were at a loss to explain much about it, so they were also unable to effectively address other elemental problems. In developing his theory of the electrodynamics of moving bodies, Einstein simply ignored the aether as a hypothesis, construct-ing his hypothesis in terms independent of it. As a result of the verified success of his theory, the aether became irrelevant in all future discourse. Also—most importantly—entirely new vistas in physics, such as quantum theory, were opened for exploration.

A less exalted example is everyday algebra. If you have an unknown in an equation that you cannot solve for, you simply define it in terms of what you do know, and you will solve for the problematic unknown by indirection. A down-right vulgar example comes from American football. If you have a great runner who keeps slamming into a wall of defensive players without any forward progress, you devise a play where he runs around the end of the defensive line, effectively avoiding the problem at the center.

Science and art and daily life are filled with such end runs, and that is what Yendo does with his projects. Rather than throw up his hands in frustration over running up against intractable social and economic problems, he chooses to work with the given conditions and make of them the best he can in human terms. The structures he has designed under the general title of *Exprosthesis* are spatially cramped and aesthetically ugly by contemporary standards. Still, they emanate a peculiarly affirmative quality related to their necessity and not their desirability. The inventive human spirit can and will prevail, Yendo seems to tell us, under even the most limiting and difficult conditions.

Why I Became an Architect, Part 1

I would like to tell a short story—or perhaps not such a short story—about the reasons why I chose to become an architect. Exactly why this blog's readers should be interested in my recollections about such a matter I cannot say, and perhaps I am mistaken in spinning out such a story here. Still, I feel compelled to do so and can only hope for the readers' tolerance.

I'll quickly pass over my early obsession with drawing and the first time I saw Gustave Doré's engravings for Dante's *Inferno*, however pleasurable it might be to linger on the great illustrator's use of pure line in his startling visions of hell. I will pass just as quickly over my childhood memories of the engineering works built by my father, comingled with memories of jet bombers and fighters that enflamed my imagination, as I have already spoken of them.*/ Instead, I'll take up the story at age sixteen or seventeen when, some years after my father's death, I—an only child—lived with my mother in Indianapolis, Indiana, and attended high school. This was the mid-1950s.

For whatever reason, I had taken up oil painting. Setting up my easel in our modest living room, I painted pictures of everything from copies of paintings in a how-to book of bowls of fruit to images of pure light, that is, light that emanated from within the little canvas boards I'd bought at an art store. Where the impulse to make such images came from I cannot say, but oil paint was perfectly suited to the task (acrylics had not yet been invented). I recall that I tended not to blend the strokes into smooth transitions, but preferred to build them up from separate dabs and daubs, so that the light was broken down into elements proceeding from an intensely radiant center to a gradually deepening darkness. I wish now that even one of these paintings had survived.

I cannot recall whether I painted these pure light images before or after I came across pictures published in *Life* magazine of Michelangelo's Sistine Chapel ceiling frescos. I suspect it was after, because I had been so moved by them. No doubt my light paintings were a form of imitation, without the heroic figures I couldn't draw, of the great artist's expressions of a troubled spirituality. The twisting and turning, the contrapposto (I later learned the term) of the figures portrayed an unnamed inner conflict having more to do, it seemed, with the struggle of the human psyche against itself, rather than the Biblical stories the paintings ostensibly illustrated, or against the domineering will of God.

Christianity is in some ways a religion of self-torment. Fear of afterlife retribution for our sins against the laws of the church weighs on many less heavily than the pain of personal guilt from moral failures and of an erosion or outright loss of faith. This has had a baleful effect on European society by placing conflict, as well as a mood of negation, at its core. But it's been a boon for the arts, giving them an inexhaustible source of affecting ideas. Or, to put it another way, the arts have not

*/ See "Origins" (January 2, 2012).

been merely ornamental but central to people's struggle to "find themselves" in a world without clarity, or certainty, of meaning. The very different worlds of Dante and Michelangelo testify equally to this condition and led me slowly, inevitably toward architecture.

Why I Became an Architect, Part 2

It is revealing that the phenomenon and experience of light became important to me through art rather than through direct experience. After all, the actual world is alive with light and its effects, with a vividness that no work of art can equal. But works of art, at least certain ones, pierced my consciousness with the presence of light in ways I had never experienced. Perhaps it was the focus they gave it by their emphasis on particular qualities, but looking back I think not. Rather, it was the art's celebratory aspect, its exaltation of light, uniting its presence with profoundly important concepts—the struggle to be fully human—that touched me so deeply. Works of art could lift experience out of the commonplace to a realm of meaning that, for me, would otherwise be unreachable.

From *Architecture-Sculpture-Painting*, 1979. All the ingredients are there.

Even in my teens I knew people who simply loved life as they found it and needed no exaltation to enhance or elevate it for them, but I also knew I was not among them. The reasons do not matter to this story. I can only see that I was lucky to have stumbled upon visual art as a transformative medium of my experience, even though, at that young age, I was not at all sure what to do with it. Of course, I would continue to emulate the art that inspired me, but never for a moment imagined I could become a real artist, someone who could devote his life to making art. To make a living someday, I would have to do something really useful that people would be willing to pay for in the world from which I came and in which I expected to live out my life. I had no particular encouragement to think otherwise.

About the same time, I took a high school class called "Mechanical Drawing 1." In it I was introduced to the T square, the triangle, the protractor, and the compass. It's possible that I took the course because of dim memories from my early childhood of my father's engineering work, though I cannot recall any now. While my awakening passion for art and its celebration of light and lofty concepts seemed distant from these instruments, I was immediately attracted to what could be made with them—straight lines, circles, geometric figures. There were the strict rules that governed their construction, a rigorous order that was precise, if not exactly self-evident. The order of geometry that could be made by anyone was its own form of exaltation, a lifting of thought and action out of the messiness of the everyday to a realm of truth, at least a human truth. Once again, my instincts to transcend the ordinary—perhaps escape it is more accurate—were awakened. What this has to say about my personal deficiencies is all too obvious and best saved for an analyst's couch—but they, too, are part of the story.

From the present, it's easy to see the direction this was leading, but all those years ago it was by no means clear. The marriage of light and geometry does indeed find its consummation in architecture, but for me it did not come about so easily. At age eighteen I entered a fine school of engineering, then transferred to a fine school of architecture, finishing there when I was twenty-four. After ten or so years of working in corporate offices, learning what it meant to build—and leading a rather turbulent life—I went out on my own. (The turbulence, of course, has continued, sometimes on the paper and sometimes off.) Throughout all that time, I continued to make paintings, hoping that in this way I would give worthy form to the questions that had beset me since the days I confronted the easel in the living room of my mother's house—but never doing so. It was not until I was thirty-eight that I began to put the pieces together in drawing my idea of what architecture could be and made a total commitment. It was only then that I finally became an architect.

February 17, 2012

Zaha Hadid's Aquatic Center

Why do I go out of my way to openly criticize Zaha Hadid's Aquatic Center for the 2012 Olympics in London? Actually, this is a kind of love letter, the kind that begins, "Don't you love me anymore?"

I feel abandoned and bereft because one of the most gifted architects of my time has been reduced to wrapping a conventional program of use in merely expressionistic forms, without letting a single ray of her genius illuminate the human condition. Am I being pretentious and overly demanding? Of course. But that's the way disappointed lovers behave. Exaggerated emotions. Absurd demands. Anger that transgresses all reason. She has let me down, and what makes it worse is that she apparently couldn't care less.

Did she ring me up and ask me what I thought the design should be? No. If she had I would certainly have told her to propose rethinking the aquatic events themselves, reconfiguring the competition pools or at least the relationship of spectator seating to them. How (it might be asked) can an architect challenge such rigid rules of a sport and the traditions surrounding it? Well, how can an architect challenge the equally entrenched conventions of how people inhabit their houses and the streets of their town or city? Simply by having a better idea. Hadid has done it before.

And did she consult with me about the way the center's form should somehow express the "fluid geometries of water in motion?" No. If she had, I would have counseled her to forget this idea, because it is too easy and obvious. Even if it could be achieved in architectural form (which it isn't here, because water's fluidity is formless and boundless), it would be much more compelling to competitors and their audience to be confronted with actualities of their relationship. For example, the most interesting photograph in the suite of images presented on the blog Arthitectural is the underwater shot, where the motive power of the competitors' choreographed arms and legs can most closely be observed.*/

Does every work of a great talent have to reach a new peak of achievement? No, of course not. Or wait. Maybe it has to at least aim for it. In the Aquatic Center, so prominent on the world stage just now, Hadid was obliged, I believe, to set an example measuring up to her status and, more so, to her talent. The finished design shows no signs of any such attempt. So says the dejected lover.

*/ See "Zaha Hadid Architects: London Aquatics Centre for 2012 Summer Olympics," *Arthitectural*, www.arthitectural.com/zaha-hadid -architects-london-aquatics-centre -for-2012-summer-olympics/.

February 21, 2012

Krasojević Unbound

In a recent post I spoke of drawing "what architecture could be."/36 Since the days when I first set out to do that with hand-made drawings, the digital computer has become commonplace and has enabled many architects with similar ambitions to create provocative images that 1) could never be hand drawn; 2) speak a visual language previously unknown; and 3) at least in theory promise to tie into a world of construction that is increasingly digitally controlled, making their actualization possible, if not probable. In a sense, the only thing that stands in the way of building many astonishing digital images is the question, why?

The drawings of Margot Krasojević are for me as compelling as most I have encountered in the current flood. What sets them apart is not their style or character—they have the same anonymous, mechanical look and feel as most other digitally produced drawings. And it is not their spatial accessibility—we never get inside the depicted forms, another common feature of such drawings. Rather, the appeal of her drawings is found in their playful yet refined tectonic language, which offers us big, generalized forms and a flurry of fragments that either inhabit the big forms or move in opposition to them. It is a dialectical approach that she handles in a very architectural way, embracing several different scales and speaking of the necessity for architecture to assert its presence in even the smallest details.

Margot Krasojević, *Complex Dimensions of Self-Similar Geometry Define the Elevation*, 2007

Yet the question persists—why? Could we inhabit these designs, if they were constructed? Are they meant to be constructed—and inhabited—at all, or might she intend another purpose for them? We can only speculate about possible answers.

It's intriguing to imagine that in some future time, when not only technology but also human conceptions of how to live have evolved far beyond what we now know, buildings such as Krasojević's might become commonplace. In such a world, the social and political and perhaps also the economic relationships between people and what we would call a "wider nature" would be very different from today, though in ways we can only infer from the drawings. What the drawings suggest is an isolation in which things do not interact with each other very much, but are self-contained and self-sustaining. Each building is a world unto itself, a domain of individuality. Or so I see it.

Somehow, though, I do not think the architect Krasojević sees her designs as belonging to a distant future. Her texts make no reference to this effect and seem much more focused on her concern with formal details of technique and method—"how" she made the drawings more than "why." Back at square one, we can only conclude that the drawings, and what they depict, are intended for the present, one that shares her concerns and that projects architecture as essentially self-referential—"art for art's sake." As such, architecture severs its conscious ties with other fields of knowledge, from social science to psychology to literature, aiming for a pure expression of its essence—the design of space. This perspective can be and has been justified in countless modernist arguments by the need for existential integrity: each thing must be true to itself before it can come into a true relationship with other things. This is a powerful but problematic perspective, to be sure.

In the twentieth century, modernism and its counterpart, existentialism, played themselves out against a backdrop of war, totalitarianism, social disintegration, and personal alienation. The "death of God" announced by Friedrich Nietzsche at the end of the nineteenth century was really the birth of a wholly anthropocentric society. Modern technologies were merely the enablers of a historically new form of freedom, defined in a famous pop song as "having nothing left to lose." Postmodernism in philosophy, art, and architecture emerged as a supposed antidote to the toxic and deadly consequences of the demise of moral values that had, for many centuries, given human relationships cohesion in spite of their many contradictions. In a sense, the digital computer has been the ultimate liberator, making anything possible while remaining totally amoral. The digital computer (there is also the analog computer, underused and misunderstood today) makes the work of Krasojević possible but does not help us make any sense of it./37 To do that, we have the choice of going by consensus—whatever is fashionable—or interpreting it in private terms.

This says more about our contemporary state of affairs than the works of Krasojević. I have no doubt that she presents them in the expectation that others will understand her intentions. And well they might. The constructed elements of a new world of which she has drawn glimpses reach out to those intrepid souls who know that not only the future but also the present demand our imaginative participation in continually reshaping what we already know. The answer to "why"—draw it or build it—becomes obvious: we really have no other choice. */

*/ For further reading about this architect's thought and work, this book is an excellent resource: Margot Krasojević, *Spatial Pathology: Floating Realities* (New York: Springer, 2007).

Interview with Lebbeus Woods—"The Ineffable"

JOHN SZOT: Looking back at your major building proposals—for Sarajevo, Berlin, Havana, San Francisco, and New York City—in each case there is an intense form of tension stemming from conflict, be it natural disaster, political turmoil, or otherwise. These conditions set the stage for radical intervention by identifying the ineffable as a preexisting condition. However, in "Terrible Beauty 2" you seem to advocate pursuing the ineffable as a legitimate, independent architectural enterprise.*/ Does this mark a shift in the trajectory of your work?

LEBBEUS WOODS: I believe that, in our era, architects have a responsibility to face the historically unprecedented problems confronting people everywhere. Not only that, but they have been entrusted with the social agency for doing so by virtue of their education, special knowledge, and skills, and being legally empowered to assume design stewardship over the human environment. If architects don't take on this job, who will? Politicians? Engineers? Builders? Commercial corporations? They need to help, certainly, but I have always believed that architects, with their commitment to the total situation, should be the leaders in the reconstruction of human landscapes transformed by violence and dominated by the ineffable, and therefore must take the initiative. That's what leaders do—not waiting for someone else to do so and then call them in.

JS: In your essay you establish a strong case for engaging the ineffable despite the difficulties it may present. Although you have a compelling moral argument for doing so, you also note that the intrinsic nature of the ineffable conflicts with expectations placed on the architect. Would you care to elaborate further on the difference between the values that embrace the ineffable and those that guide the way we approach building design, or is it merely about control?

LW: No, it's not about control; it's about the strength and validity of ideas. I base my way of thinking on the presumption that really good architects will have better ideas for reconstruction than other specialists, again, because of their comprehensive understanding of environments and their abilities to give this understanding concrete form. Of course, they don't do this in isolation, but working with others. That's what I meant in a recent manifesto of education, when I declared that "the era of the collaborative genius must begin."†/ The architect must be the collaborative genius who has the best ideas about how to structure the work process leading to the designs for reconstruction.

I don't want to spend the time or space here on elaborating why so few architects have acted decisively as leaders in the continual reconstruction of cities—damaged or not—up to now. Rather, I am convinced that we must concentrate our energy on changing architects' attitudes now and into the future, beginning in the schools of architecture.

JS: Many of the other creative disciplines have explored for decades the kind of trauma and anxiety associated with the ineffable. Some might argue that media with a deep virtual dimension (like film) are effective (and safe) surrogates for the ineffable experience. What is your position?

LW: Films are fine media for what Sigmund Freud called "sublimating" dreadful feelings, so their energy can be transformed into something useful, positive, even creative. But the rechanneling of emotional energy often only relieves and diffuses personal suffering, unless it is actively put to creative use. Vicarious experiences and voyeurism can lead to passivity and the acceptance of unacceptable norms far more easily and often than they inspire creative actions for changing them.

*/ See "Terrible Beauty 2: The Ineffable" (July 24, 2010).
†/ See a recent manifesto of education, "Manifesto: The Reality of Ideals" (June 6, 2011; http://lebbeuswoods.wordpress.com/2011/06/06/manifesto-the-reality-of-ideals/) [omitted from this volume].

The more hopeful outcome of films and other virtual experiences is addressed by Aristotle in *Poetics,* which explains his theory of Greek theater. In it, he states that the events and characters we see on the stage create models for our thoughts and actions in the world we actually inhabit. The aesthetical worlds of the theater have, in short, a moral and an ethical dimension in relation to the ineffable—they give us help in how to live our often-difficult lives. In the same way, the imaginary worlds of architectural design—and especially so-called "visionary" architecture—offer us similar models for everyday living. We're free to follow them or not, or to adapt them to our purposes.

JS: Today one can easily see a connection between the network culture of social media and the heterarchical organizational strategies you described twenty years ago. However, it is debatable whether our buildings have risen to the challenges presented by this use of technology. Your work emphasizes the relationship between buildings and physical phenomena. Do you believe there is a connection between your concept of heterarchical space and the social dynamic of a "wired" society, or does architecture's preoccupation with the physical world make for an entirely different set of obligations and opportunities?

LW: My work definitely aims to explore the consequences of freedom and choice, often by technological means. In my *Berlin Free Zone* project, the center of the city is regenerated not by traditionally hierarchical urban planning methods but by spontaneous architecture without predetermined purpose and meaning, evolving through the unpredictable exchanges by electronic means of people living there.

Our buildings today are still designed according to outdated models, what Paul Rudolph called "background" and "foreground" types—a few extraordinary "masterpieces" designed by star architects, set against an urban fabric of what Robert Venturi called "the ugly and the ordinary." It is a hierarchical formula that has worked throughout human history, for example in Europe's Middle Ages, when the cathedral was a brilliant jewel set off against the dark and dense texture of a surrounding town built by and for its ordinary inhabitants. It is easy to understand why this model endures—it is familiar and safe—even though the society it supported has passed. What is needed today are new models that give form to the democratic society struggling to emerge from the older autocratic, oligarchic ones that have dominated history for so long. It is a very difficult struggle because even the concepts of democracy inherited from the past are outmoded and must be reinvented for the present and coming age of technological revolution. The "wired" society and its imperatives for architecture are a good place to begin. */

*/ This interview was conducted on November 14, 2011 and was published in the journal *MAS Context.* See Lebbeus Woods and John Szot, "Terrible Beauty," in "Aberration," ed. John Szot, special issue, *MAS Context* 12 (Winter 2011), 65–67.

Slow Manifesto

Saarinen's Last Experiment

Occasionally, history comes back and gives me a slap in the face. The slap in this instance came in the form of an article on innovation that appeared in the *New York Times* recently.[*]/ It recounts the all-too-familiar story of how a giant American corporation sponsored some of the most important research in science and technology in the 1950s, 60s, and 70s, establishing the United States as the world leader in innovation, at least in that era.

Eero Saarinen, Bell Laboratories Building, 1962

The Bell Laboratories—initially the research and development subsidiary of the monopolistic American Telephone and Telegraph Company (AT&T) and located in Holmdel, New Jersey—was the epicenter of this story.

But this wasn't the sting in the slap. Rather, it was that the Bell Labs Building was designed by Eero Saarinen, for whose firm I worked, beginning two years after the completion of this building in 1962. By then, Saarinen was dead of a brain tumor at age fifty-one, and his practice was in the hands of his partners, Joseph N. Lacy and John Dinkeloo, and his design protégé Kevin Roche. Saarinen's great fame was founded on exciting curvilinear buildings like the Yale Hockey Rink and the TWA Terminal at New York's Idewild (now JFK International) Airport. The Bell Labs Building was the very opposite, an immense glass box relentlessly organized on a Cartesian grid.

As an architect, Eero Saarinen was a shameless experimenter. He had no signature style, which might be the reason historians have not treated his work with much interest—they tend to favor trademarked brands, as they are easier to package and sell. I tend to think of him as an expressionist: each of his buildings expresses what he saw as the essence of its function. A hockey rink is about gliding and flow; an airplane terminal is about arrivals and departures and the symbolism they evoke; a research laboratory is about logic. His many other buildings, such as the CBS Headquarters in New York, an unassailable black granite column—express Saarinen's ideas of their very different purposes. The lesson we take away from his work is that one style cannot fit all. We can only wonder at how successful he would have been today.

Did the ultra-rational design of the Bell Labs contribute at all to the innovative work carried on there? From this article it would seem so. Yet I have some doubts. Does creative thinking in any field have any relationship with the architecture in which it takes place? It's a hard case to prove, one way or the other, but architects are continually claiming the connection. In the case of Bell Labs, the argument is made that the layout of the building encouraged interdisciplinary contact that led to the most productive, innovative collaborations. If this is

[*]/ See Jon Gertner, "True Innovation," *New York Times*, February 25, 2012, www.nytimes.com/2012/02/26/opinion/sunday/innovation-and-the-bell-labs-miracle.html.

true, what does this tell us about the most celebrated architecture of today, with its eccentric, computer-generated complexities? What about the creativity of everyday life? "Dumb boxes," as I have written elsewhere, may be the wave of the most creative future.*/ Whether yes or no, the sharp sting of Saarinen's Bell Labs Building, and the story behind it, lingers on. We must not avoid the questions it raises, especially those of us who have made considerable effort to explore other ways of thinking. */ See "Dumb Boxes" (April 8, 2008).

February 29, 2012

The Next Revolution?

In a recent panel discussion with Hernan Diaz Alonso, we exchanged differing opinions about digital computers but agreed on one crucial point: debates about computer-generated drawings versus hand drawings are over. The digital computer is not only an established part of architectural practice, but also is central to it. This is because it can do things that hand drawing cannot do and in particular facilitate a type of construction ever more prevalent in the building industry. Then our discussion turned in another direction: the future development of computing machines in architecture.

My contention, with which Diaz Alonso did not disagree, was and remains that there will be a resurgence of analog computers. The digital revolution is over. While refinements in software and hardware will continue, digital computers have won their central role and will not lose it, short of a collapse of the present civilization. However, they have their limitations, and these are already becoming clear. Breaking the world down into infinitely manipulable bits and bytes leaves a vast empty space in human thought that cannot be filled, or should I say "represented," in that way. Without representation in some form, thought cannot exist. This is where analog representation comes into the story.

First of all, what is an analog? An analog is something that shares certain qualities with a subject or an object under consideration but not others. In other words, it is not a literal, "virtual" representation of the subject or object, but rather a symbolic one. Analog thinking is thinking in symbols and produces representations or (a better term) descriptions. The advantage analogous thinking has over literal descriptions is, in the first place, that it can describe things that have not been known or described before: types of space, systems of order, even emotions. While this same possibility is often claimed for virtual representations or descriptions, I contend that every virtual invention has a history of models on which it is based. Let me give a small example.

I once asked my students, as an overnight sketch problem, to make a drawing of a being from another, very different world—an alien. The next day, the drawings they showed me looked like fusions of human beings and snakes, beetles, various plants, and so on. The point is, my students—very bright and creative—could only create hybrids of living things they already knew. Part

Slow Manifesto

of the reason for this, I concluded, was because they made representational, "virtual" drawings. If they had given me a mathematical equation, or a matrix of different colors, they would certainly have been able to make aliens we had never seen before. At the same time their description would have had to be translated—interpreted—to have resulted in a conventional representation or portrait of the alien. Then again, why would we need to render them conventionally?

The answer to this question is: we are used to it. The rendering of what a thing looks like is the way we are accustomed to getting descriptions. The digital computer is so popular and accepted because it specializes in exactly this kind of description. However, it can describe what we don't already know only in very limited ways, usually by montage or collage, that is, by combining things that we do know into descriptions of something we don't. This is a serious limitation when we are exploring the unknown. In that situation the analog computer is a far superior tool.

The most powerful analog computer known is the human brain. Consisting of millions of neural nets—electrical circuits—it can compute numerous complex operations simultaneously. It allows for not only walking and chewing gum at the same time, but also many other involuntary and voluntary body functions, while working through subtle emotions and complicated philosophical questions—all at the same time. Minute after minute, day after day, throughout a lifetime. Some two billion neurons comprise the circuits in a nearly infinite number of continually changing interactions. The statistics go on, but the point remains that the analog computer works by abstract descriptions, not literal ones.

Now, if the world inhabited by human beings could be controlled only by electrical impulses that could command bricks to be moved, concrete to be poured, steel to be made; or crops to be planted and harvested; or laws to be enacted and enforced, then the story could begin and end with the human brain. Perhaps that will be the future direction of human technological evolution on the planet. But until such a time, it will remain for us to interpolate between the analogical and the digital, between abstract descriptions and the literal representations of things. To a large extent, the task of this kind of interpolation makes up the history of science and art.

The "education" of the human brain is an ongoing, increasingly important task. But so is the invention and development of the technological prostheses we require to interpolate, to bridge the gaps between abstractions and representations. With digital computers advancing so rapidly, we have neglected the potentials of their analog cousins, such as those that would enable slum dwellers to analyze their own complex communities, the better to organize politically and economically; urban planners to understand the continually changing layerings of human activities within a dense city center; architects to incorporate available recyclable materials in the design stages of their projects.

A coming generation of analog computers will differ from digital computers in many ways, but the most crucial is that they will each be designed and built for a particular situation and task, rather than as a generalized machine

usable for all situations. If we think about it, this follows the example of our brains, which would not serve
a cheetah very well. Indeed, my brain would not serve
you very well, as it is continually being constructed by
my unique life experiences. But this takes us in a direction this text cannot go. It must serve here to say that
the analogical might well be and perhaps should be at
the center of the next great technological revolution.*/

*/ Worth reading: though not
directly related to the above, a
recent article by Allison Arieff about
writing architectural criticism raises
some worthwhile points. See Allison
Arieff, "Why Don't We Read About
Architecture?" *New York Times*,
March 2, 2012, http://opinionator
.blogs.nytimes.com/2012/03/02/why
-dont-we-read-about-architecture.

March 7, 2012

Theoharis David's Built Ideas

It was in the winter of 1988. Theoharis David,
then the director of Pratt Institute's Graduate
Design Program, had hired Michael Webb, of
Archigram fame, and me as adjunct teachers
in the design studio, where he was also teaching. At the outset of our one-year tenure,
the three of us sat down and discussed the
overall direction we wanted to take. Webb
and I—architects who had no realized buildings to our credit—suggested that it would
be great if we could focus on "science and
architecture." David, a gentleman through
and through, asked if we meant exploring the

Theoharis David, Bleu Residences, Protaras,
Cyprus, 2011

relationships between technology and architecture, a topic worn thin over the
decades but still, he supposed, always worth another look. No, we answered,
it was pure science—its concepts and methodologies—that we thought would
open up fresh perspectives and possibilities. Relativity, thermodynamics, evolution, cybernetics. David's eyes brightened and he smiled in his nuanced way. A
great idea, indeed, he said—let's do it. And so began one of the most memorable
teaching years in my experience and, I believe, that of many of our students.

Science and architecture was a risky direction to take. This was not only
because other faculty were vocally skeptical of how it would lead to buildable
architecture and how it would be taught by two non-building faculty, but also
how, or if at all, it would be accepted by our students, many of whom had traveled
far and were paying dearly for this conclusion to their professional education.
Nevertheless, it was a risk that David took because he believed in its premises
and potentials. It was then that I realized what kind of man David is and came to
value his integrity as a friend and educator.

It was more recently—I am chagrined to say—that I discovered his
architecture. The fault is mine but was abetted by his innate modesty and the

fact that many of his projects are in Cyprus. My fear that many others might share my ignorance is relieved by a current exhibition and catalogue.*/ In them, we find projects of a high order of thought and design informed by a brave and compassionate spirit. Working with known building types, he has transformed their conventions into inventions animated by new readings of their traditional meanings and purposes. The boldly abstract volumes of the Ayia Trias Church; the contrasts between delicacy and mass in the Bleu Residences; the soaring, sheltering lightness of the GSP Stadium; the open courtyards of the Stylianos Lenas School, playfully painted with light and shadow—all are unique interpretations of ideas vital to contemporary living that seem at the same time both familiar and, in these works of architecture, wholly original. It is their unforced, unpretentious character that gives them strength and poetry, a naturalness that imparts to us a sense of well-being and enablement.

As it is with the man, so it is with his works. Theo David is deeply committed to his students and his colleagues and to the architecture that embodies ideas celebrating their community—indeed, community itself. In my view and from my experience, he is an architect setting for all of us an example for a better, more affirmative future.

*/ *Built Ideas: A Life of Teaching, Learning, and Action* (New York: Pratt Institute School of Architecture, 2012). Published in conjunction with the exhibition of the same name, shown at the Hazel and Robert H. Siegel Gallery, Brooklyn.

March 8, 2012

Lower Manhattan Revisited

GEOFF MANAUGH: Could you explain the origins of the *Lower Manhattan* image? †/

LEBBEUS WOODS: This was one of those occasions when I got a request from a magazine—which is very rare. In 1999, *Abitare* was making a special issue on New York City, and they invited a number of architects—Steven Holl, Rafael Viñoly, and, oh God, I don't recall. Tod Williams and Billie Tsien. Michael Sorkin. Me. They invited us to make some sort of comment about New York. So I wrote a piece—probably a thousand words, eight hundred words—and I made the drawing.

I think the main thought I had, in speculating on the future of New York, was that, in the past, a lot of discussions had been about New York being the biggest, the greatest, the best—but that all had to do with the *size* of the city. You know, the size of the skyscrapers, the size of the culture, the population. So I commented in the article about Le Corbusier's infamous remark, "Your skyscrapers are too small." Of course, New York dwellers thought he meant, "They're not tall enough"—but what he was referring to was that they were too small in their ground plan. His idea of the Radiant City and the Ideal City—this was in the early 1930s—was based on very large footprints of buildings

†/ See image at larger size at www .flickr.com/photos/bldgblog /1454491228/sizes/o/in/photostream/.

Lower Manhattan, 1999

separated by great distances. In between the buildings, in his vision, were forests, parks, and so forth. But in New York everything was cramped together because the buildings occupied such a limited ground area. So Le Corbusier was totally misunderstood by New Yorkers who thought, "Our buildings aren't tall enough—we have to go higher!" Of course, he wasn't interested at all in their height—more in their plan relationship. Remember, he's the guy who said, "The plan is the generator."

So I was speculating on the future of the city and I said, well, obviously, compared to present and future cities, New York is not going to be able to compete in terms of size anymore. It used to be a large city, but now it's a small city compared with São Paulo, Mexico City, Kuala Lumpur, or almost any Asian city of any size. I said maybe New York can establish a new kind of scale—and the

Slow Manifesto

scale I was interested in was the scale of the city to the Earth, to the planet. I made the drawing as a demonstration of the fact that Manhattan exists, with its towers and skyscrapers, because it sits on a rock—on a granite base. You can put all this weight in a very small area because Manhattan sits *on the Earth*. Let's not forget that buildings sit on the Earth.

I wanted to suggest that maybe lower Manhattan—not lower downtown, but "lower" in the sense of "below the city"—could form a new relationship with the planet. So in the drawing, you see that the East River and the Hudson are both dammed. They're purposefully drained, as it were. The underground— or *lower Manhattan*—is revealed, and, in the drawing, there are suggestions of inhabitation in that lower region.

It was a romantic idea—and the drawing is very conceptual in that sense. But the exposure of the rock base, or the underground condition of the city, completely changes the scale relationship between the city and its environment. It's peeling back the surface to see what the planetary reality is. And the new scale relationship is not about huge blockbuster buildings; it's not about towers and skyscrapers. It's about the relationship of the relatively small human scratchings on the surface of the earth compared to the earth itself. I think that comes across in the drawing. It's not geologically correct, I'm sure, but the idea is there.

There are a couple of other interesting features that I'll mention. One is that the only bridge I show is the Brooklyn Bridge. I don't show the Brooklyn– Battery Tunnel, for instance. That's just gone. And I don't show the Manhattan Bridge or the Williamsburg Bridge, which are the other two bridges on the East River. On the Hudson side, look carefully at the drawing—which I based on an aerial photograph of Manhattan, obviously—and the World Trade Center... something's going on there. Of course, this was in 1999, and I'm not a prophet and I don't think that I have any particular telepathic or clairvoyant abilities, but obviously the World Trade Center has been somehow diminished, and there are things floating in the Hudson next to it. I'm not sure exactly what I had in mind—it was several years ago—except that some kind of transforma- tion was going to happen there. [End]*/

Epilogue: Once we begin to consider what lies below Manhattan, it is hard to know where to stop. The immense masses of rock on which the city rests are extremely stable, but they are moving slowly, very slowly. The Earth's mantle—of which the bedrock of Manhattan is a part—is floating on an under- ground sea of semi-liquid rock, known as the "outer core," and its movement is a natural consequence of the planet's continuing geological evolution. Earthquakes are simply a normal phenomenon in regions of the Earth's surface where two tectonic plates meet and one slides slowly, slowly under the other. This is a process that takes tens of millions of years to make a noticeable difference in human terms. And, by then, will there be human beings as we know them today to appreciate it? Certainly not.

Yet, these epic changes to come affect our expe- rience of Earth today. A year ago, an earthquake and resulting tsunami devastated the coast of Japan, as have

*/ This text is excerpted from an interview published on BLDGBLOG. See Lebbeus Woods and Geoff Manaugh, "Without Walls: An Interview with Lebbeus Woods," *BLDGBLOG*, October 3, 2007, http://bldgblog.blogspot.com /2007/10/without-walls-interview -with-lebbeus.html.

earthquakes and the eruptions of volcanoes, not to mention related severe weather, throughout recorded history. Humans may not be able to see the mountains rise and the seas fall (as they did by hundreds of feet during the last Ice Age), only to rise again. But their knowledge that it is happening affects at the very least their understanding of the world they inhabit and consequently their thoughts and plans for the future./38

Celebrating Death

Hangar 17 at the JFK International Airport in New York City contains some of the strangest objects we might expect to encounter under the description "artifacts." Twisted steel beams, battered and burned cars and ambulances, odd personal items bearing the traces of violence, items from a mall once lively with customers but no more—this is the stuff of many possible memorials to the 9/11 terrorist attack on the United States, collected and preserved for that very purpose. This hangar, in all its unpretentious modesty, may be the best memorial of its kind to the event that will ever be devised. Unsentimental yet heart-wrenching to anyone with imagination, the straightforward presentation of these artifacts speaks directly to the impact of the attacks on ordinary people who were killed in the course of their ordinary lives. As we know in the years since the attacks, the impact has been enormous on everyone's life, ordinary and not.

This raises a question: what is the purpose of the artifacts in Hangar 17 and the anticipated memorials for which they are intended? To stir the memories of people in diverse places of the terrorist attacks? If so, how can these strangely anonymous objects awaken such memories? And if that is the goal of displaying the artifacts, what is the point of awakening these memories, assuming that this is a good and necessary thing to do?

It is obvious, I think, that the events of 9/11 opened a new period in the history of human society, one still clouded by an ambivalence of meaning. The victims of the attack didn't willingly sacrifice their lives for a noble cause, but were innocent bystanders who happened to inhabit buildings that were symbols the terrorists—who did willingly sacrifice their lives—destroyed for symbolic reasons.

I personally have no sympathy for mass murder in the name of symbolism and denounce the attacks on the World Trade Center. Still, it is hard for me to escape the feeling that the twisted steel, crushed vehicles, and scraps of clothing can too easily be understood as memorials to the terrorists as much as to their victims, because the terrorists can display the same artifacts from the places terrorized by those we presume to be "good guys."

But the important point here, I believe, is that memorials cannot any longer commemorate death and destruction in the name of noble causes but must somehow affirm the ultimate value of human life, under whatever name it goes. So let these artifacts stay in Hanger 17, where they can be pored over by specialists for their various purposes. Or—more difficult—let them be creatively transformed into a new generation of memorials that celebrate the living.*/

*/ Photos of these objects by Francesc Torres are published in his book *Memory Remains*. See Francesc Torres, *Memory Remains: 9/11 Artifacts at Hangar 17* (Washington, DC: National Geographic, 2011).

March 22, 2012

Beyond Memory

Human memory is an especially contemporary mystery. For all the advances in knowledge in the past century or so, we really don't know how memory works, that is, how we are able to remember things that happened in the past. For much of that past, it had been assumed that memories were stored in the brain, much as in a storage cabinet or, more recently, in a digital computer. And yet the more we understand about the brain, the less likely this seems. For one thing, there is sim- ply not enough neural capacity in the brain

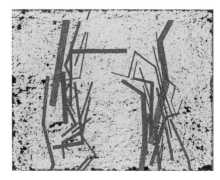

Memory Field 1+n, 2002

to store a lifetime of memories, if we consider them as discrete little packages that we retrieve on demand. For another, if memory were simply a matter of retrieval, then memory would be more nearly perfect than it is. Not only do dif- ferent people have different memories of the same past things, but also each of us remembers the same thing differently at different times. This suggests that memories are not discrete packages but fluid in their form and content, and that the act of remembering is almost a matter of their being assembled anew for every recollection. This, in turn, suggests that memories are not stored at all, but rather continually reinvented from some kind of mental raw material available in the brain at any given time. There is no accepted scientific theory of memory that would explain such a process.

Jorge Luis Borges, in his short story, *Funes the Memorious,* forcefully introduces the antithesis of memory, which is forgetting. His protagonist is a man who has locked himself into a completely dark and silent room because he remembers everything and can't forget anything. Overwhelmed, he is sim- ply unable to endure any new experiences and the memories they produce. It's a nightmarish dilemma, one that makes us realize how important forgetting is and also gives us some insight into how memory might work. Whatever the neural mechanism, there is a limit that can be reached emotionally: each of us can only cope with so many memories before a breakdown looms. The human psyche is limited by the personality of the individual who possesses it, which is formed by precise, unique experiences, different for each of us. Funes had his limits—we will certainly have our own, different ones.

Our limits are significantly defined by our capacity for forgetting. Funes could not forget. Fortunately, most of us can. What is the mental/neural process of forgetting? How do we un-remember? This is equally important as how we remember. Whether forgetting clears neural space for more remembering or whether it prepares us emotionally to handle new memories is not clear. Indeed the processes of remembering and forgetting may be linked in ways we do not yet know or imagine, but they are almost certainly mutually interdependent.

In a recent review of the book *Memory: Fragments of a Modern History*, by Alison Winter, author-critic Jenny Diski writes a summary of findings by neurophysiologists of the chemistry of remembering: "A traumatic experience is accompanied by a surge of adrenal stress hormones which increases the strength of the memory. And each time the event is recalled, a renewed rush of epinephrine and cortisol reinforces the event's emotional impact and its ease of recall. In other words, each time you recall something awful, the memory and its associated distress are strengthened. The trauma is recreated and enhanced with every recollection."/[39]

If this is true, then forgetting is especially important in our coping with traumatic experiences, such as those arising from 9/11, written about in my previous text. Memorials celebrating death, destruction, and loss keep the wounds caused by the trauma they cause painfully open, rather than help heal them. Whether this is desirable or not is a matter of personal and social choice and how important it is for individuals and their community to keep feeling the pain caused by particular experiences. This choice will shape the character of an individual and his or her community.

Learning—the creation of knowledge—often emerges from painful experiences. We learn not to put our hand in a fire because, no matter how tempting it is to find out what fire feels like, the pain has taught us that it doesn't feel good. That is a memory we would do well not to forget. But there are other painful experiences that have taught us little or nothing, or have taught us something we don't know what to do with, such as being caught in the crossfire of a war-zone. This situation has nothing to do with our volition or choice, but with decisions made by others. The only thing we can learn from the experience is how to recover from it, and that is a creative act of our choice that requires our transcending the pain—that is, not merely reliving it by remembering, but transforming the memory into something entirely new and affirmative.

This is what I had in mind in the *War and Architecture* projects of the 1990s, which addressed war-damaged buildings and their reconstruction.*/ The scar constructions don't celebrate violence, destruction and death, but rather the creative healing of the wounds they have caused.

This is a critical distinction to make and I must admit that many have had trouble making it. Perhaps only artists of one sort or another—including what might be called "artists of life"—can make the distinction and act upon it. I was convinced when I made the projects—but not so now—that those who had lived through the trauma of war were best able to understand deeply its losses and

*/ See "War and Architecture: The Sarajevo Window" (December 2, 2011).

also the necessity to transcend them—in short, to build a new society and its city. It was a romantic and much-too-heroic vision that badly underestimated most people's need to regain what had been lost, impossible as that is. For this reason, the *War and Architecture* projects and those for the reconstruction of Sarajevo have not been useful in the reconstruction of that war-damaged city. People have preferred to remember what they lost through war than to cut their losses—forget it—and move on, making for themselves and others to follow something new from the ruins of the old.

April 18, 2012

Science to Art

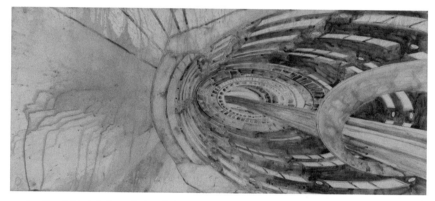

Jonathan Feldschuh, *Large Hadron Collider #20*, 2010. A painting related to the Large Hadron Collider

The interplay between science and art is fascinating but ill defined. Does science produce a kind of art almost incidentally, for example the images of subatomic particles colliding in a linear accelerator? They certainly look like art—abstract and evocative. But doesn't a work of art have to be created with an intention to be so? If not, then any interesting image would be art and that would disturb the existing social system of values that insists that art be created by artists and science by scientists.

Not to digress too far into such questions, but several times in the last century this system has been challenged by artists themselves. Most notably, the Futurists proclaimed the cacophony of factories and of the noisy machines inhabiting the streets to be the truest forms of modern music. The Dadaists likewise proclaimed ordinary objects like urinals and hat racks to be sculptures, which they called "readymades." These and other similar redefinitions of art were based on a belief that the modern age was grounded in the commonplace and the everyday and not in the narrow, over-cultivated tastes of a social elite. Together with this was the belief—or the hope—that machine technology and industrial mass production were liberators of humankind and were creating a great new phase of human history, which needed its unique artistic expressions.

Meanwhile, back in the science laboratory—say, a very particular one called the Large Hadron Collider (LHC), a giant machine under the border of France and Switzerland built to hurl protons at each other at extreme velocities, producing collisions that reveal the very smallest and highest-energy subatomic particles—scientists study computer imagery to interpret, or understand, the most fundamental realities of the physical world. From that understanding new technologies will emerge, by which we humans will interact with the natural world and, so to speak, with ourselves. The LHC is, in short, an important source of new knowledge and will have a significant place in our history and—to the extent that we influence our world—the history of the planet.

My point here concerns the role of imagery in the creation of knowledge. The imagery of the LHC is computer generated: largely, arrays of numbers. The patterns recurring in these arrays are mathematical in that they can be converted to algebraic expressions, and at the same time visual, in that their structure can be converted to logical expressions much as, say, a painting by Leonardo da Vinci. These "critical" expressions are primarily verbal and, being in a common mode, contribute to shaping our cultural values.

However, apart from the direct output of the LHC, which can only be interpreted by specialists, the physical presence of the machine is expressive. The underground spaces it occupies, the tectonics of the machine itself, the iconic impact of its geometry—each and all are part of an aesthetic that is as much a part of our visual, hence cultural, sensibility as the streamlining of airplanes and the uniformity of mass-production was to an earlier generation. Visual artists such as Jonathan Feldschuh are interpreting in traditional art media the very untraditional world of the LHC in order to give all of us access to it.*/ His paintings combine the literal and the abstract, the representational and the symbolic in a needed synthesis of the known and the as-yet-unknown, or even the ultimately unknow-able realities, that lure us on.

*/ See Jonathan Feldschuh,
www.jonathanfeldschuh.com.

Measuring Light

It has long been my contention that light does not reveal the presence of objects, but the other way around: objects reveal the presence of light. This flipping of the phrase is more then a trick with words, though it may seem like that at first. What it does is shift the emphasis of meaning. If light reveals the object, then it is the object that is important. But if objects reveal the light, it is the light that is important. In other words, the simple turn of phrasing changes the relative values of objects and light.

For me, light is the main thing. Light is a natural physical phenomenon the complexity of which reveals the structure of human consciousness. Objects, including buildings, in their absorption and reflection of light stimulate a human brain's neural networks, in effect activating the brain. The more

Lebbeus Woods in collaboration with Leo Modrcin, *Light Metrical Instruments* (details), 1987

complex and nuanced the stimulation, the more fully the brain comes to life. Shape, edge, texture, color, shadow, highlight—playing with and against one another—effectively enable the brain to make the most subtle distinctions, thereby imbuing human experience with a richness and complexity that defines it. Whatever else is involved, the perception of light is central.

Details from the *Light Metrical Instruments* series are shown above. If we can think of architecture as an instrument revealing the presence of light and therefore giving it a precise measure, then these instruments are proto-architectural. With their richness in variation of shapes, colors, and textures, they inform the design of more complex programmatic structures.

May 22, 2012

Michelangelo's War

In 1528, when the Papal armies were threatening to attack Florence and restore the Medici family to autocratic power, the Florentine Republic gave Michelangelo Buonarroti the responsibility of strengthening the city's fortified defenses. By the time the attack came in 1529, he had designed and overseen the construction of a number of bastions at crucial junctures in the existing defensive wall around the city. These were so effective that the citizens of Florence were able to repel the superior attacking troops for nearly eleven months, until—through an act of political treachery—the city finally fell in 1530.

The design drawings Michelangelo made for the bastions considered two main functions. First, to provide protected openings for the defenders to fire their muskets at the attackers; each opening covered a relatively narrow field of fire, but together they must cover the widest possible field of fire. Second, to deflect incoming cannon fire in the form of cannon balls, which were as yet nonexplosive. To accomplish both of these purposes, the walls had to be not only thick but also relatively short and angled sharply with adjoining walls, creating a "corrugation" that would conceal gun ports and better resist the impact of cannon balls. In his drawings, Michelangelo primarily studied possible variations on this fundamental idea.

For all their practical purpose, these drawings have uncommon aesthetic power. Of course, this is because they are made by one of the greatest sculptors and a self-taught architect—an "amateur of genius," as he has been called—but it is also because the bastions required had too short a history as a building type to have ossified into a rigid typology. Michelangelo was relatively free to invent strong new forms and didn't hesitate to do so. Using straight and curved lines in various combinations, these designs assume—to the contemporary eye—the character of plans for buildings belonging to our era rather than his; or, at the very least, they anticipate expressionistic architecture of the present and last centuries that has been realized because of advances in building technology.

This bit of speculation is not, however, at the heart of the drawings' emotional and intellectual power. For that, we have to look to a fluidity of invention captured in the drawings. Michelangelo's mastery of mostly freehand pen and ink drawing (each line is precise and cannot be erased) gave him the freedom to experiment with form. Without this mastery, he would have sought, as any artist would, the safety of more familiar forms. We are struck by the *élan* of the designs as much as by their visual coherence. We are moved by the seemingly effortless way they undertake the always-risky task of invention. Not least, the fortification drawings inspire us to equip ourselves with the skills necessary to explore daring new possibilities for architecture, ones that engage the daunting challenges we—as Michelangelo—must confront.

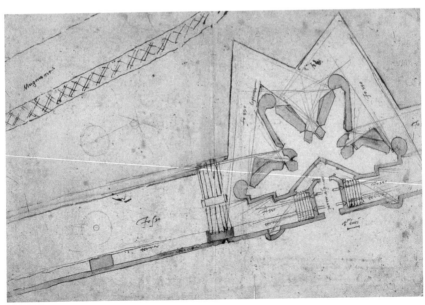

Michelangelo Buonarroti, drawing for the fortifications of Florence, 1528–29

Slow Manifesto

Oyler Wu Collaborative: Screenplay

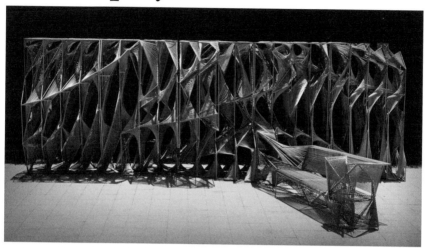

Oyler Wu Collaborative, *Screenplay*, 2012

Screenplay is conceived of as a play on one's visual perception. This twenty-one foot long screen-wall is constructed of forty-five thousand linear feet of rope strung through a series of lightweight steel frames. The wall is designed with the intention of provoking a sense of curiosity by slowly revealing its form and complexity through physical and visual engagement with the work. It is made from a repetitious steel framework with rope infill that varies over the length of the wall in three dimensions, forming a thickened, undulating screen made up of dense line-work. In its orthographic, or "straight on," view, the wall forms a meticulously organized series of patterns easily recognized by the viewer. As the viewer moves around the wall, its three-dimensional qualities reveal a more complex system of deep sectional cavities, twisting surfaces, and material densities. The experience is meant to build on an on again/off again system of pattern legibility using optical effects as a means of provoking engagement in the work.*/
Text by Oyler Wu Collaborative

*/ *Screenplay* by Oyler Wu Collaborative was on view from June 22, 2012, to June 24, 2012, at Dwell on Design 2012 at LA Convention Center. Project design and fabrication team: Dwayne Oyler, Jenny Wu, Huy Le, Sanjay Sukie, Yaohua Wang, Qing Cao, Farnoosh Rafaie, Jie Yang, Clifford Ho, Joseph Chiafari, Tingting Lu, Qian Xu, Mina Jun, Vincent Yeh, Kaige Yang, and Shouquan Sun.

In the perilous game of speculation about the design of space for human use, Dwayne Oyler and Jenny Wu have often insisted on constructing what they have conceived at 1:1. Drawings and scale models have not been enough. Consequently, the size of their speculative projects has been small. In their latest, *Screenplay*, we are given, as I read it, a domestic setting—let's call it part of a room—defined by a wall and a piece of furniture. What is remarkable about the project is the way the architects have reconceived these conventional elements and invented new techniques of construction to realize their new ideas. The wall becomes a three-dimensional screen into which is projected a complex network of spaces, a transformative sequence that—like Kurt Schwitter's *Merzbau*—is inhabited by our own creative invention. There is a fantastical play of scales here, an architectonic drama heightened by the wall's unique construction, which hovers at the edge between transparency and solidity. It is from this vertical field that the rather conventional couch emerges, becoming radical in its familiarity.

Oyler and Wu show us here how closely linked full-scale construction and new spatial concepts always are. There is much to be learned from *Screenplay,* and much to be enjoyed.
Text by Lebbeus Woods

July 9, 2012

Inevitable Architecture

How important is it—if at all—for architects to consider the ultimate decay of the buildings they design? After all, the new building best realizes their ideas, hopes, and aspirations, and the prospect of it being diminished over time amounts to their diminishment as well. Most architects dislike the idea of buildings' decay and work hard to avoid it by carefully selecting materials, systems, and methods of assembly that will withstand the forces of nature, chiefly those of weather, continually attacking them. Nevertheless, inherent in materials and systems themselves there is a

Christopher Payne, *Coal House in Summer,* from the series *North Brother Island,* New York, NY, 2010

tendency to decay—an entropy—that no amount of care in design or maintenance can overcome. Buildings will inevitably decay, and there is nothing architects or those charged with a building's upkeep can do about it. So what is an architect to think or do?

The most common thing is to forget about it. Or, to put it in psychological terms, to deny it, much as we put out of our thoughts our own inevitable decay and extinction. We tend to proceed in life as though we will live forever, thereby remaining optimistic enough to believe what we do has some enduring value and meaning. Without this capacity for denial, most would become paralyzed by despair. If architects did not believe their designs had some enduring qualities, it would be difficult to believe in what they do. Even the designers of temporary architectural installations believe they will endure through various forms of documentation—photos, film, even reconstructions—and thus find sanctuary in denial.

There is, of course, a less common and more difficult way to address the situation, and that is to embrace or at least accept decay from the start. I personally find the Romantic fascination with ruins problematic. From works by Caspar David Friedrich to Albert Speer (Hitler's architect and town planner), the evocative power of ruins has worked to produce powerful emotions, often for ideological—religious and political—purposes, making the motives exploitative, at the least. As a marketing device, nostalgic emotions of loss can sell paintings and politicians and their policies, but do little to advance knowledge.

Still, there is a tougher, more critical edge to accepting the decay of buildings and their inevitable ruin that places architecture in a unique position to inform our understanding of the human condition and to enhance its experience. Chiefly, this is to include in design a degree of complexity, and even of contradiction, embodied in the simultaneous processes of growth and decay in our buildings—a complexity that heightens and intensifies our humanity. Thankfully, there is no stagy, contrived method to accomplish this in architecture. All architects must find their own, unique ways.

August 11, 2012

Goodbye (Sort Of)

The days of regular posting on the Lebbeus Woods blog are over. There are several reasons for this. For one thing, at my age and stage of life, with various health and other issues, my time and energy are limited. For another, I have begun writing a book that soaks up what time and energy I have for writing. It is not a compendium or collection of earlier work, but rather a new piece of work in itself, having to do with how World War II shaped the architecture of the later twentieth century. The ideas are fresh and the writing brand new. Oh, and it's not a picture book. I've never done anything like it.

From time to time, I will post an article on the blog. I certainly don't expect readers to check into the blog regularly, as they have been able to do over the past four years. Readers who subscribe to the blog will get these occasional postings.

I must say that it has been a privilege to have communicated with so many bright and energetic readers. It has been a unique experience in my life that I will always value highly.

Thank you for all you have given.

Afterword

Aleksandra Wagner

At the rarest brunch we've ever attended—in a post-bohemian SoHo sprinkled with snow—I first heard Lebbeus say that he cared not for drawing any longer. The date recorded in my now faintly inked Filofax is January 2, 2010. Ours was a very fine, very small crowd. Eggs, juice, black coffee.

"I am not interested," he said.

No longer interested. Period.

The statement aroused some laughter, a bit less than comfortable. There was a woman there who laughed with the enthusiasm of an "Aha." Given her smartness and the precision of her laughing style, I listened with special attention. What does she get that I don't?

Maybe this book is about that kind of knowing laughter. What did he get that we don't?

In case you ever knew how to draw and did it magnificently....If you were over sixty-five and labeled, if only enviously, a "master draftsman."... In case you decided not to participate in any mastery....What would be your next move? You'd stop and think, especially if you drew for a living—if drawing was your means to continue to live on.

It all started with him saying, "What I do—have done—in my lifespan means one thing now, or it means nothing. What it may mean later will be another thing, or none."

Let's get to the Thing.

The Thing is, you have to know what it is to feel alone in that celebrated if repressed "existential" sense, for which no good party and no great contract can serve as a rescue. And yet the Thing requires you to be a believer in the tenuous tenderness of the social bond. The Thing is also about an unimaginable time, when an encounter with planetary wonders happened first by opening a large-format book in a provincial public library. When architects from far away but close to your own age sent urgent missives to an indifference they felt compelled to stir, through an invocation of a telegram or aerogram.

The Thing, then, was no duck and cover. It was to send a line and to keep sending. An ethics of persistence.

To whom the line is sent, however, is a different Thing. Indeed, how does anyone manage to send a lone line into the world, expecting it will reach more than a few of its inhabitants, if that? The Thing is, one expects little. One trusts that the world is an essentially friendly place—a place hungry for a quietly subversive and an ever-unfashionable mix of intelligence and sincerity. Whatever the medium, one always does the same: insists on residing in the resistant. A blank paper with its blank stare. A solidly flickering instability.

Having been around through many a morning and evening when these blog entries were born—of a dawn and a dusk; of a twilight, not of a midday—having often served as their first reader, I had little to say about them then.

Across two tables and two computer screens, there was a vibrant man who cared not for drawing any longer. He drew a line of another kind, charting and delimiting some equally unexpected territories. A proof that we all make only one book in a lifetime, this volume spells out how certain Things came to be. With characteristic gentleness, it also instructs how it came about that other Things never happened.

Were I to suggest, now, a formulation of the blog's program as it unfolded, I'd choose two of its midpoints. February 12, 2009, "Real Time"—there is no "spare time" that would enable anyone not already and always thinking to return to a more basic questioning of what architecture is and can be, even what it should be. March 15, 2009, "Notebook 97–3"—a notebook is not made of "sketches." Here Lebbeus greets one of his favorites, D. H. Lawrence, who reflected in *Apocalypse* on a difference between two ideas of completeness: the ancient circular or spiral approach, following thought deeper and deeper to some point of "fullness," and today's linearity, the "logical chain." To think them through and to fuse them was the aim of a Woods notebook, of its digital analogue, and of its present transformation.

A decision—or, just maybe, an unintentional choice—to allow a third party to be the host makes lebbeuswoods.wordpress.com endure beyond any posting to come. Lebbeus, who knew when to put the Thing down (a true master of the goodbye), wrote slowly: January 28, 2009, "Architecture School 101"—"there is nothing more discouraging and dispiriting than work left unfinished."

No fast last word will do.

Which is where the laughter comes in. As it should.

Notes

1. Comments to "Blooms(birth)day Bash" (July 21, 2011). Question posted by metamechanics on July 21, 2011, response posted by lebbeuswoods on July 21, 2011.

2. Lebbeus Woods, email to Clare Jacobson, May 13, 2009.

3. For more on Einstein's critique of the "aether" concept, see "Yendo's Exprosthesis" (January 20, 2012).

4. Francis Fukuyama, "The End of History?" *The National Interest* (Summer 1989): 3–18.

5. See Herbert Muschamp, "The Miracle in Bilbao," *New York Times*, September 7, 1997, http://www.nytimes.com/1997/09/07/magazine/the-miracle-in-bilbao.html.

6. Two previous posts on this topic—"Slums: The Problem" (January 18, 2008; http://lebbeuswoods.wordpress.com/20a08/01/18/slums-the-problem/) and "Slums: What to Do?" (January 28, 2008; http://lebbeuswoods.wordpress.com/2008/01/28/slums-what-to-do/)—have not been reproduced in this volume. As their titles suggest, they introduce the social issues that create slums (Woods notes that "some prefer the term 'squatter communities'") and suggest internal empowerment instead of imposed "urban renewal."

7. The influence of these observations can be seen in Common Ground, a seminar run by Woods and Christoph a. Kumpusch at Cornell University in the summer of 2009 and documented in "Common Ground: The Seminar" (June 17, 2009; http://lebbeuswoods.wordpress.com/2009/06/17/common-ground-the-seminar/) and "Common Ground: The Seminar Work" (July 14, 2009; http://lebbeuswoods.wordpress.com/2009/07/14/common-ground-the-seminar-work/); both posts are omitted from this volume.

8. Lydia Goehr, *The Quest for Voice: On Music, Politics, and the Limits of Philosophy: The 1997 Ernest Bloch Lectures* (Berkeley: University of California Press, 1998), 94.

9. Additional words contributed in the blog comments section include "architect," "revolution," "ideology," "context," "history," "sustainability," and "diagram."

10. Immanuel Kant, *Ethical Philosophy: Grounding for the Metaphysics of Morals and Metaphysical Principles of Virtue*, trans. James W. Ellington (Indianapolis, Ind.: Hackett, 1994), 30.

11. The comments include one from an architect claiming, "I was damn near fired" for forwarding the post to his office colleagues.

12. For information on a building that Woods realized "in the usual sense," see "A Space of Light" (February 15, 2011).

13. See "Integrity" (March 20, 2008).

14. Examples of these works appear throughout this book. In illustrating this blog entry, Woods used instead works by other architects: Kurt Schwitters's Merzbau and Michael Webb's Drive-in House.

15. Three additional posts from this series have been included in this volume, "Architecture School 201" (February 16, 2009) concerning the content of architectural education, "Architecture School 301" (March 18, 2009) concerning the design studio, and "Architecture School 401" (May 15, 2009) elaborating on collaborative analogical studios. Two posts from this series have been omitted: "Architecture School 202" (February 27, 2009; http://lebbeuswoods.wordpress.com/2009/02/27/architecture-school-202/) concerning changes at schools due to political circumstances and "Architecture School 302" (March 26, 2009; http://lebbeuswoods.wordpress.com/2009/03/26/architecture-school-302/) introducing the idea of a collaborative studio.

16. The post that addresses education at the Bauhaus, "Architecture School 202" (February 27, 2009; http://lebbeuswoods.wordpress.com/2009/02/27/architecture-school-202/), has been omitted from this volume.

17. Two additional entries in this series, "Notebook 97-3" (March 15, 2009) and "Notebook 01-3 (The Last)" (October 6, 2009), are included in this volume. Entry "Notebook 01-2" (March 22, 2009; http://lebbeuswoods.wordpress.com/2009/03/22/notebook-01-2/) has been omitted. All four posts include many more images than this volume allows.

18. D. H. Lawrence, *Apocalypse and the Writings on Revelation*, ed. Mara Kalnins (Cambridge: Cambridge University Press, 2002), 93.

19. This text is the first in a series. The posts "Zaha Hadid's Drawings 2" (March 27, 2009; http://lebbeuswoods.wordpress.com/2009/03/27/zaha-hadids-drawings-2/) and "Zaha Hadid's Drawings 3" (March 30, 2009; http://lebbeuswoods.wordpress.com/2009/03/30/zaha-hadids-drawings-3/) have been omitted from this volume.

20. "AS401: Buffalo Analog" (May 15, 2009) is included in this volume. "AS401: MU Analog" (June 1, 2009; http://lebbeuswoods.wordpress.com/2009/06/01/as401-mu

-analog/), "AS401: LA Analog" (December 7, 2009; http://lebbeuswoods.wordpress.com/2009/12/07/as401-la-analog/), "AS401: Vertical Manhattan 1" (August 15, 2010; http://lebbeuswoods.wordpress.com/2010/08/15/as401-vertical-manhattan-1/), and "AS401: Vertical Manhattan 2" (August 17, 2010; http://lebbeuswoods.wordpress.com/2010/08/17/as401-vertical-manhattan-2/) have been omitted.

/21 See "Ars Brevis, Vita Longa" (August 12, 2009).

/22 The blog post includes works by Felix Candela, Konrad Wachsmann, and Frei Otto in addition to Torroja and Nervi.

/23 A lengthy comment by composer Svjetlana Bukvich-Nichols is included within the body of the blog post.

/24 A previous post announcing Abraham's death—"Raimund Abraham, 1933–2010" (March 4, 2010; http://lebbeuswoods.wordpress.com/2010/03/04/raimund-abraham-1933-2010/), omitted from this volume—received an outpouring of comments on the Woods blog.

/25 This discussion continues in "Terrible Beauty 2: The Ineffable" (July 24, 2010) and "Terrible Beauty 3: I Am Become Death" (September 14, 2010).

/26 For more on Woods's visit to Sarajevo and the work that resulted from it, see "The Reality of Theory" (February 6, 2008), "Metastructure" (February 7, 2009), "High Houses" (February 23, 2010), "War and Architecture: The Sarajevo Window" (December 2, 2011), and "War and Architecture: Three Principles" (December 15, 2011).

/27 Images from this filmstrip are included in the blog post.

/28 A section of text that relates to specific photographs reproduced in the blog has been omitted here.

/29 In his blog post, Woods shows images of manuscript pages of Charles Dickens's *A Christmas Carol* with handwritten corrections by the author, a manuscript page of Albert Einstein's paper on the general theory of relativity with handwritten corrections by the author, a typescript of a manuscript page of T. S. Eliot's poem "The Waste Land" with handwritten critical comments by Ezra Pound, and a typeset version of the latter, including Pound's comments.

/30 Sections of text that relate to specific drawings reproduced in the blog have been omitted here.

/31 A section of text that relates to specific photographs of the Deepwater Horizon explosion has been omitted here.

/32 A subsequent post, "Solidarity" (February 27, 2011; http://lebbeuswoods.wordpress.com/2011/02/27/solidarity-updated-226/), concerns the rebellion in Libya; this has been omitted from this volume.

/33 Woods discussed the destruction of Ai's studio in Shanghai in "Ai Weiwei's Courage" (January 13, 2011; http://lebbeuswoods.wordpress.com/2011/01/13/ai-weiweis-courage/) and Ai's arrest in "This Cannot Pass" (April 3, 2011; http://lebbeuswoods.wordpress.com/2011/04/03/7669/), "Salman Rushdie: Dangerous Arts" (April 20, 2011; http://lebbeuswoods.wordpress.com/2011/04/20/salman-rushdie-dangerous-arts/), and "Ai Weiwei: What Is to Be Done?" (June 7, 2011; http://lebbeuswoods.wordpress.com/2011/06/07/ai-weiwei-what-is-to-be-done/). These posts have been omitted from this volume.

/34 See "A Space of Light" (February 15, 2011).

/35 Projects for Sarajevo that demonstrate exactly what is meant by "radical reconstruction," accompanied by extended captions, are presented in the blog post but omitted from this volume.

/36 See "Why I Became an Architect, Part 2" (February 8, 2012).

/37 For more on the topic of analog computers, see "The Next Revolution?" (February 29, 2012).

/38 Drawings and texts from the blog post on the theory of tectonic plates and their effect on Manhattan have been omitted from this volume.

/39 Jenny Diski, "The Me Who Knew It," *London Review of Books*, February 9, 2012, http://www.lrb.co.uk/v34/n03/jenny-diski/the-me-who-knew-it.

Contributors

The following people, under their names or their pseudonyms, contributed texts to the Lebbeus Woods blog. While most of their writing has not been reproduced in this volume, it was instrumental to the life of the blog.

Writers
Raimund Abraham, Peter Cook, Corrado Curti, Per-Johan Dahl, Manuel De Landa, Cheng Feng Lau, Leo Gullbring , Zvi Hecker, Jay Mark Johnson, Lars Kordetzky, Sotirios Kotoulas, Christoph a. Kumpusch, Diane Lewis, Geoff Manaugh, Shannon Mattern, Thom Mayne, Kimberli Meyer, Sebastiano Olivotto, Oyler Wu Collaborative, George Prochnik, Jack Self, Michael Sorkin, Neil Spiller, John Szot, A. Tehrani, Anthony Vidler, Les von Losberg, Aleksandra Wagner

Commenters
A_D_E_, A. Tehrani, Aaron, aaronnajera, AAscapes, aborham, acatects, AD, Adam, adam grassi, Adam Koogler, Adam Ryder, Adam Smith, adamwiseman, adamx, aes, Ahmad Borham, Aida Miron, aitraaz, aiweiwei, aiww, AJ, Ajay Manthripragada, akaak, AL, Alan, Aldrossi, Ale, Alejandro, alejandrodiazbarrios, Alessandro Orsini, Alex, Alex Bowles, Alex Gil, Alex L, Alexander Gorlin, Alexander Strugach (SPb, Russia), Alexandr, Alexandre Mendes, alfonso, algabus, Ali, ali soltani, Alicia Breck, allan areano, Alvaro Garcia, Amber, Amin, Amir Shahrokhi, amp, ampexian, Ana D'Apuzzo, Ana Maria Leon, Andrei, Andres Souto, Andrew E, Andrew Ferentinos, Andrew McCauley, AndrewC, andy Hickes, anette brunsvig, anil kumar.n, Anna, Anne Romme, Anne Zeng, Anonymous, Anthony Matters, Anthony Titus, Anthony Vidler, Antoine, Antonio, aqua alta, aranka, Arash Basirat, arcajb, ArchForm, archinthebay, architectural ruminations, archiz, arete design, Ark, Arman, Arman Bahram, arronouri, Arsalan Rafique, Art, Arthur McGoey, arun sawant., as, ashuraiw, atlatl2, augustan, aurora, austinsakong, Awax, ayuna mitupova, B. Nory, Bauhaus Design, bboyngui, bdotq, bdpog, ben, Ben Dai, Ben Dronsick, Bernadette, Bernardo BRUNO, betadinesutures, betamagellan, bhb, Biel, bigasong, Bill M, BinMar Leto, birdseeding, blackdog, Bob, bojana vuksanovic, bomoc, Bong, bosevan, BP2, Brad, Brandon Bergem, Brett Holverstott, Brian Kaye, Briana, Bright Garlick, Brook, Brooke, Bruce F, Bruno, Bryan, bryan cantley, Bugregen, C, c.smith, Caleb Crawford, Camilo, campion platt, Cara Armstrong, carlhigdon, Carlos Alberto León González, CCKL, cclee, CDC, cem özgüner - istanbul, certificazione energetica,

Cesar Cheng, Chad Brown, chaldea, channa newman, chaosW, charles, Charles Matter, Charles Roche, Charlie Anderson, Charlie Brown, Charlie 阿理, chaz, chelko, chen, Chenoe Hart, chenoehartc, Cheri, Chest Rockwell, Chinese, chiwan, chld, chlee19, Chris, chris hamby, Chris Landau, Chris Teeter, Christian, Christian Molick, Christian Peter, Christina McPhee, Christophe DM BARLIEB, Christopher, Christopher Lauriat, Christopher Otterbine, citacionista, citizenjoe1, Clinton Cole, Clover, Cody Derra, Cole Slaw, Colonel Willard, Commenter, Conrad, cor, Cory, CP, crista, Cristian Pandele, Cruz, csmith, csxlab. org, Curtis, CW, cygielski, D. Buonfrisco, D. Coulombe, Dag, Dale Nason, damien, Damir, Dan, Dan Coulombe, Dan Lenander, dan lenander uhrenholt, Dan Sherer, dana, Daniel Jacobs, daniela, danielamonaco1, Danlrene, Danny, Dante Straw, Dario Nunez-Ameni, Darrin Harvey, Dave, Dave "Diamonds are forever", Dave Chernin, Dave D, Dave Irwin, David, David A. Palmieri, David Alan Ross, David Bowman, David Burns, david gersten, David J, David Long, David Pearson, David Reid, David Ting, David Zilber, davidbburns, davidhuang, Davis, dazed, DB, Dean Morrison, Deema, deepa, Del. Irium, Den, der flaneur, Derek Fekkai, Desert dweller, DesignerGuy, designlevelzero, devdutt shastri, DHL, Diamond, Diane, Diego, Diego Peñalver, Diehl Art Gallery, difference, Dimitris, dina, djeak, djuro, dkzo, dog, dokclab, Dom Moisan, Dominique Lamandé, Donatella, doublethinker, Dover, dpr-barcelona, Drafter, dude, Duncan, durere, durganand balsavar, Dustin, Dustin Unrau, dy, Dylan Fan, dzko, e fuller, earlstvincent, eco3, eduardo blanco, edward, egrec, ehud rostoker, Eimear, ekkehard rehfeld, Elan, elan fessler, ele, Eli K., elijah, Elisa N., Elizabeth P., Ematheus, Emily Marchesiello, Emmanuele, emmanuele pilla, Eric Chin, Eric Kahn, Eric Ross, Ethan Kent (@ebkent), euphemus, Evan, Evan Bray, Ezinne Lily, Facundo, fairdkun, faizzohri, Fay Kirsten, Federico Lepre, Feroz, ff, FH, Fine Alleydone, Fine Line, Firas, Firat, FJ, Flavin, Flavin J, Flavio, forkfingers, Francesco F., Francisco, Francisco Vasconcelos, Frederieke Taylor, G MOON, gaguri, gareth lloyd, Gary He, Gavin Keeney, gb427, General, General.la, generall, George Knight, george smyrlis, George Wilson, geraldine, gerri davis, gerridavis, GhostZodick, Giancarlo M, Gio, gk-out, glen, Godofredo, golittlebook, Gong Szeto, goochin, Gr, Graham, grahame, Greg, Greg Miller, Gregory Hurcomb, Grullone, gsidari, guest, Guilherme Cartaxo, Guillermo Núñez, Gulliver, Gustavo, Gustavo B, Guy, H, Hal, Hamis, Hamish Buchanan,

Harald Brynlund-Lima, harman, harmann, harrison, haveacupoftea, HDWu, Helder, helen, hen, herman, homeless, Honus Wagner, htce, http://phenomenon-s.ru, huangdou, Hunter Bater, i.slover, ian, Ian Christopher Thomas, Icreeight, ID, if, Igor, iheartmies, Ilision, ilze, Immanuel Kant, Individuos opacos, insurrectionnow, Ipek Ek, Isil, itsme, Ivan Ostapenko, J Ingold, J.p. Sara, J.Stinson, Jack, Jack Self, Jackie Luk, Jackson, Jacob A. Bennett, Jacob North, Jacquie, Jah, Jamal Stephens, James, James Bezek, James Groundes, James Polachek, james richards, Jami Primmer, jamiesaker, jamin, Jared Karr, Jason Lee, JC, Jean Paul Sara, Jean-Paul Sara, jeff, Jeff Brown, Jeffrey Li, Jeffry Burchard, Jemuel Joseph, jenkins, jenny, Jeremy Ashkenas, Jerry, jes, jghunter, jgrzinich, JIC, jilu wu, Jim Meredith, Jim Moses, jimmy the bat, JimTwixt, Jiri Boudnik, Jiri K., Jo, joão antunes, joe, joe schmoe, Joe Viola, joehagedorn, Joel, Joey Sarafian, joeyjoseph, John, John Doe, John K, john m, John M., John Maas, John Young, johnkariyannis, Jon, Jonathan, Jonathan Feldschuh, Jordan, Jordan Johnson, jorge javier, Jos Bosman, jose, José Nascimento, joseph, Joseph Clark, Joseph Sarafian, Josh, Josh Horowitz, Josh V, Joshua Nason, Joshua Perez, Joshua Ray, JoshuaV, JRO, JS, JSavage, jtotheviss, Julia, Julia Weber, Julian McCrea, Justin, Justin Boland, K. Bradley, K.S., kabunik0, Kamil, Kamyar Fanaei, katerina, Keith, Ken Jones, Kenneth Howe Jones, Kent @ Whey Protein Review, Kevin, Kevin H., Kevin Rhowbotham, Kevin Slavin, kh, Kiel, Kiel Bryant, Kimberli Meyer, kkoense, km, Kojiro No-se, korzac, kristoferkelly, Kroy Wen, Krystina Kaza, Kuangjuan, kuniaki, Kush Patel, Kyle Schroeder, Kyu Kim, L_Son, L. L., lakin, larry rinder, Laura, Laura Blosser, Laurence Turner, Lawrence Lek, le145minimalist, Lee Becton, leezee, LeMonde, Leon, Leon_London, Leopold Lambert, lepo, leslie, Less is more, Lewis Wadsworth, Liam Ahern, lígia milagres, LIMBO, limon, lin, lin y., Linda Nochlin, lindsey, Lior Galili, liren, Lis Cena, Lisa Dublim, Liz Snow, Liza, Loaei Thabet, lorbus, Lorenzo, Lost-InPlace, lotus, LoveWW, LOW, lturner, Lucas W, Luis, luke, Luke Pulliam, L'ulu Jackson, LV, m, M Dub, m jesus huarte, m.byrne, m.hitscherich, m(odm), macmini, MadProphet, Mafalda Gamboa, Magic Whiskey, mailinator, Manel R, manolo marquez, manuel delanda, Manuel R, Marc K, Marc Lewis Krawitz, Marcello, Margot krasojevic, Maria, Maria del vicente, Maria Fueyo, marik, marin, Mario, Marius, mark, Mark Bank, Mark Bates, Mark George, Mark Jackson, Mark Keller, Mark Morris, Mark Primack, Mark Webster, markw, marmelic, Marshall Shuster,

martin, Martin Taurer, marwin bald, mary, marzipan, Mason White, matei23, Matias, Matt, matt bua, Matt Lewis, Matthew, Matthew Allen, Matthew Chen, Matthew Weinreb, Matthew Yungert, matthewdarmourpaul, Matthias Slavens Contrael, maude orban, Maurice Omollo, Maurits, max, Mazin, mbachic1, mchart, mchart929, McIng, me, Mehran, mel, memo, mero, Mersiha Veledar, mgerwing, Mhuett, Micah, Michael, Michael Cranfill, Michael Gibbs, Michael Hays, Michael Knutti, Michael Phillip Pearce, Michael Sorkin, Michael Wagner, michaelotchie, Mick, Miguel Jaime, Mik, Mikael Pedersen, Mike, Mike Clemens, Mike Geary, Mike White, Mike Wong, Mikey, milena, Millenium People, Miller Taylor, Ming, miran, miss representation, Mitch, Mitch McEwen, MLA, MM Jones, Moi, Monica Effendy, Monumental International Ltd., monumentalinternational, Moody834, moon hoon, Mou, Mr Black, MrvA, mu, Mustafa Teksoy, Naeem Mohaiemen, namhenderson, Napolesander Mina, Natale, natchard, Nathan, Nathan Bishop, Nathan_B, Nathaniel Schlundt, nemethrolanddaniel, Nenad A. Stjepanovich, Nenad Stjepanovic, neon, nexalist organization, nfgayle, Nicholas Pevzner, Nick, Nick Pevzner, Nick Porcino, Nico, nikkie, Nikola Gradinski, Nimai, nina b, nina barbuto, nolandlab, Nora, normaldesign, Noticias de Arquitectura, nucleus, null, Nuno Raphael Relvão, Nuno Varela, Nyvang, oa, ogawa, oletto, Oliver, Oliver Zarandi, olivier, Olla, omaraza, organicMobb, orhan ayyuce, oscar falcón lara, Oscar Reyes, Oscilloscope, OX, P. Garcon, P'lala, Pablo Garcia, Pablo Lara H, palace, paolo polledri, parkergarden, Pato, Patricia Deveraux, Patricio De Stefani, Patrick, Patrick Girvin, patz, Paul, Paul Anvar, Paul M. Rodriguez, Paulina Wilkowska, paulo, paulo miyada, pdx, PE, pearce, Pedro Esteban, Pedro P, pedrogadanho, PEJA, Penelope, Penley Chiang, Penny Bittone, Per-Johan Dahl, peridotlogism, pete wenger, Peter, Peter Hendry, Peter Kneiber, Peter Willis, Peter Zaharatos, Petronius Maximus, pheadx, Phillip Brunk, pixo, planement, plemeljr, Pop-Rouge, powerlessness of perspectivse, ppli, Pradheepa, Prasad, pratik, progressive reactionary, Pyracantha, Quadrus Penseroso, R MacTague, R. Y., r.c. reid, rachel jin, Raed, Rain Slowe, Raintea, RaiulBaztepo, Rand Pinson [Romulus], randy, Randy Deutsch AIA, LEED AP, Randy Nishimura, Rat Fink, Raul, Ravneson, ray, RDGarcia, Rellim Mada, Rene Peralta, Rex Thomas, Rhino, Richard, Richard Joon Yoo, Rios, river, rkirankumar, rmark, rob, Rocky Patel, Rodger, Roger Broome, Roger Kopet, rolando rojas, Romulus, Ronald Bentley, Roobarb, RosCon, Rothko George holden manz, rov,

Roxingyoursox, Roy, RS, rui, russellclark, Ryan,
Ryan J. Simons, ryanadoyle, s, S. v. Stuckrad,
sahand, Sainchi, Sakshi Gupta, Sally Bowles,
Salvatore D'Agostino, Sam, samanthaff, sander
boer, Sander Woertman, sandrine von klot,
sangahsuh, sara tilley, sarahhalford, saurabh,
Sayem (rajit) Khan, scott, Scott R, scutanddestroy,
scyg, Sean, Sean P Murphy, Sebastian Vidal,
seier+seier, serapahtar, sergio machado, Seriously,
serraglia, Severn Clay-Youman, shandor hassan,
SHANGYLCHEN, Shila Abdula, Shlomo Korzac,
shreyank, shyarc, sidahmed9, Siddid Srivastava,
signe schmidt, Simon, simongrew, 660, SJ Lee,
Slam, slothgut, smallestforest, smoghat, Solly,
some guy, Sophie, sos, Sotirios Kotoulas, Spencer,
ss, Stan Wiechers, stefan, stefanus hadi nugroho
kurniawan, Stephen, Stephen Games, Stephen
Korbich, Stephen Lauf, Stephen Mohn, Steve, steve
leitch, Steven Chou, Steven Harris, steven holl,
Steven Millan, Steven Pitera, Steven Shimamoto,
Stratis Mortakis, Stratmort, straykatstrut, student,
studentwithoutaclue, Suchitra Van, sueb, sun,
T. Caine, T.K from China, tabb, Talya Nevo-
Hacohen, tami, Taryn, Tee, teresa, Terrapol, terry,
thais, thanasis, The Sesquipedalist, the0utfit,
theblobbyblog, Thom Brady, Tima, timlan,
Timothy Latim, Timothy Mendez, TK Robinson,
TMU, todd, tofu, tom, Tom Brooksbank, Tom
Gallagher, Tomek Gancarczyk, tomer, Toni, Toralf,
torossian stephane, Trumbo, 2002–2007, Tyler,
Ugljesa Janjic, underscore, Uri Wegman,
vanderleun, Velton, ver, Vick, vicki, Vico, Victor
Linus Engels, Victor Liu, Victor Navarro, Viet Do,
Vlad, voidinbetween, Vonlrminger, w, W. Bradley,
WA Sulaiman, wang, watchzerg, Waterboy,
wave, Wayne White, wazeone, wes, Wes Rozen,
Wien 8836, wildoo, wilfingarchitettura, Will,
Will Vachon, will2build, William Astor, William
Kirby, William Stout, wing, wm, wmwm, wwcc,
xianql, Xiaohu Wang, xMoDx, y, Yan, yc, Yeang
Hong Ngui, Yefim Freidine, Yorik, youarch_01,
youssefnabil, ysgs, ytiffanie, z, Zach, Zach
Emmingham, Zach V, zaire sais, zale, zari, Zena,
Zhiwei liao, Zion luo, zk, zo, Zoran, купон
безлимитные тарифы, 中国屁民, 刘洪军,
古灵, 吉软糖, 艾的门徒, 记得, 赵雷, 道哥, 邹冉,
陈狗二, 隔壁老王, 马研, 马腾, -----, -------------, …

Published by
Princeton Architectural Press
37 East Seventh Street
New York, New York 10003

Visit our website at www.papress.com.

Printed and bound in China
18 17 16 15 4 3 2 1 First edition

This publication is supported in part by a grant from the Graham Foundation for Advanced Studies in the Fine Arts.

Editor: Megan Carey
Editorial Assistant: Marielle Suba
Archive Liaisons (Lebbeus Woods):
Ellen E. Donnelly and Leandra Burnett
Designer: Jan Haux

Special thanks to: Nicola Bednarek Brower, Janet Behning, Erin Cain, Tom Cho, Barbara Darko, Benjamin English, Jan Cigliano Hartman, Lia Hunt, Mia Johnson, Valerie Kamen, Stephanie Leke, Diane Levinson, Jennifer Lippert, Jaime Nelson, Rob Shaeffer, Sara Stemen, Kaymar Thomas, Paul Wagner, Joseph Weston, Erika Wilder, and Janet Wong of Princeton Architectural Press
—Kevin C. Lippert, publisher

Library of Congress Cataloging-in-Publication Data
Woods, Lebbeus (1940–2012).
[Works. Selections]
Slow manifesto : Lebbeus Woods blog /
Clare Jacobson, editor. — First edition.
pages cm
ISBN 978-1-61689-334-7 (paperback)
1. Woods, Lebbeus—Blogs. I. Jacobson, Clare, 1965– editor. II. Title. III. Title: Lebbeus Woods blog.
NA737.W665A35 2015
720.92—dc23

2015003037

All cover images by Lebbeus Woods (from top to bottom):

Flow, from *Slipstreaming*, c. 2005
Light Pavilion design sketches, 2007
DMZ, from *Terra Nova*, 1988
Sketchbook, 1997
Memory Field 1+n, 2002

All images courtesy Estate of Lebbeus Woods unless otherwise noted. 2: Wladyslaw; 15: Shandor Hassan; 20: Zoran Kanlić; 23: Kevin Bone; 26: Raimund Abraham; 31: Pratt Institute; 36: Margherita Spiluttini; 57: Sotirios Kotoulas; 71: Zaha Hadid Architects; 74: © Christoph a. Kumpusch; 81: Buffalo School of Architecture and Planning, University at Buffalo, the State University of New York; 85 (left): Aleksandra Pawloff; 85 (right): © Christoph a. Kumpusch; 91: © Kiki Smith, courtesy Pace Gallery. From the collections of Brooklyn Museum; 108: Tom Bonner Photography; 111: © Daniel Libeskind; 124: Public domain; 157: Corine Vermeulen; 158: Morphosis Architects; 160: Public domain; 171 (top): Steven Holl Architects; 171 (bottom): © Iwan Baan, courtesy Steven Holl Architects; 175: © Ross Racine (http://rossracine.com); 177: Michael Krüger, courtesy Zvi Hecker; 185: RIEA Archives; 187: © Iwan Baan, courtesy Steven Holl Architects; 189: James H. Ward III; 190: Collection Salvatore LaRosa and Ronald Bentley, courtesy Peter Rowe; 192: Albatros Publishing; 195: Filip Dujardin; 207: Masahiko Yendo; 213: Margot Krasojević; 217: Bill Wetzel (http://flickr.com/photos/wrwetzel); 220: Yiorgis Yerolymbos; 227: Jonathan Feldschuh; 230: Public domain; 231: Oyler Wu Collaborative; 232: Christopher Payne

Keeping in touch

sing interactive writing with young children

Edited by Nigel Hall & Anne Robinson

Heinemann

PORTSMOUTH, NH

HEINEMANN
A division of Reed Elsevier Inc.
361 Hanover Street, Portsmouth, NH 03801–3912
Offices and agents throughout the world

Copyright © 1994 Nigel Hall and Anne Robinson

Published simultaneously in the United States of America
in 1994 by Heinemann
and in the United Kingdom by
Hodder & Stoughton Educational
a division of Hodder Headline Plc
338 Euston Road
London NW1 3BH

Library of Congress Cataloging-in-Publication Data

Keeping in Touch : using interactive writing with young children/
    edited by Nigel Hall and Anne Robinson.
        p.   cm.
    Includes bibliographical references.
    ISBN 0–340–58735–0
    1. English language—Composition and exercises—Study and
teaching.   2. Dialogues—Authorship—Study and teaching.
3. Diaries—Authorship—Study and teaching.   I. Hall, Nigel.
II. Robinson, Anne.
LB1576.K385   1993
372.6'23—dc20
                                                                    93–48129
                                                                        CIP

Typeset by Wearset, Boldon, Tyne and Wear.
Printed in Great Britain for Hodder & Stoughton Educational, a division of Hodder Headline Plc, 338 Euston Road, London NW1 3BH by Thomson Litho Limited.

CONTENTS

ABOUT THE EDITORS AND CONTRIBUTORS

Nigel Hall is a lecturer in The School of Education at Manchester Metropolitan University and a specialist in early developmental literacy. He is the author of *The emergence of literacy* (Hodder and Stoughton) and co-author of *Literacy in action* (Falmer Press) and *Some day you will no all about me* (Mary Glasgow Publications). He is the editor of *Writing with reason* (Hodder and Stoughton), and co-editor of *Play in the primary curriculum* (Hodder and Stoughton).

Anne Robinson is a lecturer in The School of Education at Manchester Metropolitan University. She is the co-author of *Some day you will no all about me* (Mary Glasgow Publications).

Rita Adey is a member of Doncaster Teaching Support Service's 'Early Intervention' team.

Karen Bromley is Professor of Education at The School of Education and Human Development, State University of New York at Binghampton.

Leslie Crawford is Professor of Education, State University of New York at Potsdam.

Rose Duffy is a teacher working for Manchester Education Authority.

Shelagh Hewitt is a teacher at Cavendish Road School, Manchester.

Diane Mannix is a reading teacher at Glenwood Elementary School in Vestal, New York.

Finian O'Shea is a teacher at St Benedict's School, Dublin.

Glenise Sinnott is a classteacher at Station Road Junior and Infant School, Doncaster.

INTRODUCTION

There are few practices in teaching which are always taken up enthusiastically by children and which offer them a stimulating challenge, have powerful educational consequences, offer teachers increased insights into the lives and feelings of their pupils, give a high degree of authenticity, and are always fun to carry out. Such a practice sounds a bit like a magic trick and teachers know that there are no magic tricks to help children develop their learning. However interactive writing comes close.

In the past eight years we have introduced hundreds of teachers and student teachers to interactive writing and almost all of them have found it a positive experience. Time and time again teachers have told us that interactive writing has made a significant difference to them and the children they teach. They have reported discovering hidden abilities in their children, have experienced wonderful changes in their relationships, have found out many fascinating things about their children's lives, have obtained great personal satisfaction from writing, and have witnessed substantial improvements in the children's attitudes towards, and interest in, writing.

Because interactive writing is not a magic trick, it works only because teachers put care and concern into ensuring that it is a positive experience for their children. Like all the best teaching practices it needs some effort and time, both of which can put burdens on already over-stretched teachers. However, almost all the teachers with whom we have worked have declared that it has been worthwhile. Interactive writing represents a powerful and satisfying experience for all people involved with it.

This book provides an introduction to interactive writing. Although the chapters run continuously, they fall into three sections.

The first section, represented by Chapter 1, has a general overview of the whole area of interactive writing and is the most theoretical part of the book. This chapter analyses the nature of interactive writing and seeks to justify its educational value. It raises a whole range of important issues. If you wish to get straight into more practical issues then you may wish to leave this chapter and come back to it later; in which case start with section two.

The second section, represented by Chapters 2 to 8, contains a set of case studies about using interactive writing with young children.

Each chapter gives an account of a particular use of interactive writing. The authors explain the procedures they used, the type of children they were working with, give examples of the exchanges that occurred, analyse some of the writing, and discuss the advantages and disadvantages of the experience for both the children and the adult participants. These case studies offer a range of examples, from children writing to teachers, to children writing to prisoners convicted of serious crimes. They involve children of different ages and abilities and use a variety of techniques for exchanging their correspondence.

The third section, containing Chapter 9, answers a whole set of questions about the practical aspects of starting interactive writing with young children. If you want to get going immediately with interactive writing then start with this chapter.

Whatever the order in which you read the chapters of this book they add up to a fairly detailed presentation and assessment of using interactive writing with young children. All the authors represented in these chapters believe very strongly in making early communicative experiences as valid and authentic as possible. They also believe that powerful learning experiences can be fun and immensely enjoyable. Their chapters demonstrate very clearly that interactive writing can be all those things, but above all, in an educational system which is becoming increasingly conformist, it gives each child a chance to make his or her own voice heard clearly.

1 INTERACTIVE WRITING: ITS NATURE, PURPOSE AND SCOPE

Nigel Hall

Introduction

What is interactive writing? To a large degree this question is most easily answered by saying 'read the whole of this book', for throughout this book the reader will be shown many different types of interactive writing and a variety of ways of carrying it out, both inside and outside the classroom. However, to start with, the following statement offers a working definition:

> Interactive writing is writing involving the participation of two or more friendly correspondents who exchange meaningful and purposeful texts across an extended period of time.

Because this book is about interactive writing in educational contexts, some types of interactive writing will be less frequently encountered. However, even in school interactive writing can vary in many ways. Children can write to class friends, to older or younger children, to teachers, to parents or to other adults. The exchanges could be through written conversation, dialogue journals, or letters and the communications could be exchanged by hand, by post, by computer or by fax. Thus variation occurs in relationship, time and medium.

Staton, in discussing specifically dialogue journal writing claims:

> *Dialogue journal communication is written conversation between two persons on a functional continuous basis, about topics of individual (and eventually mutual) interest. (Staton et al., 1988, p.312)*

The notion of 'mutuality' is a very important one. Interactive writing offers a meeting place for minds. At the heart of interactive writing is the social relationship between two people and as Shuy (1987) points out:

> *There is nothing more social than dialogue: two people interacting through the medium of language. (p.890)*

But as Lindfors (1988) pointed out there is:

> *A distinction between 'talking together' and 'being together' in talk. (p.135)*

Therefore mutuality means so much more than just sending messages or letters to each other. Robinson, Crawford and Hall (1990) asked:

> *What kind of conversation would it be if people simply talked at each other with no regard for each other? Would it even be called dialogue? (p.118)*

'Mutuality' is rendered most powerful in interactive writing when it is developed within five central precepts.

1 *Mutuality is strengthened when the written exchange extends over time.*

One-off letters or messages are not as interesting, meaningful or motivating as extended dialogue. Of course, discrete writing activities have a place in life but the achievement of mutuality requires real time. Participants must have the chance to get to know each other, to develop a style of exchange, and to understand the varied obligations of a sustained relationship.

2 *Mutuality is strengthened when there is a high degree of authenticity in the relationship between the writers.*

Authors should engage in dialogue where each participant has equal rights. Although some interactive writing may take place between mature writers and young children, it is vital that the experienced writers do not use their competencies in a didactic way. It is not the function of any one party in a dialogic exchange to exert continual control over the dialogue. When participants have equal rights in the dialogue they each have the freedom to select and introduce topics, to avoid or reject topics, and together they negotiate the development of the dialogue.

3 *Mutuality is strengthened when it is the meanings of the exchanges which are significant rather than the form.*

Friends do not normally correct, mark, or grade each other's letters. Friends write because they have important or interesting things to say to each other; they want to know about each other's lives, feelings and thoughts. Each accepts the other's letters as they are.

4 *Mutuality is strengthened when there is trust between the writers.*

Friends do not seek to embarrass or humiliate each other. Equally dialogue between friends is private until both correspondents agree to what they write being made available to others; people who 'tell all' find fewer opportunities to engage in mutual exchange.

And, particularly where children are concerned:

5 *Mutuality is strengthened when children are 'invited' to correspond.*

The achievement through writing of an honest relationship with a child is impossible if that child has been forced to take part in the exchange or is made to respond for didactic reasons rather than because he or she finds the dialogue rewarding and intrinsically interesting.

Interactive writing is writing for real and is thus a very functional form of authoring. In interactive writing children can use language to accomplish many things.

> *People use language to get things done. They promise, deny, complain, predict, report, request, warn, thank, and everything else that gets done when we talk. (Shuy, 1987, p.894)*

Interactive writing can be one of the most powerful ways to encourage children to exercise all those language functions in written text. Indeed there are few forms of written language which can offer so many opportunities for engagement in a wide variety of language functions.

What is it about interactive writing that makes it such a powerful experience for all those contributing to the dialogue and for those privileged to observe or read the dialogue? What is it that makes it so attractive, meaningful and rewarding to young children? Why does it result in young children maintaining dialogue over long periods of time, sometimes to people they hardly know or may never have met? What is it that makes it such a powerful learning experience, and one which encourages children to persist when other forms of writing would have been laid aside?

There are at least seven reasons why interactive writing is so powerful. The danger in identifying them as discrete reasons is that the reader may be led to see them as quite separate. They are most certainly not; they intertwine and cohere. The absence of any one of them inevitably weakens the impact of the rest. It is simply an administrative convenience that they are, in this chapter, teased apart for more detailed examination.

It is inevitably the case that most references will be to studies of dialogue journal writing. This area has been examined much more frequently than any other, and it is probably true that dialogue journals or written conversation with a teacher will be the most common sustained experience of interactive writing. However, where possible, references are drawn from other studies which examine other forms of interactive writing and with audiences other than teachers.

Interactive writing offers reasons for authorship

Rosen and Rosen (1973) started a chapter on writing by saying:

> *It is easy to think of many reasons why a young child should not want to write and very difficult to think of reasons why he should. (p.85)*

What might have been the case in 1973 may be less the case in the early 1990s. However, the second sentence of Rosen and Rosen makes it clear why they thought young children would not want to write. They say:

> *Even more baffling is the problem of what a young child thinks he is doing when he is writing, other than submitting to the will of adults and putting writing in the same category as potty training, kiss grandma and grace before meals. (p.85)*

What kind of experience is it, for young children learning to write? There is no doubt that the nature of the experience is fundamental to a young writer's conception of what writing is, what it is for, where one does it, and what is important about it. The experience people have of something plays a major role in helping them define both the 'something' and the doing of 'something'. As Gundlach, Litowitz and Moses said (1979):

We suggest that a child's theory of writing evolves as he develops as a writer, informed along the way by his experience in writing and reading, both within the activity and in relation to other activities; by what he is capable of doing and what he feels is important to do; and by what he derives from writing instruction and guidance he is given at school. (p.128)

What they fail to make clear is that for many children most of their early experience of writing is contained within the final aspect – the child's experience in school. And what happens in school? In April 1990 a report from Her Majesty's Inspectors Of Schools claimed that two thirds of activities in English were pitched at the most basic level and that 'Standards of work were unsatisfactory when children were required to complete undemanding tasks set in isolation from other aspects of language development.' Such comments have been a constant theme of HMI reports going back over many years. In 1982 (DES) the inspectors wrote that 'Copying from workbooks and cards occupied too great a part of the time of some 5 and 6 year olds.'

A study of 'good' teachers of six-year-olds (Bennett, Desforges, Cockburn and Wilkinson, 1984) found that:

The predominant aim expressed in more than 70% of tasks intended to promote writing was to 'practise' writing and to use some aspects of grammar, especially capital letters and full stops as sentence markers. (p.101)

Requests for spellings constitute the predominant teacher/pupil exchanges in language lessons. (p.128)

It was impossible to distinguish between tasks aimed at developing imaginative writing and tasks aimed at writing reports. (p.103)

What beliefs about writing will children have if they experience it as nothing more than ritualised, routine practices with no apparent function other than providing practice on skills because the teacher demands it? Are they likely to conceive of writing as something interesting, worthwhile, fun, rewarding, explorative, enjoyable, purposeful, or useful? And are they likely to learn to write effectively if the experience is meaningless, routine, mechanical, lifeless, boring, fraught with fear of failure, undemanding, or restricted? Why are so many children given negative and meaningless experiences of writing? If children have experiences like this then it is easy to agree with Rosen and Rosen's claim that it is difficult to see why children should want to write.

If one takes away the teacher-imposed structures, removes the fear of failure, and takes out the ritual then the situation changes rather dramatically. Children do not avoid writing; they do not see it as some kind of punishment; they do not see it as an imposition. In such circumstances children function as authors creating meanings. This is particularly true when interactive writing is involved.

In schools, children's experiences of writing are often rather solitary, with the principal audience being the class teacher in the role of assessor. Such a state of affairs is almost a total contradiction of the nature of writing as it is experienced by writers and readers in the world outside of school. Outside of school we read material written for a huge variety of audiences, and we contribute material ourselves for a whole variety of audiences. We always do so for a purpose. There are always reasons for our writing and those reasons are almost always tied up with the social/communicative nature of literacy; we want people to know things. Interactive writing, at its heart, is about wanting other people to know things: about us, about the world, about feelings, attitudes, and emotions. Providing that the exchanges are set up in an open way then interactive writing is purposeful from the start. There is a reason for writing. Dialoguing with other people seems a most natural way of using writing in that it matches skills with processes already well understood by children.

Writing in general, and interactive writing in particular, becomes a more valid and meaningful activity for children if the adults involved in it recognise certain basic tenets:

- That children have the ultimate responsibility for their texts. They are the authorities on their writing. It is no accident that 'author' and 'authority' are related terms. Children who 'own' their texts will write meaningfully and will want to use their skills purposefully. In interactive writing children write with their own voice about interests, concerns, attitudes, values and beliefs.

- That authorship is given a certain 'bite' if the young author understands that an audience exists for his/her text, and if that audience is interested in, and cares about, the meanings generated by the writer.

- That the most convincing demonstration of an interest in, and care for, a child's texts, is to respond to them by using the same medium. In other words for the reader to give a concrete commitment to their response. It is not the writing of a letter that makes interactive writing a powerful experience; it is getting a reply. Getting a reply means that someone else has cared enough about your writing to invest time and effort in responding by using the same medium.

Children who can see a purpose for writing will write. The children featured in this book did not need false encouragement to dialogue with their correspondents. There was an eagerness to participate in the exchanges. This keenness is particularly noticeable when other children, not part of exchanges, virtually demand to be a part of what is going on. Lyons (1987) commented on her dialoguing with children:

> The correspondence between the children and myself very rapidly came to include a number of other indirect participants. These included other children in the class who enclosed notes to me in their friend's journals. There were other children who sent messages to me which were reported in the letters. In addition I was asked to pass messages on to a student of mine whom the children also knew. Others outside the school also began to send messages which were reported. These were usually from mothers or sisters.

Similarly Robinson, Crawford and Hall (1990, p.102) reported how when Les, one of the adult correspondents, had returned to the United States he started to get letters from children other than those to whom he wrote. These letters began with sentences like:

> I have a friend called . . . She writes to you. It's easy for her because she has a brother who writes to you. I don't know what to write.

> My brother writes to you. He pins his letters from you on his noticeboard.

> My sister writes to Nigel. She writes to him a lot and he writes back. She has got a lot of things off him like letters, postcards and Christmas cards. She keeps them in a brown envelope. When she has gone I have a look at all her things. It's fun to have a look.

These children did not need invitations to write. Interactive writing seems to carry its own hook. The hook is getting replies – genuine, meaningful replies. Receiving a reply is the most powerful motivator possible. It tells a child that someone has taken very seriously what they have written. Wanting to respond to such an interested audience is one of the most powerful reasons for authorship.

Interactive writing provides a transition from oral language to written language

Many forms of written language in school make a narrow range of linguistic demands upon children, but at the same time those demands are often highly specialised. The degree of specialisation means that, where written language is concerned, children are often grappling with the unknown rather than drawing upon the known. The genres of school frequently deny children the right to use the language they already posses. As a result children often have to write very tentatively (or more likely very safely) when they use those other genres. Shuy in Staton *et al.*, (1988) claims that in so much school writing 'Children are asked to write using a stage for which they have not passed through earlier developmental stages.' (p.73) Thus they are pitched into more complex genres before they have had a chance to write in genres more closely related to those they already know. And what they already know about is oral language! This does not mean that interactive writing is simply talk written down. Written dialogue may share many relationships with talk but goes well beyond being simply talk put into words. Interactive writing links talk with literate language, and allows a more gradual move towards mastery over the formal requirements of literate language.

It is part of the powerful potential of interactive writing that it can mediate between a child's existing language knowledge and the ways of using written language that are characteristic of more formal written texts. As Braig (1986) puts it:

Dialogue journal writing may be an important link between oral language competence and written competence: an oral and written language support where assisted writing occurs before independent formal writing. (p.111)

It has long been an adage of educational practice that one moves from the known to the unknown. What is known at age five is how to use language orally. In particular 'Children's casual speech contains practically all the language functions necessary for getting things done in the real world.' (Shuy, 1988, p.79) Children at age five are also tuned in to many aspects of social relationships:

Four-year-olds were even shown to have a social sensitivity which enabled them to vary their strategies for giving directives, depending on how they perceived the status of the persons to whom they addressed these directives. (Staton et al., 1988, p.79)

Interactive writing allows children to employ many of their known language strategies. The written dialogue of the exchanges can draw upon what children know about the exchanges of oral conversation. Those exchanges allow them to interrogate, demand, explain, clarify, deny, apologise, joke, complain, request, categorise, argue, recount, describe, sequence, persuade, and offer. It is when those functions have to be used in letters or journals to a relatively unknown audience that children are forced to modify the oral nature of those functions, and are pulled forward as authors. This 'pulling forward' can be particularly powerful where the children are dialoguing with more mature writers.

If children write to peers within the classroom then the notes and letters are rooted in shared experience, and the context within which they are created is part of that shared experience. How much do you need to write to someone who sits on the same table, plays with you at break time, and walks home with you after school? Young children should, of course, have opportunities to write to children in their class (see Greene, 1985; Karelitz, 1988; Bromley, 1989; and Chapter 4 in this book). However, it is likely that the implications for developing as an author may be different, and possibly considerably different, if the respondent is a mature writer.

Robinson, Crawford and Hall (1990) claimed that corresponding with mature writers helped the children move into a more formal use of language. They say:

Because Les and Nigel were more distanced correspondents the children had to face the fact that they could not write the same kinds of things that they would have written to a classmate. The situation drew them into attempting to be more explicit about events recorded in their letters, to offer explanations about their own activities, and to write about things in which their correspondent would be interested. The children were able to use existing conversational strategies but at the same time were led to explore ways of organising their letters which took them beyond oral conversation. (p.119)

Participation in dialogic writing, while rooted in many of the characteristics of oral language, can nevertheless 'Provide a natural bridge from interactive communication to the unique demands of essayist writing' (Peyton, in Staton *et al.*, 1988, p.106). Thus engagement in interactive writing has a potential that goes well beyond simply corresponding for enjoyment or generating a need for positive personal relationships.

Interactive writing offers an introduction to different forms of written language

Most people would probably identify letter writing (whether in dialogue journals or as separate letters) as a distinct form of writing. Certainly there are usually some features which are typically found in letters such as salutations, dates, closures, signatures, and addresses. However, these features surround the body of the text rather than exist as a constituent part of it. Because of their 'surrounding' qualities these features are, in a way, only superficially part of the form of a 'letter'. It would be a serious mistake to place too much emphasis on these surrounding features and to conclude that letter writing was a rather narrow form of linguistic exercise. Inside the main body of a letter the text can vary considerably depending upon the purpose of the letter. Indeed it would seem to be inappropriate to view letters as a genre of written language. Martin (1990) claims:

> *It is important to note however that the term letter refers to a mode and not a genre. We write lots of letters for different reasons: job applications, party invitations, thank you notes, personal letters to friends, and so on. As a channel, letters can be used to transmit all kinds of different genres. (p.17)*

and Collerson (1988) said:

> *There are several different kinds of letters with different purposes; the genre differs according to the purpose. A personal letter usually includes something of the recount as well as bits of what you could call 'written conversation'. A business letter is usually rather different (for example, a request for goods or services or a complaint). Then there are thank you letters, letters to the editor (which may include explanations or even exposition) and so on. Thus letters may involve different genres depending on their purpose. (p.21)*

The examples given by Collerson and Martin separate out the

purpose of personal letters from the purposes of other types of letters. The letters for 'other purposes' are much less likely to be interactive in the sense used in this book. They are often interactive only in that they are directed to another person and, indeed, may often not even solicit a reply. They have a one-off quality which generates a demand for greater precision and explicitness than may be the case in personal letters.

Nevertheless, personal letters can also cross genre boundaries and it seems somewhat unfortunate that Collerson seems to dismiss personal letters as containing 'something of the recount as well as bits of what you would call "written conversation".' Personal letters reach out into almost all aspects of human life; they do not exist simply to recount events. In personal letters recount may be a common feature, but equally in personal letters people frequently offer advice, comment and report on significant issues and events, provide procedural advice, seek to persuade their friends of alternative viewpoints, explain positions, and describe people, events and views. In this way mature and experienced correspondents demonstrate time and time again moves into description, procedure, explanation and exposition. In other words they are, by virtue of needing to satisfy a multitude of requirements, forced to undertake the writing of a whole variety of forms of text. When Lord Chesterfield wrote letters to his son it was not for the purpose of recounting events. It is because correspondence involves transactions across space and time that moves into many genres become a necessity. Of course, in personal letter these frequently may be mixed in longer texts, but is that so different to many texts written on more formal occasions?

As young writers grow more experienced and confident so they are better able to incorporate other genre characteristics into their letters. The existence of a correspondent who does not share exactly the same life world demands that writers are forced to consider the needs of their audience, and to expect that their own needs are recognised by their audience. Satisfying those demands necessitates moves into many forms of written text. It is inevitably the case that where younger children are concerned these 'moves' may be limited and will seldom lead to the construction of complete genres within interactive writing. In Chapter 2 the child Georgina can be seen to use written language for a number of purposes. She does not develop whole letters within one genre but nevertheless has to start differentiating parts of her text according to her different purposes.

In this way children begin the exploration of what it means to manipulate text in relation to purpose. Because human beings interact for so many different purposes, interactive writing offers a helpful start to producing written texts that are a response to function.

Interactive writing provides an introduction to authorship

The development of mutuality, the provision of reasons for authorship, the move into written language, and the taking on board of a variety of genres all derive from the central fact that interactive writing involves a partner; a correspondent; an audience. This apparently obvious fact can disguise the importance of the notion of 'audience' in the development of authorship. On the whole, mature authorship makes considerable demands upon the writer as it is usually the case that the audience ceases to be a physical presence and becomes a mental presence. Rosen (1971) described the writer as:

> *A lonely figure cut off from the stimulus and corrective of listeners. He must be a predictor of reactions and act on his predictions. He writes with one hand behind his back being robbed of gesture. He is robbed too of his tone of voice and the aid of clues the environment provides. He is condemned to monologue; there is no one to help out, to fill the silences, to put words in his mouth, to make encouraging noises. (p.142)*

As Robinson, Crawford and Hall (1990, p.114) put it 'To construct a text the author has to learn to play both the parts of writer and reader extremely well.'

There are two main perspectives about the role of audience in authorship. The first, the traditional view, is that the author's construction of a text is constrained by knowledge about the audience for whom the text is intended. As Kirsch and Roen (1990) point out, such a perspective rests on several assumptions:

> *That the audience is a known entity, that the values and needs of an audience can be identified, and that the audience is separable from the discourse and social context. (p.15)*

Such a position is typical of oral discourse where speakers face each other and reactions can be observed and responded to. Written language demands more complex strategies but this first perspective still assumes that the writer has knowledge of how an audience will react and builds the text taking such reactions into account. Thus a teacher can always say to a budding author, 'Don't forget to take your audience into account.'

The second, and more recent, perspective argues that authors create roles for readers within their texts. In other words any individual can, as a reader, have many different potential roles, and that an author can, through the kind of text created, influence how the reader selects and modifies their role as a reader. As Long (1990) puts it:

> The audience, like the significance of topic, is created by the writer, and to accomplish this creation successfully the writer must understand the nature of the reading act and the cues upon which readers depend to give them their identity. (p.84)

Whether one adopts a belief that writers have to react to known audiences or that writers create readers, the development of either would appear to depend on actual experience of the effects of writing and reading texts. Thus to find out if your text has been successfully moulded to your audience you need to experience the audience's reaction. To find out whether your text has created readers of certain kinds one needs to 'hear' from those 'readers'. Either way, interaction is a powerful component in understanding possible relationships between writers, texts, and readers.

For most children in elementary schooling, and probably beyond, not only is the teacher the main audience, but he/she is also the assessor of their writing. For that reason children learn not to write what they want to say but to write what they think will please the assessor. In one sense this is clearly writing for an audience and on the whole children's perception of teacher's agendas for writing emerges very early on. In this situation the experience of audience is thus doubly narrow as the nature of the audience is virtually unchanging across the school years.

Teachers do not have to function as such a restricted audience. If teachers can adopt the 'mutuality' criteria outlined earlier in this chapter then their role as audience shifts quite dramatically. When teachers cease to respond as assessors and act as 'people' then the writer/audience relationship becomes more diverse, richer, more powerful, authentic and more educative.

When more experienced writers interact with children there are a number of ways in which the children's understanding of audience is facilitated, and these are particularly related to the receiving of replies. Robinson, Crawford and Hall (1990) identified three main components in their study:

> *There were three ways in which receiving replies facilitated the children's writing development. The first was that the responses from Nigel and Les were themselves demonstrations of how letters can relate to an audience. The second was that the children could experience in a very explicit way the impact of their own strategies towards their audience. The third was that they had to learn to adapt to a changing audience for people inevitably change as time goes by.*
>
> *As the letters passed to and fro, so the the human relationship was constantly being redefined and the way the writers had to respond to each other had to shift continually. (p.117)*

There are not many forms of school-based writing which allow children such a distinct and interesting relationship with their audience. They will eventually have to learn to internalise their knowledge about audiences and how to react to them or how to influence them, but any child who has achieved 'mutuality' through writing will have a sound initial experience on which to generate future understandings about the nature of audience.

Interactive writing offers the chance to develop personal relationships

It is virtually impossible to undertake a sustained written dialogue with someone and not get to know them better. Indeed, pen pal relationships have a long history. Many dialogues have been published and some even made into films. Getting to know someone better does presume that both participants treat the correspondence as a partnership of mutual trust and respect. Personal correspondence does not survive long if one correspondent moans, nags, corrects, insults or humiliates the other. It usually takes some strong existing relationship or guilt to survive such negative contributions. Of course, friends who correspond may sometimes moan, challenge or complain, but providing these events occur as part of a mutual dialogue and are not one-sided or too emphatic the dialogue normally continues.

For interactive writing with children to succeed, it is even more important that the relationship which develops is not one where the more able writer (if there is one) controls or dictates the nature of the exchange. Where participants are prepared to forget about power and status quite spectacular changes can occur in the relationship between correspondents. This is particularly true where dialogue between teachers and children is concerned.

Traditionally relationships, especially verbal relationships, between teachers and children are marked by the children playing a rather subservient role. Teachers have power and impose that power by controlling entry to engagements, and the manner of the engagements. Nowhere is this demonstrated more than in teachers' use of questions. Children get to ask very few questions in classrooms; teachers get to ask a great deal (Cazden, 1988). Asking questions allows the questioner to shift topics or modify exchanges. By doing this teachers manage to establish clearly the roles of children in classrooms. Peyton and Semoun (1987) claim:

> *Studies of interactions in classrooms with native and non-native English speaking students show that question-asking is the most frequent act performed by the teacher, occupying 95% of the teacher talk. Questions usually serve to establish and maintain control and conversational domination because they guide the course of the interaction. (p.3)*

When such strategies are carried over into interactive writing then children's responses are minimal. Peyton and Seymoun (1987) comment on this aspect of dialogue journals:

> *We have seen dialogue journal interactions in which the teacher's primary contribution is to ask questions. We have observed, or heard from teachers informally, that student writing in response to those questions is often brief and even elliptical, a simple answer to the question. In these cases the writing takes on the quality of an interview consisting of teacher questions, brief student responses and then more teacher questions. (p.3)*

Hall and Duffy (1987) examined the consequences of shifting from asking questions to simply making statements. The kind of writing in the journals changed. Suddenly 'here they were branching out on their own and engaging in meaningful written conversations' (p.527). They commented on one child:

Aileen had discovered her voice in writing as a result of communicating to a real audience, someone who was not standing over her shoulder as she wrote, and someone whom she knew would be interested in what she wrote and would treat her words with respect. (p.528)

The consequence of being treated as a person is powerful. The research literature is full of comments by both students and teachers which demonstrate how important this changed relationship is to both student and teacher. One older second language learner wrote:

I learn one person I never saw before. It's not the same I talk to you like a teacher. We are in the classroom okay, but when I write in the journal it's different. You are not a teacher and I am not your student. You are Henry. I am Juana. (Gutstein, 1983)

This mature student was perhaps more able to reflect on this sentiment than younger children would, but one only has to look at the quality of exchanges between Rose Duffy and her children (see Chapter 2) to see how this ease of relationship manifests itself in good quality interactive writing. When the teacher of a group of eight-year-olds asked them to write about their experiences with dialogue journals one child wrote:

I like dialogue journals because it is fun. It is useful to tell what things I don't want other people to know. And to talk but on paper. We can express feelings and thoughts.

Kessler (1989) comments on the ensuing teacher/child relationship:

She came to know and trust her teacher on a personal level, forming that special rapport which allows for expression of feelings and thoughts. (p.2)

Teachers respond positively to the closeness of this relationship. Two student teachers who dialogued with young children commented on the experience. One wrote

I feel this activity developed a trusting relationship between us that may not have otherwise have been developed through a teacher/student relationship. (Rasinski, unpublished paper)

The other said:

Sometimes we would finish reading each other our entries and then just continue talking to each other about things in our lives and about what we like to read. (Rasinski, unpublished paper)

Another teacher commented that 'Exposure to the children's authentic language richly broadened my perspectives.' (Wilson, S., 1989, p.5)

This sense of knowing other people better can also be reflected by participants other than teachers. Stoneham (1986) wrote about her second graders who had been corresponding with younger children. She said:

> *After the initial class sharing, I asked my students to write about receiving letters. What had changed? Had the partner become more real? The students writing was honest. Almost all felt a tremendous responsibility to the partner. Kari said it best in her writing. 'I love my letters from my pal. Now her is a person instead of just a name. It's very exciting to get a letter from a little person.' (Stoneham, p.283)*

The change in knowledge and relationship that occurs as a result of genuine dialogic experience has positive benefits for many aspects of classroom life. A number of teachers have commented to me that the whole ethos of a classroom has seemed to change after such experiences. This is probably because the teachers have managed to relax, have felt more secure in their understanding of the children, and have more trust and confidence invested in the children. Interactive writing is unlikely to be the sole cause of better relationships but it can make a positive and very powerful contribution.

Interactive writing provides opportunities to explore world and self-knowledge

It seems self-evident that interaction with other people increases one's knowledge about them. At its simplest level this may involve no more than observing people and learning about how others dress, talk, behave etc. As the level of interaction increases so there develops a more intense interaction between personal worlds. This usually results in greater knowledge about someone else's beliefs, values and attitudes; the essential factors of mutuality. However, when life worlds intersect it is not just beliefs, attitudes and values that are shared; knowledge of a more objective kind is shared. As correspondents tell each other what they have done, where they have been, what they saw, when events occurred, so the objectified knowledge that this represents is made available to the other person. Equally correspondents can learn from the reactions of other people to their own explorations and discoveries.

As two people correspond so knowledge about the ways in which the world exists, or operates, becomes shared and extended. Both in oral and written conversation these instances are announced explicitly by questions such as 'Did you know?', or 'Have you heard?' and implicitly through general comments and observations.

The children who wrote to Les Crawford (Robinson, Crawford and Hall, 1990) had plenty of opportunities to explore their knowledge of the world. These five- and six-year-old British children had to make sense of where Les had disappeared to when he returned to the United States after working in Britain. When a child asked in one letter where Minnesota was he received a clear description from Les. Unfortunately this description was based on a misplaced assumption on the part of Les. The child's next letter began: 'Dear Les – Where is America?' (p.89) Another five-year-old, whose knowledge about the United States was drawn from watching 'Nightrider' and similar TV programmes, wrote: 'I bet you have a posh car. I bet it has a jet engine and fancy wheels on the car. What colour is the car you've bought?' (p.90)

The replies written by their correspondent did much to help these children develop a sense of a different culture. An equally clear example of a child, through his questions forcing a correspondent to make knowledge explicit, is shown in Chapter 7 in this book. Leonard is given a powerful lesson in some economic facts of life, although it was his questions which brought the explanations out into the open.

This emphasis on knowledge is very clear in those interactive writing events which focus around subject areas in classroom life. There are many reports about children and teachers dialoguing about books and literature (Atwell, 1987; Dillard, 1989; Wollman-Bonilla, 1989) and as many where teachers of other subjects have used dialogue journals to discuss both the topic being learned and the children's reactions to it (Kessler, 1989 and Rose, 1989 – and see Chapter 6 of this book).

In most of these cases it is the teacher who is using the journals to find out about the children's reactions and learning. However, there are instances where children themselves have made content type demands upon teachers. A case in point has been written about by Gunkel (1991). In this instance a third grade child with limited English demanded in a letter, 'Please teach America.'

It is not only knowledge about the world that can be developed as writing transactions occur. Clearly self-knowledge can change as well. A six-year-old was recently engaged in dialogue journal work when the end of the Gulf War was announced. As the war was discussed in the journal the teacher asked the child if he knew who had made the Iraqi army move into Kuwait. The entries continue:

Child   Yes I do. He is called Sudam Hussain. He is a very naughty man moving into Kuwait wasn't he? He made everybody fight.

Teacher   Do you think he did it on purpose? I wonder what it is like in Kuwait?

Child   Yes I do think he moved into Kuwait. I wonder if Kuwait has got a hundred fires? I wish nobody fighted because you get killed. If I was in a war I would be very frightened wouldn't you?

Previously the entries had concentrated on the child's understanding about the war but in that last entry the child moved to think about his own reaction to it. The teacher's questions shifted to maintain this theme.

Teacher   I certainly would. I wonder how the soldiers feel?

Child   I think they would be very frightened. If I was a soldier I would be so frightened that I would be so frightened I would drop my gun.

Thus exploration of world knowledge turns to become, in a modest but possibly powerful way, exploration of self.

Interactive writing has great promise for forcing a certain amount of self-evaluation and self-examination. Apart from the basic fact that writing in itself elicits a focusing on how one feels about what one writes, so responding to a correspondent's perspective influences one's own views about many things.

For some children written dialogue can offer the only channel for reflecting upon problems relating to personal circumstances. One British teacher found an entry in a dialogue journal written by a ten-year-old child who did not normally make much use of interactive writing and usually only wrote a couple of rather perfunctory lines. The entry read:

> I am having a problem at home. My mum and dad have split up. They've parted friends but whenever my dad comes down to see me they always go in the kitchen and all I can hear is mumbling and I get scared because I think that they are arguing or thinking about a divorce. Can you tell me any way to get them back together again.

This is not exactly an easy letter to which to write a reply. For three months the teacher and child wrote to each other about this and a whole set of consequential issues. As part of a later letter from the teacher indicates, the existence of the dialogue journals was vital for this child.

> It might help if you were prepared to talk to me about it – but if you don't want to, that's quite OK.

It may seem strange that the child could be in daily contact with the teacher and yet never mention his problems, but that is what happened. It may have been that the child saw this as a totally private channel where he could discuss things in total security. During the three months the child asked a whole set of unanswerable questions of the kind illustrated above. Fortunately, the teacher was highly skilled and was married to a social worker; many hours were spent together working out highly sensitive replies. Clearly the teacher could not solve the child's problems but through extraordinarily careful writing the child was helped to understand the feelings of the other people involved as well as being helped to understand about his own feelings. Three months later the child wrote a very brief, but to the teacher wonderful, entry:

> No more problems at home now. I quite like S. . . now and I'm seeing my dad every weekend. Thanks for all your help.

From then on the child went back to writing the usual two lines. The journals had served his purpose.

The kind of knowledge this child had gained is difficult to quantify or even identify in any specific way. But clearly the child knew much more about himself, about his parents and, inevitably, about his teacher.

Interactive writing offers the opportunity to develop as a reader

Most of the work done on interactive writing concentrates on the writing. In a direct sense everything a child writes has implications for his/her development as a reader, for as Hirsch (1977) commented, 'No one can write better than he can read, since he must be able to read his own text.' (p.168) However, interactive writing has a special relationship with reading in that all the correspondence received by children has to be written by someone else and read by the children. This does not just mean 'read' in the sense of deciphering someone else's handwriting, although in many cases that is inevitable. It does mean reading to make a more effective response. Engaging in interactive writing demands critical reading; it means following arguments, reading between the lines, spotting jokes or irony, gauging intentions – in other words wrestling with meanings. Interactive writing represents a true fusion between reading and writing.

Only if children can gain access to the meanings of their correspondent can they learn anything from those responses. Of course younger children may sometimes need help in deciphering text, and even older children may require aid with new or unusual words, but children usually go to great lengths to work things out for themselves. If they do need help, their next strategy is to ask each other, and only if this fails, do they then ask the teacher. The words of their correspondent are frequently read and re-read. Children who would be grateful to put a book down saying 'I've finished', will go back time and time again to their letters or replies, and often take great delight in reading them to other people. If a child does ask for help with reading a text, it should be given. The important thing is to help the child focus on the meanings so that it is the generation of meaning which follows when the child replies.

When children interact with skilled writers, they are the recipients of extensive demonstrations, simply by being correspondents rather than as a result of deliberate instructional policy. Sensitivity on the part of the skilled partner can make for 'scaffolding' certain aspects of the children's development. Mature writers can make requests which elicit different and more extensive replies than might otherwise have been the case, and can comment in ways which expand, and sustain, ideas and themes initiated by the children. They can show how texts can be interrogated and are able to do this in a situation which is, for the children, without threat or fear of failure. This has clear implications for the development of the children as readers. There does seem to be a relationship between something even as apparently trivial as the length of the mature writers reply and the response of the child. Bintz (1989) found that:

Students who wrote least were the ones least written to by the teacher; students who wrote most were always the ones most written to by the teacher. (p.19)

and:

The type of response the teacher made influenced the length of the response the student wrote. For example, the students wrote little in response to teacher writing that was introduced by a personal fact and followed by a closed-ended question, i.e. 'I like your story. Which one is the funniest?' Conversely students wrote extensively to teacher writing that was introduced by a personal fact followed by an open-ended question, i.e. 'I love book chats. Tell me something about your book.' (p.19)

Clearly the children were doing more than simply decoding the text. They were reading into the symbols different levels of meaning. On the one hand the teacher's questions elicited straight factual replies. On the other hand the children were reading the text for evidence about a teacher's stance towards them as people, towards the activity of writing in general, and to interactive writing in particular.

The sensitivity of the responses is important. Through them one can affirm children or put them down. One student learning English as a second language wrote in a journal, 'I know that you thought about what I wrote when I wrote something.' (Gutstien, 1983, p.10)

Clearly, for this older learner, reading what was written was a highly significant part of being a correspondent.

The reading demands of interactive writing can be considerable, yet they are seldom seen by children as a burden. The activity is not 'reading': the activity is 'getting a letter or a reply'. The reading is incidental; it is occurring as a means to an end. It is reading for meaning. So much of what goes on in classrooms is explicitly claimed to be leading towards reading for meaning. Children don't have to aim for it at some point in the future. Interactive writing makes it happen in the here and now.

Some cautionary points

While interactive writing can be a wonderful experience for all participants there are a number of factors which may need to be thought about.

All may not be sweetness and light for teachers when undertaking interactive writing. There are possible consequences of a freer relationship with children which may be more than bargained for. The children who wrote to Mrs Reed (Staton, Shuy, Kreeft, and Reed, 1988) felt able to criticise their teacher, sometimes rather vehemently. One child wrote:

> Between me and you is pure hate. Hate, Mrs Reed get that through your brain. I hate you. I know you well enough to hate you. Special class was kind of fun today. I finished reading *The Black Stallion* – it was very good and exciting. I like math better and better . . . boy do I need help in math. (p.23)

Such honesty was not a problem for the teacher who used the dialogue journals, not for teaching writing, but as a way of facilitating: 'the development of their ability to be autonomous in managing their academic and interpersonal life.' (p.36) She claimed that her main aim for each student by the end of the year was for them:

> To know that they can make choices – that they have a choice in everything they do. I don't care if they always make the right choices – what they need most is to know that they can make choices. And I want them to accept responsibility for their choices. (p.36)

Such openness, while perhaps frightening to many teachers, does have the virtue of allowing difficult issues, like relationships with teachers, to be made explicit and dealt with in a non-threatening, and reasoning context.

To enter into any form of extended written dialogue with children is to take on both a physical commitment and a moral one. There are a number of significant moral issues which are central to the context of undertaking personal correspondence with young children. If written dialogue allows special personal relationships to develop between adults and children, then adults cannot simply use the children as devices for their own learning. To have a personal relationship with a child is to accept the trust of that child. This can be a wonderful thing but it does entail moral obligations towards the child who trusts you.

In some circumstances this can raise very serious issues.

If a teacher and child have engaged in a genuine and free expression, it is possible that a dialogue journal can become a cumulative document of evidence to be misused to incriminate both the teacher and the child. (Seme, 1988)

The above sentence was written by a black South African teacher. For her it was very difficult to ask children to be open and trusting when it was impossible for her, as a teacher in South Africa, to guarantee to a child that anything written might not become the subject of critical scrutiny by people who could use the document to impose sanctions on both child and teacher. The teacher concluded by saying:

To say that black students can engage in this written conversation freely in South Africa today is to delude myself because I know very well that this is not true.

It would be too easy for Western teachers reading this to simply acknowledge the issue as one pertaining to repressive governments and say 'it does not apply to us'. Can we really be certain that in inviting our children to trust us and write in ways that are highly personal we will not abuse their trust? Letters and dialogue journals are private documents. Does any adult have a right to expose a child's private writing to any external scrutiny without the approval of the child? I believe not. Fortunately for us most children are very willing to allow others access to their work if the purpose is explained. This book could not exist if the children had not been willing to allow their work to appear in print.

Not abusing the trust that children have in us as correspondents does raise an issue to do with who does have rightful access to the correspondence. If the correspondence is to be written in school, is it then to be accessible to other teachers, the headteacher or principal, school inspectors and advisers? If a headteacher or principal claims that they have a right to see any work done in their school do you release the child's private correspondence with you? If the dialogues are part of the children's 'education', do parents have a right to read the journals or letters? What does one do if children reveal highly sensitive information, perhaps about child abuse or about criminal activity? Clearly teachers will have to determine their own stance upon these issues but it is important to recognise that undertaking this kind of work can bring these issues to life.

There are few reports of difficulties occurring providing teachers are honest about their intentions. There are few children who have minded their letters or journal entries being read by other people.

Children frequently share them with each other anyway (Robinson, Crawford, and Hall, 1990). When Robinson, Crawford and Hall were developing their project they asked all the children if they minded their letters being put, anonymously, into the book. One child objected saying that letters were personal; they were his. This wish was respected. However, at the launch of the book every child, including the one who had objected, was given a copy of the book. As soon as that child got his copy, he, along with many others, came up excitedly wanting to know which were his letters. Fortunately because the authors had, in the end, decided to use the letters anonymously, he was unable to tell that none of his were represented. It must be the case that if a child does object then those child's feelings must be paramount.

Teachers also need to be sensitive to the commitment of children. There is an extensive literature on written dialogue which on the one hand goes on about the benefits of the personal relationships engendered, and then reveals that the study was carried out for a month or shorter period. What does one say to the children at that point – 'So long its been nice knowing you!' A child writing to a student teacher wrote: 'Dear Miss D – What will you do with our letters?' (Rasinski, 1988) The exchange had been planned as a three-week exercise for the student teachers (which seems to be a dubious commitment to the children). Fortunately, this student teacher was sufficiently committed herself to give the child her home address so that the correspondence could continue. There seems little point in saying, as another student teacher did, 'I feel this activity developed a trusting relationship between us that may not otherwise have been developed through a teacher/student relationship', if after three weeks the student steps out of the child's life. Children who are used as fodder for researchers, students or teachers will soon learn to mistrust people who claim to offer them a commitment. Adult correspondents have to be led by the children. It must be the children who decide enough is enough. After all it was not the children who decided they needed to engage in letter writing or dialogue journals.

This raises another critical issue. All the chapters in this book, and indeed almost all interactive writing reports and studies have one thing in common; the activity was introduced to children by teachers or other adults. It is relatively rare to come across interactive writing that was originated by a child. Thus virtually all interactive writing is introduced for educational reasons. This is not problematic. Indeed anything which can facilitate educational development as effectively as interactive writing is to be encouraged. However, it does mean that whenever we talk about 'authenticity' in the context of interactive writing, and however meaningful, personal and purposeful the interaction becomes, we must remember that it arose in an educational context. Therefore the 'authenticity' that we feel, should not delude us into thinking that we have truly escaped the world of schooling. Underneath all the lovely things that can happen in dialogic writing lies a pedagogic practice. We are still being teachers and we are still operating in school contexts. There is a hidden agenda even in the most meaningful of interactive texts that are constructed in schools.

The existence of this hidden agenda means there is a danger that, without wishing to, we begin to manipulate interactive writing in more directive ways. Equally it may appear to less experienced teachers that it 'should' operate in more explicitly educational ways. Such moves or beliefs would be terribly counter-productive. Hidden agendas are never actually hidden from children and they would soon indicate their unwillingness to put their souls into manipulative interactive writing. It is when teachers take over interactive writing that the children cease to write meaningfully and complaints start to arise that interactive writing doesn't work. It does work but it is easily killed by insensitive teaching. It works best when teachers stop acting as teachers and become partners in exploring meaning making.

To achieve mutuality is, of course, very difficult. Teachers wear an invisible cloak; the cloak of teacherness. However we may try to be people to children, we cannot escape that all embracing cloak. We are bigger than they are, we are more powerful, we are more skilled, we work in institutions which disempower children, and we have been socialised into the discourse of schooling. As a consequence we may find it less easy than the children to actually be honest. As Brodkey (1992) illustrates, teachers, without even being conscious of what they are doing, resist the intrusion into dialogue of many aspects of life. The discourses of which teachers are part are immensely powerful in very subtle ways, especially in respect of gender and class.

While I am being realistic, we must also accept that the notion of 'mutuality' does not mean that children are totally revealed by what they write. I am not sure that I understand what it means to claim that one really 'knows' someone. One can learn more about children through their writing but it is important to be wary of making claims as if there was nothing more to be said. Children's lives and meanings are every bit as subtle and complex as those of teachers.

Conclusion

It would be outrageous to claim that interactive writing is some kind of universal panacea; that it solves all educational problems, washes whiter than white, reaches the parts that other educational practices don't reach. Nothing in education will work for all children, or for any child all of the time. It is the nature of interpersonal writing that it has ebbs and flows. Sometimes we have a lot to say and sometimes not so much. Sometimes we are keen to write and sometimes we cannot be bothered. Children experience these same feelings and we cannot even attempt to make claims about offering children an authentic experience if we are not prepared to offer them the same freedoms as we would want to have ourselves.

It would be unfortunate to end this chapter on a negative note. It is certainly the case that compared with most school practices interactive writing is a wonderfully meaningful experience for children. When 'mutuality' is close the resulting writing transcends classroom constraints. The children's voices that can be heard emerging from the pages of this book are the products of interactive writing processes which have freed children's minds and allowed them to write with intensity and feeling.

A British government report (DES, 1988) stated that, 'The best writing is vigorous, committed, honest and interesting.' (p.48) There is not a piece of child's writing in this book which does not count as 'best' writing. Every piece is saturated with vigour, commitment, honesty and interest. Interactive writing is one of the most powerful human and educational experiences that we can offer young children. It is an equally powerful experience for adult correspondents. Adults want to be liked, they want to feel needed, they want to feel that they are noticed, and they want to be recognised as people. Interactive writing does not simply affirm children; it affirms adults too.

References

Atwell, N. (1987) 'Building a dining room table: dialogue journals about reading' in **Fulwiler, T.** (ed.) *The Journal Book.* Portsmouth, New Hampshire: Heinemann Educational Books.

Bennett, N; Desforges, C; Cockburn, A. and **Wilkinson, B.** (1984) *The quality of pupil learning experiences.* Hillsdale, New Jersey: Lawrence Erlbaum Associates.

Bintz, W. (1989) 'Learning how to study dialogue journals: a researcher's perspective', *Dialogue,* **6,** (1), 18–20.

Braig, D. (1986) 'Six characters in search of an audience' in **Schiefflen, B.** and **Gilmore, P.** (eds) *The acquisition of literacy: ethnographic perspectives.* New Jersey: Ablex Publishing Corporation.

Brodkey, L. (1992) 'On the subjects of class and gender' in 'The literacy letters' in **Shannon, P.** (ed.) *Becoming political.* Portsmouth, New Hampshire: Heinemann Educational Books.

Bromley, K. (1989) 'Buddy journals make the reading-writing connection', *The Reading Teacher,* **43,** (2), 122–9.

Collerson, J. (1988) *Writing for life.* Rozelle, NSW: PETA.

DES (1982) *Education 5 to 9: an illustrative survey of 80 first schools in England.* London: HMSO.

DES (1988) *English for ages 5–11.* London: HMSO.

Dillard, J. (1989) 'Learning from first graders how to use dialogue journals: a teacher's perspective', *Dialogue,* **6,** (1), 15–17.

Greene, J. (1985) 'Children's writing in an elementary school postal system' in **Farr, M.** (ed.) *Advances in writing research Vol 1: children's early writing development.* New Jersey: Ablex Publishing Corporation.

Gundlach, R; Litowitz, B. and **Moses, R.** (1979) 'The ontogenesis of the writer's sense of audience: rhetorical theory and children's written discourse' in **Brown, R.** and **Steinemann, M.** (eds) *Rhetoric 78: proceedings of theory of rhetoric: an interdisciplinary conference.* Minneapolis: University of Minnesota Center for Advanced Studies.

Gunkel, J. (1991) 'Please teach America; Keisuke's journey into a language community', *Language Arts,* **68,** (4), 303–10.

Gutstein, S. (1983) 'Using real English: writing a dialogue journal'. Paper presented at the annual meeting of the teachers of English to speakers of other languages. Toronto, March 15–20.

Hall, N. and Duffy, R. (1987) 'Every child has a story to tell', *Language Arts*, **64**, (5), 523–9.

Hirsch, E. (1977) *The philosophy of composition*. Chicago: The University of Chicago Press.

Karelitz, E. (1988) 'Note-taking: a neglected genre' in Newkirk, T. and Atwell, N. (eds) *Understanding writing: ways of observing, learning and teaching*. Portsmouth, New Hampshire: Heinemann Educational Books.

Kessler, C. (1989) 'Interactive writing in the content areas: a promising practice for all learners', *Dialogue*, **6**, (2), 2–4.

Kirsch, G. and Roen, D. (1990) *A sense of audience in communication*. Newburry Park, California: Sage Publications.

Lindfors, J. (1988) 'From "talking together" to "being together" in talk', *Language Arts*, **65**, (2), 135–41.

Long, R. (1990) 'The writer's audience: fact or fiction?' in Kirsch, G. and Roen, D. *A sense of audience in communication*. Newburry Park, California: Sage Publications.

Lyons, H. (1987) 'Keeping in touch: developing writing through the use of dialogue journals with second year children', *Primary Contact*, **4**, (3), 29–38.

Martin, J. (1989) *Factual writing: exploring and challenging social reality*. Oxford: Oxford University Press.

Peyton, J. and Seyoum, M. (1987) 'Teacher strategies and their effect on student writing', *Dialogue*, **4**, (1), 3–5.

Rasinski, T. (undated) 'Literacy learning: building relationships through dialogue journals'. Unpublished paper.

Robinson, A; Crawford, L. and Hall, N. (1990) *Some day you will no all about me: young children's explorations in a world of letters*. Portsmouth, New Hampshire: Heinemann Educational Books.

Rose, B. (1989) 'Dialogue journals in mathematic courses', *Dialogue*, **6**, (2), 6–7.

Rosen, C. and Rosen, H. (1973) *The language of primary school children*. London: Penguin Books.

Rosen, H. (1971) 'Towards a language policy across the curriculum' in Barnes, D; Britton, J. and Rosen, H. (eds) *Language, the learner and the school*. London: Penguin Books.

Sema, N. (1988) 'A black South African perspective on dialogue journals in mother-tongue language', *Dialogue*, **5**, (1), 5–7.

Shuy, R. (1987) 'Dialogue as the heart of learning', *Language Arts*, **64**, (8), 890–7.

Staton, J; Shuy, R; Peyton, J. and **Reed, L.** (1988) *Dialogue journal communication: classroom, linguistic, social and cognitive views.* New Jersey: Ablex Publishing Corporation.

Stoneham, J. (1986) 'What happens when students have a real audience?', *Journal of teaching writing,* **5**, (2), 281–7.

Wilson, S. (1989) 'Interactive writing: the key to unlocking a shy second grader', *Dialogue,* **6**, (1), 5–6.

Wollman-Bonilla, J. (1989) 'Reading journals: invitations to participate in literature', *The Reading Teacher,* **43**, (2), 112–20.

2 'IT'S JUST LIKE TALKING TO EACH OTHER': WRITTEN CONVERSATION WITH FIVE-YEAR-OLD CHILDREN

Rose Duffy

I have already explored, in my teaching, the use of dialogue journals with very young children (Duffy, 1989 and Hall and Duffy, 1987). I gave my five-year-olds a journal in which I wrote to them and they replied to me. The children wrote their entries unaided and unseen by me. The books were then put on my desk and I took them home and wrote my replies. In many respects this was highly successful. The children's writing developed, the children exhibited great enthusiasm and I began to learn much more about the children I taught. There were, however, a few aspects which I felt could be improved.

The first related to my workload. Initially I was taking thirty books home each evening, such was the children's enthusiasm. Although I was not having to write a lot in the books, completing thirty nevertheless took up a considerable amount of time. The second was that even with a daily return of the book from me the children's willingness to hang on to topics and develop them was restricted. Each day's entry of a single sentence or paragraph had its topic and this topic rarely extended into the next day. Despite these minor issues the experience was highly satisfactory and made me realise that I did not want to lose the sense of involvement with the children that had developed through sharing the dialogue journals. I was convinced that a situation which allowed the children to have, what was in effect a private correspondence with their teacher was highly beneficial to them as growing authors.

My initial experiment had taken place in the final term of the school year, and when the new academic year started I was resolved not only to develop dialogue journals with my new class but to make them more immediate, and to attempt to reduce the workload on myself. As the new term began I decided to adopt a modified approach; a difference which I would characterise as a shift from dialogue journals towards written conversation.

My class was divided into groups and at most times of the day each group would be following a different activity. I made my way around the class working with groups or individuals. Some of the activities required less attention than others so I had a little more time to spend with some groups. One of these would be a writing group. I would start work on their conversation journals by writing a sentence in each of their books. Depending upon the time available I would either sit with them and respond when they had replied, or I would visit some other children and return to the writing group once they had written their replies. In this way I was able to have a written conversation with each of the children, while at the same time continue to monitor, and be involved with, the work undertaken by other children in the class.

The conversation journals described in this chapter were written during the children's second term in school. At the time they were somewhere between five and and five-and-a-half years old.

As with any new activity children are initially unsure what they are supposed to do. This problem can be even greater if a teacher has been very directive and the children are completely unused to being allowed to write on their own. Such children inevitably respond by saying 'I can't' or 'You'll have to write it for me'. From the beginning my children had been encouraged to write on their own and it was therefore not a dramatic change for them to begin to write to me in their conversation journals. There was an initial phase where the children explored their freedom to write anything and to write in any way they wanted, but for most children this settling in period was very short, and they soon began to use the conversation journals as if they had been writing them for years.

Most children arrive at school as fairly fluent and successful language users. For several years they have been engaging in conversation with parents, peers, other adults, and most probably themselves. It seemed a natural move to allow them to carry out conversations in writing. They did not have to wrestle with finding a subject and organising a text to fit a particular genre. They already knew the genre. They knew how to take part in a conversation. All they had to do was to write it down.

The advantage of multiple entries made on one day was that the written text could really begin to take on the characteristics of

Figure 2.1

What a nuisance:
My car would not start
this morning. my daddy
hat to tek it to
the ghj
Why? biy cos the
tajr wondt go
My tyre was flat too!
did you tek it to the
garj
I couldn't drive it there!
You Cod of rigb upthe
man huw ges the cars
I'll do that next time.
I am worried about my
dog. It Cod of gt Sold
Los nat
No! She was sick!.
War wos She Sick
She was sick on the carpet.
did you have to Wosit
Yes! Wer did you put your dog
afd you had wosd the Capt
I took her to the vet.
Wot did the doctr Sey a bant
hr
He gave her some medicine.
Wos it nac medicines.
I don't think she liked it much.
I am worried now

conversation. For example, let me examine one dialogue between Georgina and myself (Figure 2.1).

Georgina, 12 March (translation)

Me	What a nuisance! My car would not start this morning.
Georgina	My daddy had to take it to the garage.
Me	Why?
Georgina	Because the tyre wouldn't go.
Me	My tyre was flat too!
Georgina	Did you take it to the garage.
Me	I couldn't drive it there!
Georgina	You could have rung up the man who gets the cars.
Me	I'll do that next time. I am worried about my dog.
Georgina	It could have got stolen last night.
Me	No! She was sick!
Georgina	Where was she sick.
Me	She was sick on the carpet.
Georgina	Did you have to wash it.
Me	Yes
Georgina	Where did you put your dog after you had washed the carpet.
Me	I took her to the vet.
Georgina	What did the doctor say about her.
Me	He gave her some medicine.
Georgina	Was it nice medicine.
Me	I don't think she liked it much.
Georgina	I am worried now.

This extract was one day's exchange with Georgina. There are a number of points worth making about this extract, the first of which must be that it is more like conversation than any other genre.

The topic derives from the everyday experience of both of us. The exchange contains twenty-two turns of about equal length. (In fact Georgina's sentences are a little longer than mine: hers are, on average, 6.9 words long and mine are 5.5.) As conversation, however, it is much more like everyday conversation between two adults than a conversation between a child and a teacher. Most conversations/discussions involving teachers and children are grotesquely one-sided, instructional, and ritualised in their structure (Cazden, 1988).

In the above written conversation Georgina has equal

participatory rights, and could even be seen to be the controller of the dialogue. It is true that I initiated both the topics of this exchange (although this was not always the case as can be seen later). However, even a very simple look at the exchange shows that the rest of the dialogue was directed by the questions from Georgina. In my previous work with dialogue journals I had found it a bit of a struggle to get the children to ask questions. Previously the typical dialogue journal exchange was for me, being the teacher, to ask the question and the child to act solely as a respondent. It took some time and some learning on my part to discover ways of avoiding the typical teacher/pupil dialogue. The answer when it came was for me to stop asking questions. In the conversation journals I worked hard to curb my natural instincts to ask questions and attempted to start each exchange by making a statement, as I did in the above exchange. This strategy seemed to work and in the exchange with Georgina I asked only one question. She asked six questions. The topic was mine but the direction was hers.

Another side of this control is evident in her freedom to write whatever she wants. She was not prevented from writing her part of the exchange by having to find a word book, queue up to get my attention, and then copy it out. She did not have to avoid using a word because she was unsure how to spell it. She was not worried that if she had a go at a spelling I would criticise her. It is important to understand that I care very much about spelling; I want my children to develop confidence and competence in spelling, but I do not wish them to become spellers at the expense of being authors. I view the development of spelling and authorship as reciprocal experiences. These conversation journals were for exchanging meanings, for being authors, for having things to say. The conversation journals were not the only writing that these children did. Indeed it was a relatively small part of their writing and those other aspects offered opportunities to explore language in more formal ways. The children understood perfectly well that the journals were for conversation not instruction.

An important feature of the above example is its length. Georgina wrote seventy-six words during this conversation. Too often children of this age are reduced to copying out very short single sentences and often copy no more than six or seven words a day, and never actually write any for themselves. How can children learn to write if they don't write? When I looked across the exchanges with the children it was not unusual for the children's contributions to range between twenty and eighty words. Thus, even discounting all the other writing the children were doing, within these conversation journals the children were getting substantial experience of writing. But they were not only getting experience of writing; my contributions were about the same overall length as theirs so each child had to do quite a lot of reading. Sometimes they needed help in reading my sentences but it was all extra experience of acting as a reader.

The final point I will make here relates to what Georgina is doing with the words she writes. Instead of a typical diet of copying teacher-influenced short recount or declarative sentences (the sort which go 'Last night I . . .' or 'This is me and . . .', she is ranging across a variety of functions. I have already noted that she asked six questions. She is prepared to hypothesise 'It could have got stolen last night', she is prepared to argue 'You could have rung up the man who gets the cars', and she is prepared to respond affectively 'I am worried now'. In one day's dialogue Georgina has had a rich, powerful and demanding writing experience.

Once the nature of the dialogue journals was understood by the children they did not wait for me to initiate the conversation. I would arrive at the table and sentences would be waiting for me. The next day's exchange with Georgina illustrates this clearly.

Georgina	I got a baby doll for Christmas.
Me	What is she like?
Georgina	She is like a real baby. Her name is Charlotte.
Me	Is she good?
Georgina	Yes she doesn't cry.
Georgina	I had toast and cheese for dinner when we had to go home. What did you have for dinner?
Me	I had soup!
Georgina	What kind of soup?
Me	Tomato soup.
Georgina	I like tomato soup too.
Me	So do I.
Georgina	I like noodle soup. What other kind of soup do you like?
Me	Chicken.
Georgina	I like bringing messages.
Me	I like reading them and I like writing to you.
Georgina	It's just like talking to each other.

Although containing slightly fewer turns Georgina still manages to write over seventy words. She not only initiates the conversation she redirects it twice by bringing in new topics. The final topic leads on to a statement, 'It's just like talking to each other', which, perhaps more than anything I could write, serves to sum up the precise quality of these exchanges. Georgina was not merely engaging in conversation she was becoming aware of the special quality that made these 'conversation' journals work so well.

Georgina was a child who had moved fairly easily into authoring experiences: Nathan was not. I made a note when he had completed a conversation journal that 'prior to starting off in this book Nathan was most reluctant to write anything, I am overwhelmed by his exuberance!' It was as if Nathan, given a more authentic context for his authorship was prepared to make that extra effort. Nathan's attendance was, for a number of reasons, somewhat sporadic yet the conversation journals enabled him to establish some continuity in his experiences. Through the conversation journal Nathan and I could sustain topics which carried over his sometimes extended absences from school. As all the previous entries were accessible to both of us, topics were easily perused and continued. The next few extracts offer an example of one such extended topic. This set of exchanges covers a period from the middle of March to the beginning of May.

Nathan, 17 March

Me	Nathan, I am glad you have come back from Kent.
Nathan	I am glad I have come back with Heather to school.
Me	Who is Heather?
Nathan	She is my Aunty. Guess what?
Me	I can't guess. You will have to tell me.
Nathan	She is going to have some kittens.
Me	Who? Auntie Heather! Is she going to have some kittens?
Nathan	No silly. Snowy is going to have some kittens.
Me	I'm not silly. You are.
Nathan	I'm talking about Snowy.
Me	Who's Snowy?
Nathan	She's my pussy.

23 March

Me	Look at that rain!
Nathan	Yes isn't it horrible.

Me I forgot my wellies!

Nathan So did I.

Me I'll have to be careful of the puddles on the way home!

Nathan I will as well.

Me How's Snowy?

Nathan She is waiting for her kittens.

Me How many is she waiting for?

Nathan I don't know yet because they are all in her tummy.

Me How many would you like?

Nathan Ten. How many would you like?

Me I prefer puppies!

Nathan The kittens are puppies.

Me Kittens are not puppies silly! Kittens are baby cats and puppies are baby dogs!

Nathan Are they?

24 March (extract from start of the day's journal)

Nathan I love Snowy to bits.

Me I bet Snowy loves you to bits too!

Nathan Yes she does love me to bits.

Me How do you know?

Nathan Because she always licks me.

9 April

Nathan Guess what?

Me What?

Nathan Snowy had her kittens.

Me How many did she have?

Nathan Snowy had four.

Me Tell me about them I feel excited.

Nathan You can come to see the kittens to look if they're nice. And two are black and grey and two are like Snowy. Two and two make four.

1 May

Me Hello Nathan. You have been away for a long long time.

Nathan Yes I have. Guess what?

Me What? I can't guess!

Nathan The kittens have opened their eyes.

Me That's good news. When are you going to give them names? Who looked after them when your mummy was in Portugal and you were in Ireland?

Nathan Maran minded the kittens. I called one of the kittens Bob. I haven't given all of the kittens a name.

The physical act of writing was not easy for Nathan. However, at the same time, he was not going to be put off from generating his messages because of those difficulties. It would have been easy with such a child to have insisted that he had a massive amount of handwriting or copying experience rather than be allowed to author his own texts – but so much would have been missed. Nathan has things to say and indeed almost forces me to listen. When Nathan writes 'Guess what?' he is really saying 'Hey, listen to what I've got to say'. It was worth 'listening'. Nathan was anything but a passive contributor to the journal. When I wrote 'Look at that rain', his return was not a simple 'Yes' but 'Yes, isn't it horrible'. Although I had generated the topic he could develop it in a distinct way. It was very gratifying that a child who had previously avoided writing anything could now hold a good written dialogue with me and in the process write unaided between thirty and forty words. Nathan's entries over those weeks allowed him to return to a highly significant event in his life. He did not need me to keep asking him about Snowy.

The written conversation with Nathan demonstrates two other powerful features of the conversation journals. The first is that some opportunities for helping children clarify thoughts, expressions or knowledge occur within the dialogue. There are two examples in the dialogue with Nathan. The first occurs in the entries for 17 March. My responses force Nathan to face up to the ambiguity of his sentence 'She is going to have some kittens'. Young children's explanations are frequently abbreviated and make assumptions about the reader's knowledge of the subject. My requests for clarification were a demonstration to Nathan that his reader did not share all his knowledge about Snowy or his aunt. The second event occurs at the end of the entries for 23 March. Nathan seems to have the impression that puppies are the same as kittens. I am not sure whether he really did not know or whether it was just a temporary confusion. Whichever it was, additional information was made available to Nathan from my response. It is vital to point out that I do not see the conversation journals as excuses to engage in instruction. On the whole I would strive to avoid behaving like a teacher intent on imposing instruction. It would conflict with my principal aim of having a medium where the children and I could meet on equal terms. However there were times and places when it seemed quite natural to pick up on a point and to clarify it.

The second major feature of the conversation journals is that because the nature of the relationship is often less formal, a sense of jokeyness can emerge. Nathan feels quite happy to call me 'silly', and I was quite happy to respond in kind knowing that he would not take it as a personal insult. The more relaxed relationships of the journals frequently lead to the children and I making jokes against each other or name-calling in fun. This is exemplified more clearly in the final extract from a dialogue between Louise and myself.

Louise, 11 March

Me	Have you any news for me Louise?
Louise	My daddy is an army man.
Me	What does he do?
Louise	He shoots people.
Me	Are you sure Louise?
Louise	Yes.
Me	Why does he shoot people?
Louise	I don't know.
Me	That's not very nice is it?
Louise	No.
Me	I think you are telling fibs.
Louise	I know that.

12 March

Me	I am going to visit my friend tonight.
Louise	I went to see my daddy at work and he gave me a cuddle and a kiss.
Me	Where does he work?
Louise	I don't know.
Me	What does he do?
Louise	He mends trucks.
Me	Does he mend only trucks?
Louise	No he mends cars too and vans too.
Me	What will he say if I ask him to mend my car?
Louise	He will mend it.

Me   How much will it cost?
Louise 2p.
Me   That's not much!
Louise I meant 3p.

In the first extract the joke is deliberate. The humour in the second is probably unintentional but one cannot be sure. In looking back at these entries it is clear that I am the one asking all the questions. However, Louise uses me to create a fiction – she leads me on. Thus, although using questions is normally a way in which teachers control dialogue, Louise has very cleverly turned the tables and made my obsession with questions into a weakness. She is the one who controls the dialogue. I am the stooge.

All the children who participated in these journals did so with evident enjoyment. There was never any of the sighing and resignation that often accompanies requests to young children to write. The activity was a highly purposeful one for them. It may seem somewhat strange that children in a classroom with a teacher should so enjoy a written conversation with that teacher. After all, writing is not easy for young children and why should they write what they want to say when they could just tell the teacher orally? I have no precise answer to that point but I suspect that for children the written dialogue represents a private channel of communication with a teacher. It offers them the undivided attention of the teacher, and it offers them the teacher as a person rather than as a teacher. Whatever the reason it seems to work and the enthusiasm generated is intense.

The rate of working in the conversation journals varies. Sometimes children are desperate to tell me something, sometimes the spaces between dialogues grow into a week. It is vital to maintain a high degree of flexibility. Anything which is worked on simply because of the day or the hour will soon lose the freshness which characterised these written conversations.

These conversations seem to me to be particularly appropriate for children just beginning their authoring careers. To write long sustained texts would demand a very high degree of effort and concentration. The written conversation allows them to write probably as many words but in a more natural way. Such dialogue is not a substitute for experience of writing more extended texts. It is, however, a means of offering children support in their efforts to become more experienced and competent writers. It is only one strategy for use in a classroom but it does seem a very effective and beneficial authoring experience for young children and for their teachers. From the teacher's perspective the advantages in terms of increased knowledge of one's children, and the increased personal relationship are enormous.

References

Cazden, C. (1988) *Classroom Discourse.* Portsmouth, New Hampshire: Heinemann Educational Books.

Duffy, R. (1989) 'Dear Mrs Duffy' in **Hall, N.** (ed.) *Writing With Reason.* London: Hodder and Stoughton.

Hall, N. and **Duffy, R.** (1987) 'Every child has a story to tell', *Language Arts,* **64**, (5), 523–9.

3 'IT'S REALLY OK. HE'S A NICE PERSON': CHILDREN WRITING TO PRISONERS

Rita Adey and Glenise Sinnott

When eight-year-old Neil was asked by a radio interviewer what he felt about the prisoners with whom he had been corresponding he replied, 'Some people are bad because they are in prison and some people are nice but they've just done something wrong.' The statement demonstrates the depth of feeling and understanding which we have come to expect from the children involved in the project and also reveals that the resulting learning experiences go much deeper than the improvement of literacy skills.

Neil, and most of the children in his class are indeed exchanging letters with prisoners from a local prison. The prisoners, who had all committed serious crimes, were people that the children did not expect to meet, who for many years had experienced little contact with ordinary people and never with children, were not familiar with modern life as we know it, and would usually be considered unlikely or even undesirable pen pals for the young and impressionable. But as Gemma commented in her interview, 'It's just like writing to a normal person that you don't know and you get so friendly it's like talking to your parents in a letter. It's really OK. He's a nice person.'

The exchange started because writing letters was the only way the children could express their thanks and appreciation for all the hard work that was being done in their school by inmates from the prison. The prisoners had volunteered to give up their weekends in order to renovate, decorate and refurbish the school library. The prison's community project programme was designed to give the men the opportunity to utilise the skills they were learning in prison workshops as well as providing a means of re-integrating the men into society after their long prison sentences.

From the earliest planning meetings with prison officers some form of written communication between the children and the prisoners had been envisaged. This was initially seen as involving simple notes, messages and drawings expressing thanks from the youngest children. However, it soon became clear that the letter writing enthusiasm of the older children should be given expression, opportunity and a real audience.

The children were already keen letter writers because the central theme of our library campaign had involved writing lots of letters to famous people asking for memories of their favourite children's books. Many wonderful replies had been received and during the summer vacation some of the older children had even set up their own letter campaign.

The parents were aware, and supportive, of the prison's involvement with the school. They were also fascinated by the success of the children's letter writing. Although extending the activity to include all those involved from the prison seemed to us a natural progression, two questions were in our mind. Would the parents support the children writing to the prisoners, and would the children actually want to write?

The parents' reaction was, not unreasonably, varied. Many were sceptical 'because of who they were', but nevertheless were prepared to allow it to go ahead. Some parents preferred their children to write only to the prison officers and one child's parents declined to have their child involved. When the proposal was put to the children, no one wanted to be left out.

During the early days of the work in school one of us made the first of many visits to the prisoners. During the course of that meeting the prisoners and the officer were told that the children would be writing to thank them and, although it was not compulsory in any way, the children would love to get a letter in return.

As a result of that meeting twelve names were secured – six prisoners, three prison officers and three governors. Our immediate problem was one of numbers; we had too many children and too few prisoners and officers. As a consequence we decided that the children should write in pairs. The children chose their own partners and it was interesting that all the children chose friends who were also of approximately similar ability. Although we would have preferred partnerships of differing ability, time has proved the children right. All the original partnerships have remained solid and have served to provide mutual support, consultation, discussion, and decision making.

From the outset the children were given maximum possible responsibility for what they wrote. The only rule ever issued (and it was adhered to) was that 'all letters must be readable'! The only formal guidance given was for the initial letter of thanks. After that the content, style and length was never subject to teacher control. The role of the teacher was always seen as facilitator and optional advisor.

The choice of pen pal was left to the children. At our next meeting with the prisoners twelve similar (although individually written) letters were handed to the officer for distribution to the men. The initial thank you letters were rather barren and stilted. All contained the same question 'What was your favourite book when you were a little boy?' All the children thanked the prisoners for the work that was being done and most of the children added their age after their signature. With one exception the average length was about thirty words. Katie and Louise's first letter was typical:

> Thank you for letting your men do our library for us we appreciate it. We would like to know what your favourite children's book was. Our favourite book is Frog and Toad.

Their letter was answered promptly but not as fast as the reply received by two of the other children. The original letters had not been distributed until all the men were back at the prison. One of them had immediately sat down and written a reply. The following day Tommy very proudly handed me a letter for Neil and Rebekah saying 'I've written to the kiddies. I said I would. It took me a long time. I hope it's OK. I hope they've got a sense of humour.'

The expression 'OK' proved to be an understatement. Tommy's letter not only amazed the class teacher and myself but gave a history lesson to Neil and Rebekah and the other thirty children in the class. He told his readers about his childhood, the cost of bread and ice-cream, and about going to the 'picture house'. He gave details of his first job as a bakery boy, his life down the mine, and his travels with the Royal Navy. His long reply was hand-printed in order that the children 'could read it for themselves rather than the teacher have to read it to them'. It contained everything possible to hold and encourage the children's interest: personal details, humour, questions and opinions, and an obvious desire for the correspondence to continue.

During the following two weeks answers to all the original letters were received. Many were hand-printed, some were beautifully illustrated with cartoon figures or flowers, and most gave indications that they wished the correspondence to continue. Every letter reflected the time, care, and consideration which had been given to the content, and exhibited the Prisoner's respect and appreciation of the children as individuals and as partners.

To Neil and Rebekah from Tommy:

In 1940 I could go on the bus for two pence. Three pence for my ticket to any picture house. Ice-cream was two pence and a bag of chips two pence or three pence.

Sorry I'm not famous but I have won a gold medal for 'clog dancing' and 'shoeing a race horse on the gallop'. I hope both of you have a sense of humour.

To Gemma and Claire from George:

When I was a small child as you are now I also went to a small village school very much like yours. When I walked through your school it brought back very fond memories.

To Gary and Jamie from John:

It is a long, long time since I myself was at school but I do remember that my favourite book was about a horse. A beautiful black horse. Perhaps that was the reason Anna Sewell the author named it 'Black Beauty'. Did you see it on television? I still like animals and work on a farm looking after lots of pigs, a bull and chickens.

To Natalie and Warren from Paddy:

Be good, work hard, be happy, be wise and take good care of yourselves always and keep away from strangers it's wise.

The children were used to sharing with the rest of the class any letters they received, usually reading their letters out aloud. The prison letters were no exception. The whole class sat mesmerised and spellbound as their own personal storytellers enriched their experience of life. From that point on the correspondence became a routine part of classroom life.

The prisoners' letters gave rise to a lot of questions from the children about life in prisons as well as specific questions about their own pal: What does he look like? How long has he been there? What do they do all day? Why don't they run away?

As a result of our own contact with the prisoners and prison staff we were able to answer these questions accurately and give the children an honest view of the realities of prison life. Prison life and the problems of being confined were never glamorised or made amusing. For their part the children accepted the details but we think they found it difficult to understand that most of their correspondents had been in prison longer than they, the children, had been alive.

The only question we found difficult to answer was 'What does he look like?' We had been using a video camera to record the work on the library and it was easy to divert the video and capture most of the workers on tape. After the children had pointed out that the prisoners did not know what they looked like we gave each partnership one minute of video time to introduce themselves.

The children had few constraints about asking the prisoners personal questions. Any reservations were ours and, more often than not, totally needless. Questions such as 'Do you like it in prison?' or 'Do you want to go home?' or 'How long have you been in?' became the norm. However, none of the children ever asked why their pen friend was in prison. Recently we asked the children why not. With everyone nodding in agreement Rebekah replied, 'For him. We thought it would upset him if we did and then he wouldn't write to us any more.'

One prisoner did volunteer that sensitive information:

I am sure you will both be wondering what I am in for. Well I did some work for somebody and they would not pay me for the work I did, so I went about getting my money back the wrong way. I took it from him, which was wrong of me. I should have gone to the police and reported him but I didn't. I did it all wrong and I finished up here. So you see it does not pay to do wrong.

As the exchange of letters progressed we became increasingly amazed and delighted by the quality of the response from all the participants. After the initial somewhat staid texts the children's letters became longer and were more interesting; they shared experiences, personal details, asked questions, provided information and shared jokes. The letters became a means of 'knowing people'. These qualities were reciprocated in all the letters written by the prisoners. None of them has ever talked down to the children or criticised them in any way. From their experiences 'inside' some have expressed concern about the children's safety and offered advice. As one said, 'so they don't make the same mistakes as I did'. One confessed that he had 'got out of the habit of writing letters' and another 'found it very difficult at first' to write his letters in 'simple language that the children would understand'.

In order to convey a clearer impression of the actual exchanges we have selected just one for more detailed presentation. The exchange which has generated the most text is the one between Neil, Rebekah, and Tommy. Neil and Rebekah's first letter was longer than the other children's but was just as formal and typical, and had no voice that could be said to be distinctly theirs. Once they received Tommy's speedy reply, that all changed as the following extracts show:

> I received your letter. I thought it was very interesting. I thought it was good that you could get a ticket for . . . Most of all I liked the bit where it said that you worked down a mine when you were seventeen. Also you asked us what we wanted to be when we grow up. I want to be a secretary or a nurse . . . Anyway that's enough of me now, let's go on to Neil. He wants to be a footballer or a policeman . . . let's jump the conclusion of that now let's talk about you. When you worked at the bakery shop was your boss strict? When you worked down the mine did you think that it was exciting or did you wish that you didn't go down it?

In all they wrote over three hundred words. In that letter they responded to the information given by Tommy, asked for more details, answered questions, gave personal details and displayed a chatty, friendly, conversational style.

Tommy's response was even longer. He answered their questions in great detail, telling them all about his life in the Navy and offered encouragement for their chosen careers.

> I enjoyed my four years at the colliery . . . I just felt that I was wasting my life down a big black hole so I enlisted for the Royal Navy. I could not swim . . .

> Rebekah nursing is a wonderful job to go into and I hope and wish you all the best in the future . . .

> Neil you do realise all bobbies have to wear size 14 boots. Anyway I hope you make the right choice when you are about eighteen years of age. If you are a good footballer then keep it up.
> I don't think I will find a job at my age do you?'

Tommy was sixty and had been in and out of prison for twenty-six years.

In their reply the children demonstrate the difficulties of sorting out the voices in their letters. This was a problem with two children having to write a joint letter. In itself it was a very interesting writing exercise.

> We received your letter. We thought that it was very interesting and some bits were funny. We are sorry that you did not succeed on many jobs . . . I am glad to hear that you will be able to come out soon. I am a little bit sad because we will not be able to write to you . . . We have got a joke for you . . . Neil's mum thinks you have a very funny sense of humour. It is Neil's brother's birthday on Friday and it is Rebekah's Grandma's anniversary on Saturday. What war were you in? Thank you for your lovely letter.

By now the children were learning quite a lot about Tommy but they did misinterpret one thing – Tommy was not due for release! Before Tommy could reply the children were interviewed on a national BBC radio programme about the letter writing exchange. Tommy wrote:

> I listened to the tape which was broadcast on Radio 4 from the school. You were very good all of you. I am now famous because you mentioned my name on Radio 4. The only other famous member of my family was my great grandfather who crossed the Gobi desert on a Pogo stick in 1820.

> I will be staying in Lindholme until I hear from London about my release date so I will continue to write to you for some time yet.

He went on to tell the children about his childhood – the clogs he used to wear, his first pair of black shoes, the hard times of the war years and his adventures with the Snerpers (rabbit catchers), his fishing adventures and bank holiday outings. For the first time he asked the children to do something:

> Today in 1992 life is much different for you children. You have everything we never had TV, video, games, new bicycles, all the modern clothes and yet I don't like to read in the newspapers and see on TV when children are sniffing glue and solvent because they are bored and some die through sniffing glue. Promise me none of you will ever sniff glue or solvents because it is very dangerous.

Their long reply featured a decorative border and like Tommy they began to number their pages.

> Rebekah was born in London and we came up to Yorkshire because my grandad is very old and has had a few strokes. Rebekah has got two sisters and one brother . . .

> Neil has got one brother called Carl. He is six. There are only four people in Neil's family. In your letter you asked us if we would promise never to sniff glue well we promise that we won't. Did you hate working all day very hard or did you think it was exciting? When you leave prison will you still write to us? . . . Did you have any pets when you were young? . . . We thought it was very interesting that your great grandma had twenty children and four had to get in one bed.

They have now almost sorted out the 'I' and 'we' problem. Their letters are becoming more orderly and they are eager to extend Tommy's knowledge of them and to know more about him. They are learning how to organise lengthy texts and to construct text for a non-present audience by using contextualised comments and maintaining themes and topics across several letters.

In his reply Tommy told them about his love for his alsatian dog, Major, and that 'he was the best friend I ever had. I preferred Major to other human beings.' He also spoke of his love of birds and gardening and told the children about his job as a 'tea boy' for the prison officers.

The children's reply was one of the shortest they ever wrote to Tommy.

> Sorry it has taken us so long to write back to you. It is our sports' day on the 10th July. We had a muesli contest. Our muesli won two times and our muesli box won 1st two times. We went on a trip to Jorvik Viking Centre and went on the time cars. We went to the shop and bought some things. Rebekah's mum is pregnant.

Shortly after that the work on the library was complete and the school held a 'grand opening'. Tommy was allowed to come to the grand opening and actually met the children and Neil's mother. On his return to prison he immediately sat down and wrote to the children.

> It was nice to meet you both at the school. I was very impressed with you both. It was a pity we could not have stayed a little longer and had a look around your classrooms.

I hope the photographs come out alright. Pleased to hear Rebekah will have a sister or brother in the near future. It was nice to meet Neil's mum.

Thanks for the drawings and the paintings. They are very good especially the rabbit hutch. I have some coloured pens for you both. I will try and pass them on to you, then you can colour a painting for my tea room wall.

I am hoping to get hold of a couple of drawing blocks from education. Then I will try and paint some water colours for you to put on your classroom walls.

The summer holidays intervened but the enforced summer break had little effect on the children's writing; they even recalled Tommy's reference to how long it had taken him to write a letter – and returned it. Their reply was enquiring, reassuring, and contained lots of jokes to cheer him up. Rebekah started the letter:

I received your letter but Neil was on holiday so he has not read it yet but he is going to very soon. We are now in Mr Andrew's class. After playtime we are going to do some painting. Hurray! . . .

Gary is going to send some pictures to John so ask him if you can have a look at them . . . Will you be able to come to our school to see us again? Do you know when you will be let out of prison?

They also enclosed the requested picture for the tea room wall – a picture of Tommy in a smoke filled kitchen burning John's toast! His reply was short but he did enclose the coloured pens and two beautiful water colours for the children.

Thank you for your letter and jokes. I am enclosing a couple of water colours I have painted. You can put them on the classroom board. I don't know if I am moving from Lindholme or not. I will let you know when I hear from London. You ask when I am coming out, I should be out in about eighteen months with luck. I enclose some coloured pens for you both. This will be an early Xmas present. I will write more when I hear from London, at the moment I don't feel too good in myself.

It was at this point in the exchange that the children began to write separate letters. The cooperative writing had worked well for a long time but in all the pairs the children were striving for more individualism. It was easiest to allow them to write separately but for them to accept that their correspondent would continue to write one reply to both of them. Neil wrote:

> How are you? I hope you don't have to move from the prison . . . Thank you very much for the pens and the painting . . . My mum said you look very nice. What is Christmas like in prison? What sport do you like best? Did you play in any teams?

In an earlier letter Tommy had mentioned that he was going to try and give up smoking. Neil finished his letter with a large 'and remember NO SMOKING' sign. He also made and enclosed a get well card with the message 'I hope you feel better soon. Keep burning John's toast, it might make you feel better.'

Rebekah wrote:

> Thank you very much for all of your presents. Especially for the pictures, they are brilliant. I wish I could draw as good as you! Did you use paints? or felt tip pens? I am going to play the violin as well as the guitar now. When you were young did you play any instruments? . . . Sorry it has taken me so long to write to you. Please will you forgive me!!?!? . . . I have got one more joke for you – Save accidents. Drive on the pavement!

> Love from Rebekah, not Neil!

Rebekah had started her letter in school and then, because of illness, finished it at home. It was two pages long and very intricately decorated with flowers and patterns. We can only ponder at the reasons for the use of so many question and exclamation marks after 'forgive me'.

Tommy's reply took the children by surprise:

> I am leaving Lindholme . . . I will drop you a few lines when I have settled in . . . I will take the burnt toast drawing with me and put it on my wall. I will hang my stocking up on Christmas Eve. Last year I put one on the end of my bed. I had an apple and a bag of sweets. I still don't know who put them in the sock – it must have been Father Christmas . . .

> Christmas is a very sad time to be in prison. You would like to be with your family but that's not possible. I make the best of it and enjoy the Christmas dinner they usually put on for us.

> God bless and hope you have a very merry Christmas.

Included with the letters were photographs for the children. Without any prompting they immediately pooled their resources and set about making a pop-up good luck card for Tommy. The front of the card was covered in flowers which when opened showed a piece of burnt toast popping out of the toaster with a message 'Oops, it's burnt again'. It also included the following note:

> We wish you good luck at Rudgate. We are sure you will like it very much and will make new friends. You will miss all your friends when you get out. When you get out will you visit our school? We would like to see you again.

In less than a year the relationship had developed from one which simply engendered a polite thank you letter to one in which the children could write an incredibly sensitive note and send a very thoughtfully developed card. It was now a relationship in which both parties could offer friendship, support and encouragement.

There is no doubt of the benefits the correspondence brought to all the children, not just Neil and Rebekah. They have learnt to construct sensitive written language. The improvements in their handwriting, spelling and punctuation have been considerable.

We strongly believe that the benefits go much deeper than simply those relating to writing skills. It is easy for busy adults to forget that young children are thinking, feeling individuals in their own right and if given the opportunity and the means to express themselves write with conviction and dedication.

We have all learnt. Seventy per cent of the prisoners who received letters remain in regular contact with the children, even those who have now left prison. George, who had been corresponding with Claire and Gemma, wrote not long after he had been released:

> Hello again! Well I am back home with my little girls and boys. I have grand-daughters about your age and it is lovely to be back home with them again so we can laugh and play together. I missed them a lot when I was in prison. It was not nice at all being there.
>
> I read in the newspaper that you enjoyed meeting and talking to me. Well, I feel the same! You were both nice and polite. I enjoyed your company and the jokes and secrets you told me. I will always remember you both.

It takes two to correspond and the immense contribution of the prisoners cannot be underestimated. They have helped to formulate and change the opinions and attitudes of the children, parents, staff, families and friends. They have increased the children's knowledge and understanding of the world around them, helped prepare them for the opportunities, experiences and responsibilities of adult life, and tried to impress upon them the importance of participative citizenship. They have proved to all of us that as Tommy said, they 'are not all bad'.

The children have never seen the writing as a chore and now willingly give up their lunch times to participate in the newly formed 'Letter Club', in order to start or complete letters, drawings, puzzles and cards for their pen friends. Their new teacher confirms what we had both suspected and hoped – that the improvements in literacy skills observed in the children's letters were transferring to their other school work. Their work was neater, clearer, better organised, and they needed less help with spelling and punctuation. They also now write more freely and with confidence that the content of their work is interesting.

All the children treasure the letters they have received. They all keep them in a 'safe place', usually in their own rooms at home, and many confess to reading them again 'before I go to sleep'. One child told us 'I've always kept my letters in a plastic folder, so they don't get torn or anything. I'm going to keep them forever so I can show my own children.'

We hope that in some small way our venture has also helped the prisoners. We certainly respect and value their efforts, their friendship and their individuality. Rebekah recently echoed the sentiments of most of the people involved when she said, 'When I thought about Tommy yesterday, I forgot he was in prison.' To us and the children the prisoners are not numbers; they are friends. Tommy once wrote, 'Thank you for coming into my life. Although I have a family I don't hear from them very often', and Tom said 'When I read the girls' letters, tears come into my eyes – somebody cares.'

All the children agree that the nicest thing about writing is 'when they write back and you can read their letters'. When asked why they kept writing, the reply was simple and unanimous – 'because we want to'. The enthusiasm of the children and prisoners has exceeded everyone's expectation and shows no sign of waning.

Tommy wrote recently, 'I will continue writing to both of you so don't think I will forget about both of you.' George said 'As long as the girls enjoy corresponding, I will continue to write.' And Tom wrote to his children 'I hope you are my friends for good.' The children have also expressed their opinions. In Rebekah's latest letter to Tommy she wrote, 'We are always going to be writing to you even when we go to comprehensive school or a different country!' And Gemma commented 'We could still be writing when we go to college.'

Who knows? We trust that by then the children will have accepted full responsibility for their own writing. Until that day we shall continue to support their authorship and hope that for them at least, the art, and pleasure, of letter writing will never be lost.

Acknowledgment

The authors would like to acknowledge the help and support of Doncaster Education Authority, HMP Lindholme and especially Prison Officer Graham Parker.

4 BUDDY JOURNALS IN THE CLASSROOM

Karen Bromley

My work with elementary school teachers and an interest in exploring peer interactions as a way of building literacy have led me to explore an idea I call 'buddy journals'. This chapter is a case study of buddy journals and their use by a teacher named Carol with some of her third grade eight- and nine-year-old children.

What is a buddy journal? It is a diary that a pair of students keeps together in which they write back and forth to each other, conversing in writing. It is a variation of a classroom dialogue journal in which the student and teacher converse together in writing. The buddy journal has many parallels with an oral conversation two children might have with one another. It can be a stimulating way for children to read and write in a purposeful and personally meaningful context as they interact socially with each other.

My development of the idea of buddy journals arose from previous work I had done with young children who were considered 'at risk' and who needed to develop positive self-esteem, see themselves as able to learn, and see a value in their lives for literacy. I was keen to explore a process that might help such children see more purpose in learning to read and write. I also knew that making connections between reading and writing for children promotes the growth of literacy because these two language processes can develop simultaneously and reinforce each other in the process.

The idea of buddy journals made sense since most of the teachers with whom I work are eager for practical strategies to help build meaningful literacy learning experiences, and some of them were already using journals in their classrooms. Buddy journals had the potential to build self-esteem, to help children become literate as they learned about each other, and to build relationships among children that might positively affect their attitudes toward school.

But first I needed to know whether the idea would work with any children.

Introducing buddy journals

Carol, a teacher with six years of experience, was enrolled in her final course in our university's master's programme in reading and language arts. She was an enthusiastic and thoughtful teacher; one who throughout her graduate coursework was usually eager to try new ideas that translate research and theory into instruction to benefit her students. Carol and her class of twenty-two children were happily in the midst of using dialogue journals when I introduced her to the idea of buddy journals in her graduate course.

Normally, when a particular idea or strategy is the focus in lectures, one or more people will try it, come to class the next week, and report their success or problems in implementation. For a number of reasons, no one tried buddy journals, nor did anyone during the succeeding few weeks. Carol discussed her hesitation with me after class one evening. She said she was satisfied with dialogue journals, and she hesitated to remove herself from this opportunity for written conversations with her children. She felt that through dialogue journals she knew her children better, and that the content and conventions of their writing had improved.

As with any new idea, I was eager to try buddy journals to see what children would do with them, whether they would like them, how they might use them, what process might work best, how collaboration might affect interpersonal relationships, and also how Carol might react to them. So, I asked her if during my next scheduled visit to her classroom we might talk with her children about buddy journals in the hope that some of them would be interested in having a try. Carol agreed and so we began to explore buddy journals together.

When I arrived in the classroom one morning in December, the children were just reading Carol's latest entries in their dialogue journals. Carol used journal writing for about ten minutes three times a week as a break in the morning between reading and math. She introduced me as her teacher, which surprised some of the children and gave her an opportunity to explain her graduate work. We talked about buddy journals, saying that we wondered if they would work with third graders, and asked for volunteers. Everyone volunteered and within a few minutes had found a 'buddy'. The children chose their own partners so that the experience would be more fun and less threatening. Carol planned to be a buddy herself if an odd number of children volunteered, and she offered to continue the dialogue journal for any child who still preferred to write to her.

When everyone had a partner, the buddy journal writing began. Children used the same journals in which they had been dialoging with Carol. Buddies eagerly wrote back and forth to each other about three times a week. Each child wrote in his or her own journal one day and then exchanged journals, read the buddy's entry, wrote a response to that entry, and then exchanged journals again. The remainder of this chapter explores selected journal entries of six children over a two-month period and Carol's observations of their interactions.

The children's writing

Matt and Greg were both reading above grade level and were considered by Carol to be bright students. They were best friends who spent a lot of time together, both inside and outside school,

> 11/30
> Today at school our reading group had to make a poem. I think that was nice. My poem was about reading and how fun it can be.
> M.

> That's great. I enjoyed your poem very much. We will be doing a special unit on poems this year.

> 12/2
> Dear, Greg How's it hanging. can you come to my Birthday party? We are going to chiChi's. after that we are going home and we will play football and open the presents. I invited you, Jared, Todd, Jessey and Ryan. Who is your best Frend you are one of mine.
> M

> Matt you are one of my best friends and it's hainging fine. I can come to your party.
> G

Figure 4.1

and were curious and eager to learn. Matt and Greg immediately turned to each other when we told them to pick a partner. They used buddy journals in the context of an already well-established friendship.

In Figure 4.1, the two top entries are the last two exchanges in the dialogues between Carol and one of the children. The two remaining entries are Matt and Greg's first buddy journal writing and show immediately a shift in both the content and language from that used in the dialogue journal with Carol.

Matt invites Greg to his birthday party which will be held at a restaurant called 'Chi Chi's' and Greg assures Matt that he is one of his best friends and can come to the party. These entries read like a spoken conversation in which the boys ask and answer questions and use current slang as they converse together. (British readers should know that in the US we write our dates differently; thus 11/30 at the top of Figure 4.1 means 30 November.)

In Figure 4.2, Matt repeats the invitation to his birthday party and Greg repeats his answer, suggesting that perhaps in their eagerness to write they were not yet reading each other's entries. In Greg's first entry he shows an awareness that his cursive signature, identified as his 'doctor sign' or doctor's signature, is not very legible. In Matt's last entry he is curious to know whether or not Greg enjoyed the party and thanks Greg for his gift of 'micro machines' which he says he likes.

Figure 4.3 shows the boys beginning to read each other's entries before writing. On 13 January Greg lists his Christmas gifts and Matt's next entry asks Greg how he likes his gifts. Matt also inquires about what Greg is reading for SSR (Sustained Silent Reading), and Greg answers that it is *Mr Popper's Penguin*. Greg includes the authors' names and gives the book an enthusiastic plug by writing 'It's a great book'. The boys also converse about the 'Pinewood Derby', a forthcoming event in which children race small carved wooden cars against each other.

Matt and Greg continued buddy journals for two months and then returned to the dialogue journal with Carol. They remained close friends throughout the year. In some respects it is difficult to evaluate the place of the buddy journal in the lives of these two boys. For the most part they are doing little more than passing low-level pleasantries and cataloguing their presents. Given that these two boys were already close friends it is difficult to believe that these things were not already being said to each other in the course of

Figure 4.2

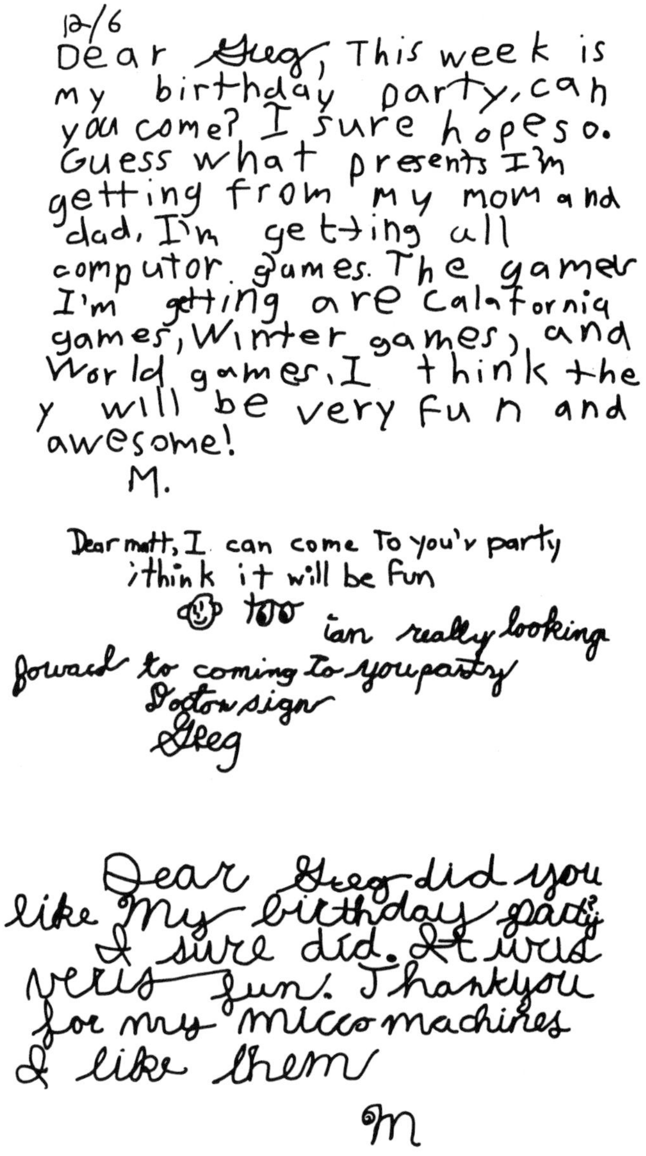

> 12/6
> Dear ~~Greg~~, This week is
> my birthday party, can
> you come? I sure hopeso.
> Guess what presents I'm
> getting from my mom and
> dad, I'm getting all
> computor games. The games
> I'm getting are California
> games, Winter games, and
> World games, I think the
> y will be very fun and
> awesome!
> M.

> Dear matt, I can come To you'v party
> i think it will be Fun
> ☺ too ian really looking
> foward to coming To youparty
> I don sign
> ~~Greg~~

> Dear ~~Greg~~ did you
> like My birthday party
> I sure did. It was
> very fun. Thankyou
> for my micco machines
> I like them
> M

their normal talking, playing, and working together. For these friends, the written buddy journal may not have offered them enough that was new and intellectually challenging.

Their difficultly highlights one major potential problem with the notion of buddy journals – if you see someone everyday and are already a friend, what is it that you can say to each other in writing that you have not already expressed orally? Perhaps children who are very secure in their friendship would be better off dialoguing with children that are not known so intimately. Certainly Matt and Greg did not seem to have need to explore the meanings of their

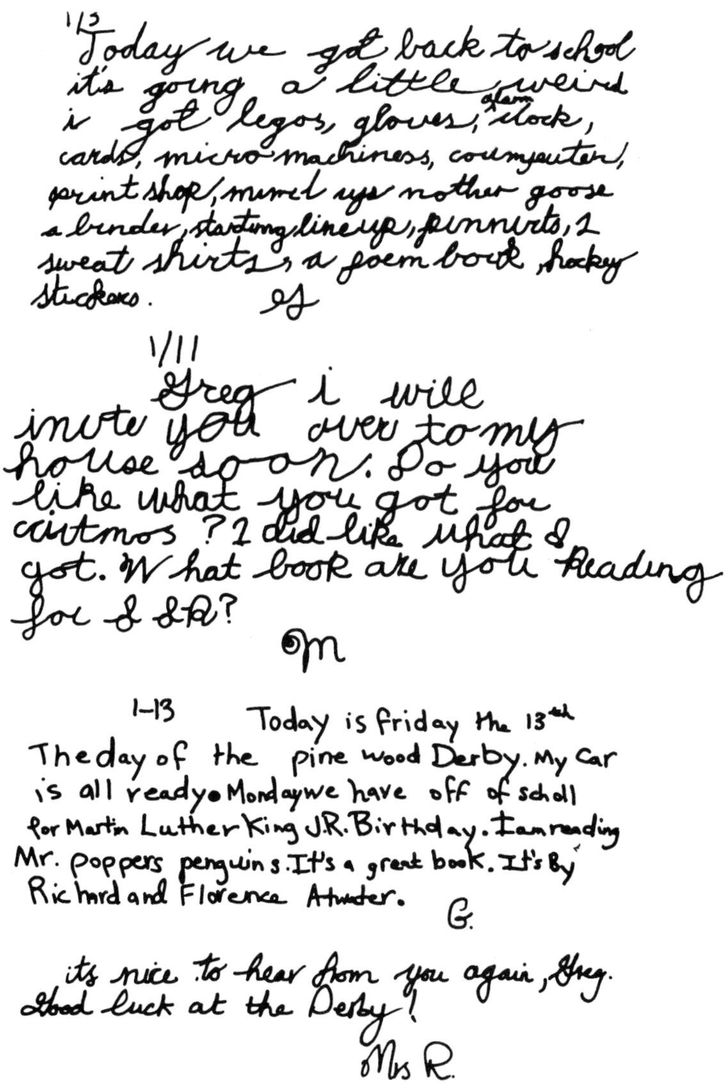

1/3

Today we got back to school it's going a little weird i got legos, gloves, clock, cards, micro machiness, coumpeuter, print shop, mumel ups nother goose a binder, starting lineup, pinnerts, 2 sweat shirts, a poem book, hockey stickers. — J

1/11

Greg i will invite you over to my house soon. Do you like what you got for cristmos ? I did like what I got. What book are you reading for S SR ? — m

1-13   Today is friday the 13th The day of the pine wood Derby. My car is all ready. Monday we have off of scholl for Martin Luther King JR. Birthday. I am reading Mr. poppers penguins. It's a great book. It's By Richard and Florence Atwater. — G.

its nice to hear from you again, Greg. Good luck at the Derby ! — Mrs R.

Figure 4.3

relationship with each other. For them dialoguing with their teacher may have been more interesting, challenging and ultimately satisfying. Their own dialoguing probably did not seem to have much purpose and thus the exchanges lacked dynamism, and they were happier when they returned to dialoguing with their teacher.

Candis and Nichole were both reading on grade level in the same group. They were seated beside each other and chose one another as partners quickly at the start of the buddy journals. They were both popular and seemed like typical third-grade girls. Their buddy journals do, however, show a greater sense of usefulness than those

Figure 4.4

12-2
My new sister is a pain
She wakes me up at night
all the time. mostly at.
3:30 in the morning Then
she gas back to sleep
and wakes me up at 7.00.

C.

she shire
is a piane. you,
stile love her don't
you? do you have eney
older sisters or
brothers? N

12-6
my mom dos't pay
any atenchen, to me
she pays most atenchen
to Jennifer. C.

that's not far is it?
if she pase more aten.
to Jennifer.
N

of Matt and Greg. Candis and Nichole did have areas of their
relationship that needed exploring.

Candis' and Nichole's entries in Figure 4.4 show the disruption
that the new baby named Jennifer causes in Candis' life and her
feelings of diminished importance in her mother's eyes since her
mother 'pays most atenchen to Jennifer'. Nichole demonstrates her
understanding of Candis' feelings and supports Candis while she
tries to learn more about her family. Carol was surprised that in
December these two girls still did not know who each other's
siblings were, but she made the observation that children had very
little time for personal interchanges in the crowded curriculum of the
classroom.

In Figure 4.5, Candis' entry dated 16 December is written in
cursive and Nichole follows the lead, writing her entry in cursive.
When Candis goes back to print-script in her entry dated 3 January,
Nichole also writes her next entry in print-script. Candis's second
entry shows the use of 'Chapter 1', 'Chapter 2', etc. to mark each
sentence she writes about Christmas gifts. At about this time Carol
was reading *Little House on the Prairie* to the class and Carol felt that
Candis may have transferred the idea from that book.

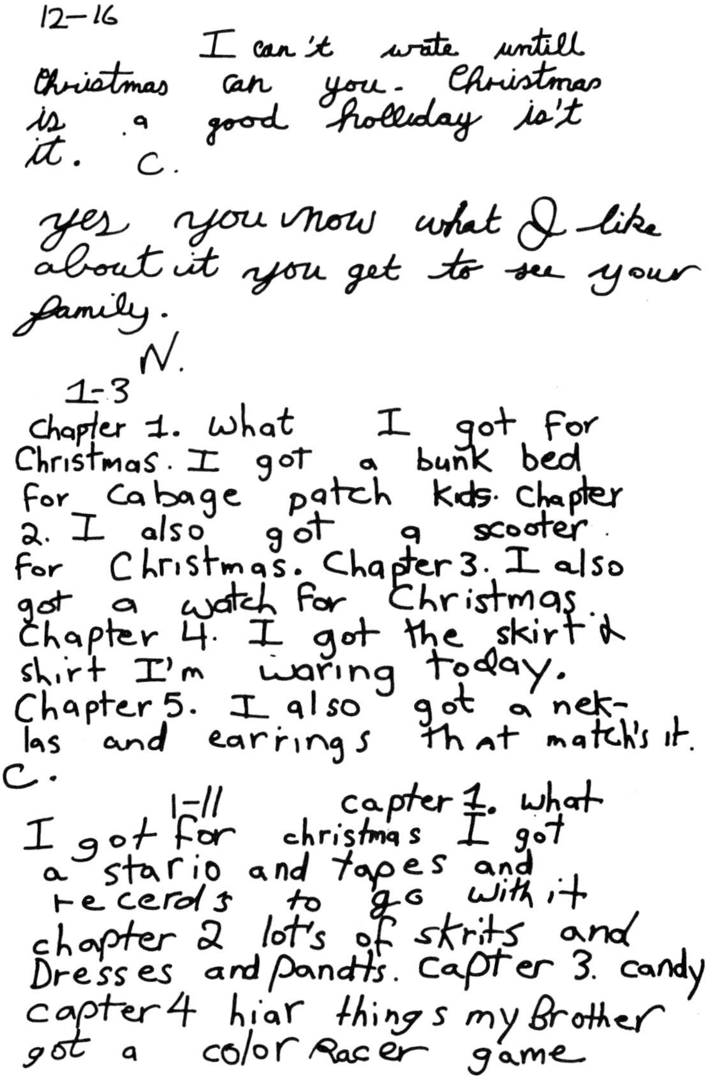

12—16
I can't write untill
Christmas can you. Christmas
is a good holliday is't
it. C.

yes you now what I like
about it you get to see your
family.
N.

1-3
chapter 1. what I got for
Christmas. I got a bunk bed
for Cabage patch kids. Chapter
2. I also got a scooter.
for Christmas. Chapter 3. I also
got a watch for Christmas.
Chapter 4. I got the skirt &
shirt I'm waring today.
Chapter 5. I also got a nek-
las and earrings that match's it.
C.

1-11 capter 1. what
I got for christmas I got
a stario and tapes and
recerds to go with it
chapter 2 lot's of skrits and
Dresses and pandts. capter 3. candy
capter 4 hiar things my Brother
got a color Racer game

N.

Figure 4.5

In Figure 4.6, Candis accuses Nichole of being a 'copy cater' because Nichole also uses the 'chapter' idea in her journal entry. At this point the two have a spat and the name of a third girl, Sona, enters their journal. Nichole appears to feel threatened by Candis' friendship with Sona and tells Candis to 'brake up with Sona or brak up with me'. Again, Nichole demonstrates an understanding of a difficult situation with 'I know it's hard to geuss (choose) you got take side'. Six days later on 26 January Candis marks the 'surcle' indicating that she intends to 'brak up' with Sona. But then she tries to make peace with 'Nichole you are my friend but Sona is to. I want

Figure 4.6

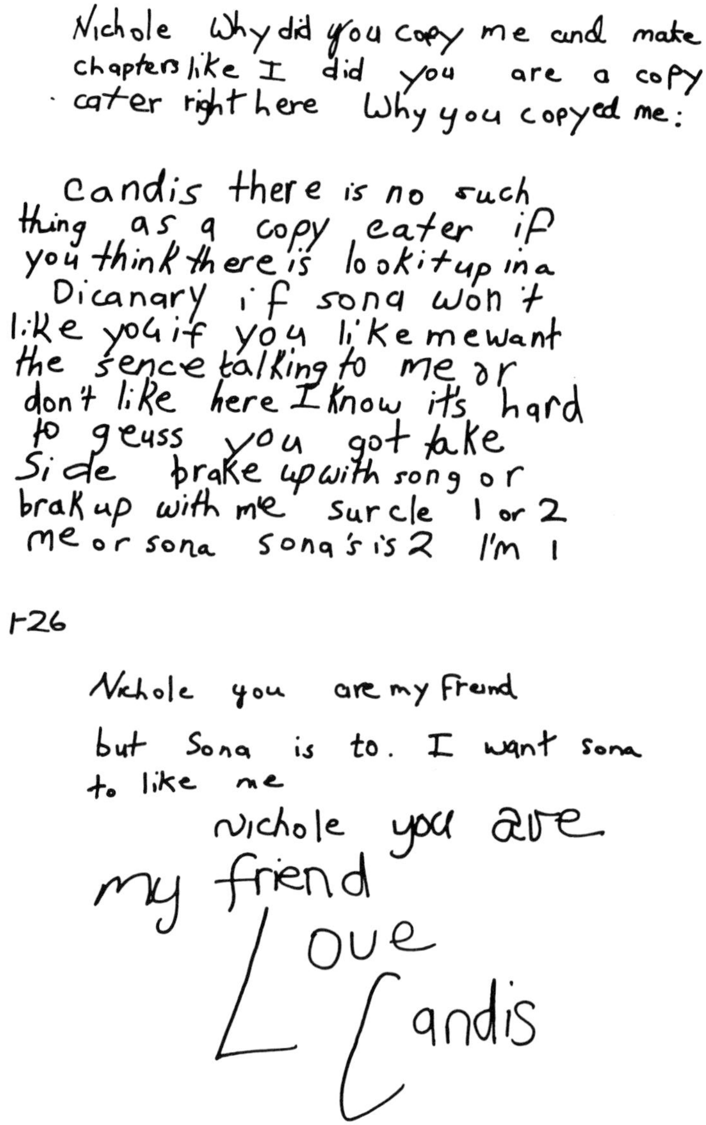

Nichole Why did you copy me and make chapters like I did you are a copy cater right here Why you copyed me:

candis there is no such thing as a copy eater if you think there is look it up in a Dicanary if sona won't like you if you like me want the sence talking to me or don't like here I know it's hard to geuss you got take Side brake up with song or brak up with me surcle 1 or 2 me or sona sona's is 2 I'm 1

⊦26

Nichole you are my Frend but Sona is to. I want sona to like me
Nichole you are my friend Love Candis

Sona to like me.' Candis' final entry, 'Nichole you are my friend. Love Candis' shows that they have made their peace with each other. Through their entries these two girls explore a friendship and the normal changes a third person causes when she tries to enter the 'best friend' relationship.

Candis and Nichole continued with their buddy journals for another month and then changed partners. Candis teamed with Jessica, and Nichole with Michelle, both other girls in the same reading group. Carol reported that the new buddies continued for the remainder of the year and all the children were quite satisfied with their arrangements.

Although Candis and Nichole had sat next to each other and chosen each other as partners it is clear that theirs was an insecure relationship. The tensions of this relationship created a topic of substance to be explored in the buddy journal. That the buddy journal was effective in this instance was probably because there were things that these two friends did not know about each other, and because some interpersonal tensions can be dealt with more easily through writing than they can in face-to-face communication.

Initially, Mike and Shannon had both asked other children to be their buddies but neither found a partner until Carol suggested they team up. Mike was a good student, a fluent writer and an avid reader who was reading far above his grade level. Shannon was reading a bit below grade level, was not as fluent or fast a writer as Mike, and seemed emotionally younger than the others in the class, openly sucking his thumb the morning I was there. The two amicably agreed to be journal buddies.

Mike initially wrote a long entry demonstrating his involvement with books and reading. Shannon did not respond. Carol felt that perhaps initially he lacked the self-confidence. Mike writes again (see

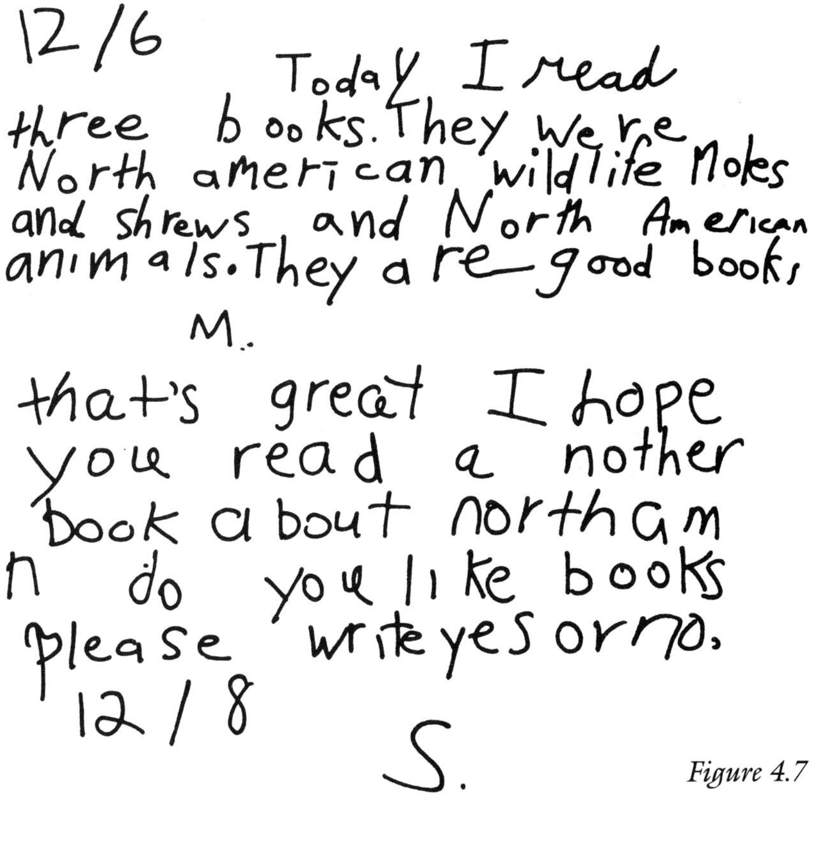

12/6
Today I read three books. They were North american wildlife Moles and shrews and North American animals. They are good books
M.

that's great I hope you read a nother book about north am n do you like books please write yes or no.
12/8
S.

Figure 4.7

Figure 4.7) and finally Shannon replies and requests a 'yes' or 'no' answer to his question. It is difficult to interpret Shannon's comment. On the one hand it does represent an initiative to take some ownership of the dialogue but on the other it seems the response of someone who does not really know how to respond – possibly both interpretations are correct.

Figure 4.8

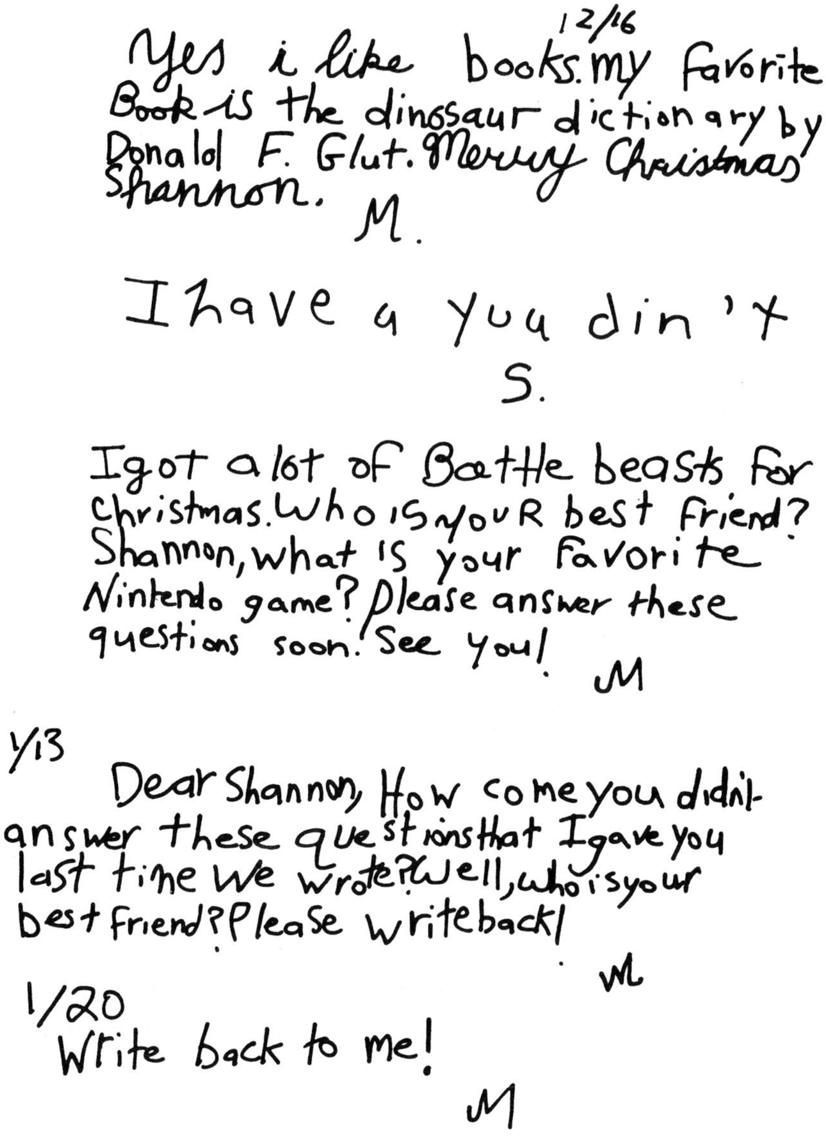

Yes i like books. my favorite Book is the dinosaur dictionary by Donald F. Glut. Merry Christmas Shannon. M.

12/16

I have a you din't S.

I got a lot of Battle beasts for Christmas. Who is your best friend? Shannon, what is your favorite Nintendo game? Please answer these questions soon. See you! M

1/13 Dear Shannon, How come you didn't answer these questions that I gave you last time we wrote? Well, who is your best friend? Please write back! M

1/20 Write back to me! M

In Figure 4.8, a week later, Mike answers the question and continues to ask Shannon questions. But Shannon stops writing in Mike's journal. Mike demands a reply, first with 'Please write back!' and finally 'Write back to me!' Mike makes strong attempts to maintain the dialogue offering straightforward questions as well as making those strong demands.

Mike, I did not writ with that mike, you britty make some thing so. I can writ some thing bretty nixe time.

I'm sorry, Shannon. What have you been doing at home? Have you been playing with youR friends! Answer this question. What is the Longest dinosaur?
  M.

brontsers Mike does that answer your question I have a question for you how many dinssaurs
  S

12/23
Wrong! the longest dinosaur is Mamenchisaurus. There were over 3,000,000,000 dinosaurs! did you have fun at the party yesterday.
  M

Figure 4.9

Shannon finally replies (Figure 4.9). He tells Mike 'you britty (better) make something (some questions) so I can writ something bretty (better) nixe time.' Mike apologises to Shannon and immediately asks him three questions. When Shannon answers one of the questions incorrectly, Mike rather deflatingly corrects him, 'the longest dinosaur is mamenchisaurus'. It is clear that Shannon has a very fixed notion of how the journals should work but it is also clear that Mike, as the superior writer, makes considerable efforts to accommodate Shannon's ideas and adjust to his level.

By the end of February Mike chose to return to the dialogue journal with Carol. Shannon also began to dialogue with Carol when Mike stopped the buddy journal. Carol used the opportunity to converse with him about his thumb-sucking in school, which she hoped to help him stop before he went to fourth grade. She was unsuccessful however, reporting that he was not able to break the habit that year.

Reflections

After examining the buddy journal entries of these three pairs of third grade students and talking with Carol about what she saw, as well as her beliefs and feelings about buddy journals, I have some observations to make about the use and value of buddy journals.

Carol was initially hesitant about buddy journals because of her positive experience with dialogue journals, even though they took a lot of time. She said she felt closer to her children, knew them much better as individuals, and enjoyed the private exchange with each child. She tried buddy journals and was convinced by the end of the year of their usefulness for some children in promoting their interactions and enhancing purposeful, meaning-centred reading and writing.

According to Carol, ten children stayed with buddy journals for the next six months, while the rest of the class returned to dialogue journals with her. Carol saw her children getting to know each other better through the buddy journals and felt that for the children who continued with them, the experience was clearly satisfying and worthwhile. She felt that buddy journals would be popular and effective with older students as well. She remembered a fifth grade class she had taught previously in which the boys in the class wrote to her in their dialogue journals about sports and the status of various players and teams, a topic about which she knew little. She felt buddy journals would allow those boys to communicate with peers who might possess knowledge and interests she did not (although, of course, her lack of knowledge might have been what prompted the boys to write about those topics).

Carol felt the need to monitor buddy journals by regularly reading them to ensure that content and language were appropriate. It is important, however, that the children understand that this is going to be the case – if a teacher monitors the journals then they clearly do not belong to the children in the way that they could if only the children were to read and write in the books. In the case of Mike and Shannon, Carol felt Shannon may have needed some help from her to understand that the kind of response and amount he wrote might affect his buddy's enthusiasm and willingness to write and continue writing. Carol said she felt somewhat left out of the children's buddy journal time, and was actually pleased when, after two months, six of the original buddy pairs chose to return to dialogue journals with her.

Thinking ahead to the following year, Carol said she planned to begin the year as she had this one, by orally reading *Dear Mr Henshaw* by Beverly Cleary, a book composed of letter and journal entries written by a ten-year-old boy. Then she planned to have the children begin journal writing, moving into dialogue journal writing with her for a period of time before giving the children the option to try buddy journals. So, for Carol, buddy journals are a worthwhile adjunct to dialogue journals.

For some of the children, buddy journals provided an avenue for peer interactions through personal written conversations. Children could share interests and knowledge, discuss problems and gain insights, explore relationships, and build friendships. In those journal entries the children showed how they could sustain meaningful written conversations over extended periods of time. Buddy journals gave them an opportunity to explore and practise writing for a real audience of peers. In their buddy journals these children shared the remarkable and unremarkable observations and events of their lives with each other.

What does seem to be clear is that buddy journals met a need for some of the children for a long time, some for only a short time, and some hardly at all. Thus buddy journals, just like all other forms of interactive writing will not work for everyone all the time. However, if the opportunity is available for those who wish to try it then some children will find great pleasure and satisfaction in exploring through writing about each other's lives. The availability of the option extends the range of meaningful writing opportunities for young children. For these reasons, buddy journals may make sense as a way of helping many students extend their interaction with their peers, build positive self-esteem, and become literate as they learn about each other. My beliefs about the potential of integrating reading and writing were confirmed and I have a richer appreciation for the importance of written peer interactions in children's learning.

5 A YEAR IN THE LIFE OF A CORRESPONDENCE: 'I'LL TELL YOU ALL ABOUT IT'

Anne Robinson, Leslie Crawford and Nigel Hall

In many accounts of interactive writing authors select extracts from the correspondence in order to illustrate particular features of their argument. Indeed the authors of the chapters in this book have not included all their available data. This is usually a straightforward logistical problem; there simply is not enough space. Inevitably, readers always gain only a partial view of what went on within the written interaction. An examination of the complete exchanges would show the ups and downs, successes and failures, changes, developments, and limitations which are a natural part of a developing correspondence.

In this chapter, by providing access to a substantial amount of continuous written interaction, it is hoped to partially redress the balance. It is still 'partially', because even the one year record presented in this chapter represents only one year of what was a three-year exchange.

All the children in a Year 1 infant class started writing to one of two adults (Nigel Hall and Leslie Crawford) who visited their classroom during the study of a topic on 'Communication'. Although the topic itself only lasted a few weeks, the children continued to write for a number of years. The collection of letters has provided a rich resource of details about the development of young children as letter writers (Robinson, Crawford and Hall, 1991). While the children were given every support and encouragement in the form of opportunities to write, access to materials, and interest in their efforts, no assistance was given with the actual writing. The children were offered help with reading the letters received if they requested it, but the selection and organisation of the content of their replies was left entirely up to them. They were working in a classroom where they were encouraged to use their own knowledge and resources to create text. Their own spelling attempts were accepted, encouraged and respected; they were expected to make their own decisions about what they needed to write. As far as the letter writing was concerned this resulted in sets of letters which were unique to each pair of correspondents.

Because each set of letters revealed a child's individual style, choosing one set out of all the sets was not easy. All were worthy of discussion but in the end Marie was chosen. She could be described as average; average in that she was in the middle of the age range – she was five years and nine months at the start of the correspondence. She was also average in terms of her performance compared with children in her class; she was not one of the best writers but neither did she have any particular problems. Like many other children in the class her interest in, and enthusiasm for, literacy was growing rapidly as she was given choice in selecting reading materials and topics for writing.

She was similar to the other children in many respects, but in one way she was quite distinct. Although she was attending school in a semi-rural situation, Marie was the only child in her class who had direct experience of rural life; she lived on a farm. This background was clearly reflected in her letters and allowed her correspondent access to information which was different than that provided by the other children. However, it is important to stress that for Marie, life on the farm was simply her life. She was writing about her home and family just as other children wrote about theirs.

The correspondence

In common with all the children in class, Marie received a letter from one of the adults (Nigel) who visited her class. The letter was given to her when the two men (who were strangers to the children but friends of the teacher) spent the morning joining in class activities and making friends with the children. The letter extended an invitation to write but did not prescribe what form or content any reply should have. Marie was free to write or not write, and if she chose to respond was free to choose what she wrote about and how she wrote it. (For the sake of brevity almost all salutations and 'sign-off' statements have been ignored. To allow concentration on the meaning, the spelling has been corrected but the punctuation left untouched.)

Marie's first letter (4.3.87)

Dear Nigel did you like being in my class and have you got any children and would you like to come to the Strawberry Fair

Nigel's second letter (13.3.87)

Thank you for your very lovely letter. I think you write ever so nicely. When is your Strawberry Fair? What happens at a Strawberry Fair? I have never been to one so perhaps you can tell me about it. Do write to me again. It is very nice to get letters.

Marie's second letter (18.3.87)

Dear Nigel
The children are going to the museum do you know a museum and I almost forgot are you coming to the Strawberry Fair and I know you have got snakes but I do not know what they are called.

Nigel's third letter (23.3.87)

Thank you for such an interesting letter. I shall try to answer all your questions. My snakes are called Orson, Elvis, Buddy, and Marilyn. I used to have one called Eddy but he died. We buried him in the garden. I will not be able to come to your Strawberry Fair. Perhaps you will be able to tell me all about it? Did you enjoy your visit to the museum? What did you see? I like museums.

Marie's third letter (26.3.87)

I did not go to the museum and one of our dogs has died and it is called Rover and we buried him in the garden too and we have got some lambs and I have got a white lamb and Sally has got a white one too.

Nigel's fourth letter (1.4.87)

I really loved your letter. I am very jealous because you have some lambs. I think my wife would like a little lamb as a pet but we have no room for one in our garden. Why don't you draw me a picture of your lambs. It would be nice to see them. You are very lucky to live on a farm. I don't live on a farm – I live in an ordinary house and it only has a small garden. I do have a big greenhouse. It is full of cacti. Do you know what cacti are?

Marie's fourth letter (6.4.87)

> I do not know if my dad will let you have a lamb but I will tell my dad when I go home if Peter says yes I will send it to you and I feed the lambs with a bottle and a frame.

Beginnings are never easy. Here were two people who did not really know each other; they had met only once and even then Marie had been just one person amongst the whole class whom Nigel had seen on his visit. Nigel did not know anything about Marie as an individual and he did not know what her reaction to the letter writing request would be. While he had written many letters before he had limited experience of writing them to children of this age; he did not know what would interest Marie or how she would cope with the demands of reading his text. Marie had little experience to inform her letter writing. The early letters show Marie and Nigel coming to terms with the new experience.

The task at the beginning of any dialogue is to establish a feeling of personal and interpersonal comfort; to discover what one has in common with one's partner, and to find a tone for the dialogue which enables interaction to proceed. The beginning of a letter writing exchange is really no different except in one major respect. In face-to-face conversation the dialogic relationship can be negotiated fairly quickly. There is virtually instant feedback and continual re-adjustment. Thus all it takes is a couple of minutes for two people to decide whether a conversation is worth continuing.

Letter writing cannot proceed at this pace (although letters via fax offer a reasonable chance of achieving speed). Time and distance both affect the rate at which dialogue develops. Letters have to be sent through the post and this takes time. They have to be sent to a non-present audience and therefore feedback has to be waited for. This causes many difficulties and complications, and they are compounded where very young children are concerned. Will they remember what they wrote in previous letters? Will topics be sustainable across time?

To some extent these difficulties were reduced by Marie's correspondent being an adult writer who could anticipate some of the problems. He allowed the agenda in these early letters to be set by Marie. From her initial response in which she used questions to refer back to the visit, to seek personal information about Nigel and to proffer an invitation, she initiated the topics of Nigel's letters. This was not because he had nothing new to contribute, but as he had to have regard for her age, her reading ability and stamina, and her interests, it was easier for him to be led by her. As Marie asked questions to be answered and provided new information which required comment and clarification, she made it easy for him to follow her lead.

What kind of relationship had been established by the end of the first four letters? It must have been a satisfying one from Marie's perspective. She did not have to continue writing but continue she did with eagerness and considerable vigour. Part of this enthusiasm would have been the novelty of the experience of receiving letters. However, we also believe that the content of Nigel's letters helped. Marie was continuously affirmed as a writer by Nigel. Her letters were 'lovely', and 'interesting'. Perhaps even more importantly Nigel responded to her questions and in the process told her something about himself. By the fourth letter both know quite a lot about each other and the tenor of the letters is open and friendly. Marie seems to have responded to Nigel as a friend as indicated by the offer of one of her father's lambs

However, some of the problems can also be seen in these early letters. Although Nigel picks up on the topics raised by Marie she fails to answer his request for information about the strawberry fair. She even asks him again about coming to it. As can be seen from the dates at this point in the exchanges, the gap between sending a letter and receiving a reply was about a fortnight and it may well have been a week or even a fortnight after that when a response was written; quite a long time in a young child's life. Despite this there is clear evidence of continuity of topic within the dialogue. Marie asks about the snakes and Nigel responds by telling about the burial. Marie responds with information about her dog Rover, 'and we buried him in the garden too'; in other words one good story deserves another. The all important 'too' could so easily get lost in the unpunctuated sentence but is vital for the continuity of the correspondence. Thus the relationship is developed partly through topic coherence.

As well as developing a relationship Marie was also having to cope with the technical demands of writing to a relatively unknown audience. Such writing demands more explicitness than speech, and there was a very clear demonstration of the need for this in Marie's second letter (18.3.87). When she wrote about children going to the museum she neglected to mention it was a class of older children and Nigel (23.3.87) mistakenly thought that she had been to the museum. The need to correct this assumption in her next letter

(26.3.87) would be a valuable experience for Marie.

Even in these early letters where Marie was writing relatively little, it is possible to see that she is using interesting strategies to maintain the dialogue. For example, the reference to Nigel's snakes in her second letter (18.3.87) where she could have simply asked their names. She initially tells him 'I know you have got snakes' (through discussion with her classmates) 'but I do not know what they are called'.

In the final letter of this section, Marie is shown using a very complex construction 'I don't know if . . . but . . . when . . . if . . . I will'. It is doubtful whether any other writing experience in school at this time would have provided the opportunity or necessity for such a complex sequence. It is also unlikely that she had seen such a sentence written in her reading books. Attempting to write what she really wants to say forces her to adopt a complex construction, a choice which is available to her because she is not limited in her willingness to 'have a go'.

We will comment only briefly on the surface features of Marie's letters as they are of secondary importance to the main purpose of our discussion. She concentrated her efforts on conveying her meaning; her address was not included in any of the letters she wrote during the first six months, nor was the date. Although this convention was demonstrated in all Nigel's letters, she, unlike other children, chose not to use it. From the beginning her messages were readable, although no awareness of punctuation was shown. Her spelling was a mixture of known 'sight' words and her own attempts (which showed some knowledge that spelling is more than transcribing sounds), but in the main she used simple phonic strategies.

Nigel's fifth letter (27.4.87)

Thank you for such a special letter. Did you have a nice Easter? I'm sure you had some Easter eggs. Did you go anywhere nice? I went with Les to see a butterfly farm. Have you ever been to one? It had hundreds of spectacular butterflies flying around. Do write and tell me what you are doing.

Nigel's postcard (5.87)

This is a very pretty butterfly. Have you ever seen one like it?

Marie's fifth letter (6.5.87)

Thank you for the postcard and at Easter we did not go anywhere and the Book Week has started and we started the Book Week by doing a play and I will tell you all about it at first we Started when Mrs Robinson said today we are doing a play and Mrs Robinson said give me a 'B' give me an 'O' give me another 'O' give me a 'K' give me a 'S' what have we got 'BOOKS' and then some people did characters but I did not have a character but I had a book and at the end we showed the postcard and at the end of the assembly Mrs Megson told us to leave

Nigel's sixth letter (11.6.87)

Thank you for your wonderful long letter. It must have taken a long time to write it all. It was 120 words long, and it was very interesting. Are you looking forward to your half-term holiday? I wonder if you are going anywhere nice? If you do you could always send me a postcard. I am hoping that Les and I will see you all on Wednesday this week. Do write me another lovely letter soon.

Marie's sixth letter (15.6.87)

Kim and Graham have got married and me and Sally was a bridesmaid and Vee and Helen were a bridesmaid and when it was the anniversary it was a long time and I almost fell asleep and Sally and Helen were doing the hokey cokey and Vee and Helen were trying to catch up with Sally because Sally was catching up with other people but Vee and Helen did not.

Nigel's seventh letter (No date)

Guess what? I have just had a phone call from Les. All the way from America. He said that he had a very long journey back to America but guess who was on the plane with him? Have you heard of the pop singer 'Prince'? Well he was on the plane as well. Les got his luggage mixed up with theirs so he was a long time getting off the plane. He said that he will be sending postcards to all those people that he writes to so tell them to look out in about a week's time. Did you have a nice holiday? Did you go anywhere special? If you did, do write and tell me all about it. This weekend I have been sitting in the garden sunbathing. So far instead of going brown I'm more a red colour. If the good weather continues perhaps I'll end up having quite a nice suntan. Do write to me again and let me know all that you have been doing.

Marie's seventh letter (25.7.87)

When it was the school holidays I did not go on holiday or anywhere nice but we did help David and Jane move house me Sally daddy and mummy and when we got it to the new house David and Jane did not know where to put it and after we went home.

(Marie enclosed a story)

I am going to tell you a story of the wobbly men once upon a time there was a house and that house was sold and when a family went in the house they were called the wobbly family so they called the house the wobble house and The wobble family was a big family and I will tell you what is in the family two big girls two big boy and one baby and soon The wobble lady had another baby and they lived Happily ever after

Nigel's eighth letter (31.7.87)

Thank you so much for that wonderful story. I enjoyed reading it so much. This week I am in Scotland. The bridge in the picture is a railway bridge. It takes four years to paint it. Then they have to start all over again. Why not send me a postcard during your school holiday. Have a nice time.

Considering the likely impact of receiving a letter in which one is promised a lamb, it is somewhat surprising to find that Nigel (24.8.87) referred to it only as 'a special letter'. He made no other mention of lambs or the farm. The reason for this was that the Easter holidays had intervened and Nigel was not sure that Marie would remember the topics raised by her letter. He chose to initiate new topics for the new term; this is the first time he has attempted to set the agenda. This was a successful strategy as Marie did indeed 'tell what she was doing' by providing a very detailed account of Book Week, and even prefacing the account by an announcement 'I will tell you all about it'.

In this group of letters 'telling you all about it' seems to sum up the stance taken by both writers. Marie seems to have abandoned asking questions as a letter writing strategy. Was this because she had independently decided that this was what was needed in a letter, or was it a more literal response to Nigel's frequent request to 'write and tell me what you are doing'? It is perhaps appropriate to raise here the issue of how Marie came to have a concept of what made an appropriate letter.

It is unlikely that Marie would have had much experience of letter writing prior to her correspondence with Nigel. She may have copied 'thank you' letters or cards at Christmas or birthday time but few young children get regular letters at a time when most potential correspondents would not expect them to be able to read them or write replies. Marie's notion of what was an appropriate letter must, therefore, have derived directly or indirectly from her correspondent or from her working out for herself an appropriate strategy.

Marie would have been reading not only the letters Nigel wrote to her but also letters written by either Nigel or Les to all the other children in the class. All the children shared their letters with each other. At one point the teacher (Anne) had the class create a 'What we know about Les and Nigel book' which involved examining a lot of the letters. Marie would, therefore, have had access to quite a lot of models of letter writing.

If we look at Nigel's letters during this section it is clear that most of them have large chunks of what we might call simple 'news' (Nigel's sixth letter was an exception consisting mostly of general observations). This was not untypical of the content of both his and Les' letters to all the other children in the class. It would not be surprising if Marie decided that this was exactly what one should do in a letter.

However, as indicated above, it may have represented a more independent strategy than that. It has already been mentioned that quite long gaps occurred between letters. Marie was writing about once a month and Nigel was not asking specific questions which would influence a particular content for Marie's replies. When faced with the task of filling a certain amount of space when writing to a distanced correspondent, Marie might well have worked out for herself that 'news' was a useful way out of the problem.

One consequence of the 'telling news' strategy is that the letters stand more independently than the early letters. Nigel and Marie were still corresponding in the sense that they wrote letters to each other and made polite reference to those, but the topics they chose to explore were largely independent of each other's letters. Marie was writing about Book Week at the beginning of May; Nigel's reply came just over a month later. Marie was writing about the wedding in June; Nigel responded in July. While both these were of obvious interest to Marie at the time of writing the time delay meant that Nigel did not feel the topics merited any continuation.

Whatever the reason, the sense of real contact seems diminished in these letters. But this does not necessarily mean that they were not read with real interest and enjoyment at the time. The information about the visit to the butterfly farm created lots of interesting discussion between the children in the class, as did his contact with Les. Marie's own letters, each in their own way, captured so well the essence of the situations she was describing. The Book Week letter (Marie 6.5.87) gives a vivid account of the big performance assembly, with the teacher telling children to do things and children following the set routine. There is no danger that Nigel would misunderstand what happened here!

At this point there was a long gap in the correspondence as a result of the summer vacation. The correspondence had, in effect, to begin again. Nigel initiated the contact with a letter and later a card.

Nigel's ninth letter (26.9.87)

How are you? Did you have a nice summer and go anywhere exciting? I bet things are busy on your farm. In a couple of weeks I am going all the way to America to see Les. It is going to take me 22 hours to get there. Do write to me again.

Nigel's postcard (10.87)

I am in Arizona. It is very, very hot. All around me is desert. Yesterday I went to a lovely zoo. I will write properly when I get back.

Marie's eighth letter (17.11.87)

Thank you for the postcard that you sent to me. and I want to ask you a Question have you still got all your snakes. Because I have got five more calves but I do not have to feed them if I do not want to. and I have a bull and we called it Woolly. and we have three more calves and I have not seen them yet but Sally has seen them Because Sally and my daddy bought them and there are two red and white ones and one black and white. and I do not think that mummy has seen them or not. and our teacher is called Miss S. . . and we have done lots of autumn pictures and autumn poems and I like my friends best and she is called Sally and I like David next and I like mine last and our teacher is called Miss S. . .

Nigel's tenth letter (2.12.87)

It was so lovely to get such a long letter. I bet your hand was tired after you had written it. I do not have all my snakes. I gave two away. I still have Elvis and Orson. Your calves sound so nice. I wonder how old they are? What happens to them when they are grown up? Do you like feeding them? Do you think they get cold during the winter. Christmas will be here soon. I expect you will get lots of presents. Do calves get presents at Christmas? Do write to me again.

Marie's ninth letter (5.1.88)

Thank you for the letter and thank you for the postcard me and my sister have got the the biggest present it is called My Little Pony Paradise Estate and we have a game called Ping Pong and I have got a knitting set and yesterday we had a cafeteria and two new people have come and the boy is called Ben and the girl and we are going to a Pantomime and it is called Prince and the Pauper and we have a lot more presents I will try and tell you all the presents I got I got Ping Pong and Dial a Disc and Connect 4 and acrobats sorry I can't tell you anymore

Nigel's eleventh letter (24.1.88)

Thank you for such a long and interesting letter. I did enjoy reading it. What an enormous number of presents you got. Do you and your sister share the 'My Little Pony Paradise Estate'? Don't you quarrel over it sometimes? When I was young I was always fighting with my brother about who was allowed to play with toys. What are the two new children like? Have they settled in? It must be very strange to have to go to a new school and meet strange people. I hope everyone in your class is kind to them. Do write and tell me about the pantomime.

Marie's tenth letter (8.2.88)

Thank you for saying my letter was such a long letter and me and Sally always share the Paradise Estate and we have a My Little Pony Castle and a Lullaby Nursery or have I told you that and we have some Pearl Sea Ponies and the float that Sally has got is a crocodile float and I have a frog float but I have forgotten what their names are and we have some baby twins and mine are unicorns and Sally has fly ponies and we have a new track suit and now we have two track suits and in summer I am going to Helen's house and we have done winter scenes and that was easy to do.

Nigel's twelfth letter (29.2.88)

My word – another lovely long letter from you. You say you have done some winter scenes, and that they were easy to do. What kinds of work do you find easy and what do you find difficult? When I was at school I used to find maths difficult (I still do). How is life on your farm? I expect your mum and dad are delighted that we have had such a mild winter. When do the new lambs come along? I expect it must be soon – or have you got some already? Did you know we have been writing to each other for over a year now? Perhaps I should bring in all your letters for you to have a look at.

The new school year saw new influences on Marie's letters. The new class teacher introduced the use of the full address, date, and punctuation. The first two of these Marie adopted and continued to use in all her future letters. She attended to punctuation in the early part of her eighth letter (17.11.87), placing some full stops before her own boundary markers, for example, before 'and'. Generally, though, this teaching of punctuation had little effect for a long time as subsequent letters show.

For this session's letters Nigel seems to have virtually abandoned 'news' as a focus in the text. He uses mostly general observations and asks quite a lot of questions. It may be his questions which move Marie into answering at greater length and with a greater sense of topic completeness. Marie's focus is more on events at home than on events at school, and in the process begins to offer Nigel real insight into her life as a child on the farm.

Marie was able to help re-establish the relationship with reference to shared interests. She was not only writing longer letters but also showing signs of her increased awareness of the social obligations towards her reader. She was invariably using some form of conventional opening in her letters. While she continued to write at length about her own topics of interest, she now did not ignore Nigel's questions, comments, or his needs as an audience. Of course, partly due to the fact that the partners were writing at increased length, both continued to be selective when picking up or maintaining topics. A growing ability to handle the selection process can be seen in Marie's first letter of the term (17.11.87), where she used her question about Nigel's snakes to lead into giving information about some new calves. In the following letter from Marie (5.1.88) she did not ignore school-based events, although the main focus was on her Christmas presents.

As the year of corresponding drew to a close, Nigel's letter drew attention to the length of time they had been writing. Marie was now aged six years, nine months and as her final letters show, she had come some way since the beginning of the correspondence.

Marie's eleventh letter (8.3.88)

Thank you for the letter and my dad has bought us five lambs and one is very cheeky and that is my sisters and one has a brown face and one did not used to drink and the fifth one has three legs and a half and Sally's is the fastest drinking and we go to school and we have the alarm after my mum and dad have gone on the milk round and we have the alarm being set off at 7 o clock and we take turns in making the breakfast and it was my turn to make the breakfast and I hope it will snow a lot because I do not like school very much and when Mrs S. . . shouts at Jonathan she makes me Jump and we have got a cat and when you annoy her she scratches you or bites you and we have another cat and if we put them in a room they always fight and the littlest had to have stitches in her side but that still did not stop her from scratching and clawing and biting you and number is a bit hard and I am on page 22 I think and David is on page 62 and I am the highest in my group and I am in green group and I will tell you all the people who are in my Group Kelly and Grace Tom and Paul Christopher and Ben and Rachel and Vicky

Marie's twelfth letter (21.3.88)

Yesterday Rachel had a birthday and Jenny went and Kelly went as well and lots of other children went and me of course and it was good and a bit of bad news one of our lambs has died but my dad has made one invention and that has five teats on it and bits of wood in between and the teats are fastened to a bucket and I get the the little scoops of lamb milk and I think they have six scoops of lamb milk and the big ones have ten scoops of lamb milk and I think we have fifteen calves and yesterday in our bedroom the drawer fell down with the television on top and I was sick in my bed and the cover is still hung above the bath and is still dripping wet and in the washer and when the clothes come out the things are full of piles of stuff but I do not know what they are called and this is the last week at school to have Easter and I Like Easter because I like chocolate and some Easter eggs have sweets and I hope there are buttons in because I love buttons that are full of chocolate yum all that talking about eggs has made me hungry and on the farm we have a calf and in the night it Jumps into another pen and when we go and feed the lambs we get mad so we tell daddy and daddy puts it in to its own pen and that is called Skipper and he is usually naughty and stupid and they knock the ladder that is used for giving corn in and milk every set of calves has one and when they knock it down my dad has to knock it back up and Skipper pokes his nose in and my dad says Sally get Skipper away because he might get hit with the hammer but before that Skipper was chewing my dads coat

Extract from Nigel's thirteenth letter (11.4.88)

Thank you so much for your two enormous letters. I am amazed that your hand doesn't drop off with all the effort you have put into them. I was absolutely delighted to get them and was very excited to read them.

These two letters form the grand finale to the 13 month correspondence. Their length alone forms a marked contrast to Marie's first letter, but her development as an author is demonstrated in other ways too. Admittedly she had still not adopted conventional punctuation, she over-uses 'and' which can be seen as her sentence boundary marker. However, she was also using a wide range of writing strategies which could be transferred to writing a variety of genres.

In thirteen months Marie had moved from being a typical 'two-liner' to an adventurous, confident author. There is interest, commitment and honesty in her writing. She was clearly happy with the writing relationship she had with Nigel. Those last two letters contained between them 600 words. Both seem to be mostly just 'news', but on the other hand in her eleventh letter (8.3.88) her text could be seen as a kind of description. After all, Nigel had asked her a whole series of questions about her life and she seems to have answered many of them in that letter. She was now able to give a clear picture of the new lambs and follow this with a recount of the morning routine. As a result Nigel was provided with considerable insight into the responsibilities which she and her sister shared. She reacts to Nigel's comment about 'the mild winter' with 'I hope it will snow a lot' and her reasoning is clear, if not explicit.

The twelfth letter was sent despite the fact that Nigel had not yet replied to the eleventh. As a self-initiated text it cannot be a response to questions asked previously. Marie has to formulate her own topics and while she uses well established ones she manages to invest the letter with a considerable sense of relaxation, even fun. The sections 'and me of course', and 'yum all that talking about eggs has made me hungry' demonstrate an intentional humour. The story of being sick and 'piles of stuff' is probably less intentionally funny but nevertheless is a sign of a laid-back writer. This was a letter written for pleasure and it certainly gave much pleasure to its reader. Marie seems confident that Nigel will be interested in her daily life (as he certainly was) and takes care to render it in great detail both through description and the recounting of events.

Marie's letters were by now much more interesting than some of Nigel's to her; the pressures of time and the complexities of trying to write full, individual letters to fifteen children meant that corners were sometimes skipped. Fortunately these occasional lapses did not seem to inhibit her. Marie seldom wrote again at the length of those two letters but nevertheless was for three years a committed and energetic correspondent.

During the thirteen months of the exchange detailed here Marie had many and varied literacy experiences of which the letter writing formed only one small part. Even so, it provided the opportunity to develop and practise a wide range of writing strategies, to learn about the needs of an audience, to recognise the responsibilities of being a respondent, and it also provided a means of her writing with authority about what was relevant to her.

Conclusion

Looking at the full texts of all the letters of the first year allows us to see how both Marie and Nigel developed their relationship solely through print. While one cannot help be aware that one correspondent is an adult and the other a very young child, when it comes to being ready to contribute, being willing to write honestly, and being prepared to keep at it, there was no significant difference between the two writers.

Looking back at the letters shows the amount of reading involved in this kind of dialogue. Although Marie did not respond to everything written by Nigel, she did read it all. Even when choosing not to make a written reply she responded with interest, pleasure and through mentally reflecting on what was read.

The whole set of letters reveals times where the dialogue was alive, with real interaction taking place; and other times when it was as if no correspondence in the real sense of the word was happening. It is important to remember that writers get tired, have other demands on their time, can have moments of disinterest, or can feel enough has been said on a topic. Real writing is like that and for both writers this was an authentic communicative exchange. We have to accept that continuous exchanges will produce varying quality of writing and levels of commitment.

The effort of sustaining a written relationship demands special skills as well as considerable commitment. It requires a sense of obligation, the ability to recognise what will interest the reader and maintain the relationship, and it demands a certain level of give and take in the expectations for what will be written. No one letter can demonstrate these qualities. The proof comes only from an inspection of all the texts written across a length of time. The letters displayed in this chapter allow such an inspection and it is clear that for both Marie and Nigel this was a very powerful, demanding, at times exhilarating, and definitely pleasurable, experience.

References

Robinson, A; Crawford, L. and **Hall, N.** (1989) *'Some day you will no all about me': young children's explorations in a world of letters.* London: Mary Glasgow Publications.

6 'LET'S EAT A SUNBEAM': DIALOGUE JOURNALS IN THE SCIENCE CLASS

Diane Mannix

While pursuing graduate degrees, a fellow student, Sandra Whitehouse, and I decided to collaborate on a project which required us to teach a content area which would be integrated with the language arts, in particular children's literature. We obtained permission to work with a fourth grade (nine- and ten-year-olds) science class in a local elementary school. In the course of this unit we engaged in a three-way written interaction in which the children wrote in their daily logs which were then read by both teachers and responded to by the one who had taught that day's lesson. This rather complex arrangement kept both teachers in tune with each other's lessons and with the children's developing understanding of a science unit on food chains and food webs.

The children had no previous experience of using logs in this way. They had used journals before but those had not been interactive; they were more in the nature of personal journals. Neither had they used their journals to comment on what they were learning.

Both of us were engaged in a new teaching experience and were trying out a whole range of ideas. Before we taught the unit, detailed plans were made of the projected content, and lists were drawn up of the necessary resources and activities to be used with the children. We listed fiction and non-fiction sources and explored how to include the widest possible range of uses of oral and written language.

What follows is an exploration of the experience documented by the diary I kept of what happened, and from extracts from the interactive logs maintained by us and the children. On one level it is a simple story but at the same time for us, and we believe the children, it was a powerful, intense and productive experience.

8 November

Today Sandy Whitehouse and I made our long-awaited debut in Mrs Schmidt's class. Our integrated unit for Language Arts is officially underway. We decided to split teaching duties on the first day, but after this we will be teaching alternate lessons.

This fourth grade class was enthusiastic, and everyone seemed eager to participate. I was amazed at some of the students' ideas when they brainstormed the word 'chain'. Timing chains, pocket watch chains, and the chains on the back of oil trucks were among the responses that neither Sandy nor I had anticipated. I told the students that they had taught me a few things today!

All of the children listened intently as Marcia Brown's *Once a Mouse . . .* (1961) was read, and afterwards they showed they had listened to my pre-reading instructions by listing the foods mentioned in the story. As I went through the links between the foods, the students joined in, obviously thoroughly enjoying this concept.

At this point, Sandy took over. The students worked well in groups, and both of us were surprised at their answers which used information learned in previous units, as well as that presented in this lesson. A few groups even offered simple food chains! I think that this introduction to the unit on food chains and food webs may have been even more effective than Sandy and I had expected!

The class seemed excited when we passed out the dialogue-learning logs which will be an important part of our unit. The logs will allow the students to respond to each lesson by writing information learned, or questions, ideas, or thoughts about that lesson. Either Sandy or I will read and reply to each entry.

The unit's theme – Let's eat a sunbeam! – is on the cover of each log. The students were intrigued when we said we weren't going to tell them yet what it means. Actually, we hope they will be able to figure out its meaning as they learn about food chains.

I think we made a good start. I can't wait to read the logs and see the students' reactions to this first lesson.

(See Figures 6.1, 6.2 and 6.3.)

16 November

Tomorrow is my second time in the classroom. Sandy taught on the 14th. I was interested to read in the students' logs about the photosynthesis experiment she set up. These logs help me to be a part of

Links-food chains-animals diets plants

This is a good list, Ehren. It covers just about everything we did today. You were certainly paying attention!
— mrs. Mannix

Figure 6.1

Links: owl - snake - frog - fly

Brainstormed what things have chains and words that have Chain in them. It was neat. Animals eat something and then it eats another animal.

Erin, you picked an excellent example of a food chain to include in your log. I'm glad you enjoyed learning this today. There is a lot more to come!
— Mrs. Mannix

Figure 6.2

Do fish really eat crabs?
everything was intresting.
I like how the things commebind
that is neat
I liked the story.

Lisa, I know my dad used to use crabs for bait
when he fished, so some fish must eat them.
I'm glad you liked the story. I did, too!
— Mrs. Mannix

Figure 6.3

the entire unit, even though I am not teaching every class. They also serve to unify the unit for the children. It can't be easy for them to have two different teachers in the same class.

(See Figures 6.4 and 6.5.)

17 November

Today we read *Where Do Animals Get Food?* (Cohen *et al.*, 1987) using a three level guide. It involved literal and interpretive comprehension, and the ability to relate to their own experience those things they had read. The students worked in groups. The three level guide appeared to be new to the students. They had no problems with levels one and two, but level three caused some discussion in most groups. Finally, one group called me over to tell me that they just could not agree on an answer. When I told them that was all right, they were relieved and rather pleased. Finally, a question that everyone could answer correctly!

The vocabulary in this unit is very difficult for these fourth graders. Will they be able to master it? I hope the logs help with this. Using the vocabulary in their own writing should reinforce the meaning. I'll have to wait and see . . .

After the group work, each student individually rated his/her behaviour in the group. They were eager to write in their logs.

(See Figures 6.6 and 6.7.)

29 November

Vacation and scheduling problems have combined to keep me out of the classroom for twelve days. Sandy has taught both of the last two classes. Thank goodness for the logs! They keep me in touch with the students and what they've learned when I'm not there.

Today we reviewed omnivores, carnivores, and herbivores with an Every Pupil Response activity. I identified an animal and read a list of the foods it eats, and each student classified it by holding up a card on which an 'O', a 'C', or an 'H' was printed. They enjoyed this, and I was very excited when I saw their answers, especially since they were answering quickly without looking around to see what cards others were holding up. They certainly seem to understand these words.

I read a short selection from *Scavengers and Decomposers: The Cleanup Crew* by Pat Huey (1984), and we had an interesting discussion about scavengers, predators, prey, and decomposers.

I now know all of the children by name. The learning logs have helped

Today I learned about Chlorophyl and Photosynthesis We are also doing an experiment.

Shark → Mackerel → Prawn → Phyroplankton

It will be interesting to see what happens to each of the plants. Thanks for the food chain. In a few weeks we will be studying about ocean food chains. You can share this one then. What is a prawn? A prawn is a mrs. whitehouse Shrimp-like crustacean, but is larger.

Figure 6.4

We'll learned photosynthesis. We rubbed spinich on a piece of paper and the chlorophyll came out and the paper was green.
The main product is simple sugar that is neat. I didn't know that. The plant needs water, carbon dioxide, and sunlight.
We're doing a little experiment One plant has no water, one has no CO_2, one has no sunlight Also there's a control plant which we're doing. One table is putting foil on the leaves It was neat!!
Glad you liked it. You certainly learned a lot, and I'm glad you learned something you didn't know.

Mrs Whitehouse

Figure 6.5

Figure 6.6

herbivor-carnivor-omivors-gr-
ouping animals- working in groups

Well, Ehren, which are you - herbivore, carnivore,
or omnivore? Have a nice Thanksgiving!
Omnivore Mrs. Mannix

Figure 6.7

I glad that you came and talk about
all the stuff. I can not belive that
we eat omnivore. I Learned alot
to work with groups.

Lisa, I'm glad I came, too. Yes, you are an
omnivore if you eat meat and vegetables and fruits.
I'm an omnivore, too. In fact, I'm looking forward
to eating turkey and vegetables on Thursday!
Have a nice Thanksgiving! _ Mrs. Mannix

with this. I also know something about what each child is like because of the logs. I am so pleased we decided to use them to fill the writing requirement for our unit!

One of the boys has been trying to figure out what 'Let's eat a sunbeam!' means. He has written about this in several log entries. Today he called me over, and we talked about it. I gave him a hint, and he worked out the meaning. He was so happy! I noticed that he told his friend, because this boy put it in his log also.

(See Figures 6.8, 6.9 and 6.10.)

1 December

Today was busy, but fun. I felt like I needed to be in twelve places at once while the pairs were working on making models of food chains. The students worked well together and thoroughly enjoyed applying what they have been learning.

I had given the students homework to do for today. They were to keep a list of all the foods they ate for two days. Time ran out today, so the activity using this homework was postponed until next week. I

Figure 6.8

17/11/89

learned that animals are
all consumers—

lets eat a sunbeam— try to do
yourbes at what you do
Try to do diffucult things

Greg, I'm glad you tried to make sense out of
"Let's eat a sunbeam!" Keep thinking about it.
You are the first one to try to figure it out. Good
for you! Think about how the sun is important
to plants. Then listen carefully in class. You
may be the first to know what it means!
— Mrs. Mannix

Figure 6.9

21/11/89

learned how plants need everything
to live
lets eat a sunbeam — means try to
belive you are aplant. Try to
reach asunbeam

Yes, our plants need sunlight, CO_2, + water
to live and our experiment will show what
happens if a plant doesn't get all of those
things. I'm glad you are still thinking
about "Let's eat a sunbeam."
Mrs. Whitehouse

Figure 6.10

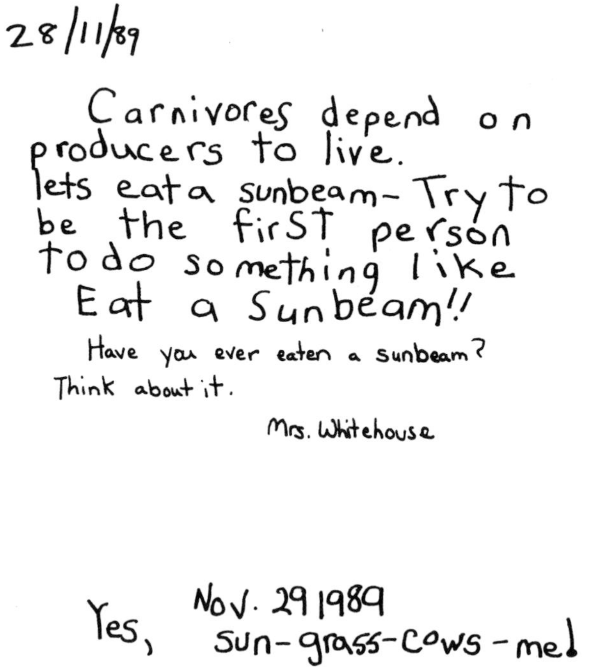

28/11/89

Carnivores depend on producers to live.
lets eat a sunbeam— Try to be the first person to do something like Eat a Sunbeam!!

Have you ever eaten a sunbeam? Think about it.

Mrs. Whitehouse

Yes, Nov. 29 1989
Sun-grass-cows-me!

collected it and will staple the food lists in the logs and comment on them when I write in the logs.

The logs have been so successful that I have decided to try something new. I have started a log of my own. The ideal thing would be to write in it while they are writing in theirs, so I could model journal writing. However, I am always so pressed for time that this is not feasible in this class. So, I wrote my entry at home last night. I also included my list of foods for the past two days.

I am going to leave my log in the classroom and see if anyone dialogues with me. Some of the students seem very interested in the idea. We shall see.

6 December

Today's lesson was truly wonderful from start to finish. I was met at the door by Harmony who was holding my learning log. She wanted to make sure I didn't forget it. There are six entries. None of them is long, and they are all quite similar. However, I did notice that four were made by the quietest students in the class. Perhaps a teacher's log gives this type of student an opportunity to reach out for the teacher's attention.

It's awfully easy for a quiet student to be lost in the crowd.

(See Figure 6.11.)

7 December

I finish my work with this class on Friday, but I have time to leave my log for student response once more. I wonder if the same students will participate.

The pre-reading activity for *The Day They Parachuted Cats on Borneo* by Pomerant (1971) was excellent. Very few students had ever heard of DDT, but one boy was able to tell me exactly what it was. They enjoyed the article from the *New York Times*, and they could barely contain themselves when I told them we were going to read a play based on this story.

The students did a fine job both in the groups and when we read as a class. I'm so glad we found this book. The lessons it teaches will remain with the children for a long, long time because it tells such an unusual story in a fun way.

8 December

My last day! Our unit ended with the students writing to organisations or government agencies to ask for information about endangered species. The children loved this activity. Some of them even included their phone numbers in the letter in case someone needed to call them!

We finished the period with a review of the Borneo play by means of a web. Then all of the students wrote in their logs one last time. I noticed that the activities of the past few days have excited them, and some entries are longer than usual. Some students are still figuring out 'Let's eat a sunbeam!'

(See Figures 6.12 and 6.13.)

21 December

I made my last visit to Mrs Schmidt's fourth grade science class today. Katie rushed up to me with news that she had already received an answer to her letter to the Whooping Crane Conservation Association. She was one excited girl!

I wanted to take the class a present, and I finally decided on an amaryllis. What better gift following a unit on food chains than a green plant! When I presented the plant to them, I said that I had brought

Figure 6.11

November 30th

I have been enjoying my time with this class I especially like reading the learning logs. I wonder if anyone will write in mine

Tomorrow we're going to make models of food chains. I think each group will do a good job if the students carefully read the directions. I can't wait to see how they turn out

I don't think too many know what "Let's eat a Sunbeam!" means yet. Will they figure it out?

I You shure have a long list I hope I behave, Shaun

WOW What a lot
to Wright you
Shure wright nice. Harman

Hi! Yoasurehavealong list itisreally long. Your nice Erica

Hi yousure have alot of stuff to write. I figured out what the front met. Lisa

You stare have a lot of stuff
Katie

Hi I havent found out about Let's eat a sunbeam means but I will soon Kim

Wrote a letter to people who are trying to save the endangered species. figured out what lets eat a sunbeam means. It means that the sun grows the plants and when Humans eat plants we are eating a sunbeam.

Matt.

Very good! Now I have a question for you. Are we eating a sunbeam when we eat meat?

— Mrs. Mannix

Figure 6.12

December 8, 1989
lets eat a sun beam means, the sun gives off energy that makes the plants grow, and the herbavoires and omnavoires eat the plantes. then the carnivoirs and omnivoires eat the othe animeles and so on. Is the test easy? When is the last day you will be here?

Figure 6.13

Katelyn,
You sure *do* Know what "Let's eat a Sunbeam" means!
As you probably Know by now, the test is next week. I think you'll do fine.
I don't think I'll be back to teach, but I will be back to say goodbye! Mrs. Whitehouse will be teaching a few more times.

— Mrs. Mann

them a producer. Ehren raised his hand and said, 'Why didn't you bring us a consumer?' I told him, 'You're lucky; it could have been a decomposer', at which the entire class went 'Eeeeewwwww!!' I am glad to see that they have learned the vocabulary in this unit.

I was sorry to say goodbye to this class. It has been a rewarding experience. The best part of the unit for me has been the learning logs. They helped me get to know these children in a short time. Without the logs I wouldn't have realised Michael's great interest in science because he's rather quiet in the classroom. Or that Greg was the one willing to take a guess and perhaps be totally wrong – at least in his log. Or that shy Lisa was very interested in and involved with the whole unit. Or that Shawn was concerned about his behaviour, which surprised me because he had never done anything in science to warrant such concern. I could go on and on. I think I would learn these things in the course of events if I were in the classroom for a longer time, but the logs have been very helpful during this short teaching stint.

The logs also gave the children opportunities to use the vocabulary they had learned and to record their observations of the photosynthesis experiment. Many asked questions about material that perplexed them, and Sandy and I were able to clarify these concepts with our answers. Through the entries we also found that some things needed to be reviewed or even re-taught! The logs allowed the students to give their opinions about class activities and helped them explore their own thoughts in a non-threatening atmosphere.

I had certainly not forseen how these logs would affect the children, their learning, and their relationship with us. The use of interactive writing added to the creation of an exciting environment in which teachers and students communicated daily about what was happening in the science lesson. This communication offered Sandy and me a glimpse of the effects of this unit and of classroom dynamics on each of our pupils. We discovered more about these nine- and ten-year-olds from their logs than we did from the final test we administered. We saw our students wondering, reflecting, questioning, struggling, reacting, thinking and exploring. They shared their thoughts, ideas and knowledge with us, and we, in turn, shared our thoughts, ideas and knowledge with them. Moreover I believe that these fourth graders learned more about us than they would have without the logs. Finally, meaningful written dialogue created a bond between these students and their two short-term teachers.

(**Note:** Sandra Whitehouse is a graduate student in the School of Education and Human Development at the State University of New York at Binghamton.)

7 'WE WRITE OUR DIALOGUE JOURNALS TO HAVE FUN'

Shelagh Hewitt

The authors of most of the other chapters in this book will feature fairly explicitly the benefits for children of undertaking interactive writing. In this chapter I want to take a slightly different stance and concentrate on what *I* have gained from interactive writing. I shall not ignore the children's development but I want to emphasise just how much I have benefited from writing to the children in my class.

We started dialogue journals early in the year. The pattern, once it had settled, was that the children would have about an hour (more if they wanted it) to write to me. I would take all their books home at the weekend and write my replies. On Monday morning I would give them all back their books. I had started by writing far too much and asking too many questions. I found I was getting replies which consisted of little more than 'yes, I did', and 'no, I didn't'. I realised how dependent they were on my questions when one day a child said to me 'I can't answer you because you've not asked me any questions'. After a few weeks we had a class discussion about the dialogue journals and we talked about asking and answering questions. As a result the level of communication improved. I had learned to let go of some of my 'teacherness' and found that as a consequence I started to know my children a lot better. The whole process also became more enjoyable and was more fun for all of us.

I certainly got closer to some children who in the normal course of classroom life did not find it easy to communicate orally. One such child was Leon. He liked to listen but did not feel very comfortable talking. The dialogue journals allowed him to reveal himself as quite a reflective communicator.

One of the most penetrating exchanges of all took place with Leon across a four week period. I had started the new year by writing a letter to each of the children telling them about my Christmas. I asked Leon a few questions. Little did I realise that I had started a train of enquiry for Leon that would have me having to explain very carefully some the economic facts of my life. Leon took very seriously my somewhat throwaway comment about not liking going shopping for food.

Shelagh (10.1.90)

. . . Where did you go shopping and what did you buy? I don't like going shopping for food but I like buying clothes and earrings – what about you? Please tell me all about it.

Leon (undated)

Thank you for your letter. I went shopping at Kwik Save. If you don't like buying food what will you eat for breakfast, lunch and supper? I got a Christmas card which sings when you open it. My sister got one.

This very literal interpretation of my comment was a surprise. It was probably the last part of my letter that I expected to gain his interest. I had some explaining to do:

Shelagh (19.1.90)

Thank you for your letter. You are right. If I didn't go shopping – what would I eat? What I mean is I think shopping for food has to be done but its boring because you have to go again the next week! Then again.

Do you have any hobbies that you do out of school? I like sewing and reading. Please tell me about them if possible. Did you have a good weekend?

Leon (undated)

Thank you for your letter. I know you have to do it but why didn't you buy lots of shopping and [then] you don't have to go every week.

Clearly a simple explanation was not going to satisfy Leon who was demonstrating unanticipated logical ability.

Shelagh (23.1.90)

Dear me – thank you for your letter – but are you very rich? I cannot afford to buy a lot at one go!!

Do you have any spending money? What do you buy with it or are you saving up for something? How good are you at saving money? Please tell me all about it.

Leon (undated)

Thank you for your letter. But don't you get any money? If you get any money you can save it and then you can buy lots and lots of food and then you don't have to go every week.

Leon was ignoring all the other parts of my letter and with considerable determination seemed intent on forcing me to explicate a whole range of aspects of my life.

Shelagh (29.1.90)

Thank you for your letter. Yes I get money – but I also have a lot of other bills to pay every month. Also greengrocery stuff doesn't last a long time. It has to be bought every week.

What do you spend your money on? Did you have a good weekend?'

Leon (5.2.90)

Thank you for your letter. Which other bills do you pay? I pay bills for the flat I live in. I spend most of my money on my toy cars and some of my stickers. On the weekend I went to the B.O.C. to see a lot of cars and my dad said he is going to buy a Renault 25.

Shelagh (5.2.90)

Thank you for my letter. I have to pay my rates, gas, electricity, insurance and car bills every month.

Leon had pursued his enquiries for a whole month, determinedly hanging on the the topic. I am unable to account for his interest in this aspect of life, but what is clear is that he was having to think about some crucial economic issues. Quite probably, even within his own family life, he had never given any thought to how one manages a budget and plans expenditure. It is possible that for Leon this exchange was a powerful learning experience.

From my perspective it was also a powerful learning experience; it revealed a whole new dimension of Leon. It was also very enjoyable to see him doggedly seeking a resolution to a problem and forcing me to be more and more explicit about my meanings and the economic facts about life in our modern world. Although it appears as if Leon was giving me an interrogation I am unsure who got the most pleasure out of the experience. Certainly I enjoyed very much seeing him think so powerfully.

However, it is not only children who can learn about the world from teachers: teachers have things to learn as well, as this extract shows:

Adam

I thought the visit to Whitworth Art gallery was badly wicked . . .

Shelagh

. . . What does 'badly wicked' mean. I am old fashioned and don't understand all these new words!

Adam

. . . 'Badly wicked' means better than good . . .

Many of the children through their use of language in the journals, and their efforts to explain some terminology to me, contributed to my more informed view of their culture. The journals were very definitely an exchange.

Some children were less sure about the dialogue journals, but one advantage this medium has is that it can be used to investigate itself. Harry never wrote very much.

Shelagh (29.1.90)

Thank you for your letter. Brief as usual! I wonder why?

I don't have a pet any longer. He died last June. He was a corgi called Bryn Dai and he was very good natured and he liked playing with children! Crazy dog! I went to see my neighbour this weekend. She has 16 cats – a terrapin and a gerbil.

Harry (undated)

Thank you for your letter. My letters are brief because I don't have enough information to write.

Shelagh (2.2.90)

Thank you for your letter explaining why it is usually so brief. Perhaps – if you made a comment about what I have written to you. Then ask me some some questions that I have to consider. I don't find it easy either because I've got 28 different ones to write. Think yourself lucky.

Harry (undated)

Thank you for your letter. Miss Hewitt have you noticed that all the letters in this book begin with 'Thank you for your letter'. I am sorry about my letter before this one. I am sure I did intend to write more.

Shelagh (14.2.90)

Merci bien pour votre lettre. Well – does that at least make a change? Do you realise that you really do have lots to write about if you really think. When I write letters – it's not just about what I've done but about what I think and feel. Emotions are important.

PS Did you have a good holiday?

Harry (undated)

Thank you for your letter. I'm sorry I could the first 4 words in a definite . . . Yes I did have a nice holiday. I did nearly everything that you can think of. What did you do at the holidays?

Shelagh (2.3.90)

Cheat! You are supposed to tell me what you did. Very clever twist. I went collecting pebbles and shells off the beach in a howling wind and rain!! I did the usual boring things too – like the washing and the ironing!!

Harry (undated)

I can't think what to write so thank you for your letter. When you mean clever twist do I have to write what I did in this letter? Tell me if I'm wrong but I don't know about beaches in Manchester.

Clearly one cannot win them all, but if Harry wouldn't be persuaded to recount events from his life, he was clearly able to explore ways of writing that cleverly avoided the need for news. It was fascinating to watch him wriggle as he explored every way of avoiding writing. In fact, he probably ended up writing just as much as he would have done if he had told me some news.

Harry was unfailingly honest about his understanding of the problem as was another child when asked about the brevity of one of his letters.

Adam (undated)

Thank you for your letter. I'm sorry I did not write much. I was too busy chatting to get on with my work.

Some children found writing difficult but were prepared to have a very good try:

Shelagh (19.1.90)

Thank you for your letter. I know you don't like writing to me – but it will help you. Honestly. Please tell me about the things you like doing and making.

Mustaq (undated)

I like your letter. It is nice to know that you want me to read and spell and be clever from you. It's very kind of you and I like making things out of paper.

PS What do you like doing?

Mustaq was a quiet child who did not find writing easy. It was, therefore, doubly pleasurable when he made an effort. In fact time and time again the letters which gave me most pleasure came not from those who were already fluent writers but from those, like Leon, Harry and Mustaq, whose initial reluctance to communicate shifted as the academic year moved on.

Another aspect of the letters that I enjoyed was the honesty of children which, in turn, made it very easy for me to be open and honest with them.

Lucy (29.1.90)

. . . It's my birthday (and Clara's) on February 8th. I'm having it on 11th February. I don't think I can invite you though. Should I save some cake? . . .'

Shelagh (1.2.90)

Thank you for your letter. Why can't you invite me? Yes please – save me some cake . . .

Lucy (5.2.90)

I am going to ask about you coming too, it's just that last time I asked the teacher said, 'No, I have something else to do.' and the same every time. Please watch out I'm very sleepy today. I stayed the night at Geneva's.

Shelagh (8.2.90)

Thank you for your letter. I'm sorry I couldn't come to your party but you didn't ask me soon enough. I always try to go to a party if invited but I tend to get booked up very quickly. What did you do at Geneva's? Last weekend I went to visit a friend – we went out for a meal at an Indian restaurant.

Lucy (12.2.90)

Thank you for your letter. You do not know how it feels to write 'Dear Miss Hewitt' every time you write in a dialogue journal. Quite a mouthful compared to what you write, huh? . . .

The honesty of their writing was important to me. It was a sign that they saw the dialogue journals as something to be treated seriously, even though we could also have fun with them.

I was confident from having participated in the dialogue journals that the children enjoyed the experience as much as I did. I told them I had a friend who was interested in their views about the dialogue journals and asked if they would write some reactions for him.

Two made me wonder:

We have dialogue journals to keep us busy and occupied.

I think we do dialogue journals for handwriting practice.

The children in my class never need excuses to keep busy and anyone who has ever seen the actual journals will know that they were certainly not for handwriting practice. The rest of the comments echoed my own feelings.

Some took a fairly serious view of the experience:

I tell Miss Hewitt lots of things and she tells me about her so that we know a bit about each other.

I think we do it to get used to telling people things you would normally be too shy to tell in words.

It helps you explain things you can't say.

You can express yourself privately.

I tell Miss Hewitt about me and she can tell me some things about her so we know bits about each other.

While others picked out the fact that it was fun:

Sometimes Miss Hewitt puts funny things in our books and we all laugh.

When we do our dialogue journals it makes me happy because I like reading them.

I think we do dialogue journals so Miss Hewitt gets to know us and we get to know her. But I like it and I enjoy it and I think it is good.

I enjoy doing the dialogue journals because they are fun to read.

We write our dialogue journals to have fun.

My theme in this chapter has been the pleasures I have had from engaging in a dialogue journal exchange, and hearing the children's voices in their writing. Let me finish with an extract from the dialogue with Matthew. I had told him about getting some presents for my birthday and had commented:

When you are old like me you don't expect birthday presents. If you do get them it is a lovely surprise . . .

Matthew's modest response read as if it had come straight out of the pages of one of Richmal Crompton's William stories.

I don't think I would be surprised if I got a present when I am old because I have never been surprised before when I have got presents. So I don't think I will be surprised because I'm not that suprisable.

It made me laugh with delight and I can think of no finer reason for interactive writing than the fact that it is immensely pleasurable for both my children and myself.

8 'DEAR SIR, WHAT IS A REPLY ANYWAY?'

Finian O'Shea

When I was appointed as 'remedial teacher' in 1987, I inherited a room full of graded readers and a 'working tradition' developed by the previous holders of the post. At the beginning of the school year the children were screened on standardised tests and those showing up as being 'significantly behind' were assigned a daily period of remedial teaching. For this they would leave their classes and come to my room for half to three-quarters of an hour.

I had been working in the school since leaving college in the early seventies and had built up a reputation as being a mite 'unconventional' in some of the approaches I used with my classes. It was broadly based on my allowing the children to have some say in what they learnt and how they learnt it. It required a lot of responsibility from the children and they rarely failed to rise to the task.

Within the first couple of weeks I got rid of all the graded readers and replaced them with as many real books as I could forage. Because I had small groups I was able to get to know the children quite well and build up relationships with each of them. It didn't take me long to recognise the tremendous sense of failure they all shared. This was most evident when it came to reading and writing. All of the thirty-eight children (aged between eight and twelve) had registered as being a minimum of two years behind on a standardised reading test.

I did a lot of story reading and story telling and many of the parents did 'paired reading' with their children. I tried to provide experiences which would interest and stimulate the children but most of all give them confidence in themselves.

During the first two terms the children engaged in a variety of written work: composing, editing and publishing their own books.

As with the classes I had taught previously, the children adapted to having responsibility for their work and gradually their self-esteem began to grow.

There was a great sense of community in the room. Displays of their books and artwork filled the shelves 'vacated' by the graded readers. Teachers, parents and classmates were invited to see these displays. 'Not knowing' and 'not being able to do' had become a challenge rather than a status. Gradually I became less of a direct instructor and more of a facilitator of the children's learning.

In the final term I decided to try and correspond in writing with the children. I had read about similar projects in the UK (Robinson, Crawford and Hall, 1989) and was attracted by the possibilities it opened up for my children.

Apart from providing another opportunity for engaging in a different type of reading/writing activity, I had vague aspirations that it might also allow them a greater sense of dialogue with me. The removal of the parameters set by having to use correct spelling and punctuation would also provide an opportunity to concentrate on the message they wished to convey.

I discussed the idea with the children. The older ones were immediately attracted by the chance to write to an adult but some of the younger ones needed reassurance. They were uncertain about what it would entail. I assured them that they could write whatever they wanted and I would respond. I presented each child with a writing book and asked them to write to me. They all wrote, although at first some of them had to sort out what kind of activity this was. When I received a response which said 'Dear Sir, what is a reply anyway' I could see some discussion was needed. I had certainly not been prepared for the amount of work involved; most of the children wrote daily. Though I had begun with a particular educational context in mind the children seemed to come at it from a different angle; they were intent on engaging me in a personal relationship as though they were aware that they now had a person to write to rather than a teacher to write for.

Practical reasons dictated that I conducted the correspondence in writing books as I didn't see myself being able to cope with a folder filled with pieces of paper going home each evening. We drew up some ground rules:

1 *Notebooks would be private property.*
2 *All correspondence would be confidential.*

3 *Spelling/grammar/punctuation, would not be marked.*
4 *There would be no compulsion to write.*
5 *All subjects could be discussed.*

The younger children developed and maintained the personal relationship mainly through a question and answer technique. This was sometimes through reference to classroom based topics:

Phil (8–9 years old)

> I'm reading Mrs Frisby and the Rats of Nimh. It is a very good story. I like it. Mr O'Shea, do you like Mrs Frisby and the Rats of Nimh? Did you like the story? Tell me in your letter.

Sometimes it was through more personal questions about what I had been doing out of school:

Josh (8–9 years old)

> Did you live over in London? Was it good . . . did you have a nice time?

From the beginning, though, a number of children used the correspondence to inquire about their progress:

Dilly (9–10 years old)

> Are we doing well in this class? Are we good at stories?

Kathy (9–10 years old)

> I hope my writing is getting better. And also my behaviour things are not working out too well for me lately. I think the idea of the notebook is very good. Nathan is doing art today.

For these children, who had been labelled as failures, the dialogue was providing an opportunity to discuss in private their concerns about their own performance. We often imagine that children such as these 'don't care', yet the stress and uncertainty they suffer can be as disabling as their learning problems.

Other children found the correspondence provided a chance to write at length about their own personal lives. Julie's letters were always a delight to read as they gave a running commentary on her life outside school.

> Dear Mr O'Shea
> How are you! I'm fine. Yesterday I went to Howth. I had a great time. I came home at 6.00 o'clock. My tea was ready. Do you like the sea side? I got a gold ring yesterday and I am not allowed to wear it because it is too big for me and my mam is going to change it today. It is a sovereign ring. I like it very much.
> Thank you

For Paul, another eleven-year-old, the experience was positively liberating. He had been diagnosed as being severely 'dyslexic' and we were told that he would always find both writing and reading a great problem. During the previous term I had had to listen to him read his stories out loud in order to understand them. I would then transcribe his efforts. But his first letter did not appear to contain many mistakes:

> Dear Mr O'Shea
> Did you know that my dog was killed on April the first and either today or tomorrow I will have three dogs or two dogs. Oh yes, sir, Happy Birthday.

The following day the writing book disappeared and I later found it hidden at the back of the cupboard. Paul had received great mileage from his disability and was not about to give it up! He proved an avid correspondent over the term and though continuing to exhibit difficulties with spelling, I had no problem reading his letters.

There was a more intimate aspect to the correspondence in the letters from the older children. My working relationship with them had a far greater social dimension than with the other class groups. There was also a perception that I was somehow inviting them to be more adult in their transactions with me and this they took rather seriously. The correspondence was an extension of the relationship I had built up with children and was now being taken on to an individual level.

This aspect of being on a one-to-one basis in the letter writing was very important to the older children. There is also an awareness of their status vis-à-vis me. This is evidenced in their revelations about themselves in the anticipated belief that I will accept their viewpoint about themselves! Informing me about the things that were going on in their lives was of paramount importance. So was their commenting about the revelations I made about my life outside school: my mother's illness, the antics of a rather stupid dog I rescued from the dog's home, the books I was reading and the music I listened to, concerts I went to, and places I visited.

The case studies which follow provide a glimpse of how four of the older children used the letters for their own individual purposes.

Conor

Conor's first letter read:

> When I go home I like to do my homework and then look at my book. After that I play with my soldiers. What is bothering me is that I can never sleep at night. I do get very hot. I can't help listening to people talk either. And my big sister is not at home, neither is my brother. I have only six friends. One lives in the country. My Dad has not got a job. He just works for himself.

Conor was eleven and often appeared to be one of those children that only a mother could love! He whined and whinged, was always unpleasant to the other children and never mixed really well with them. For the first couple of weeks I really had to work at liking the lad; my attempts at befriending him were often rebuked. He was extremely overweight and had a problem with body odour. In a small room this became a problem for everyone and I had to talk to him about it. There was a temporary improvement during which I managed to get him working with a group but within weeks he was isolated again and the process was to be repeated almost on a monthly basis. Trying to involve his parents proved futile.

Conor refused permission for me to use any but the first of his letters in this article, but said that I could refer to them . . . and if I was really stuck, I could quote 'little bits'. From his letters I discovered that he was, in fact, repressed; given the eventual picture of home which emerged, I was not surprised! He wrote:

> There is nothing to do in this boring world. And when I go home I just stare at something.

In subsequent letters he was to tell me about his father's drinking, his mother's over-protectiveness (which meant that he was not allowed out to play), and his sister's running away from home. Conor commented:

> I hate living. Life is boring and so are my mam and dad.

This troubled me quite a lot. My initial reaction was to try and ignore Conor's evident unhappiness but as I had invited the correspondence, I had the responsibility of being as concerned as Conor was. I sought help from a psychologist friend and on her advice I worked as a counsellor with Conor using letters instead of face-to-face counselling sessions. His biggest single worry was his lack of friends; this was a subject which came up time and time again.

Conor worked through a lot of his frustration and unhappiness in his letters. He frequently documented rows between his parents. His sister's return to home lead to many parental rows concerned with apportioning the blame for how the children were turning out; each parent blamed the other and this upset Conor greatly. I had quite a time of it to help him see that his parents' problems were not his responsibility. My ill-advised offer at one stage to broach the topic with his mother lead to a panic reply asking me not to. For a while his letters became mundane and I had to work hard at assuring him that he could trust me.

Gradually his odour problem disappeared and I noted that he was getting along better with the other children though he did not seem to have established any real friendships within the class. Conor left the class at the end of the term with a far happier notion about himself and who he really was. His final letters were quite 'up tempo' as he told me about new friends and how he was looking forward to his new school and learning how to operate computers.

Writing to Conor was not an easy task; having to be aware of my role as counsellor meant that I had to think seriously about how I responded to what he wrote. This raises the whole question of confidentiality and the care which has to be taken in the sensitive handling of such personal and sometimes disturbing information. It is important to recognise that once the personal relationship is invited it cannot be entered into lightly. I was glad that Conor had found a way of sorting out his feelings and was quite proud of how he used the correspondence rather than becoming dependent on it.

Jenny

Jenny, aged eleven, was the busiest of all my correspondents. We exchanged some thirty-four letters over the term and covered the day-to-day events in her life.

Dear Sir
Did you enjoy yourself on your holiday, and are the people nice? or kind

there. For my exams test my teacher said I done well in my English test, and fair in the other three. Thanks very much for the book-marker.

Her letters included the worries she had about leaving primary school and going into secondary but there was absolutely no request for advice at any stage. The problem was simply stated as being something she had on her mind and that was it.

We discussed granny's ulcer, her big brother's demands on the home finances to complete his karate training, her younger sister's being bullied while out playing and the purchase of the new school uniform for secondary school:

> I put on one that was great in length and in width it wouldn't fit me and it was too small, and then I tried on another one and it was terrible in length and great in width – what a mess! If that wasn't enough I tried on a coat and it was great but the shoulders were too big. I was tired and had had enough by the time my mam had everything fitting me . . . then she decided that my Auntie Ann could make them on the machine!!!!

We went through her fears about going to hospital for tests because she had 'a big fat knot in the stomach at times' and still she found space to identify and notice things around her and write with a certain amount of humour about them! On 7 June the budgie's egg finally hatched; the build-up to this event had gone on over six letters as Bubbles and Goldie awaited the arrival of their baby. Jenny wrote:

> My dad's budgies are real parents! The girl budgie is very cruel. If she thinks that her baby budgie is bad in any way she kills him or the daddy. I don't like her one bit. I will tell you about what will happen, OK?

Reading Jenny's work I was struck by the wonderful capacity she had for telling a tale. She had a way of using words which made everyday events take on a new exciting perspective. In fact her letters made it quite difficult to imagine that she had a problem with language. This form of writing had provided her with the chance to use oral language skill and exploit it to its full capacity.

Kate

Kate was aged twelve and had moved to the school in the middle of the second term. She came to live with her grandmother after her parent's marriage broke up. She quickly established her reputation as a 'somebody' within her brief period in school; even the bravest of the senior boys had a healthy respect for Kate.

Two major events happened to Kate in the final term: she was picked for the school athletics' team and she established her first real friendship with Tracey. Tracey was nobody's fool and adopted Kate as sheer protection.

However, Tracey soon discovered boys, fluorescent T-shirts and Bermuda Shorts and Kate did not fit in with this new image and was dropped! Kate became friendly with Lisa. The boys weren't all they were cracked up to be and Kate tried to reinstate their relationship. Eventually she and Kate made up. Kate wrote about all that was going on!:

> Dear Mr O'Shea
> Did you ever win a race? It is very exhilarating. When I ran I felt I was never going to win. I thought it would never going to end.
>
> Tracey and I got back together as friends. We are finding it a bit difficult. We can't put all the pieces back together the way we had before. It is different.
>
> Dear Kate
> Thank you for writing to me. I'm afraid I was never too good at sports of any kind – I never won races or anything like that! I was very interested in what you had to say about your friendship with Tracey. When we fall out with friends, the whole thing becomes different. We have seen a different side to the other person – and so the relationship changes! We might pick up all the pieces, but like Humpty Dumpty, they'll never fit together the same way again. But that does not mean that the friendship is no longer good . . . it is just different!
>
> Dear Mr O'Shea
> I know what you mean. Yes, we are still good friends. We can turn to each other. I made friends with Lisa. We have been friends for about five months now. We get on great. She went to England for two weeks and came back. I was delighted to see her again on Thursday. We had great fun together.

Some days later she wrote that Lisa and her family were going to emigrate to England and we finally (two pages later) get to the actual moment of parting.

> . . . I could not look at her and so I walked quickly away. I walked into

my room and started to cry and looked out the window and just kept crying and crying! I ran down stairs to see where the taxi had gone but I did not get back there on time so I walked slowly back up the stairs. I just kept crying until half-past three.

There followed a lengthy description of a conversation with a cousin of Lisa's confirming the leave-taking and the promise of visiting Lisa in England this forthcoming summer, and then the dashing of this hope with the realisation that the family could not afford such expense. All this was written in fine melodramatic style:

. . . though my heart is broken in two, I will miss her!

You might think that this is a bit over the top but it is so typical of the emotional mayhem of the young teenager, especially a teenager who loved TV soaps. Replying to her lengthy letter took some time as I was not sure how best to deal with it but I wrote:

It is very hard to be parted from our friends, isn't it? It makes you feel very sad inside – like you said, as though your heart was being broken in two. Being sad is not a nice feeling but it does show that we care about people and what happens to them. In the beginning it seems as though we will feel like this always but as time goes by it does get a little easier. There are no 'instant cures'! It is good to cry about sad things. That way the hurt does not get locked up inside us. Hurt, when it is locked up inside, keeps on hurting for a very long time. Thank you for trusting me with your sadness.

By the next letter the passions had abetted and we were back to discussing the training for the athletics in Santry Stadium and the intensity of the possibility of winning and losing and would she get her hair messed up if there was to be a photograph in the newspaper!

Writing to Kate was a wonderful experience. The Kate in the letters was so real; the tough exterior she maintained with the other children was such a contrast to the 'feeling' human being that it hid. At no time did she drop the mask with the other children; to them she was to be admired and respected.

For Kate the letter writing provided the opportunity to write at length about important events in her life. While the extremes of emotion would be out of place in the routine writing tasks set for her in other classes, they are perfectly acceptable here.

John

John's nick-name was 'Haze'! He seemed to be away in a world of his own a lot of the time and would reconnect with reality from time to time with a 'What did he say?' usually at the top of his lungs and scaring the wits out of me and everyone else in the room! John was fine as long as I didn't try to get him to work. Any attempt at this would lead to immediate conflict; I soon learnt to see the thunder in his eyes and quickly learnt to back off. I knew that he had a normal range of abilities but was not interested in learning. I had become used to his rather eccentric behaviour over the first two terms and accepted him as being a little 'different'. Essentially John dictated his own curriculum.

His mother firmly believed that John was given to her to make up for his five older brothers and sisters who had never given her a 'moment's trouble'. By the time he was ten and in my class she was at the exasperated stage. Over the years his parents had trundled John to a succession of child psychiatrists and psychologists. Their reports made about as much sense as John's behaviour. All of his former teachers seemed to get a glossy look in their eyes when I tried to find out what made John tick! Most admitted that they had endured rather than taught John!

The exchange of letters was to reveal a rather different ten-year-old; a youngster who was painfully normal and sensitive to much that was happening in his world.

Dear Mr O'Shea
I read James and the Giant Peach as well. I did not know that he write some episodes on TV. I did like it very much in Spain. It was very nice. Sometimes I go to the country and I do not like the journey to Wexford because I always get sick. It is real far away.

Dear John
Thank you for your letter. I was sorry to read that you get car sick. It can be very upsetting. Wexford is a long long way away. Who do you visit there?

Dear Mr O'Shea
When I go down to Wexford I visit my grandad and my uncle. I do like it down there. My uncle's dog died down there about a month ago and when I get bored I get my fishing rod and go fishing on the bank.

Dear John
Thank you for writing to me. Aren't you lucky to have such a nice grandad to visit? I was sorry to read about your uncle's dog. Were you sad when you heard about it? I didn't know that you liked to go fishing! What kind of fish do you catch?

Dear Mr O'Shea
My grandad is my mam's dad. He has a lot of cows and he had about twenty sheep and ten lambs. I was very sad when the dog died. My uncle was crying. They are getting a new dog. I will see it when I go down to Wexford.

This correspondence lasted right through the term, his letters revealing a John who was very much in touch with the reality which mattered to him and also connected to the emotions which were relevant to him. Initially I found myself looking at John and wondering where this 'normal' John had come from. Gradually the eccentric behaviour became less and less evident and John began to relate to his peers; a change which was to spill over to his relationships with his classmates and his teacher and eventually with home. The conflict ceased and John and I had become friends.

I avoided drawing conclusions as to how all this took place. I suppose that there is the subject matter for a treatise on John but I think that it shall be up to him to write it.

Conclusion

One morning in early June I arrived at school to find two letters on my desk. By that time I have to admit that I was a little wary of anything which was put in writing and with a certain amount of trepidation read the contents!

The first came from a child in another class:

Dear Mr O'Shea
Will I be able to join the English class please? I was eleven last May the 13th. It was a Friday so it was bad luck for me. I have three brothers and four sisters and myself still to count. So there is ten people in our family including my mam and dad. My brother Paul is 21 this year and my brother David will be 13 on Hallowe'en night. My brother Sean will be 2 in September. I never been to Spain or France and things like that. I was never out of Ireland. But hopefully this year my family and I might be going to Spain or Canada

PS I like reading books. I am also in the club you are doing. I also go to Donaghmede Library. I go every Saturday. I hope you enjoy reading my letter. Good bye for now . . . and I will be looking forward to hearing from you soon.

The second letter was not quite so subtle! T had graduated earlier in the year and was no longer in need of Remedial Education!

Dear Mr O'Shea,
I would be grateful if I could come back. Because I think I am getting worse at Maths and I am too slow. I need some help . . . please Sir, can I? Pretty please. Thanks sir, you're the best. Thanking you in anticipation, I will let my teacher know everything.

It turned out that though the children had kept the content of their correspondence confidential, they had made sure that their classes became aware that there was something out of the ordinary going on in my room! For once the remedial children were a source of envy in the school!

By the end of the term I had written some 400 letters to thirty-eight children. Only one child had opted out of the project and already this year it is the one activity that all the children have inquired about!

The greatest lesson I learnt from the project was that those aspects of learning which cannot be measured on tests and scales are probably the most important. Tests reveal scores while the letters revealed real children – real human beings! The improvement in self-esteem and the development of the feeling that school was not all negative made a powerful difference to the children's engagement with many other aspects of their work in school. It was a privilege to play a part in their development and have them trust me enough to be open with their feelings, opinions, curiosity and hopes.

I'll not deny that there was a tremendous amount of work involved and that I was not always in the form for replying to the letters. But looking at the stack of writing books and knowing how much confidence the project gave the children, I know that I will continue to use letter writing as a central part of both the children's learning and my own education!

9 STARTING INTERACTIVE WRITING: SOME PRACTICAL CONSIDERATIONS

Nigel Hall and Anne Robinson

For many years now we have been working with teachers and children engaged in some form of interactive writing. In the course of that time we have explored many different procedural aspects of undertaking interactive writing. We have given many talks about this topic and have been asked a wide range of questions about it. In this chapter we try to address some of the most common questions asked by people who would like to start interactive writing with children. There is no 'best way' to organise these questions. We have chosen to group them under three headings: 'Initial choices', 'Getting started', and 'Later issues'.

Initial choices

Why do I want the children to engage in interactive writing?

In a general sense this question has already been answered by the previous chapters, particularly Chapter 1. However, no written interaction operates solely at a general level and there are some points worth thinking about. Whatever agenda you have in mind we believe it is critical that you think carefully about it before you start. Are you doing it because you want to develop your relationship with the children? Are you doing it because you want to help the children learn something? Are you doing it to develop their confidence as writers? The answers to these questions are not necessarily mutually exclusive. However they may imply differences in the starting point, the procedures you use, and how you are going to respond. It is as well to be as clear as possible about what you want.

Can I do interactive writing with any children?

The answer, both from our own experience and from that of other people, seems to be yes. We have come across interactive journals with children as young as three (although in this case pictures replaced words), primary-aged children, secondary-aged children, college and university students, adult basic education students, second language learners, deaf students, and special needs students. If you have students who do not fit into any of the above categories then try it and let us know what happens.

To whom can the children write?

Who would you like them to write to? We would not want to exclude any possibility. Before editing this book we may not have thought that eight-year-olds could write to convicted murderers – yet, as you will have seen from Chapter 3, it has been done.

The critical question is not to whom can the children write but 'Can I make sure that my chosen correspondents are prepared to take the task seriously?' Are they prepared to give a commitment to corresponding with the children?

What does this commitment involve? We believe that anyone engaging in correspondence with young children must agree to:

- write regularly;

- write for as long as the children wish to write;

- treat the children's writing as meaningful and honest communication;

- avoid talking down to the children;

- write honestly to the children.

Even if the correspondent is yourself – still ask yourself if you are prepared to make the above commitments.

A range of ideas for correspondents can be found in this book. In addition we can suggest: overseas pen pals, grandparents, senior citizens, long-stay hospital patients, people in the armed forces and merchant navy, teacher education students, school principals, and parents.

Can the children write to an imaginary correspondent?

It has been fairly common in Britain for teachers to write in the guise of an imaginary character to young children. These disguises take many forms. One of the first to do this and document it was Price

(1989). Her four-year-olds had been reading *The bad-tempered ladybird* (*The grouchy ladybug* in the US) and had made a large ladybird. One morning when the children came in they found a large letter propped up by the ladybird. When they asked their teacher to read it they found it was from the Ladybird. The children wrote back and the dialogue continued for about six weeks.

Since that time we have come across a vast range of characters being used as correspondents. There was the British classroom which, typically, had a large hole in the ceiling. The teacher convinced the children that there was a ghost which came out at night and would write to them. In another classroom the radiator used to make a strange noise every now and then. The children were persuaded that the noise was made by a little mouse running through the pipes. Needless to say a correspondence began. We have seen children writing to soft felt toys, stuffed animals, monsters, fairy-tale characters (see Pearson, 1989), Puff The Magic Dragon, the Iron Man, historical and other characters reached through a play time-machine, and many, many more.

There are a couple of points that need to be made. Clearly the older the child the less likely it is that the character will be believed in as a real character. It may be better to introduce it as a game; indeed the older children may enjoy writing in character themselves. The younger children (under sixes) mostly appear to believe with only slight doubts. Prices' children, for example, wondered how the ladybird managed to write the letters.

The second, and more important point, is that if you, or someone else, is going to write in character then the writer must make the effort to really write as if they were that character. It is all too easy for a teacher to carry on writing just as a teacher. If your letters read like: 'How are you? Do you like school? What is your favourite lesson? What did you do at the weekend?', then you will not sound like a mouse, a stuffed hippopotamus or Puff The Magic Dragon; you will simply sound like a teacher.

One teacher we know had been having her children write to fairy-tale characters. One child wrote to the 'Beauty' who married the 'ugly beast' who turned into a prince. Here is the reply the child received:

Dear Sally
Fancy you knowing all about me. I do like it in the Palace. I am quite used to it now because I lived here when the Beast was still a Beast. I

was surprised when the Beast turned into a Prince. We have a baby now.
When he was born the Prince said the baby looked just like him and I
must say for a few days I was quite worried that we had got a baby
beast. Now he is growing up he is quite a nice baby to look at but he is
sometimes very naughty so he is a bit like the old beast. Do you know
anything about any of the other people who live here. If you have read
about us you might know some of our friends.

A little bit of effort makes the difference between a correspondence
which scrapes along and a correspondence which zings with energy
and excitement.

What medium should be used for interactive writing?

There are as many choices as there are ways of exchanging written
and illustrated communications. It is clear that the most frequently
occurring modes are the dialogue journal and written conversation
journal. However, as the chapters in this book illustrate there are
other ways including letters being posted, and at the moment we are
investigating the use of fax. This has some wonderful advantages for
younger children; they keep their originals, they can send
illustrations and the communication can be achieved very quickly.
The disadvantage is that very few schools have fax machines
(although the inevitable march of technology will no doubt lead to
such reductions in prices so that schools will soon feel isolated
without them).

Should I tell the parents?

At a fundamental level we believe that teachers should always strive
to keep parents informed about the experiences their children are
having in classrooms. However, such a principle operates at different
levels of significance. If the interactive writing is going to be no
more than exchanging letters between children in the class or school
then there is probably no need to give it any special status. If you are
going to engage in dialogue journals or written conversations with
the children then you may want to let the parents know, but such an
activity probably still falls within the remit of normal teacher
classroom practices.

If the children are going to write to someone outside the school
then we believe it is vital that parents are invited to approve and
given safeguards about the choice of correspondents. It will be clear

from Chapter 4 in this book that the choice of some audiences can be a very sensitive issue.

Even in the correspondence detailed by Robinson, Crawford and Hall in Chapter 5 a problem arose. Although the teacher sent a letter home with every child which explained what was going to happen, she forgot to give one to a child who was absent on that day. That child, when he returned, heard all about the letters from his classmates and was determined not to be left out. Consequently he wrote to Nigel when all the other children did. Because the child had been absent on the day Nigel had visited, Nigel decided to describe himself in his reply. A couple of days later a very worried mother appeared in the headteacher's room wondering about this strange man who had suddenly written to her son! It pays to be very careful in ensuring that parents are fully informed about external exchanges. Our experience has been that they are almost always very supportive.

It goes without saying that it is not only parents who should be informed. No teacher should ever start an external exchange without getting the agreement of the headteacher or principal.

Should what is written be confidential?

This is a difficult question to answer and teachers who ask it are usually concerned that children may begin to operate outside the normal teacher/pupil relationships. The question would not normally arise in relation to the routine writing done in class. It would be generally assumed that children's writing would be public and anyone could see it. Parents, for example, would normally expect to have reasonable access to the children's work and teachers would not expect otherwise.

However, it is in the nature of interactive writing that the relationship between the correspondents is a close one. Within this close relationship children sometimes feel relaxed enough to reveal things which worry them or which worry the teacher. The problems themselves may not be particularly serious but nevertheless may need sensitive handling. A teacher may feel that a parent could help but we think this must be discussed with the child and their permission gained before the problem is taken outside the correspondence. The children should normally be the ones to decide who should have access to the contents. In our experience this has very rarely been a problem; children usually show everyone what they have written and what has been written to them.

Sometimes, the problem itself is very serious, so serious in fact that a teacher feels compelled to take some action. Problems of physical or sexual abuse would fall into this category. There are no easy answers to what to do in this case. The best advice is probably to seek expert help while keeping the child's name a secret. Some teachers may ask the child if the revelation is a cry for action to be taken or may give advice on where the child can seek further help. If in doubt seek advice from your headteacher or principal, but do make sure they understand the essentially confidential nature of the exercise.

Should you ever wish to use any of the children's work for any public or semi-public purpose you must ask their permission and respect their wishes. 'Public purposes' may include writing for publication (as in this book for instance) and 'semi-public purposes' may include conducting a staff seminar or workshop exercise. In our experience it is rare for children to object. All the children in this book are happy for their teachers to use their work in print.

Where am I going to find the time to do interactive writing?

The flexibility of interactive writing means that it can be used in many different ways within classrooms. It is inevitably the case that this question is a bigger issue for teachers who have very tightly organised classrooms than for those who run a more open system.

Clearly, the issue is one of priorities. If you feel that interactive writing has something powerful to offer your children and can fulfil some of your other objectives for developing children's writing abilities in the process, then finding time is most unlikely to be a problem. If you feel it is an utterly fringe activity and not as important as all the other things you are doing then you are best to avoid interactive writing. It will not work unless it is given some time and commitment from teachers who can believe in it.

Within this book a number of people have shown how they organised interactive writing within their school day. Rose Duffy (Chapter 2) managed to contain it all (including her replies) within a normal working day. Sheila Hewitt (Chapter 7) allowed the children to write their dialogue journals during a fixed time each week. She took them home to write her replies. The children featured in the Robinson, Crawford and Hall chapter (Chapter 5) chose their own times to write their letters. The more formal requirements of electronic mail communication probably means more precise timetabling. Each teacher can make their own choices. You might have to try a few different procedures to find one with which you are really comfortable.

If you need to justify finding time to undertake interactive writing do not forget how much experience of reading the children will gain from it.

Getting started

Should I involve all the children at the same time?

If you have arranged for the children to write to a range of external correspondents, or to another class then there is no reason why all the children should not be involved at the same time. This does not mean that they all write at the same time. The writing can be staggered across a few days, a group at a time.

If you are going to be the correspondent and you have never done interactive writing before then our advice is to start with just one group of children. It may be the most able writers who need pushing forward in their writing, or it may be a group of less able children who need to develop confidence in writing. The group you chose does not matter but by choosing one group you allow yourself some time for exploration of the technique without binding yourself too tightly into a method that might not work well for you. If things work out, then add another group or move onto another group. If it does work you may find it difficult not to end up corresponding with the whole class.

What should be my first move?

In some cases the first move is simply to begin the correspondence. The five-year-olds in the study reported in Chapter 5 were simply handed letters after a visit by two adults. The letters invited them to write to the two adults. No child had to, but they all did. The children who wrote to the prisoners (Chapter 3) started corresponding by writing thank you letters for some work that had been done in the school.

Starting is probably more difficult when a teacher decides to introduce dialogue journals half way through a year. Children may be unsure what is expected of them as the journals are a new feature of classroom life. If you are a teacher who would normally mark every piece of children's work, then they might be very suspicious about believing you if you suddenly tell them they can write how they like in these books.

Our suggestion is that you give each child a small plain-papered booklet. On the first page you write a simple letter to them. Do *not* ask any questions. This will feel psychologically disturbing to teachers who probably use questions more than any other group of working people. Nevertheless, our experience shows clearly that simple statements telling the children something about you, and a short sentence saying you would pleased if they would write back, are very effective. Do not make the opening letter too long or too complicated. You may find that children are still unsure about their role in the process. Plenty of reassurance and a certain amount of experience should sort out that difficulty.

We do feel that it is important to explain to the whole group that they can write whatever they like in the journal and that you will not be marking it or correcting it. They may not believe you at first. You will have to show them that you mean it by avoiding any written or oral comment on the secretarial aspects of their work. (For some thoughts about these issues see a later question.)

What if I can't read what the children write?

This question most often comes from people writing to beginning writers. In written conversation (see Chapter 2) the easiest way is to simply ask the children to read what they have written. The child may need to ask you what you have written. Just tell it! We have never found that it has had any inhibitory effect on the dialogue; on the contrary it can free the child. Where very young children are concerned the writing may be mostly drawing or collections of letters or letter-like shapes. In these cases conversation is a necessity. It is, however, vital that the child's communication is taken seriously and the child made to feel that he/she is a writer who can communicate meanings.

There is more of a problem if the teacher, or correspondent, is not present when the children write their text. Teachers who are used to young children doing unaided writing have developed all kinds of tricks to gain access to their children's meanings and it may well be the case that a teacher's general knowledge of the children may help when interpreting the writing. It may be necessary to wait and find time to talk to the children individually or it may sometimes be the case that one simply affirms the child in question and generates new topics.

When children are a little older it is usually possible to have a guess at what is being said. Do not worry about it, and if you feel you want to be sure then just ask the children to tell you what they have written.

What should we write about?

This depends to some extent on the kind of interactive writing which you are engaged in. If we are working with dialogue journals which are concerned with one or more subject areas then to a large extent the content mostly takes care of itself. Although children who are new to this idea may need some help to know just what is expected, teachers, who are the usual correspondents, will have to structure their responses carefully to guide their pupils towards aspects of the subject being learned. Teachers have a choice to make too, about how much to dwell on the content area and how much to 'socialise' in order to establish the relaxed relationship.

If the interactive writing is not directed towards a specific subject the question is rather like asking 'What do I say?' in a conversation with a friend. The answer is anything and everything. There are no rules about what each party might find interesting or think is important; you just have to see what develops.

Should I try to control what the children write about?

Anyone who has engaged in interactive writing will find this question amusing. It is very difficult to determine what someone else will write. Interests come and go and topics important one week may be unimportant the next week. On the other hand, some things are key topics for a long time in spite of not being encouraged by the partner. Even when the subject of the writing is pre-determined, as in content learning logs (Chapter 6), individuality emerges and all kinds of interesting and unexpected things get included. As this is part of the fun of interactive writing, it certainly should not be discouraged. Children new to interactive writing may need guidance about the things which are possible and skilful correspondents will make openings for their co-writers. Exploration rather than control is what interactive writing is all about.

Should I worry about the children's errors?

It will be clear to readers of this book that we see the primary function of interactive writing as exchanging meanings. Thus it is content rather than form which is important. This is not because we believe form is unimportant. Children are going to be disadvantaged if they cannot write neatly or develop strategies for spelling and punctuating. However, the evidence from many studies shows that if teachers make demands for conventional accuracy in interactive writing they can almost certainly say goodbye to vigour and commitment in the child's writing. What would Georgina (Chapter 2 pages 33–7) have done if her teacher had corrected every error she made, and asked her to do something about them? The next time Georgina was invited to write to her teacher she would have either declined or would have written only those words she knew were correct. Instead of commitment and interest we would have found tedium and safety.

We believe teachers would do much better to use interactive writing as a source of knowledge about not only what the child knows about writing but what the child sees as significant in writing. The teacher can then devise appropriate teaching strategies based on good information about the child. These strategies can be carried out at other times in the classroom.

The stance we are taking does not mean that children should not be left unaware of the importance of writing so that their audience can read what they have written. Nor does it imply that they shouldn't be expected to write correctly (or be corrected) in their other written work. Teachers must make their own choices about these issues. Interactive writing offers a pretty powerful display of the need to write clearly and accurately and children are capable of understanding this. If they really care about what they are writing (and in a good writing relationship they almost always do) then they will take pains and will care very much that their reader is able to understand the message. By engaging in interactive writing children will learn about the needs of audiences.

How much should the children write?

As much or as little as they feel appropriate. We do believe respondents can have a considerable influence on the length of children's letters. If their partner writes at length, writes interestingly and does not structure texts so as to induce a passive response from their correspondent, then children's texts tend to get longer and longer. It is important though to remember that all relationships have their good times and their bad times. Not everyone has always got a lot to say. The good thing about a sustained correspondence is that it allows these variations to be evened out across a whole correspondence.

What if the children don't want to write?

As we believe that children should be invited to correspond it stands to reason that we do not think they should be forced to write if they do not want to. We believe they should be encouraged and should be written to; but if in the end they do not want to correspond then let them have some alternative writing experience. In our experience children who are initially reluctant soon feel they are missing out on something once the other children can be seen to be enjoying what they are doing.

Some practitioners do make formal demands on children to write. Mrs Reed (Staton *et al.*, 1988) did insist on each child writing a certain amount in the dialogue journal every day. She was prepared to live with the ups and downs that such pressure brings. Clearly, the children did write their entries and the wealth of evidence from that study is that most of the children enjoyed what they were doing.

Later issues

How long should the exchanges continue?

The simple answer is as long as the children continue to want to write. It is important to remember that it is unlikely that the children asked to engage in interactive writing. They were invited or persuaded to have a go; they were invited to make a commitment.

However, it is inevitably the case that even if children wish to continue, it is not always possible. If an end-point can be forecast then it is imperative that the children are told this from the start. It is easier for them to bear the end of a good relationship if they know it is going to happen. They can even begin to explore how one writes towards the end of relationships. Honesty in the correspondence is an overriding principle for us and we do not think it helps children's commitment to writing if they suddenly get cut off from a correspondent.

Sometimes these things do happen despite the best of intentions. In such instances the teacher must then help the child understand the circumstances which led to the conclusion of the correspondence and wherever possible help the child find another correspondent as soon as possible.

What is my role if I am not a correspondent?

In some situations the teacher is not one of the corespondents (see Chapters 3, 4, 5, and 9). The teacher, nevertheless, still has a critical role to play in ensuring that the exchanges work well.

Initially a teacher will be involved in planning and organising the exchange. They may act as an initial point of contact and provide information for all those who need to know about the writing. Later they may act as facilitators providing material, resources, space and time. Throughout the correspondence they can offer interest and support. It is so important that the teacher is always ready to listen, to read and, if necessary, encourage. Whilst it is true that children almost always participate readily in interactive writing, they do so more eagerly if the teacher has a genuine concern for what is happening. A teacher may also have a logistical role, distributing letters and arranging for children's contributions to be collected and passed on. It may be necessary for the teacher to act as translator. Correspondents may not be experienced in reading the writing of young children and a pencilled translation could make a great difference to the ease with which something can be read. This, of course, works both ways; children cannot always read what they are sent and help may be needed.

In some situations teachers may wish to participate in class discussions about the nature of writing letters, or may help, if the children are willing, to share or even display some of their letters. This may not only be within the classroom; the children involved in the Robinson, Crawford and Hall (1991) study used to talk regularly in school assembly about what they were learning from their correspondents.

Teachers who are not contributors need never fear being left out. Providing the children are happy for the teacher to read and listen, then much will be learned about the children and their skills as writers.

Will it change my relationship with the children?

If you are one of the correspondents then you can influence the tenor of the conversation, just as you can in speech. The relationship between you and your children can be maintained just as it always has been, if this is what you wish. Many teachers engage in this activity to try to develop a rather more relaxed interaction, to get to know the children better and also to let the children know them better. In this case you have to decide how much of yourself as a person you wish to reveal. Many teachers report on improved relationships in class as the interactive writing develops. But you have to ask yourself if you are ready for this. We are talking about a more open friendly relaxed atmosphere outside the writing as well as within the privacy of the text. This raises a related question – what if the children are cheeky? Obviously if you invite a more open relationship you have to be prepared for the consequences. Some children may see this as a softening of discipline and take it further than you intend. As with many things in class you need to set the boundaries clearly. It is important to remember though that friends can be a bit cheeky with each other, they can have a joke.

References

Pearson, N. (1989) 'A journey into authorship' in **Hall, N.** (ed.) *Writing with reason: the emergence of authorship in young children.* London: Hodder and Stoughton.

Price, J. (1989) 'The ladybird letters' in **Hall, N.** (ed.) *Writing with reason: the emergence of authorship in young children.* London: Hodder and Stoughton.

Staton, J; Shuy, R; Kreeft Peyton, J. and **Reed, L.** (1988) *Dialogue journal communication: classroom, linguistic, social and cognitive views.* New Jersey: Ablex Publishing Company.